WHAT HAPPENED TO
SERIE A

THE RISE, FALL AND SIGNS OF REVIVAL

STEVEN G. MANDIS

THOMAS LOMBARDI

SARAH PARSONS WOLTER

First published in 2018 by

ARENA SPORT
An imprint of Birlinn Limited
West Newington House
10 Newington Road
Edinburgh
EH9 1QS

www.arenasportbooks.co.uk

Hardback ISBN:9781909715622
Paperback ISBN: 9781909715639
eBook ISBN: 9781788850940

British Library Cataloguing-in-Publication Data
A catalogue record for this book is available on request from the British Library.

Designed and typeset by Polaris Publishing, Edinburgh

Printed in Great Britain by TJ International Ltd, Padstow

This book is dedicated to the people of Italy.

We admire your beautiful and fascinating culture, history and language.

Most of all, we appreciate your warmth and kindness.

'What happened to Italy's Serie A football? It's complicated. It's Italy.'

Serie A football club executive

Dear Reader,

The book is dedicated to the people of Italy. We understand that *calcio* is interpreted as an element of Italian identity and pride. We hope the book helps improve football in Italy as well as your understanding and passion for *calcio*.

As you read the book, please keep in mind that we are using our best efforts to draw on our academic training and 'outsider status' to shed light on a fascinating topic via a scholarly framework. We tried to stay as independent and neutral as possible. We did not receive any payment or reimbursement of expenses from any club. We donated all of the money we received from the publisher to charity.

The book provides exhaustive research, lots of data and plenty of analysis. We are the first to use a 360-degree approach and framework to rigorously analyse both the on-the-pitch and off-the-pitch (business) aspects of Serie A and Italian clubs. What we learned is completely unexpected, raises new ideas and challenges many popular explanations and conventional wisdom.

After the national team of football-crazed Italy failed to qualify for the 2018 FIFA World Cup, Italian football was in existential 'crisis'. While many challenges still exist and serious reforms are required, we found there are signs of optimism for Italian football overall. Generally unnoticed in the last few years, signs of a revival are taking place. For example, certain Italian football clubs, led by innovative owners, are adapting and developing new ways to compete on and off the pitch with some success, even though they have to overcome many challenges unique to Italy.

We anticipate that we will take criticism from many sides because of the content of the book. We readily admit we are not European football experts, let alone Italian football experts, and have many limitations. Our only response to criticism is that we genuinely tried our best with the resources and access we had. We did all of this work primarily to satisfy our curiosity, make an academic contribution, donate to a charitable cause and help organisations improve. (We also had a lot of fun working together and meeting extraordinary people who kindly helped us.) We do think approaching this study essentially as 'outsiders' can help produce fresh and original ideas, research, analysis and conclusions.

Readers may agree or disagree or even feel like other aspects should be mentioned or examined further. We genuinely welcome constructive feedback. As academics and curious people, we are always learning and trying to get to the most reasonable conclusion.

If you would like to contact the authors, please feel free to email Steven G. Mandis at his Columbia University Business School email: sgm2130@columbia.edu.

We can't promise that we will respond to every message, but we can promise you that we will read each one.

Warmest regards,

Steven, Thomas and Sarah
August, 2018

CONTENTS

PART THREE: REVIVAL
NEW APPROACHES, OWNERS AND INNOVATORS

PART FOUR: THE FUTURE

INTRODUCTION

THE EUROPEAN professional football industry is a big and growing business. It brings in €24.4 billion of revenue per year, which is larger than the major North American sports leagues, the NFL, MLB, NBA and NHL, combined. The top five European football premier leagues (English Premier League, German Bundesliga, Spanish La Liga, Italian Serie A and French Ligue 1) alone had €12.3 billion in revenues in 2015, more than the NFL's €11.7 billion. The 2015 UEFA Champions League final had an estimated global TV audience of 380 million, compared to 120 million for the Super Bowl. The winner of the Champions League final received around €97.3 million in prize money, while the winner of the Super Bowl made €13.5 million. The 2015 Champions League finalists had a total of 101 million Facebook and 25 million Twitter followers, outnumbering the Super Bowl finalists' total of 9 million and 2 million, respectively.[1] No longer is football restricted to the sports pages of newspapers. The *Financial Times* and *Wall Street Journal* now have sports sections and journalists specialising in coverage of financial issues in sport. There are sports management classes at top business schools and even Master's degrees in sports management itself.

[1] http://www.marketwatch.com/story/the-nfl-made-13-billion-last-season-see-how-it-stacks-up-against-other-leagues-2016-07-01; http://www.vocativ.com/news/198079/the-super-bowl-is-no-match-for-the-uefa-champions-league/index.html

Football (*calcio* in Italian; although 'calcio' literally means 'kick'; the Italians preferring not to Latinise the word 'football' like the Spanish did with 'fútbol') is the most popular sport in Italy. The 25 most watched television programmes in history in Italy are all football matches. It has been estimated that Italian football generates aggregate revenue of nearly €7 billion per year to the Italian economy. However, football in Italy is more than a sport or a business or entertainment; *calcio* is interpreted as an element of identity and pride. This is one reason that made studying Italian football in particular so compelling and engrossing.

After Italy won the FIFA World Cup in 1982 and hosted the tournament in 1990, Italian professional football dominated Europe. Every year from 1989 to 1999 Italy's Serie A had at least one finalist in a European competition. In four of those years Italy had a finalist in all three UEFA club competitions (1989, 1990, 1993, 1994), and in 1990 Italian clubs won all three competitions (Milan in European Cup, Sampdoria in Cup Winners' Cup and Juventus in UEFA Cup beating fellow Italian club Fiorentina). Italy's Serie A clubs also dominated off the pitch. In the Deloitte Football Revenues Rankings in 2000/01, five of the top ten clubs were Italian. Only three of the top ten were in the English Premier League.

By the turn of the century, things off the pitch slowly started to decline for Italy's Serie A. And eventually the on-the-pitch results suffered. The 2010/11 season will probably go down as the worst continental season in Italian professional football history with no Serie A clubs progressing past the last 32 in the Europa League or the quarter-finals in the Champions League. By 2011, Italian clubs were playing so poorly Serie A fell behind Germany's Bundesliga in the UEFA mathematical coefficient rankings, dropping from third place to fourth and thereby losing one of its guaranteed qualifying slots for the Champions League for the 2011/12 season. In 2014, the Portuguese Primeira Liga overtook Serie A in UEFA's league coefficient ranking system. By 2014/15, only one Italian club, Juventus, was in the top ten in the Deloitte Football Revenues Rankings. Five of the top ten were in the English Premier League.

While not directly tied to, but certainly connected with and a barometer for the state of, the Italian professional football league Serie

A, Italy's national team didn't advance out of the group stage in the 2010 and 2014 World Cups, finishing in 26th and 22nd places, respectively. If there were any Italian football fans or decision-makers denying a decline, they certainty had to admit there were serious issues and a decline when four-time (1934, 1938, 1982 and 2006) World Cup champions Italy failed to even qualify for the 2018 World Cup, the first and only time since 1958. After Italy failed to qualify for the 2018 FIFA World Cup, the media claimed Italian football overall was in existential 'crisis'.

Generally overlooked, a relative decline off the pitch in financial power had started well before the on-the-pitch decline for professional Italian football's Serie A. In general, most Italian clubs and the league believed football in Italy should be owned by, and played for, Italians and only matchday's results mattered. However, the world had changed both on and off the pitch. The Italian league and its clubs didn't adapt to changing market conditions forced by competitive, organisational, regulatory and technological changes. For example, European professional football became a global entertainment business with global community brands that required significant investment and professional management both on and off the pitch. As competitors built sustainable economic-sport businesses or found new capital and business strategies, rich Italian owners just funded the losses and investments. However, this was unsustainable as the financial commitment became bigger and bigger, especially as the costs of star players grew exponentially. Additionally, many of the Serie A clubs were handicapped by historical, cultural, league, management, regulatory, economic and other challenges unique to Italy. For example, generally, potential investors with more resources and new ideas were both unwelcomed and hesitant to invest in, or buy, a football club in a country with challenging business, financial and legal transparency and practices, not to mention a language barrier. It was much easier to invest in, or buy, a football club in the English Premier League. With a relative decline in financial power, there was a decline in the overall talent and fan experience in Italy's Serie A. However, while many challenges still exist and serious reforms are required to rebuild Italian football overall, we found there are signs to be optimistic.

Generally unnoticed in the last few years, signs of a revival are taking place. For example, certain Italian clubs, led by innovative owners, are adapting and developing new ways to compete on and off the pitch and having some success. Postive signs on the pitch include Juventus reaching the Champions League finals in 2014/15 and 2016/17, and Roma's incredible comeback to defeat Barcelona to advance to the 2017/18 Champions League semi-finals.

Italian football is notoriously opaque. Utilising exhaustive research, lots of data and plenty of analysis, we shed light on questions and topics that have never fully been investigated and explained. Our 'outsider status' and 360-degree academic approach allows us to challenge many popular explanations and conventional wisdom.

What happened to Italian football and what is now happening, revealed here, is a fascinating story, with implications for industries and organisations worldwide beyond just sports.

*

In 2015, I was doing research for a book titled *The Real Madrid Way*. For only the second time in my life, I was watching a UEFA Champions League final match on TV – Barcelona versus Juventus in Berlin. The TV presenter stated that this was the first time Juventus had advanced past the quarter-finals in the Champions League in 12 years and only the fourth time an Italian Serie A club had been in the finals since then (Milan in 2005 and 2007 and Inter in 2010 were the others). I wasn't really a passionate fan of football, but I remembered Italy's Serie A clubs dominating European competitions and Juventus being one of the top clubs in Europe. Therefore, the lack of positive results surprised me. Curious, I looked into the history books.

Of the 44 possible places in European finals (Champions League and UEFA Cup) across an 11-year period from 1989 to 1999, a remarkable ten different Serie A clubs (Fiorentina, Inter, Juventus, Lazio, Milan, Napoli, Parma, Roma, Sampdoria and Torino) occupied 23 of them. Comparing this to the 11-year period of 2004 to 2014, there were only two Serie A clubs (Inter and Milan) who advanced to three finals. [2]

---

[2] Since 2014, Juventus advanced to the finals of the Champions League in 2014/15 and 2016/17, and in 2017/18 Roma advanced to the semi-finals. This will be discussed later.

Finalists in the Champions League
or Europa League/UEFA Cup
1989–99 Finalists (If Winner, in Bold)

Year	Champions League	UEFA Cup
1989	**Milan**	**Napoli**
1990	**Milan**	**Juventus**, Fiorentina
1991		**Inter,** Roma
1992	Sampdoria	Torino
1993	Milan	**Juventus**
1994	**Milan**	**Inter**
1995	Milan	**Parma**, Juventus
1996	**Juventus**	
1997	Juventus	Inter
1998	Juventus	**Inter**, Lazio
1999		**Parma**

2004–2014 Finalists (If Winner, in Bold)

Year	Champions League	Europa League/UEFA Cup
2004		
2005	Milan	
2006		
2007	**Milan**	
2008		
2009		
2010	**Inter**	
2011		
2012		
2013		
2014		

Since 2007, Milan have not advanced past the Champions League quarter-finals stage. From 2007 to 2014 only one Italian club managed to get past the quarter-final stage – the title-winning Inter Milan of 2010. Since 2010, Inter have not made it past the quarter-finals, when they have even qualified, which has been only twice – 2011 and 2012. From 2003 to 2014 Juventus did not advance past the quarter-finals. In addition, since 2000, no Italian club have even made the finals of the UEFA Cup or Europa League. It is all a far cry from the 1980s and 1990s, when Italian clubs were consistently in the final rounds of the Champions League/ European Cup and the UEFA Cup.

When I reviewed the Deloitte Football Revenues Rankings, I couldn't believe what I saw. I stared at one page for 2015/16 and then flipped back to compare it to another page for 2000/01. In the 2000/01 Deloitte Football Revenues Rankings, five Italian football clubs were in the top ten: Juventus #2, AC Milan #4, Lazio #7, Roma #8 and Inter #10. In the 2015/16 Rankings, only Juventus placed in the top ten, at #10. And Juventus had just been in the final of the UEFA Champions League the previous year and benefited from the corresponding prize money revenue. I was amazed at the drop-off.

Deloitte Football Revenues Rankings
2000/01

Rank	Club	Revenues	European Cups (at the time)
1	Manchester United	€217.2 million	1968, 1999
2	**Juventus**	173.5	1985, 1996
3	Bayern Munich	173.2	1974, 1975, 1976, 2001
4	**AC Milan**	164.6	1963, 1969, 1989, 1990, 1994
5	Real Madrid	138.2	1956, 1957, 1958, 1959, 1960, 1966, 1998, 2000
6	Liverpool	137.6	1977, 1978, 1981, 1984
7	**Lazio**	125.4	
8	**Roma**	123.8	
9	Chelsea	118.4	
10	**Internazionale**	112.8	1964, 1965

Deloitte Football Revenues Rankings
2015/16

Rank	Club	2000 Rank	Revenues	Rev Growth Since 2000	Since 2000/01 UCL Cups
1	Manchester United	1	€689.0 mill	217%	2008
2	Barcelona	NA	620.2		06, 09, 11, 15
3	Real Madrid	5	620.1	349	02, 14, 16
4	Bayern Munich	3	592.0	241	01, 13
5	Man City	NA	524.9		
6	PSG	NA	520.9		
7	Arsenal	NA	468.5		
8	Chelsea	9	447.4	278	12
9	Liverpool	6	403.8	194	05
10	**Juventus**	2	341.1	96	
11	Borussia Dortmund	NA	283.9		
12	Tottenham Hotspur	NA	279.7		
13	Atlético Madrid	NA	228.6		
14	Schalke 04	NA	224.5		
15	**Roma**	8	218.2	76	
16	**AC Milan**	4	214.7	31	03, 07
17	FC Zenit	NA	196.5		
18	West Ham United	NA	192.3		
19	**Internazionale**	10	179.2	59	10
20	Leicester City	NA	172.1		

In the 2016/17 Deloitte Football Revenues Rankings things got worse. AC Milan and Roma fell out of the top 20. The revenue growth since 2000 for the Italian clubs is significantly below the other clubs that were in the top 10 in 2000/01. And during this time AC Milan and Inter did win trophies.

Deloitte Football Revenues Rankings
2016/17

Rank	Club	2000 Rank	Revenues	Rev Growth Since 2000	Since 2000/01 UCL Cups
1	Manchester United	1	€676.3 mill	211%	2008
2	Real Madrid	5	674.6	388	02, 14, 16, 17
3	Barcelona	NA	648.3		06, 09, 11, 15
4	Bayern Munich	3	587.8	239	01, 13
5	Manchester City	NA	527.7		
6	Arsenal	NA	487.6		
7	PSG	NA	486.2		
8	Chelsea	9	428.0	262	12
9	Liverpool	6	424.2	208	05
10	**Juventus**	2	405.7	134	
11	Tottenham Hotspur	NA	355.6		
12	Borussia Dortmund	NA	332.6		
13	Atlético Madrid	NA	272.5		
14	Leicester City	NA	271.1		
15	**Internazionale**	10	262.1	132	10
16	Schalke 04	NA	230.2		
17	West Ham United	NA	213.3		
18	Southampton	NA	212.1		
19	**Napoli**	NA	200.7		
20	Everton	NA	199.2		

The question on my mind was: What happened to Italy's Serie A football?

During my research for my book _The Real Madrid Way_, I was introduced to the president and a principal owner of AS Roma, Jim Pallotta. Jim is a successful American businessman and entrepreneur. Jim had served as vice chairman at Tudor Investment Corporation, one of the largest and most successful investment funds in the world. Additionally, Jim is a co-owner and executive board member of the NBA's Boston Celtics. Jim was born in 1958 in Boston to Italian immigrants and raised in Boston's Italian North End neighbourhood. Jim, along with three other American investors (Thomas R. DiBenedetto, Michael Ruane and Richard D'Amore), acquired Roma in 2011. In 2012, Jim became chairman of the club, succeeding Thomas R. DiBenedetto. Personally, I was also the son of working-class European

(Greek) immigrants, born into an ethnic-dominated city neighbourhood (Chicago's Greektown) and spent time in the investment management business (before going back to school at 38 years old and graduating with a PhD from Columbia University). Therefore, I immediately connected to Jim and enjoyed his passion, smarts, vision, curiosity and friendly informality. He provided helpful insights and feedback for my Real Madrid book, and we stayed in touch.

As I got to know Jim better and learned about his vision for Roma and the challenges and opportunities for Roma and Italian football, my curiosity and fascination remained unabated. The more I learned, the more I wanted to know. During a call with Jim, I asked him if he would be willing to provide me with unprecedented access to both people and data regarding Roma and Serie A. I wanted to investigate both the on-the-pitch and business aspects of the club and league. For background, I consider myself a curious academic who teaches in the finance and economics department at Columbia Business School; I grew up in America; I am not really a football fan; while I wrote a book about Real Madrid, before that book I knew very little about Real Madrid or European football; I knew very little about Italian football when I started this book; I have visited Italy on vacation about a half dozen times before starting this book; and I don't speak Italian (or Spanish).

To my amazement and great appreciation, Jim and Roma agreed. I went to Rome in April 2017 for eight days to start my research. My first trip finished with attending a Roma match against Juventus at the Stadio Olimpico in Rome. I was given complete access to the club, including being allowed to see whatever I wanted and to meet with whomever, including the players and coaches. Roma staff also thoroughly and promptly responded to many very long information request lists from me about Roma and Italian football. I was provided with financial information and statistical data. Roma also introduced me to other players, executives and owners in Italian football. I also spoke with many executives of Italian football clubs and others related to Italian football that were introduced to me by my own contacts, not Roma.

While teaching at Columbia Business School, I enlisted the help of two former Columbia Business School students to help me answer my question because the further I investigated the more daunting the research and analysis seemed. Thomas Lombardi is a French-Swiss-Italian working for a French bank. He is a passionate Italian football fan and follows Serie A closely. He was tasked to fill in the gaps and nuances about Italian history and football, while trying not to be too biased. Sarah Parsons Wolter is an American working for an American bank. She is an Olympic medallist, having been the youngest athlete on the USA's women's hockey team in the 2006 Winter Games in Turin, Italy. She is passionate about sports but knew very little about European football and Serie A before the project. She was tasked to challenge what I or Thomas Lombardi would take for granted and held no biases. We would also gather feedback and information from many others throughout the project.

Note to Reader

It is not our intention to glorify or vilify any individual, group or era, although we suspect parts will be interpreted or used to do so. When we contacted people we wanted to interview, we explained we are not reporters, would keep their participation confidential and would not quote them. We did provide drafts of the book to senior contacts at all the clubs profiled (Inter, Juventus, Milan, Napoli, and Roma) as professional courtesy and to allow them to provide feedback on any information they felt may be incorrect or misleading. Some chose to respond, others did not. We had to submit the final draft to the publisher before the conclusion of the 2017/18 season.

*

It took us many long hours of rigorous research and analysis to come to the same conclusion that a Serie A football executive told us in the first five minutes of his interview: 'What happened to Italy's Serie A football? It's complicated. It's Italy.'

The story about what happened to Italy's Serie A is messy and complex. Many seemingly unrelated changes, events and decisions over time, as well as their interdependent, unintended and compounding consequences, slowly caused Serie A to decline. The analysis is even more complicated because, as we previously mentioned, Italian football is notoriously opaque.

We developed a framework for analysis to make things clearer. To our knowledge this has never been done before for any sports league. First, we tried to divide reasons for the decline into 'on the pitch' and 'off the pitch'. This division is very difficult because, as explained earlier, the two are often intertwined, although they are often reported on and analysed separately by either 'football experts' or 'sports business experts'. Second, it became very clear that talent on the pitch and overall fan experience and engagement off the pitch are two critical issues, so we segmented those. After those two critical factors, we then divided the issues further into the following categories: the league, the management at clubs, the country Italy itself, technology and legal/regulatory. Often the reasons could easily be placed into more than one category. In those instances, we tried to place the issue into what we believe is its primary category for this analysis. Lastly, we tried to order the reasons in their primary categories to give a sense of priority.

Serie A did not decline overnight. Generally overlooked, a relative slow decline off the pitch in financial power had started well before the on-the-pitch decline. The weighting of importance of each reason changes over time generally and for each club specifically depending on each club's unique circumstances. We found that many interviewees viewed each reason differently because they view the analysis through their own experiences and the lens of their favourite clubs' history. We recognise the inclusion and importance of each reason is debatable, but after reading the analysis each one should provoke at least some thought.

On The Pitch Issues

Talent	*League*	*Management*
Less Talent	Perception of Relatively Defensive, Boring Games	Slow to Adapt to New Methods
Less Talent Development	Perception of Competitive Imbalance	Drain of Top Coaching Talent
Too Many Older Players	Fans Too Far and Attendance Too Poor to Influence Referees	
Not Enough Fast Players	Dilution of Quality with Too Many Clubs Difficulty in Passports for Players	

Country	*Technology*	*Legal/Regulatory*
Relatively Worse Income Taxes Favours Seniority	Synthetic Ball Speeds the Game	Negative Football Rule Changes to Italian Tactics

Off The Pitch Issues

Overall Fan Experience
Not Global Entertainment Brands
No Community-Centric Culture
Lack of Star Power
Poor Stadium Experience
Poor Facilities
Power of the Ultras
Clouds of Racism and Violence
Poor Online Engagement
Clubs
Players
Decentralised Supporters Clubs

League
Decisions Made for Short Term
Not for Common Good
Poor Global League Promotion
Poor Online Engagement
Clouds of Scandal
Poor Control of Ownership
Inability to Govern Itself
Lack of Collective Player Activism

Management
Tolerated Unethical Behaviour
Unsustainable Business Models
Over-reliance on TV Revenues
Poor Corporate Governance
Lack of Global Vision
Lack of Professional Development

Country
Patrimonial Ownership

Nepotistic System
Promotes Family and Friends
Favourable Regulatory Changes
Hid Problems
Lack of Transparency
Financial and Regulatory
Forgery of Football Merchandise
Strong Presence of Organised Crime
Challenging Demographics
Challenging Economic Situation
Dysfunctional Justice System
Italian Not a Global Language

Technology
Impact of Video Games

Legal/Regulatory
Italian Owners with Limited Ways
to Skirt FFP Limits

When we started the project, the easiest and most popular explanation for the decline in Serie A football was that there was a lack of money from the Italian club owners, and therefore there is a lack of talent playing in Serie A. In some ways, it is similar to the question, 'Which came first, the chicken or the egg?' If the owners don't have the money to sign the best players, then the league won't have the best talent. However, if the league had the best players, then the owners would likely have more opportunities to generate more matchday, commercial and broadcasting revenues. Both did impact Serie A, but we concluded neither is the sole nor primary cause. In many ways, the lack of money and talent is a result of the owners and league not recognising and adapting to various changes.

We also don't believe the explanation that Serie A declined primarily because of a struggling Italian economy. We actually believe this has been used as a simple to understand, and sympathise with, explanation that has been used by some parties that are actually partially to blame. In fact, we found that spending in the 2000s for a few club owners was more correlated to global factors, such as global oil prices and global economic growth, than the Italian economy. In addition, European football revenue growth was coming from global sources. Sustainable economic-sport models were not created in Italy. The required investments growing faster than, and becoming too big relative to, the commercial revenues (which needed global sources) are more of a factor for the decline than the Italian economy.

What really happened is European professional football became a global entertainment business with global community brands. At one time, the leading category of revenues for European football was local matchday ticket sales, which then evolved into domestic TV rights and then European TV rights and then to digital global broadcast rights. Commercial opportunities such as sponsorships and advertising with global sponsors eager to reach loyal and supportive fans were becoming as much or even more valuable than even the broadcast rights. Football became as much, or even more, about identity, community brands, entertainment and experiences, rather than just winning. Italian clubs didn't think of their names as global brands to market. When they won trophies, they didn't have sophisticated commercial areas to take advantage of their on-the-pitch success. Even worse, the clubs didn't even protect what they did have in brand value. For example, they allowed widespread cheap forgeries of their branded merchandise right outside their own stadiums.

The Italian league and owners failed to recognise and adapt to market changes. The owners of Serie A overly relied on revenues from domestic TV rights and debt to pay players and didn't invest in stadium experiences and take advantage of commercial opportunities, which made them financially vulnerable. For example, Italian fans primarily don't go to the Serie A games because they don't have discretionary income; they primarily don't go because the owners didn't invest in stadium experiences because, in part, they don't own the stadiums; therefore, generally the stadiums and the overall fan experience are poor. While it is true there are fewer world-class, headlining stars in the league to watch, academic research shows that stadium quality is the first predictor of sports stadium attendance and star players are the second predictor (Wakefield 2011). Many people are surprised that standings in the league (e.g. winning) was the third predictor, leading to the shocking idea to most club owners that fans care more than just about winning, which will be discussed later.

Most club owners' businesses in Italy did suffer from the downturn of the Italian economy, but the management teams never built self-sustaining global businesses. For example, they didn't successfully export the brand/identity of their clubs and league globally or raise outside capital or bringing in professional management with new ideas about sports management or push through measures to improve stadiums. Simply, Italian club owners didn't see their football clubs as true businesses that had to support themselves. They always covered the losses, which until the 2000s were relatively manageable to very wealthy and enterprising Italian owners. With a rich Italian owner to bail them out every year, the day-to-day management teams of clubs never innovated out of necessity to generate a break-even business model, let alone make a profit. Part of the reason to blame is that Italian society is based on 'neo-patrimonial' networks which typically are regional and rely on family relationships, personal contacts and a system of favours (Eisenstadt 1973; Sapelli 1995; Doidge 2015).

Italy wasn't declared a united kingdom until 1861 and has maintained much stronger regional and family communities and identifications than most European countries. Italian football clubs were typically parts of, or sponsored in some way by, regional industrial family business groups whose original purpose was to improve employee morale and pride, so industrial patronage and regional 'wars' played out on the pitches were accepted. For example, prior to Serie A being created for the 1929/30 season, many clubs competed in the top level of Italian football on a regional basis until 1922, then an interregional basis until 1929. In addition to controlling the most popular pastime, typically these regional industrial family business groups incorporated and controlled the regional media. Controlling large employee bases and extended football fans, all of whom voted, and the media also meant that these families had an influence on politics. Therefore, it was accepted that family business, corporate business, football, media and politics not only mixed, but supported each other. The idea of making football clubs economically self-sustaining was, and generally still is, a foreign idea, as was having an independent media. Such strong regional identification and historical financial and political uncertainty also created an environment where owners focused on their own short-term interests, versus making the national league stronger and more globally marketable, which may be in their best long-term interests.

The European football industry started to dramatically change in the mid to late 1990s and early 2000s into a global entertainment business with revenues from many sources, but Italian football didn't adapt. Player salaries and transfer fees went up dramatically, especially with the Bosman ruling in 1995. Competitors searched for new sources of revenue, but the Italian club owners didn't adjust. Eventually, what was once accepted as a relatively manageable loss leader for other purposes, required more and more money to compete in a global entertainment and community brand business, and the owners were losing more and more serious money. According to *The Economist*, in 2001, total player costs among leading clubs averaged 125% of revenue in Italy, 85% in Spain and 75% in England.[3]

When the owners of Serie A clubs recognised financial challenges as the industry changed, instead of restructuring, repositioning and expanding, they tried to cut expenses and raise capital by reducing compensation and selling star players. This had a spiralling negative effect on fan interest and revenues. Despite the popularity of football in Italy, the owners didn't and couldn't raise capital from foreign investors because of poor business, legal and financial transparency and practices. Italian owners kept injecting equity, borrowing money and utilising financial tricks to keep up with other European competitors that were generating revenues from other sources besides domestic TV rights. And, when things continued to get worse, some government regulations actually made the financial tricks easier. Also, instead of collaborating and taking a long-term view to strengthen the league overall, Italian owners and the league made decisions in their individual short-term best interests.

Meanwhile, many competitors of Italian clubs were busy adapting and innovating. For example, Real Madrid and Barcelona can't sell shares and raise equity due to their by-laws and do not have billionaire owners; instead, they are owned by tens of thousands of members. Without billionaire owners to fund losses, they were forced to innovate and expand revenues to build self-sustaining businesses. In 2000, before Florentino Pérez was elected president, Real Madrid were essentially bankrupt, even having won the Champions League in 1998 and 2000, demonstrating that winning doesn't necessarily lead to off-the-pitch financial success and on-the-pitch performance can benefit from last-gasp spending before drastic changes need

---

3 'Business: Players and Gentlemen: European football clubs,' *The Economist*, 9 November 2002, p 82.

to be made. Even though Real Madrid won the Champions League in 1998 and 2000, during this time (i) the number of Real Madrid owner-members actually declined; (ii) Real Madrid only sold out their stadium once per season during those seasons – for the match against Barcelona; and (iii) the incumbent president who delivered Real Madrid's first Champions League trophy since 1966 lost the election to Florentino Pérez; all three are examples illustrating that fans care more than about just winning. Today, Real Madrid are a financial powerhouse with a global community brand supported by technology and social media; Real Madrid had to stop accepting new owner-members (now only available to legacies) and have a long waiting list for season tickets. Real Madrid spent a lot of money on the world's best talent, but they carefully selected the best players with the values of its community and had them play beautiful, attacking football, which led to more fans and more passion and loyalty, which led to more commercial revenues, which allowed them to attract and retain world-class talent. The club also made significant investments in the fan experience. For example, the club invested a lot of money in their stadium and stadium experience, including a museum that is the #2 attraction in Madrid after the Prado Museum. And some of Real Madrid's growth was also during difficult economic times in Spain. Real Madrid brought in professional management to run the club like a world-class business, and they built a global community brand, not dependent on the Spanish economy or domestic TV. For example, less than 5% of Real Madrid's supporters and social media followers are from Spain, as Real Madrid looked globally. Real Madrid invested significantly in the use of technology and engagement of social media to support and grow their brand. They are able to monetise their social media followers by offering their passionate and loyal fans compelling and authentic products and services, which leads to more commercial revenues which gives them more money to spend on talent. Real Madrid spends less than 50% of its revenues on players (one of the lowest in European football), while Italian clubs spend a much higher percentage because their revenues are much less. Unable to make profit distributions to owner-members because of its by-laws and structure, today, Real Madrid has accumulated cash and is the only top football club that has more cash than debt.

Real Madrid are not alone in quickly adapting to the industry changes. Bayern Munich are majority-owned by members. With strong financial transparency and governance, they sold 8.33% stakes each to three German-based, multinational corporate sponsors (adidas, Allianz and Audi) to raise capital to invest in their stadium experience and players. Bayern Munich also sought revenues globally. For example, together with the Bundesliga, Bayern Munich have made a concerted effort to increase their exposure in the growth market of China. Today, Bayern Munich are the #1-rated club on Chinese digital media, according to the Red Card 2016 China Digital Football Index. In addition, Bayern Munich has offices in New York and Shanghai.

Several owners of clubs in the English Premier League recognised industry changes, and the significant resources required to compete. They took advantage of stronger business, financial and legal transparency and practices in England and sold their clubs, or stakes in their clubs, to foreigners with more capital and new ideas. In 2016, 57% of clubs in England's top two tiers of football (Premier League and Championship) were owned by a foreigner. In fact, 14 of the 20 Premier League clubs have foreign ownership/control with only Burnley, Middlesbrough, Stoke, Tottenham, West Brom and West Ham the exceptions (11 of the 24 Championship clubs have foreign owners/majority shareholders). While English fans didn't exactly completely 'welcome' all new foreign owners with open arms, they did not have a strong culture of 'neo-patrimonial' networks, similar to Italy's. One of the issues why Italian clubs seem not to work together as well as the UK, where the legal system – and much of civil society – operates on the basis of reciprocal trust, Italy's is based on 'una diffidenza reciproca' – essentially, mutual distrust (A. Baroncelli and R. Caruso, 2011). Also, with more owners in the EPL looking at clubs as investments (not parts of regional family businesses), they generally had common interests and therefore collaborated more and have taken a longer-term view than Italian owners. For example, the English Premier League was created in 1992 to collectively negotiate TV rights – something that was forced on Italian clubs in the 2010/11 season – and took advantage of English being a global language.

Certainly, the Italian economy didn't help. However, for the most part, Italian owners and Serie A didn't change or didn't change drastically enough or fast enough. The opportunities were there; and many still are there, although some challenges specific to Italy and the league still exist.

For example, most football clubs don't own their own stadiums and pay rent to government entities. If the clubs want to build their own stadiums and leave, then the government entities will lose income, so this is an Italian political issue. Obviously, there are also other factors distinctive to Italian culture such as patrimonial networks and nepotistic structures.

The 2006 Italian football scandal *Calciopoli* (literally 'footballville') is another common reason mentioned by experts for the decline. We found Serie A was in decline both on and off the pitch before 2006. Some blame Calciopoli for the decline in attendance, but the attendance decline started well before 2006. The scandal symbolised some of the country-specific institutional issues that were challenges to Italian football from competing on the European stage. For example, many Italian fans identify racism, violence, organised crime and Ultras in the stadium as major issues. Unfortunately, the bad actions of a few cause most of the issues, but the responses to date have not been effective enough for a variety of reasons. Serie A lags behind its rivals in the kind of infrastructure and attitudes that could help attract commercial sponsors and increase its global following, which in turn could lead to more lucrative international broadcast rights agreements. The 2016 Deloitte Football Money League report bluntly stated that Serie A's 'pattern of decline, relative to its European peers' is likely to continue, 'unless there is significant and immediate investment in both stadia facilities and improving the matchday experience'. Not only are the clubs and league, among others, to blame, but the players themselves have not collectively worked together in any effective manner to help address issues such as racism, let alone push more social media engagement to improve fan experiences.

Professors and economists Tito Boeri of Bocconi University and Battista Severgnini of Copenhagen Business School studied the economic model of Serie A in 2012. They found that out of 37 teams participating in Serie A in the period 2001/02 to 2010/11, nine, that is, 25% of the total, had to declare bankruptcy (Ancona, Como, Fiorentina, Messina, Perugia, Piacenza, Torino, Treviso and Venezia). Second, they found an upward trend in net losses from 2001/02 to 2010/11, with an average of about €250 million of losses per year for the league, peaking above €300 million in 2002/03, 2003/04 and 2010/11, and the total debt of Serie A clubs was increasing at a faster rate. They noted that these numbers may underestimate actual losses as football clubs often used manipulated extraordinary profits to reduce the reported losses. Therefore, the financial condition of Serie A may be worse than known or estimated. The professors conclude, 'Our analysis suggests that Italian football is on an unsustainable path . . . any serious attempt to get Italian football off this unsustainable path should address the revenue side.' The differences between Serie A clubs and their European rivals are quite striking. TV and other media rights take a much larger share of total revenues in Italian clubs than in the other top European teams, while matchday revenues in Italy are negligible by top European clubs' standards. The non-Italian clubs are much more diversified in terms of the composition of revenues. The low level of matchday and commercial revenues of Italian clubs suggests that they have been severely mismanaged but also that the clubs have potential opportunities for increasing total revenues.

Today, it is much more difficult for a wealthy owner to just spend and make investments to reposition a club. UEFA Financial Fair Play Regulations were implemented in the 2011/12 football season to prevent football clubs from spending more than they earn. Therefore, clubs that don't find new ways to increase revenues are more restricted and at a competitive financial disadvantage to those that made the necessary large investments and built global brands and entertainment businesses before the rules were implemented. Therefore, more innovation and ingenuity will be required and/or clubs will need to have more commercial synergies with other related entities.

Financial Fair Play has played a significant two-fold role in improving clubs' balance sheets, firstly by limiting major losses and secondly by requiring owners to permanently inject capital rather than allowing loans to build up year after year. According to UEFA, English clubs have enjoyed the most equity increases via earnings or capital contributions totalling €2.3 billion in the last five years ending 2015. Italian clubs are the next largest beneficiaries, totalling €1.1 billion. Since Italian clubs already have significant debt, with four of the top ten largest net debt amounts being Italian clubs, owners have had to inject capital. However, unlike the English clubs where the contributions have been in earnings, Italian club owners are injecting personal capital because of losses, which at some point is unsustainable. This is what has, and will, continue to cause ownership of Italian clubs to change or sustainable economic-sport models will have to be implemented.

While we started to piece together data to answer my question about the decline of Italian football, we also found a fascinating story about how two innovative clubs, AS Roma and SSC Napoli, were using two different approaches, to challenge both an established leader, Juventus, as well as the old way of doing things in Italy. All three clubs do not want to win just in Italy, but they want to win European titles against the elite clubs, and they are making progress. Pallotta and the owner of Napoli are relatively new owners and innovate out of necessity to try to create sustainable, economic-sport businesses that consistently compete for trophies. Jim brought his passion and quantitative and data analytics approach in investing to all aspects of the club. The on-the-pitch results have been good – finishing second in Serie A in three of the last four years (with the other year finishing third).[4]

In April 2018, Roma advanced to the semi-finals of the Champions League with a dramatic win over Barcelona; it was Roma's first semi-final since 1984 when they reached the final. To provide context, in 2016/17 Barcelona's player wage bill ranked #1 and was 2.65 time greater than Roma's, which ranked #15. In addition, Pallotta brought his knowledge in, and vision from, investing in media and technology to transform Roma into one of the most innovative digital brands in football. In 2017, Roma finally received the necessary approvals to build its own stadium which is expected to be completed in 2020.

The owner of Napoli, Aurelio De Laurentiis, is a prominent Italian film producer and sees football as a form of exciting entertainment. He acquired the club in bankruptcy in 2004 and through results managed to get the club promoted from the third division Serie C to the first division Serie A in three years. De Laurentiis has put together a distinctive, identifiable, attacking type of football and culture that is fun to watch and be a part of. The football and cultural changes were so compelling that after only one year match attendance sky-rocketed, even though the club was in Serie C. In 2016/17 Napoli advanced to the Round of 16 in the Champions League, and in 2017/18 Napoli were challenging Juventus for the Italian domestic title. To provide perspective, Napoli have the fifth-highest player wage bill in Serie A, behind Juventus, AC Milan, Roma and Inter Milan, with Juventus spending more than double Napoli's total.

---

[4] Roma also had good results prior, including in the early 1980s. After winning their third Scudetto in 2001, Roma were also second in 2002, 2004, 2006, 2007, 2008 and 2010. However, most years it was not a close second.

Roma and Napoli are embracing the idea that the world has changed and continues to do so. They changed their organisations to take advantage. It will take time and execution (and most likely their own stadiums) to build commercial powerhouses to compete against the top clubs for superstar players, but they are on the right track. We suspect more Serie A clubs will need to look to new owners for the management strategies and capital necessary to compete, which will force more positive changes.

Juventus are the most popular football club in Italy and have won the most domestic trophies.[5] They are controlled by the Agnelli family (although the club is also publicly listed), which controls the automobile manufacturer Fiat and is considered one of the wealthiest and most powerful families in Italy. The Agnelli family – which also control the city's newspaper, *La Stampa* – is revered as Turin's quasi royal family. The club's nickname is the 'Old Lady' and Juventus have been trying to overcome a perception that their style is too defensive and tactical, and their black and white colours are too boring.[6]

In 2006, Juventus were relegated to Serie B from Serie A as a punishment resulting from the 2006 Italian football scandal Calciopoli. Suffering relegation to Serie B meant that Juventus lost the TV revenues of Serie A, their biggest source of revenue at the time, until they were promoted back to Serie A in 2007/08. While having immediate negative financial consequences, ironically it did cause the club's management to recognise their vulnerabilities and changes in the industry. They urgently restructured and repositioned and found new ways to generate new and more revenue beyond TV and improve their overall fan experience and engagement. They looked to their past to help define their future. Juventus became 'Newventus'. For example, Juventus built their own stadium in 2011 which led to a dramatic increase in revenue and improvement of overall fan experience. In addition, the club were the first European football club to have a Netflix documentary give fans behind-the-scenes access, which

---

[5] While Juventus are the most popular club throughout Italy, they are not considered the most popular club in Turin; Torino has that distinction.

[6] A common perception of an Italian Juventus fan's view: 'La famiglia, dolce vita, Ferrari, Prosecco and Juve.' Besides their success on the pitch, Juventus' popularity is partly explained by the fact that so many people work at companies around Italy that supply Fiat or Agnelli-related companies with products and services, who then, out of patrimonial feelings, support the Agnellis' Juventus. In addition, Juventus have traditionally had a higher percentage of players on the Italian national team, making Juventus appear more 'Italian' as opposed to regional, which also helps makes them a favourite among people of Italian background.

improves overall fan engagement. However, overcoming the old ways of doing things and the challenges the league and country generally presents, is why, in part, they only rank #10 in the 2016/17 Deloitte Football Revenues Rankings, despite their on-the-pitch success. Juventus' strong culture and leadership have helped the club reach the Champions League finals in 2014/15 and 2016/17, overcoming the financial disadvantage relative to the nine clubs ranked higher in revenues.

Figuring out what happened in Serie A is a fascinating puzzle that takes us into the heart of a dynamic and complex situation and environment. It is a story of intrigue involving a country, a sport and clubs that garner highly emotional responses. But it is more than that. It raises questions that are fundamental to organisations themselves. The book offers a glimpse into the consequences of not adapting and innovating. Juventus, Roma and Napoli are leading change in football in Italy. Milan and Inter have recently been purchased by Chinese-backed entities, highlighting some recognition that more things need to change. We expect more foreigners will buy, or invest in, Serie A clubs and bring more capital and a fresh global perspective. The new owners might see and capitalise on opportunities differently than traditional regional family industrial groups; however, the new owners still have to operate in a country and league that pose unique challenges.

In fact, the 2017 sale of AC Milan to Chinese investors by Silvio Berlusconi, who in 2017 *Forbes* magazine ranked as the 199th richest person in the world with a net worth of €6.2 billion (down from €9.6 billion in 2005), is a signal that some Italians are starting to recognise their challenges. Berlusconi posted on his Facebook page the following message after the sale: 'I leave today, after more than 30 years, the ownership and the presidency of AC Milan. I do it with grief and emotion, but knowing that modern football, to compete at the top level in Europe and in the world, needs investments and resources that only one family cannot support.'[7]

The acceleration of European football clubs' ownership changing hands, especially in Italy, is a clear illustration of the trend of European football becoming such a big and global business. Most current owners can't just simply employ family members, utilise their clubs in the same way they use their business connections and contribute more equity and borrow more

---

7 http://www.espnfc.com/ac-milan/story/3103229/silvio-berlusconi-writes-open-letter-to-ac-milan-fans-following-sale-of-club

money each year to cover losses. Today, football clubs require professional management executing sustainable, economic-sport model strategies that can support the level of necessary investment. Often, there has to be a completely different vision to how a club and the business of football and entertainment was viewed and used in the past.[8]

All Italian football clubs face very specific historical and cultural challenges, not to mention league and economic challenges and intense competition in a rapidly changing world. However, there are signs that, albeit slowly, selected clubs are adapting to changes and even taking advantage of them, so we are optimistic about the potential opportunities for Italian football. It is fascinating to examine how some top clubs are adapting and innovating in their own distinctive way to compete, and there are unexpected and valuable lessons to be learned.

Although our study focuses on Serie A, the story has much broader implications. Corporate industries and businesses as well as sports leagues and clubs face the same pressures and changes as Serie A – competitive, organisational, regulatory and technological. Leaders may not be able to see that it is happening until it is too late. Glimpses of glory because of luck or unsustainable spending and losses or industry growth may mask the changes – but slowly the changes are making their impact. Leaders need to constantly be evolving, adapting and innovating, while not losing their core principles and values that make them unique. The book will help leaders identify the pressures and changes facing them so they can adapt to changes and even take advantage of them.

Near the end of the book, we make a few observations and predictions about the future of European football both on and off the pitch. We are not making any recommendations or judgements. We recognise the inclusion and importance of each observation and prediction is debatable, but after reading the analysis each one should provoke at least some thought.

---

[8] Silvio Berlusconi was Italian prime minister in 1994–95, 2001–06 and 2008–11. He acquired Milan in 1986. Many believe that with the help of Milan's success on the pitch, he won his first general election. Milan won Serie A in 1988, 1992, 1993, 1994, 1996, 1999, 2004 and 2011 and the Champions League in 1989, 1990, 1994, 2003 and 2007. 'Football is a business that provides votes for politicians,' Marco Mazzocchi, a football analyst and television show host in Italy, said. 'All these fans can vote, and these club owners can often control votes.' When Berlusconi ran for election in 1994, his party slogan was 'Forza Italia', the saying to support the Italian national football team. The message was he would make Italy win just like he made Milan win, not only in Italy but in Europe and the world. Berlusconi announced the signing of beloved player Ronaldinho on 10 April 2008, just days before the election for prime minister. http://www.nytimes.com/2007/02/06/sports/soccer/06soccer.html

PART ONE

THE RISE IN THE 1980s AND 1990s

CHAPTER ONE

THE ITALIAN SERIE A LEAGUE'S DOMINANCE

ITALY'S SERIE A was known as '*Il campionato più bello del mondo*' ('The most beautiful championship in the world'). Football fans in Italy are notorious for their feverish support: the Italian word for fan, '*tifoso*', translates as those who have typhoid. Italy won the World Cup in 1982 and what followed were exciting battles for the Italian League Serie A trophy between AC Milan, Inter Milan and Juventus (with Fiorentina, Hellas Verona, Lazio, Napoli, Parma, Roma and Sampdoria competing from time to time).

In the 1980s and 1990s, if you turned on your TV to watch football during the weekend, there was a high likelihood that you would see an Italian team. A generation of football fans would tune in every weekend for their dose of Italian football culture, captivated by a league that was different, unique, exotic. *Gazzetta Football Italia*, a very popular free-to-air Channel 4 British show, had a youthful and charismatic James Richardson educating British and world viewers about Serie A. With the English Premier League moving to pay TV on Sky, there was a vacuum to be filled for millions of fans wanting a football fix. Italy had just hosted the World Cup in 1990 and with drama and stars it really captured the imagination. Now, Serie A was football in many of the same stadiums and with many of the same players. For anyone who enjoyed Italia '90 it was almost like a spin-off series. The football was more beautiful and different compared to a lot of football that people had been watching elsewhere in Europe.[1]

Serie A clubs were consistently in the finals of the biggest European competitions. From 1983 to 1998 an Italian club was in the final of the Champions League 12 of the 16 years (75%). In addition, Serie A had one of the greatest teams of all time, AC Milan, that won back-to-back European trophies in 1989 and 1990.

Italian Clubs in Champions League/European Cup Finals (1983–98)

Year	Winner	Runner-Up
1983	Hamburg	**Juventus**
1984	Liverpool	**Roma**
1985	**Juventus**	Liverpool
1989	**Milan**	Steaua București
1990	**Milan**	Benfica
1992	Barcelona	**Sampdoria**
1993	Marseille	**Milan**
1994	**Milan**	Barcelona
1995	Ajax	**Milan**
1996	**Juventus**	Ajax
1997	Borussia Dortmund	**Juventus**
1998	Real Madrid	**Juventus**

At the time, the UEFA Europa League Cup was a more competitive competition than today because the European Cup/Champions League had fewer clubs. The UEFA Cup invited clubs that finished second, third or fourth in their national league. From the start of the European Cup in 1955/56 until 1996/97 (the name changed to the UEFA Champions League in 1992/93), only the domestic league champions qualified for this most prestigious pan-European football club competition. The following two seasons, eligibility was expanded to include the runners-up from the largest domestic leagues. Currently, up to four teams from the domestic leagues qualify for the UCL.[2] After the expansion of the UCL, the payouts for participating clubs increased dramatically. While the

---

[1] https://inews.co.uk/essentials/sport/football/football-indepth/james-richardson-football-italia/
[2] Starting in 2018/19 the top four clubs from the top four ranked domestic leagues automatically qualify (in 2018/19 in alphabetical order: England, Germany, Italy and Spain).

Italian Serie A champions were fighting to win the Champions League, Italian clubs dominated the UEFA Europa League Cup competition. From 1989 to 1999, an Italian club was in the final ten of the 11 years. Serie A clubs were in so many UEFA Cup finals, the tournament's finals were sometimes sarcastically referred to as the 'European Coppa Italia'.

Italian Clubs in UEFA Europa League Cup Finals (1989–99)

Year	Winner	Runner-Up
1989	**Napoli**	Stuttgart
1990	**Juventus**	**Fiorentina**
1991	Inter	**Roma**
1992	Ajax	**Torino**
1993	**Juventus**	Borussia Dortmund
1994	**Inter**	Salzburg
1995	**Parma**	**Juventus**
1997	Schalke	**Inter**
1998	**Inter**	**Lazio**
1999	**Parma**	Marseille

Another important European competition at the time was the Cup Winners' Cup for clubs that won national cups the year before. Italian clubs also did well in this competition. They won the Cup Winners' Cup in 1984 (Juventus), 1990 (Sampdoria), 1993 (Parma), and 1999 (Lazio), and reached the final in 1989 (Sampdoria) and 1994 (Parma). The Cup Winners' Cup merged into the new UEFA Cup in 2000, that ultimately became the UEFA Europa League in 2004.

Most impressively, every year from 1989 to 1999 Italy had at least one finalist in a European competition. Serie A also had the highest match attendances in Europe by far. For instance, in 1992, Milan broke the world record and sold 72,000 season tickets. In 1992/93 Milan had an average crowd of 75,807 spectators for every home game, compared to 37,009 for Liverpool and 35,084 for Manchester United. In the 1992/93 season, Serie A had an average of 32,106 per game versus the English Premier League's 21,132.

There are several reasons why Serie A became the most successful league in the 1980s and 1990s. We created a framework to categorise the reasons either on or off the pitch, in order to make it easier to explain and the reader to follow along. Obviously, what happens both on and off the pitch have an impact on each other.

On the Pitch

More Talent

During the 1980s and 1990s, some of the most exciting stars of football from around the world played in Serie A. Between 1984 and 2000, the world transfer fee record was broken 12 times, nine of which were made by Italian clubs. In the 18 years from 1982 to 2000, a player from Italy's Serie A won the Ballon d'Or 13 times (72%). The next highest league was Spain's La Liga with three.

Ballon d'Or Winners Playing in Italy (1982–2000)

Year	Player	Club
1982	Paolo Rossi	Juventus
1983	Michel Platini	Juventus
1984	Michel Platini	Juventus
1985	Michel Platini	Juventus
1987	Ruud Gullit	Milan
1988	Marco van Basten	Milan (Milan had 3 in the top 3)
1989	Marco van Basten	Milan (Milan had 3 in the top 3)
1990	Lothar Matthäus	Inter (Serie A had 3 in the top 3)
1992	Marco van Basten	Milan
1993	Roberto Baggio	Juventus
1995	George Weah	Milan
1997	Ronaldo	Inter
1998	Zinedine Zidane	Juventus

Serie A also had the most World Cup Golden Ball (best player) and Golden Boot (top goalscorer) winners from 1982 to 1998.

World Cup Golden Ball Winners Playing in Italy (1982–98)

Year	Player	Club (at the time)
1982 Spain	Paolo Rossi	(Juventus)
1986 Mexico	Diego Maradona	(Napoli)
1990 Italy	Salvatore Schillaci	(Juventus)
1998 France	Ronaldo	(Inter)

World Cup Golden Boot Winners Playing in Italy (1982–90)

Year	Player	Club (at the time)
1982 Spain	Paolo Rossi	(Juventus)
1990 Italy	Salvatore Schillaci	(Juventus)

Better Coaching and Player Development

Italy has produced some of the greatest managers/coaches and players. One of the reasons is that they have had a dedicated school for teaching football since 1958, Scuola Allenatori (the Managers' School), at the Italian Football Federation's Technical Centre in Coverciano, Italy, north of Florence. It is often referred to as 'Coverciano'.

Luigi Ridolfi, born into one of Florence's oldest and wealthiest landed families, came up with the idea of creating a national training base specifically for football players and coaches – something that did not really exist in Europe at the time. Importantly, he wanted it to be a place where students would have the opportunity to interact and collaborate with other athletes and coaches from different sporting backgrounds as well. For that to happen, he made Coverciano into a place that other athletes would want to visit and train at. The presence of diverse athletes was a key element in advancing Italian coaches' understanding of what their players' bodies could and could not do and the best physical training techniques were. By the late 1960s, professors were teaching Coverciano's first-ever courses on how to prepare footballers physically to compete at the highest level. From the beginning, the underpinning ethos was one of innovation and openness to novel ideas. It owes its existence to Ridolfi's willingness to try something different.

Luigi Ridolfi travelled all over Europe before starting work on the Coverciano, seeking out the most advanced materials and technologies available at the time. For example, the window panes in the gym are made with a crystal that allows them to withstand being struck with a football, which was innovative at the time.

Up until 1998 when UEFA changed the rules, domestic football federations handled the licensing of coaches, but Scuola Allenatori and Italy were far ahead of the curve. Since the 1960s, anyone aspiring to work at the highest level in Italy was obliged to put themselves through a rigorous syllabus at Coverciano which became known as 'il Supercorso'. Students were required to attend as many as 900 hours of lessons and seminars – almost four times as many as today's UEFA requirements – over two years.

One of the final hurdles a student must clear today to graduate from Coverciano is submission of a thesis on a subject of his choosing. The requirement was and is uniquely Italian. The requirement for a written thesis was introduced in stages. In Coverciano's small library one can find copies of the work that each coach submitted before receiving their final qualification. Claudio Ranieri's dissertation, from 1990, was not truly a dissertation but rather a comprehensive diary, listing every activity he conducted with his Cagliari players over the course of a pre-season training camp. By contrast, 16 years later, Antonio Conte prepared a 38-page discourse under the title: 'Considerations on 4-3-1-2 and the didactic use of video'.[3]

In fairness, it is important to recognise a growing body of research suggests that managers have surprisingly little impact on how well a team plays. In a study of English professional clubs between 1973 and 2010, Stefan Szymanski, an economist at the University of Michigan, found that there is a 90% correlation between teams' wages and their results, and that only a handful of managers consistently performed above their team's expected level.[4]

As for players, the Italian clubs developed some of the world's best players. Overleaf is a list of some of the best players that played for Italy in the 1980s and 1990s as ranked by *Bleacher Report*.

Some of the Best Players that Played for Italy
in the 1980s and 1990s
In order of ranking by *Bleacher Report*

Player	Years in Italy	Caps	Goals	Age @ 1st Cap
Paolo Maldini	1988–2002	126	7	20
Roberto Baggio	1988–2004	56	27	21
Franco Baresi	1982–1994	82	1	22
Paolo Rossi	1977–1986	48	20	21
Gaetano Scirea	1974–1986	78	2	22
Gianluigi Buffon	1997–2017	143	0	19

[3] http://www.dailymail.co.uk/sport/football/article-4971836/Inside-Coverciano-Italian-finishing-school-managers.html; http://www.todayonline.com/sports/italian-coaching-academy-which-has-produced-winners-conte-ranieri-lippi-and-ancelotti
[4] https://www.independent.co.uk/sport/football/premier-league/sacking-managers-pointless-stats-slaven-bilic-west-ham-premier-league-a8044586.html

Alessandro Del Piero	1995–2008	91	27	21
Fabio Cannavaro	1997–2010	136	2	24
Francesco Totti	1998–2006	58	9	22
Giuseppe Bergomi	1982–1998	81	6	19
Claudio Gentile	1975–1984	71	0	22
Alessandro Nesta	1996–2006	78	0	20
Marco Tardelli	1976–1985	76	7	22

Source: http://bleacherreport.com/articles/408960-fifa-world-cups-greatest-ever-top-20-italian-players-of-all-time

It is interesting that of the 13 greatest players above, eight of them were developed by the clubs they played for most of their careers with or played for only one more Italian club for the rest of their careers.

Roma has famously developed two contemporary Italian football legends in their academy, namely Francesco Totti and Daniele De Rossi. Roma's academy will be discussed later.

Lesser known outside of Italy is the youth development at Atalanta, a football club located 40 km north-east of Milan. They established one of the first meaningful youth academies. It was set up in the 1940s by Giuseppe Ciatto. In the late 1950s former Atalanta player Luigi Tentorio (then Special Commissioner of the club) felt the need to start investing more systematically in youth development and created a youth development department, with its own independent structure from the first team. The youth development department was entrusted to Giuseppe Brolis, who created a partnership with various clubs in geographic areas that he felt had good football cultures and traditions, building a network of scouts and young coaches.

In the early 1990s, the president of Atalanta, Antonio Percassi, implemented a new investment policy and an even greater focus on youth development. The Atalanta youth system not only continued to increase the development of players for the first team but began to win several honours in the most important national leagues. From 1991 to 2014, the various Atalanta youth teams have won 17 national titles. The club has proven time and again that it has one of the best youth academies in Italy, arguably in Europe. Interestingly, the academy doesn't focus on the results on the pitch; they are focused on showing all of their youngsters how to play. When evaluating a player, the coaches consider the player's footballing ability as well as his desire to fit into the club ethos. With this in mind, Atalanta are careful when selecting the coaches, preferring coaches who have gone through their system or played for the club – those who truly understand the meaning of the academy and its significance.

Graduates from the academy include Riccardo Montolivo, Giampaolo Pazzini, Franco Nodari, Piero Gardoni, Roberto Donadoni, Alessio Tacchinardi, Gaetano Scirea, Gianpaolo Bellini and Angelo Domenghini. With relatively less investment in academy development in recent years from most Italian clubs, Atalanta has been able to sell many of its young promising players to bigger rivals. Some young players recently sold to bigger Italian clubs in the past couple of years include: Daniele Baselli in 2015 for €6 million to Torino; Davide Zappacosta in 2015 for €10 million to Torino and now Chelsea; Giacomo 'Jack' Bonaventura in 2014 to Milan for €7 million; Roberto Gagliardini in 2017 for an estimated €25 million to Inter Milan; Andrea Conti in 2017 for €24 million to Milan; Mattia Caldara in 2017 for €15 million, rising to a potential €25 million with add-ons to Juventus and loan back to Atalanta; and Franck Kessié in 2017 for a loan fee of €8 million to Milan.

Competitive Balance and Talent Across Clubs

The quality of the talent was not only very high but it was also diversified. Of the 44 possible places in European finals (Champions League and UEFA Cup) across an 11-year period from 1989 to 1999, a remarkable ten different Serie A clubs (Fiorentina, Inter, Juventus, Lazio, Milan, Napoli, Parma, Roma, Sampdoria and Torino) occupied 23 of them. In 1988 Atalanta reached the Cup Winners' Cup semi-finals while playing in Serie B, the Italian league second level. Torino, Genoa, Cagliari, Vicenza and Bologna managed to reach the finals or semi-finals in the UEFA Cup or Cup Winners' Cup during the 1980s and 1990s.

Serie A had just 16 teams – from 1967 to 1998 – before it was increased to 18. The decision to have 20 sides competing wasn't made until 2004.

The stadiums in Italy were newly built or renovated for the 1990 World Cup. These stadiums, improvements and a few side projects (some of which were never finished such as an infamous hotel in Milan) cost around €1 billion, almost twice as much as budgeted. In addition, Serie A had the greatest players in the world who played beautiful football. The attendance numbers were reflective of new stadiums and star players which led to a good overall fan experience. Even though violence would occur in certain areas, in general, games were viewed by fans as a special community event with colour and singing as well as a place to express themselves and their passion. Fans even arrived early to enjoy the atmosphere.

Big money had not flooded into football yet and the sport overall was increasingly plagued by negative incidents and stadium disasters. Generally, fans were complimentary of their stadium experiences during the 1990 World Cup. Although the often large, concrete stadiums offered few luxuries, only occasionally cover, and seats with a back were not yet a FIFA requirement, few people expected more of a football stadium at that time. Italia '90 was the tournament that was at a turning point in football history. It was the last big tournament before the commercialisation of the Premier League and Champions League set in.

A total of 12 venues had been selected for Italia '90, two more than in France eight years later and a similar amount as in Germany in 2006, though with 12 matches less to play. This meant that most stadiums hosted only three or four matches, not much for a World Cup. While few new stadiums were built for Italia '90 (this was only the case for Stadio delle Alpi and Stadio San Nicola), most stadiums did undergo significant renovations. The San Siro of today, for example, hardly resembles the pre-1990 San Siro. As a part of the renovations, the stadium became all seated, with an extra tier being added to three sides of the stadium. This entailed the building of 11 concrete towers around the outside of the stadium. Four of these concrete towers were located at the corners to support a new roof, which has distinctive protruding red girders.[5] Though Rome's Stadio Olimpico was initially only planned

---

5 http://www.stadiumguide.com/the-unfortunate-legacy-of-italia-1990/

to get extensively renovated, several redesigns later an almost complete new stadium was built, with a price tag three times its initial size. Another stadium that got almost completely rebuilt was Genoa's Stadio Luigi Ferraris, while Napoli's Stadio San Paolo and Florence's Stadio Comunale got extensively refurbished. Udinese's Stadio Friuli needed the least work as it had been completed in 1976.

Italia '90 was unfortunate timing because the early 1990s were a turning point in stadium design. English stadiums started the trend with the conversion into new and modern all-seaters following an investigation into a stadium disaster in 1989, which led to the Taylor Report. The opening of the Amsterdam ArenA in 1996, with a retractable roof and lots of premium business and box seats, was a revolution for large stadium design in Europe. The Stade de France opened two years later in 1998. However, in the 1990s Italy offered the most new, or newly furbished, stadiums that met the expectations and attitudes, at the time, of fans for a good overall experience.

Also, it is worth noting that until 1993, no Serie A match was broadcasted live. Starting from 29 August 1993, just one night-match every week was broadcasted live on Tele+, an Italian-French pay TV broadcaster. This changed radically after 2003, when Rupert Murdoch's Sky replaced Stream (Tele+ replacement) and began broadcasting more and more live games, later joined by Mediaset Premium.

Compelling Rivalries

Serie A captured the imagination and passion of football fans. Putting aside the remarkably talented stars and beautiful football being played, TV viewers could feel the intensity and passion in the packed stadiums, and especially during the Italian derbies.

Fans around the world were familiar with many of the Serie A cross-town rival derbies, such as: 'Derby della Madonnina', also known as the 'Derby di Milano' (or the Milan Derby, as it is known in the English-speaking world), between Inter and Milan[6]; 'Derby della Capitale' (Derby of the Capital) between Roma and Lazio; 'Derby della Mole'

---

[6] It is called 'Derby della Madonnina' in honour of one of the main sights in the city of Milan, the statue of the Virgin Mary on the top of the Duomo, which is often referred to as the Madonnina [Little Madonna].

(Turin Derby) between Juventus and Torino; and 'Derby della Lanterna' (the Lighthouse Derby) between Genoa and Sampdoria. Fans were also familiar with Italian regional derbies such as: 'Derby d'Italia' (Derby of Italy) between Inter and Juventus; 'Derby d'Europa' (Derby of Europe) between Milan and Juventus; and 'Derby del Sole' (Derby of the Sun) between Roma and Napoli.

Allegations of Cheating

It is very difficult to analyse past performance when there are allegations of cheating both domestically and in Europe. This is true not just for Italy but many leagues and clubs in Europe over time. Cheating may or may not help to explain Italy's dominance, but it is worth mentioning in fairness and for context. In Italy, for example, an executive of Roma later admitted to trying to bribe a referee before the European Cup versus Liverpool in 1984 and admitted to bribing a referee before its second semi-final match against Dundee United, which Roma won 3-0, after Roma lost 2-0 at United. Roma were under pressure in 1984 because the European Cup final was being played in its own stadium. Domestically, there have been many match-fixing and referee tampering scandals and investigations.

In addition, there have been allegations of the use of performance-enhancing drugs. For example, Juventus won Serie A titles in 1995, 1997 and 1998, and reached the Champions League final in three successive years (1996, 1997, 1998), winning in 1996. There were many suspicions and allegations of Juventus players using performance-enhancing drugs, which ultimately led to an investigation and trial. Juventus have always maintained their innocence. There was a fair degree of cynicism about whether the trial would achieve anything. Many view the Italian legal system as one of never-ending trials and appeals which fizzle out after years and where there are no results, in part because of relatively short statute of limitations. So, when in 2004 a judge sentenced a member of the Juventus medical team to 22 months in jail for supplying Juventus players with performance-enhancing drugs, including the banned blood-boosting hormone EPO, between 1994 and 1998, the football world and Italians were very surprised.[7]

---

[7] http://www.independent.co.uk/news/world/europe/the-drug-scandal-that-blackens-the-name-of-juves-team-of-the-nineties-728710.html) At the time, Juventus insisted it had done nothing wrong

According to a Juventus executive who was quoted after winning the appeal, anyone who thought that the investigations and trials had impacted the reputation of Juventus or the league was 'a village idiot'. From 2001 to 2003, players at Inter, Juventus, Lazio and Parma tested positive for performance-enhancing drugs. Players at clubs in England, France, Germany and Spain also tested positive. Part of the Juventus supporters' defence was that the club did not administer to players anything that was not commonly used in football at other big clubs.

In 1999, Emmanuel Petit, then a World Cup winner with France and midfielder with Arsenal said, 'We will all have to take drugs to survive the demands of domestic, European and international fixtures . . . Some footballers already do.' FIFA and the Professional Footballers' Association in England dismissed Petit's view. But he stuck to his assertion that the ever-increasing demands on players – the extension of Europe's Champions League, the addition of FIFA's tournaments, the increasing pace of the game and the expectation of 70 matches in a ten-month season – were destined to tire and injure players and cause them to consider performance-enhancing drugs.[8]

The World Anti-Doping Agency, a foundation initiated by the International Olympic Committee to promote, coordinate and monitor the fight against drugs in sports, was founded in 1999. Since it was enacted in 2003 at the World Conference on Doping in Sport, the World Anti-Doping Code (WADC) has harmonised anti-doping policies throughout the world. In the run-up to the 2006 FIFA World Cup, the FIFA Congress ratified the WADC code, being the last of the Olympic sports to agree to 'anti-doping'. Since 2008, UEFA has been blood testing for doping. In the 2014/15 season, UEFA carried out 2,318 tests – 2,024 urine tests and 294 blood tests.

During the 2000/01 Serie A season, Inter's Álvaro Recoba, Lazio's Juan Sebastián Verón and Milan's Dida were among a number of players from Inter, Lazio, Milan, Napoli, Parma, Roma and Udinese implicated in a league scandal involving fraudulent European passports

and was confident that the employee would win his appeal. In 2005, the medical staff member was acquitted of the charges by a court of appeal. http://www.independent.co.uk/sport/football/european/juventus-champions-league-final-ajax-doping-scandal-casts-dark-shadows-ahead-real-madrid-a7768061.html

[8] http://www.nytimes.com/2004/11/27/sports/soccer-juventus-doping-conviction-casts-aura-of-doubt-on-sport.html

to circumvent limits on non-EU players. First Division rules impose a cap of three non-European Union players in a single team and five in the pool eligible for one club. Clubs therefore have a vested interest in getting players registered as EU nationals. Recoba, who was reportedly the highest paid player in Italy at the time, had his one-year ban later reduced on appeal to four months. Verón, a key player in the Lazio team that won the Italian championship the previous year, was cleared.[9] Other clubs at other leagues were also investigated for fraudulent passports at various times to circumvent limits on non-EU players.

UEFA Bans English Clubs from 1985/86 to 1990/91

An unfortunate disaster at the 1984/85 European Cup final between Juventus and Liverpool at the Heysel Stadium in Brussels, Belgium changed European football. Approximately one hour before the Juventus–Liverpool final was due to kick off, Liverpool supporters charged at Juventus fans and breached a fence that was separating them from a 'neutral area'. This came after a period of hostility between the two sets of fans, which saw missiles thrown by both teams' supporters. The instigators of the violence are still unknown, with varying accounts.[10] Juventus fans ran back on the terraces and away from the threat into a concrete retaining wall. Fans already standing near the wall were crushed; eventually the wall collapsed. Many people climbed over to safety, but 39 people – mostly Italians and Juventus fans – were killed and 600 were injured in the confrontation. The match was played despite the disaster, with Juventus winning 1–0.

The tragedy resulted in all English football clubs being placed under an indefinite ban by UEFA from all European competitions (lifted in 1990/91), with Liverpool being excluded for an additional three years, later reduced to one, and 14 Liverpool fans found guilty of manslaughter and each sentenced to three years' imprisonment.

---

[9] While others used false passports, his was genuine, but based on false citizenship documents. Verón had played on an Italian passport obtained by intermediaries who had claimed that the player had Italian ancestry through a great-grandfather who emigrated to Argentina a century before. The great-grandfather used was false but Verón discovered he did have Italian descent through another great-grandparent.

[10] Some English fans believe that the tension with Italian fans was partly a carry-over of confrontations between Liverpool and Roma fans in the European Cup final in Rome the previous year.

English clubs returned to European competition in the 1990/91 season. Liverpool returned to European competition a season later in the 1991/92 UEFA Cup. On the pitch, Liverpool's domination was coming to an end by 1991.

During the ban, in 1989 and 1990 AC Milan won back-to-back European Cups and Napoli and Juventus won the UEFA Cup in 1989 and 1990, respectively. With English clubs being banned from UEFA competition, Serie A and the Italian clubs became a more attractive market for international players. Also, Serie A was able to solidify both on- and off-the-field dominance. Even after the ban on English clubs in European competitions was lifted, a number of high-profile players moved to Italy including Paul Gascoigne and David Platt.

It took time for English teams to re-establish themselves in Europe. Although Manchester United won the European Cup Winners' Cup in the first season after the ban was lifted, the European Cup was not won by an English club until 1999 – 15 years after the last triumph (Liverpool 1984).

The Heysel Stadium disaster and the Hillsborough disaster (and ultimately the Taylor Report), which also involved Liverpool, led to a modernisation of English football and English stadiums by the mid-1990s. The FA Premier League was formed in 1992. In part out of necessity, Manchester United and Alex Ferguson developed players in their youth system (Gary and Philip Neville, Paul Scholes, Ryan Giggs, and David Beckham) and then dominated English football in the 1990s (similar to Barcelona in the early 2000s). Manchester United's main challengers for the title in the Premier League's first few years were Blackburn Rovers, led by star striker Alan Shearer. Attendances were often restricted during the first two or three seasons of the Premiership, as clubs rebuilt their stadiums or relocated to comply with the requirement to be all-seater by the 1994/95 season, and most clubs were left with a lesser capacity than in the era of terracing. The Premier League was decreased from 22 to 20 clubs in 1995.

In support of how good the Italian stadiums were considered after Italia '90, despite its status as Belgium's national stadium, Heysel was in a poor state of repair by the time of the 1985 European Cup final. The 55-year-old stadium had not been sufficiently maintained for several years, and large parts of it were literally crumbling. For example, the outer wall had been made of cinder block, and fans who did not have tickets were seen kicking holes in it to get in to the final.

Importing Great 'Oriundi' Players

Starting in the 1850s and ending after World War II, poverty, lack of jobs and political turmoil caused many Italians to emigrate to South America, especially Argentina, Uruguay and Brazil. There are 25 million emigrants from Italy since unification in 1870, 9 million between 1900 and 1915. For example, in Argentina and Uruguay close to 50% of immigrants were from Italy, compared to around 33% from Spain. It is only natural that some descendants from Italian émigrés would be talented footballers.

The word *oriundo* (or *oriundi* to give it its plural form) is applied to immigrants who are of Italian descent but were born outside the country. It is a combination of the Latin word *oriri* (meaning 'to be born') and 'Orient', which is of relevance in that Italy lies to the east of South America, the place most oriundi call home. In a strictly sporting sense, the term was used to refer to only South American players of Italian descent who have returned to the mother country to pursue their careers. Over time, the word was more loosely used to include any player born abroad of Italian descent who came to Italy to play. In order to be considered an *oriundo* and thereby obtain an Italian passport, these players must prove an ancestor is or was from Italy. By gaining citizenship, these players could more easily play for Serie A clubs which had nationality quotas, and later EU quotas.

Attitudes in Italy changed regarding oriundi after a disastrous first round loss in the 1962 FIFA World Cup in Chile against the host country. The match was titled in the press as the 'Battle of Santiago', because of the level of violence seen in the match. The first foul occurred within 12 seconds of the kick-off. An Italian player was sent off in the 12th minute after a foul but refused to leave the pitch and had to be dragged off by policemen. Several players threw punches. The police had to intervene several other times. Chile won the match 2-0. There were oriundi on that national team, just as there had been on previous Italian national teams. Afterwards, the general feeling was that Italian football players should exemplify specific Italian characteristics, and home-grown Italian players should be developed. This attitude intensified after a shocking defeat to North Korea in the 1966 World Cup in England. Between 1965 and 1980, non-Italians not already in the league were completely banned from playing football in Italy despite the provisions for the free movement of labour in the Treaty of Rome (1957). This affected the development of Italian football and Serie A.

Before the rule change in 1965, Milan won the European Cup in 1963, then Inter won back-to-back trophies in 1964 and 1965. Both clubs had foreigners. During the 'no foreigner rule' from 1965 to 1980, only one Italian club would win the European Cup, Milan in 1969 (utilising two foreign players that were already in the league, and one oriundo, Ángelo Sormani, born in Brazil). In addition, only one Italian club would win the UEFA Cup/Europa League Cup, Juventus in 1977, with no foreign players.[11]

Although Italian clubs didn't win many European trophies, out of necessity, Italian clubs did become very good at developing domestic talent. Their efforts would be rewarded. In 1982 Italy won their third World Cup. The 1982 World Cup was seen as being won by 'true Italians', with no oriundi.[12]

After the rule change in 1980, strong Italian-developed players were combined with world class foreigners in Serie A, helping create the Serie A 1980s and 1990s golden age. The Bosman ruling in 1995 had an impact with EU players being equals. Clubs could have as many EU players as they wanted but a maximum of three non-EU players. With some slight differences, today it is essentially still this way.[13] Initially, after the Bosman ruling, fortunately, the costs were still manageable for Italian club owners and several competing clubs were in precarious financial positions. Over time, the Bosman ruling caused the costs of players to increase dramatically,

---

11 Claudio Gentile was born in Libya but raised in Italy.
12 Claudio Gentile was on the team.
13 It is crucial to know that, before 1992, no one could have Italian citizenship plus another citizenship. If a player decided to take Italian citizenship, he had to renounce his original citizenship, which is why the word oriundo is used less frequently. Today, players can keep both nationalities, so it's easier to qualify as an EU player without renouncing to play with their original national team. South American players with an Italian ancestor are useful to avoid the non-EU limit and they were not forced to change national teams.

and unfortunately those costs eventually got to be too much for more and more Italian owners. And their competitors had adjusted to find new and greater revenues.

Many oriundi had a meaningful impact on the quality of Serie A in the 1980s and 1990s, such as Michel Platini[14], Daniel Passarella[15], and Javier Zanetti.[16]

Today, because of generational effects, there may be fewer oriundi that qualify as Italians and feel a connection to Italy. For example, Paulo Dybala who was born in, and plays for Argentina, but also would qualify for Italy or Poland, said, 'I wouldn't be happy in a national team that didn't feel like mine, to hear an anthem that isn't my own, in colours that don't belong to me. My friend Franco Vazquez has an Italian mother. I only have an Italian passport thanks to a great-grandmother who I know nothing about. He feels Italian, I don't.'[17] A few footballers with dual citizenship/Italian passports have made an impact in Serie A (e.g. Mauro Icardi and Paulo Dybala), and help their clubs meet UEFA and league quotas.[18] However, it is too early to determine if their impact will be as great as players such as Platini, Passarella, Batistuta and Zanetti.

It is worth noting, born Lionel Andres Messi Cuccittini, the future Barcelona star had Italian ancestry. Messi would have qualified for an Italian passport through his great-grandfather, who moved from Recanati to Messi's place of birth, Rosario, in 1883. Messi, who also could have qualified to play for Spain, feels in a similar way as Dybala in playing for Argentina.

Wasn't Big Business Yet

For context it is important to understand the amount of money that was in European football in the 1980s and 1990s. We selected Manchester United, Juventus, Bayern Munich, Milan and Real Madrid because they were the top five in revenues in 2000/01. The story behind each club

---

14 French/Italian; Serie A 1982–87; Serie A's leading scorer 1983-85

15 Argentinean/Italian; Serie A 1982–88; FIFA 125 list of world's greatest living players.

16 Argentinean/Italian; Serie A 1995–2014; fourth-most appearances in Serie A behind Maldini, Buffon and Totti.

17 http://www.goal.com/en-ie/news/why-lionel-messi-couldve-played-for-italy/1gmrvshfpxk7919y a4a0g7hac2

18 Gonzalo Higuaín was born in France and has both Argentinian and French citizenship.

gives an insight into how much has changed in European football as well as when changes were starting. Not only was European football not a big business yet, the competitors of Italian football in the 1980s and 1990s were not that financially strong.

More information about each club at the time is provided in the Appendix.

Manchester United highlight how much digital TV changes the economics of the sport. In 1989, Manchester United were valued at around €29.3 million and after digital TV rights were bid on, the club received a €933 million offer in 1998. Keep in mind, in the 1970s and 1980s Manchester United didn't win England's First Division.

The Agnellis, who control both Fiat and Juventus, were able to afford talent for Juventus to win. At the time, the amounts of money paid to players was still reasonable to an owner of an industrial conglomerate. In 1990, Giovanni Agnelli had an estimated worth of €3.1 billion by *Fortune* magazine, one of the 50th wealthiest people in the world at the time.

Berlusconi bought AC Milan in 1986, and unlike traditional industrial Italian families that owned clubs, he saw Milan as complementary entertainment content with subscribers for his media business (and eventually his political campaigns). In 1990, Berlusconi had an estimated worth of €2.0 billion by *Fortune* magazine, one of the 50th wealthiest people in the world at the time.

Bayern Munich, member-owned, would need to sell an 8.33% stake in 2002 to adidas for around €75 million for capital.

Real Madrid, member-owned, would win its first Champions League trophy in 1998 (and again in 2000) in 32 years, but the player spending would leave Real near bankruptcy as the club didn't have a sustainable economic-sport model. This led, in part, to Florentino Pérez getting elected president of the club in 2000.

Notably, Barcelona wasn't in the top 10 in the Deloitte Football Revenues Rankings until the mid-2000s. Messi would start his first senior match for Barcelona at age 18 in 2005.

PART TWO

THE FALL IN THE 2000s:
HOW, WHEN AND WHY DID IT HAPPEN?

CHAPTER TWO

ITALY'S SERIE A CRISIS

THE MOST POPULAR phrase in the Italian media to describe Italian football overall and Serie A is '*la crisi del calcio Italiano*' ('The Italian football crisis'). It is easy to understand why. Italy's national team didn't advance out of the group stage in the 2010 and 2014 World Cups, finishing in 26th and 22nd places, respectively. After the Azzurri failed to qualify for the 2018 FIFA World Cup, Italian football overall was in existential crisis.

Milan have not advanced past the quarter-finals stage in Serie A since 2007. From 2007 to 2014 only one Italian club managed to get past the quarter-final stage in the Champions League – the title-winning Inter Milan of 2010. Since 2010, Inter have not made it past the quarter-finals, when they have even qualified, which has been only twice – 2011 and 2012. From 2003 to 2014 Juventus did not advance past the quarter-finals. In addition, since 2000, no Italian club have even made the finals of the UEFA Cup or Europa League. It is all a far cry from the 1980s and 1990s, when Italian clubs were consistently in the final rounds of the Champions League/European Cup and the UEFA Cup.[1]

In the 2000/01 Deloitte Football Revenues Rankings, five Italian football

---

[1] Since 2014, Juventus advanced to the Champions League finals in 2015 and 2017, and in 2018 Roma advanced to the semi-finals. This will be discussed later.

clubs were in the top ten: Juventus #2, AC Milan #4, Lazio #7, Roma #8 and Inter #10. In the 2015/16 Rankings, only Juventus placed in the top ten, at #10. By 2016/17, things had got even worse. AC Milan and Roma fell out of the top 20. The revenue growth since 2000 for the Italian clubs is significantly below the other clubs that were in the top 10 in 2000/01.

Deloitte Football Revenues Rankings
2016/17

Rank	Club	2000 Rank	Revenues	Rev Growth Since 2000	Since 2000/01 UCL Cups
1	Manchester United	1	€676.3 million	211%	2008
2	Real Madrid	5	674.6	388	02, 14, 16, 17
3	Barcelona	NA	648.3		06, 09, 11, 15
4	Bayern Munich	3	587.8	239	01, 13
5	Manchester City	NA	527.7		
6	Arsenal	NA	487.6		
7	PSG	NA	486.2		
8	Chelsea	9	428.0	262	12
9	Liverpool	6	424.2	208	05
10	Juventus	2	405.7	134	
11	Tottenham Hotspur	NA	355.6		
12	Borussia Dortmund	NA	332.6		
13	Atlético Madrid	NA	272.5		
14	Leicester City	NA	271.1		
15	Internazionale	10	262.1	132	10
16	Schalke 04	NA	230.2		
17	West Ham United	NA	213.3		
18	Southampton	NA	212.1		
19	Napoli	NA	200.7		
20	Everton	NA	199.2		

Champions League money is helping keep Juventus in the top 10 in the Deloitte Football Revenues Rankings, which also makes Juventus vulnerable to dropping out of the top 10. For example, below is how the payments added up in 2016/17. Real Madrid had to divide market pool money with Atlético Madrid and Barcelona. Juventus was the only Italian club in the quarter-finals. Leicester City was the only EPL club in the quarter-finals.

UEFA and the European Club Association have agreed on a new cash distribution model for the 2018-21 seasons when revenues are expected to rise significantly. The new formula will better reward teams that advance deeper into the competition and is weighted to favor clubs that won European titles since UEFA launched club competitions in 1955.

2016/17 Champions League Payments
€ in millions

Club	Participation Bonus	Performance Bonus	Market Pool	Round of: 16	QF	SF	Final	Total
Juventus	12.7	7.9	58.8	6	6.5	7.5	11	110.3
Real Madrid	12.7	6.7	26.1	6	6.5	7.5	11	81.0
Leicester	12.7	7.4	49.1	6	6.5			81.7

* Each club was guaranteed a minimum payment of €12.7 million. There are performance bonuses for each match win. Further bonuses are paid for each knockout round. Money from the market pool is divided according to the value of the TV deal in each country, number of clubs per country and other factors.

As for the league, not just the clubs, in the 1980s, Serie A was the highest money-generating league and the most successful in European competitions. In 1992, total Serie A revenue was €400 million, compared to €255 million in England's top league, which was emerging from a period of crisis.[1] In 1996/97, the English Premier League had €685 million in revenue with Italy dropping to second with €551 million.[2] While Serie A started to fall behind the English Premier League in the mid-to-late 1990s off the pitch, Serie A was still very much considered a power on the pitch.

In the 2002/03 financial year, operating losses of the Serie A and Serie B clubs were estimated at €1.5 billion on €3 billion of revenues. Virtually all Serie A clubs showed a net loss and the losses would have been much larger if extraordinary items had not been taken into consideration (and many of those were questionable).[3]

By 2006/07, Serie A had fallen to fourth in revenues, lagging behind in commercial and matchday revenues, behind Germany and Spain (Hamil, Morrow et al 2010). In 2015, Serie A was still fourth and had the slowest growth among the top five European football leagues.

---

[1] The English Premier League wasn't created until 1992/93.

[2] https://www.foxsports.com/soccer/story/what-caused-serie-a-to-lose-its-financial-power-081114

[3] https://core.ac.uk/download/pdf/6463357.pdf

Top Five European Football League Revenues
(1992, 2000, 2015)
€ in billions

	1992		2000		2015		Mult. Growth
	Rank	Rev.	Rank	Rev.	Rank	Rev.	Over 2000
English Premier League	#2	0.256	#1	1.3	#1	4.8	3.4x
Italian Serie A	#1	0.576	#2	1.1	#4	1.7	1.0x
Spanish La Liga			#3	0.8	#3	2.0	2.1x
German Bundesliga			#4	0.8	#2	2.5	3.1x
French Ligue 1			#5	0.6	#5	1.4	1.5x
Total						12.4	

Sources: Deloitte, UEFA, Statista.com, The Economist, and historical documents from the English Premier League (note that historical numbers do vary between documents).[4]

In general, the average attendance has been declining. In their book, Ripartenza (Reboot), Gianfranco Teotino and Michele Uva (2010) make the point that Serie A was the only league in Europe to have a decline in the average number of spectators per match from 2000 to 2010. Below is the average match attendance and stadium utilisation by league from Deloitte in 2015/16. In 2015/16, average Serie A attendances were 21,680 per match, far behind the major European leagues, apart from Ligue 1 which was 20,894.

Average Match Attendance and Stadium Utilisation (2015/16)

League	Average match attendance	Stadium Utilisation
England	36,490	96%
Germany	42,420	90%
Spain	27,626	76%
Italy	21,680	52%
France	20,894	70%

Opposite is the average attendance and matchday revenues for the top five clubs in Italy. Obviously, Juventus, with its own modern stadium, has a significant advantage in matchday revenues over other Italian clubs, even with similar attendance. With its new stadium, Juventus is able to maximise matchday revenues and make more money per attendee.

---

[4] https://www.statista.com/statistics/261218/big-five-european-soccer-leagues-revenue/ https://www.economist.com/blogs/graphicdetail/2017/08/daily-chart-21

Average Match Attendance for Selected Italian Clubs (2016/17)

Club	Average Attendance	Stadium Capacity	Utilisation	Matchday Revenues (€)
Inter	46,620	80,018	58%	28.4
AC Milan	40,294	80,018	50%	23.0
Juventus*	39,489	41,507	95%	57.8
Napoli	36,605	60,240	61%	19.4
Roma	32,638	72,698	44%	22.3

Before the new stadium in 2011, the Stadio delle Alpi capacity was 69,000. Average attendance was 21,966 in 2010, only 31% utilisation. [5]

None of the Italian clubs are in the top ten in Europe in attendance. With the exception of Juventus with its new stadium, none of the Italian clubs have high stadium utilisation, which has meaningful implications for revenues (see Appendix) and attractiveness on TV. The European clubs below have large average attendances and high utilisation rates, which make for a great atmosphere and give a sense of the passion and loyalty. All of the clubs below have invested significant amounts of money into modernising their stadiums. Some of the clubs below do not have superstars. German clubs, with their member ownership structure, have very high attendance.[6]

In general, Italian clubs have a significant disadvantage in matchday revenues. Roma's matchday revenues are €22.3 million with an average attendance of 32,638, compared to Barcelona's €137.2 million with an average attendance of 79,532. Also, keep in mind most German clubs and Real Madrid and Barcelona are member-owned and generally keep season ticket prices for member-owners low.

Average Attendance (2016/17)

Club	Average Attendance	Stadium Capacity	Utilisation	Matchday Revenues (€)
Borussia Dortmund	80,977	81,360	99%	58.6
Barcelona	79,532	99,354	80%	137.2
Man United	75,282	75,643	99%	125.2
Bayern Munich	75,000	75,000	100%	97.7

[5] Source: http://www.worldfootball.net/attendance/ita-serie-a-2016-2017/1/

[6] In May 2016, La Liga decided to impose fines on clubs if empty seats appeared on television while games were being broadcast. Sections of grounds which appear prominently on television, according to the new stipulations, must be fully populated by fans.

Real Madrid	69,736	81,044	86%	136.4
Schalke 04	60,000	60,000	100%	53.3
Benfica	55,174	65,647	84%	24.4
Manchester City	54,041	55,097	98%	60.4
Hamburg	54,000	57,000	95%	

Source: https://en.as.com/en/2016/11/28/football/1480360002_418201.html

Surprisingly, Serie A's average attendance of 21,680 per match is lower than the US's Major League Soccer (MLS) average attendance of 22,158 per game. In 2016/17 MLS had 22 teams with average attendances ranging from 15,122 for FC Dallas to 48,200 for Atlanta United FC. Serie A had 20 teams with attendance ranging from 46,620 for Inter to 8,222 for FC Crotone. Below is a list of the clubs from both leagues with attendances above 22,000. MLS attendance leaders Atlanta and Seattle have higher average attendance than Milan, Juventus, Napoli and Roma.

Average Match Attendance for Serie A and MLS (2016/17) Above 22,000

Club	League	Average Attendance
Atlanta	MLS	48,200
Inter		46,620
Seattle Sounders	MLS	43,666
AC Milan		40,294
Juventus		39,489
Napoli		36,605
Roma		32,638
Toronto	MLS	27,647
Fiorentina		26,470
Orlando City	MLS	25,028
New York City	MLS	22,643
LA Galaxy	MLS	22,246

Referee Bias Against Italian Clubs or For Other Clubs

We heard many fans complain about potential bias against Italian clubs. In response, we carefully read many academic studies on factors influencing football referees' judgement; some of the studies are mentioned in the book. Overall, we found there are many psychological, physiological and personal factors influencing referees' performance. The large number of football referee decisions during a match, about three or four decisions each minute, is quite striking (Helsen & Bultying, 2004). A lot of elements such as a team's reputation for aggressiveness (Jones, Paull, & Erskine, 2002), crowd noise, experience and anxiety (Balmer et al., 2007), a preceding foul judgement (Plessner & Betsch, 2001), the height of the players involved in a foul (Van Quaquebeke & Giessner, 2010), individual differences in referee ability to cope under pressure (Page & Page, 2010), and social pressure and nationality (Dawson & Dobson, 2010) act upon soccer referee decision-making. In the end referees are human beings. We can incorporate technology to assist in decisions, but many decisions are truly judgement (or interpretation of the rules) calls. And not only do many factors influence judgement, but the number of times judgement must be applied. For example, more aggressive, attack-oriented clubs put the referees into more situations in which a decision must be made and judgement applied.

There is no credible academic evidence at all that we could find that referees are biased specifically against Italian clubs. In our opinion, home ground advantage seems to be the biggest factor in decision-making. No matter how neutral a referee is or which country he is from, he is a human being and still susceptible to social pressure (Buraimo, Simmons & Maciaszczyk, 2011). If fans think back to when they felt a referee's call went against their team, the odds are that their club was playing an away match. This is discussed further with data and analysis from academic studies in several areas. In particular, fans of Italian clubs that play matches in stadiums with athletic tracks surrounding the playing pitch will find some studies included later incredibly interesting.

CHAPTER THREE

TALENT ON THE PITCH

On-the-Pitch Issues: Talent

Less Talent

Many experts point to the decline in talent as the primary reason for the decline in performance on the pitch. The argument is that Italian clubs, in general, sold the best players in the world to raise money and cut expenses and replaced them by buying good foreign players and trying to develop them to sell them to raise more money.

As previously mentioned, before Zidane left Juventus for Real Madrid in 2001, it was widely believed that the best players in the world played in Italy and wanted to play in Italy. Zidane leaving Italy was the signal that things were changing.[1] Since 2005, Italy's Serie A has had two players finish in the top three in the Ballon d'Or voting (Gianluigi Buffon, second in 2006 and Kaká, first in 2007), with the last one over ten years ago.[2] Since 2008, the Italian Serie A has not had one player in the top three voting for the Ballon d'Or. Since 1998, the Italian Serie A has had no World Cup Golden Ball (best player) or Golden Boot (top goalscorer) winners

---

[1] An echo effect of the Zidane move was the Brazilian Ronaldo, after winning the World Cup in 2002 and before winning the Ballon d'Or again that season, left Inter Milan for Real Madrid.
[2] Fabio Cannavaro won the Ballon d'Or when at Real Madrid in 2006, but he played for Juventus in 2005/06.

in the World Cup. In the latest 2017 Ballon d'Or nominations, Serie A is represented by only five players out of 30. Dybala (finished 15th), Džeko (28th), Mertens (29th), Buffon (4th) and Bonucci (21st). The last two are Italians, a 40-year-old goalkeeper and a 30-year-old centre back.

Since Hernan Crespo's €58.3 million move in 2000 from Parma to Lazio, Italy has not broken the world record for transfer fees. In the last 14 years, Gonzalo Higuaín has been the only player to go to Serie A for a fee that falls into the top ten biggest transfers an Italian club has ever completed. It is now an imaginable scenario that top players in Italy's Serie A consider leaving for non-contenders in the English Premier League. That sentence in the 1980s or 1990s or even early 2000s would have been inconceivable.[3]

According to transfermarkt.com in the autumn of 2017, only two Serie A players rank in the top 30 of the most valuable players – Gonzalo Higuaín at #15 and Paulo Dybala at #12, who both play for Juventus in 2017. Combined with Inter's Mauro Icardi at #34 and Napoli's Lorenzo Insigne at #48, there are only four players in Serie A in the top 50. The comparisons below with La Liga and the EPL are staggering.

Transfermarkt.com Ranking of Most Valuable Players

League	# in top 10	Top 25
La Liga	5	9
EPL	2	9
Ligue 1	2	3
Bundesliga	1	2
Serie A	0	2

Source: https://www.transfermarkt.com/spieler-statistik/wertvollstespieler/marktwertetop

There is less talent playing in Italy's Serie A, in part because talent can make more money elsewhere. The English Premier League pays more than double in total wages of any other league – and Chelsea, Manchester City, Manchester United, Arsenal and Liverpool are in the top ten spending teams. In 2015, the Premier League paid out a staggering total €3.2 billion in players' salaries – averaging €160.6 million per club. Serie A clubs paid a total of €1.6 billion (less than half), with the average wage at €78.2 million per club.[4]

---

[3] https://www.sportskeeda.com/slideshow/football-5-reasons-serie-a-decline; http://www.juvefc.com/serie-failed-paul-pogba/; https://forzaitalianfootball.com/2017/01/why-serie-a-is-not-attracting-the-big-name-players-anymore/; http://www.the42.ie/juventus-champions-league-serie-a-decline-2137803-Jun2015/

[4] https://www.thesun.co.uk/sport/football/2597657/premier-league-pays-more-than-double-in-wages-of-any-other-league-and-chelsea-man-city-manchester-united-arsenal-and-liverpool-in-top-ten-spending-teams/

Below is the average club wages and wages to revenue ratio in 2015/16. UEFA has a guideline that the wages to revenue ratio should be below 70% for each club. Generally, Serie A clubs have lower revenues, therefore the wage percentage will be larger.

Big Five Leagues' Average Club Wages and Wages to Revenue Ratio by Deloitte 2015/16
€ in millions

League	Average Club Wages	Wages/Revenue Ratio
England	€203 million	63%
Germany	100	49%
Spain	99	61%
Italy	89	70%
France	68	69%

Below is the list of Wages to Revenue Ratio by club. Obviously, the lower the percentage the more financial flexibility the club has. Generally, the Serie A clubs are higher, as revenues are lower.

Selected Club Wages to Revenue Ratio
2015/16 (alphabetical order)

Club	Wages/Revenue Ratio
English Premier League	
Arsenal	55%
Chelsea	67%
Liverpool	69%
Manchester City	51%
Manchester United	45%
Tottenham	48%
La Liga	
Barcelona	61%
Real Madrid	50%
Atlético Madrid	56%
Serie A	
Inter	69%
Juventus	61%
Milan	82%
Roma	75%
Bundesliga	
Bayern Munich	48%
Dortmund	42%

Source: https://www.reddit.com/r/soccer/comments/4rhnbm/wage_bills_as_proportion_of_revenues/ https://www.theguardian.com/football/2017/jun/01/premier-league-finances-club-by-club

None of the world's ten highest-paid players in 2016/17 played in Serie A. The top players also make substantial money in sponsorship as opposed to just wages, demonstrating their 'star power'. Serie A's two highest-paid players, Paulo Dybala, reportedly making around €6.2 million and Gonzalo Higuaín ,reportedly making around €8.8 million, have far fewer sponsorships.

Top Ten Highest-Paid Players in the World
According to *Forbes* 2017
€ in millions

Rank	Player	League	Salary	Sponsorships	Total
1	Cristiano Ronaldo	Spain	€51	€31	€82
2	Lionel Messi	Spain	47	24	71
3	Neymar	Spain	13	19.5	32.5
4	Gareth Bale	Spain	20	9.7	29.7
5	Zlatan Ibrahimović	England	24	4.4	28.4
6	Wayne Rooney	England	15.5	5.3	20.8
7	Luis Suárez	Spain	15.3	5.3	20.6
8	Sergio Agüero	England	12.9	7	19.9
9	James Rodriguez	Spain	13.2	6.2	19.4
10	Paul Pogba	England	15.2	3.5	18.7

Source : https://www.forbes.com/sites/christinasettimi/2017/05/26/the-worlds-highest-paid-soccer-players-2017-cristiano-ronaldo-lionel-messi-lead-the-list/#4b80bcc9210e

In 2016, ESPN reported that there are at least 34 players in Serie A earning more than €100,000 per week gross. The official figures from the US's Major League Soccer union show there are seven players in MLS that earned more than €5.0 million in 2016, or €100,000 per week. Five Serie A clubs have two or more players who earn at least €100,000 gross; Juventus have 13 players over that level. Manchester City, who lead that particular ranking, have 18 players making more than €100,000 a week.

Thirty-four players in Serie A in 2016 making more than €100,000 per week gross were listed by club in a survey from *Panorama*.

Panorama's List of Serie A Players Making More Than €100,000 per Week Gross by Club

Juventus: Gonzalo Higuaín, Miralem Pjanic, Sami Khedira, Gianluigi Buffon, Mario Mandzukic, Claudio Marchisio, Giorgio Chiellini, Leonardo Bonucci, Juan Cuadrado, Dani Alves, Medhi

Benatia, Patrice Evra, Andrea Barzagli
Inter: Mauro Icardi, Geoffrey Kondogbia, Gabriel Barbosa, Ever Banega, Joao Mario, Rodrigo Palacio, Stevan Jovetic, Antonio Candreva, Miranda, Felipe Melo
Roma: Daniele De Rossi, Edin Džeko, Mohamed Salah, Kevin Strootman
Milan: Carlos Bacca, Riccardo Montolivo, Luiz Adriano, Keisuke Honda
Napoli: Marek Hamsik, Jose Callejon
Torino: Joe Hart (on loan from Manchester City, who pay about two-thirds of his wages)

Source: https://www.panorama.it/sport/calcio/stipendi-calciatori-serie-a-squadre/

In the top ten teams' total wages in 2016/17, the only club in the top ten was Juventus at #10. AC Milan #12, Roma #15 and Inter #16 were the only other clubs from Italy. There were 15 clubs in the top 25 from the English Premier League.

2016/17 Top 25 Club Total Wages
€ in millions

Rank	Club	Total Wages
1	Barcelona	€324 million
2	Man United	308
3	Chelsea	298
4	Real Madrid	291
5	Man City	288
6	PSG	278
7	Arsenal	272
8	Bayern Munich	262
9	Liverpool	233
10	**Juventus**	**210**
11	Tottenham	140
12	**AC Milan**	**134**
13	Dortmund	131
14	Everton	123
15	**Roma**	**122**
16	**Inter Milan**	**119**
17	West Ham	110
18	Southampton	107
19	Stoke	107
20	Swansea	107
21	Leicester	105
22	Sunderland	105
23	Atlético Madrid	100
24	West Brom	98
25	Crystal Palace	80
NR	Napoli	77
NR	Sevilla	51

Source: http://www.dailymail.co.uk/sport/football/article-4564154/Hey-big-spenders-Palace-match-world-s-best.html

Serie A clubs have not kept up with player wage increases from other selected top European clubs.

Player Wage Changes by Selected Clubs from 2006/07 to 2016/17

Club	% Wage Change 2006/07 to 2016/17	% Revenue Change 2006/07 to 2016/17
PSG	697%	526%
Manchester City	254%	524%
Manchester United	115%	115%
Barcelona	113%	123%
Chelsea	72%	51%
Real Madrid	70%	92%
Juventus	47%	179%
Inter	-5%	34%
Milan	-36%	-16%

In *Winners and Losers: The Business Strategy of Football* (New York: Viking, 1999), Szymanski and researcher Tim Kuypers analysed ten years of English top flight football (1990–99) and discovered that the one variable with the highest correlation to winning is: the teams that pay the highest salaries for the best players win the most often. It probably doesn't take a lot of classes on data analytics to figure that out. We believe in a competitive industry with competitive owners who have lots of money to spend; a team needs a distinctive competitive advantage to maximise the performance of these best players as well as to help generate more money to pay the salaries. For example, Juventus are #10 and Atlético Madrid #24 in club total wages but have consistently beaten and challenged much bigger spenders in European competitions. Both clubs have distinctive cultures and identities that their players buy into. Culture and identity are discussed later.

Less Talent Development

Italy is historically a successful football nation but that success did not solely come from great financial resources or defensive tactics. Italian football has always developed technically gifted players. Every winning generation in

Italy had world-class Italian players that played in Serie A – from Rossi to Baresi, from Maldini to Baggio, from Del Piero to Totti or Pirlo.

Italy were European Under-21 champions (as a youth national team) in 1992, 1994, 1996, 2000 and 2004 (which is a record with Italy still being number one in Europe with five titles, all during this period, but they have only made it to the final in 2013 since then). That great generation would also win the World Cup of 2006 and have played for many Serie A clubs. Then, suddenly, success stopped after the 2004 Euro Under-21 tournament and the 2006 World Cup, with Italy not producing the kind of players they once did.

In 2017, Italy had only four players who were among the list of the top 55 footballers according to a poll to select the FIFA FIFPro World 11 – Buffon (40, Juventus), Bonucci (30, Milan), Chiellini (33, Juventus) and Verratti (25, PSG). The only Italian player under 30, Verratti does not play in Serie A, but plays for PSG in the French league. The 55 top players have 20 different nationalities. Nine of them are from Spain; Brazil and France both have seven players; and Germany has six.

Top 55 Players' Countries
According to FIFA FIFPro World 11

Country	Amount
Spain	9
Brazil	7
France	7
Germany	6
Italy	4 (only one under 30, Verratti)

As of 2017, Italy have some promising players such as Belotti (23, Torino), Donnarumma (18, Milan), Florenzi (26, Roma), El Shaarawy (25, Roma), Gagliardini (23, Inter/Atalanta), Insigne (26, Napoli), Romagnoli (22, Milan), Rugani (23, Juventus) and Zappacosta (25, Chelsea) but none have been nominated for the Best XI or Ballon d'Or, and Italy does not have nearly as many young players on the national team as some other world football powerhouses. Only one player under 23 years old, Donnarumma, a goalkeeper, was in the Italian national team for most of 2017, while Spain had seven (Arrizabalaga, Asensio, Bellerín,

Fornals, Níguez, Odriozola and Oyarzabal), France has six (Coman, Dembele, Martial, Mbappé, Pavard and Rabiot) and Germany has five (Brandt, Kimmich, Sané, Süle and Werner) on their national team.[5]

National Team Players Under 23 Years Old in 2017

Country	Amount
Spain	7
France	6
Germany	5
Italy	1

In Spain's La Liga there are many clubs' academies that produce many professional players for the top five European leagues. In the English, Spanish and Dutch leagues, clubs are allowed to have a 'second team or B team' that competes in the professional leagues which allows clubs to develop talent in close association with the first team. The one rule is that a club can only have one team in the first division. However, young players from the academy get to play against professional players and develop while still living and training in the club's academy.

In contrast, in Italy, clubs only have 19-year-old and under teams playing against each other. When a player turns 20 years old, the player must move to the first team or be put under contract and put out on loan to another club (usually outside Italy because there is a limited domestic market), taking them away from the development programme and the watch of the academy, or be released. If one were to look at most Serie A club squads, most have a much longer list of players on loan than other leagues. With so many players in other countries, they become difficult to track, control and maintain a relationship. Many times, the contract runs out and the club loses the rights to the player. Because the player is on loan, the receiving club has less incentive to invest in that player's development.

In 2016/17, Serie A clubs loaned out 485 professional football players, compared to 113 for the English Premier League, 97 for La Liga and 59 for the Bundesliga. Serie A clubs loan out an average of 24 players versus three players in the Bundesliga and six players in the EPL.

---

[5] Alessio Romagnoli, who was a youth product of Roma, has five caps for Italy since 2016 but was not called up for the last matches of 2017.

Number of Players Loaned Out By League in 2016/17

League	Total Number	Average By Club
Serie A	485	24
English Premier League	113	6
La Liga	97	5
Bundesliga	59	3

The two leagues with the lowest number of players loaned out, Spanish La Liga and German Bundesliga, have very strong national teams. One has to believe the low number of players loaned out, especially outside the home country, has some impact on development.

Research shows that the number of players in the top five leagues trained at the academies of top clubs in Italy is low. A major study of European football revealed that only Roma's youth system is among the top ten in Europe – producing more footballers playing in the continent's five best leagues than any other Italian side. But besides Roma, there are no Italian clubs in the top 15.

Number of Players in Big Five Leagues By Club

Rank	Club	Country	# of Big-5 Players
1.	Real Madrid	Spain	41
2.	Barcelona	Spain	37
3.	Manchester United	England	34
4.	Lyon	France	29
5.	Athletic Bilbao*	Spain	25
5.	Real Sociedad**	Spain	25
7.	Roma	Italy	24
8.	Arsenal	England	22
8.	Monaco	France	22
8.	Rennes	France	22

*Athletic Bilbao is known for its cantera policy of developing young Basque players, as well as recruiting top Basque players from other clubs. Since the early 20th century, Athletic's official policy is signing professional players native to or trained in football in the greater Basque Country.
** Until the late 1980s, Real Sociedad operated a Basque-only player recruitment policy but abandoned this in order to try to remain more competitive; however, their youth recruitment network is still focused around their home region and there are collaboration agreements in place with the small clubs in the region. In 2013, 22 of the 23 members of the Juvenil A squad were from their home region.

Italian clubs are underinvesting in their own academies which is impacting the development of the talent in the league. In 2015, Serie A's 20 clubs spent €55 million on their academies, an average of €2.75 million each. The Bundesliga's 18, in contrast, invested €79.3 million, €4.4 million each.

In addition, resources for development in Serie A are going to foreign players. In the 2003/04 season, foreign players totalled around 33% of the league. In 2017, that number was 55%. After England, the Italian league has the second highest percentage of minutes of footballers playing in a different association from where they grew up, as they seek development opportunities. The English Premier League clubs can use the money from their global TV rights deals to buy and retain players, so they don't need as much of a focus on internal development.

2017 Percentage of Foreign Players in the League

Rank	League	%
1.	England	61
2.	Italy	55
3.	Germany	51
4.	Spain	39
5.	France	36

Source: http://www.football-observatory.com/?lang=en

Interestingly, of the 55% of players that are foreign, around half of those featured in 15 games or fewer during the season. Therefore, they may be taking some opportunities away from local talent development.

Young Italian players are not getting enough time on the first team to develop. Players aged 30 or over total 30% of Italy's top league, and only 15% of Germany's. Younger Italian players get demoralised and some of them get lost along the way. With underinvestment in academies and players leaving, Italy's Serie A has the second lowest percentage of minutes by players who have been in the employer club for at least three seasons between the ages of 15 and 21.

Percentage of Minutes by Players At Employer Club between ages 15 and 21 for at least 3 Seasons

Rank	League	%
1.	Spain	22
2.	France	14
3.	Germany	12
4.	Italy	7
5.	England	6

Source: http://www.espnfc.com/italian-serie-a/12/blog/post/1975378/the-ugly-reality-of-italian-football-emerges

Starting in 2017, Serie A required squads to include four youth team players and four players with Italian experience. Specifically, every team must include four players who have spent at least three years, between the ages of 16 and 21, with the club's youth team, and another four players who must have spent three years with any Italian club before reaching the age of 21. Both these categories may include foreigners, though in practice the vast majority of these players are likely to be Italian. The reform is aimed at increasing the number of Italian and domestically formed players in Serie A. While the federation's move is likely to prove popular among Italian national team fans, it places many clubs in a difficult situation with regards to the transfer market, and has already been the object of some criticism. 'Italian football is not prepared for this rule,' said Juventus sporting director Beppe Marotta, as reported by the *Gazzetta*. 'It would have been best to adopt some remedies first, and then action the reform. The squad has to be reduced, penalising players who are useful over the economy of a season, especially for a team like Juventus that has to play in three tournaments and more than 50 games.'[6]

Lastly, Italian sporting directors seem more focused on deal-making than talent development,. In 2015/16, Serie A had 1,026 players leaving different clubs and 984 players arriving at different clubs. In comparison, La Liga had 357 players leaving and 371 players arriving, whilst the Bundesliga had 276 players leaving and 298 players arriving. The number of players leaving and arriving is staggeringly higher than other leagues.

---

[6] http://www.football-italia.net/85171/serie-italian-reform

2015/2016 Players Leaving and Arriving at Clubs by League

League	Leaving	Arriving
Serie A	1,026	984
La Liga	357	371
Bundesliga	276	298

Italy has not been producing the kind of players they once did and that's mainly because of Italian clubs' preference for buying players rather than developing their own. With the deteriorating finances of the clubs this is an important strategy for them to generate income, if they are to compete in the league, as well as in Europe. Italian clubs need to develop other sources of income rather than relying on buying and selling players, so they can focus more on youth development. In the long-run player development can pay off. It requires patience. The lack of stability at clubs with so many players coming and going can also impact the team's culture, and how players then view their relationship with the clubs and coaches.

Too Many Older Players

Many factors (e.g., genetics, diet, conditioning, previous injuries, etc.) determine a player's peak age, and it can vary significantly from athlete to athlete. The timing may vary but unfortunately the results are unavoidable: athletic performance declines for a player after a peak age. Also, the older a player is, the longer it takes to recover to be able to compete at peak performance. When analysing data, it is important to understand context. Age is often neglected when reviewing statistics. Sian Allen and Will Hopkins, at the Sports Performance Research Institute in New Zealand, examined scientific literature to determine the age at which athletes competing in various sports hit peak competitive performance:

Peak Ages for Male Athletes by the Sports Performance Research Institute in New Zealand

Sport	Peak Age
Sprinter	25

Olympic Distance Triathlete	27
Marathoner	30
Ironman Distance Triathlete	32

Generally, the authors noticed that athletes competing in 'sprint' events requiring explosive power peak much sooner than athletes competing in endurance or game-oriented events, perhaps because older athletes are able to use experience and savvy to their advantage. Glaringly missing from the review was football, but football peak age is probably in the middle of sprinting (25) and endurance (32), although sprinting and speed is becoming increasingly important in football, which is discussed later.

In the 1970s, an average football player ran approximately 4 km per 90-minute game. Today, an analysis of the maximum running distances of players in La Liga and Champions League games shows that the average football player runs approximately 11.4 km in a game (the minimum is 5.6 km; the maximum is 13.7 km). The largest distances are covered by central midfielders (approx. 12.1 km), followed by side midfielders (approx. 12.1 km), side defenders (approx. 11.4 km), forwards (approx. 11.3 km), and central defenders (approx. 10.6 km). A total of 188 studies have shown that with the increased distances covered today, players slow in the second half of play. Younger players tend to have more stamina, in addition to being able to recover faster.

Footballers run in short bursts, using the time when the ball is on the other side of the field to recover. During the game a player might have 35 to 50 'sprints', depending on the player's position. Most of these are of relatively short duration, less than five seconds. Taking a player's average of 45 'sprints', they 'sprint' about every two minutes. So, it's like doing 45 short sprints with probably a 90- to 180-second recovery jog in between. And as previously discussed, sprinters and Olympic distance triathletes have peak age performances of 25 and 27, respectively. In modern football, since the mid-2000s, the average number of sprints a football player performs has increased by about 33%, while the recovery time between the high-intensity sprints has dropped around 20%. With football demanding more physical exertion than ever, the sport is turning into a young man's game.

In a July 2014 article titled, 'Player age in football: the clock is ticking', *The Economist* analysed the average team age and final standing for the defending FIFA World Cup champions, and discovered that within this group, age has a remarkably strong impact.

Average Age of Team and Final Standing for Defending FIFA World Cup Champions from *Economist*

Year	Defending Team	Average Age of Team	Final Standing*
2014	Spain	27.5–28.0	20–25
2010	Italy	28.0–28.5	20–25
2006	Brazil	28.0–28.5	2–5
2002	France	28.0–28.5	25–30
1994	Germany	28.5–29.0	2–5

*Adjusted for continental advantage
Source: The Economist

After adjusting for the effect of geography, teams that played on their own continent performed six places better than those that had to travel to another continent (a one-year increase in average age for a team correlated with a four-place drop in performance). So, if a defending champion simply brought back the same players and coach from four years before, and the team's average age increased by four years, the team would be expected to finish in 17th place.

Unsurprisingly, according to CIES Football Observatory, Serie A has the oldest average age of any of the top five European leagues on the pitch.

Average Age of Players by League from CIES Football Observatory

Rank	League	Average Age
1.	Italy	27.29
2.	England	27.25
3.	Spain	26.86
4.	France	26.13
5.	Germany	26.04

Source: CIES Football Observatory

We went deeper into the analysis and examined the average ages of the starting 11 of the Italian clubs in the last three Champions League finals because what really matters are the players on the pitch with regards to being too old and tired. The result was the Italian clubs averaged 31 years old, while their competitors averaged 28 years old.

Average Birthday Year of the Starting 11
in the Champions League Final

2017	Birthday Year	Implied Age
Juventus	1986	31
Real Madrid	1989	28
2015		
Juventus	1985	30
Barcelona	1988	27
2010		
Inter	1979	31
Bayern Munich	1982	28

The culture of Italy is patrimonial, nepotistic and favours seniority, which is discussed in several areas of the book. This has led to many legendary players staying at one club for a long time. If it wasn't for this culture, it's likely more Italian players would have left Serie A. This loyalty and passion is important in building and supporting a community and identity. The unintended consequence is that legendary players staying too long can impact on their on-the-pitch performance as well as restricting talent development (especially if there isn't a second team). It is a complex and complicated balance. The ageing superstar dilemma affects every club, but in Italy it can go deeper because many of these players are beloved home town heroes. If a 'less famous', younger player is playing better than the ageing legendary player loved by the community or gives the club a better chance to win, the coach is in a very difficult position. Also, management is in a difficult position because the legendary player is a part of the brand which has matchday and commercial revenues, while placement in the league standings have broadcast revenues, including European tournament revenues. If the legendary player is rested or not regularly played by a coach that is judged by on-the-pitch performance, then the media attention is overwhelming and the media, coaches, players, etc., are left in the awkward position of choosing sides. An ageing legend can probably contribute, but maybe not at the level to start on a regular basis or play in a match where speed and work rate will have an impact on tactics and results.

Not Enough Fast Players

Speed of players has a meaningful impact on the number of goals. Jan Vecer, a former professor in the department of statistics at Columbia University who is working on an upcoming book titled *Soccermetrics: Science of Soccer Statistics*, believes, 'The sprint distances have a large positive effect on the goals.' His hypothesis is that the critical statistic is acceleration, which captures the change from fast play to sprints. More importantly, it is not the absolute value of the acceleration, but rather the difference over the opposite team. He believes that fast players benefit enormously from being able to accelerate to a level that can overrun the defenders of the opposite team. His hypothesis implies that Italian clubs' lower scoring rate in the Champions League (goals per game) is primarily due to the acceleration differential being smaller in comparison to the competition in Serie A. Speed not only helps a player score goals for himself but creates space and opportunities for his teammates. In addition, a player is able to sprint back from attack to help with defence. Speed increases the pressure on the opposing team's players and attacks and reduces their space to manoeuvre.

Italian football fans were introduced to the powerful impact of youth and speed in modern football in October 2010. In a Champions League group match between Tottenham and Inter at the San Siro, Inter took a four goals to nil lead in 35 minutes, aided by a numerical advantage after the Tottenham goalkeeper was given a red card in the eighth minute. In the 52nd minute, 21-year-old Gareth Bale started dribbling the ball inside his own half, eluded two challenges, drove into the penalty area and rifled an exquisite left-footed low shot past a stunned goalkeeper, Julio Cesar, into the far corner of the net. It became obvious that Bale possessed another speed gear that Inter's players could not defend. One of the men left in his wake was Maicon, the Brazilian international many cited to be the best right back in world football, but he had no answer to Bale's pace and power. Winning 4-1, Inter focused on defence, but once again Bale raced forward from deep, this time leaving Inter's Javier Zanetti trailing, and slotted home a carbon copy of his first goal; the resemblance was uncanny. Inter's defence knew precisely what Bale had planned to do, but simply could not stop his speed and flawless technique and finish. Now down 4-2, Bale quickly retrieved the ball from the back of the net and urged his side to rush back into position for the restart. He then eluded defenders and rifled a third goal from the left in stoppage time. Bale's blistering runs, clinical finishes and hat-trick (in the San Siro!) at 21 years old against the defending European champions from Italy, whose important starting players now averaged nearly 32 years old, was notice that skill can be possessed by youth and when combined with speed, together they would change European football.

Gareth Bale is known for his physical fitness, speed, skill, stamina, agility and acceleration. When Real Madrid were evaluating Bale, two of the technical aspects that attracted them to him were age and speed. Bale ran around 12 kilometres (7.5 miles) per game, which is a little above average. But what was remarkable was that more than one kilometre was at a speed near his maximum, which is around twice the distance of the average player. More importantly, he has the ability to perform and use his technique at that speed. Real Madrid signed him when he was 24 years old, which is consistent with their shift in signing younger players (in contrast to signing star players that were older like Figo, Zidane, Brazilian Ronaldo and Beckham who might get tired at the end of a long season). His speed not only helps him score goals for himself but creates space and opportunities for his teammates. In addition, he is able to sprint back from attack to help with defence. His speed increases the pressure on the opposing team's players and attacks and reduces their space to manoeuvre.

No Italian players or Serie A players are included in the top 20 fastest players in the EA Sports FIFA 18 game, which is based as closely as possible to players' actual speeds.[7]

---

7 Mohamed Salah #16 overall played for Roma from 2015–17 and Jonathan Biabiany #2 overall played for Inter 2015–17; Deulofeu played for Milan from January 2017–June 2017.

Top 13 Fastest Players in EA Sports FIFA 18
in Big Five Leagues

Rank	Player	Country	Club	League
1.	Pierre-Emerick Aubameyang	Gabon	Borussia Dortmund	Germany
2.	Héctor Bellerín	Spain	Arsenal	England
3.	Gareth Bale	Wales	Real Madrid	Spain
4.	Leroy Sané	Germany	Man City	England
5.	Gelson Martins	Portugal	Sporting	Portugal
6.	Sadio Mané	Senegal	Liverpool	England
7.	Jordi Alba	Spain	Barcelona	Spain
8.	Lucas Moura	Brazil	PSG	France
9.	Mohamed Salah	Egypt	Liverpool	England
10.	Raheem Sterling	England	Man City	England
11.	Gerard Deulofeu	Spain	Barcelona	Spain
12.	Bruma	Portugal	RB Leipzig	Germany
13.	Iñaki Williams	Spain	Athletic Bilbao	Spain

Source: EA Sports

FIFA started to track players' speeds during the 2014 World Cup in Brazil. It was revealed that Arjen Robben was clocked at a top speed of around 37 km/h during the group game against Spain, which is widely regarded as the fastest speed record of a footballer in a match since such data collection started. To put this speed into perspective, 35.92 km/h or 22.32 mph (10.02 seconds for 100 metres) was the speed for the last qualifier in the finals in the 2012 Olympics for the men's 100 metres race, which Usain Bolt won with a time of 9.63 seconds or 37.38 km/h (23.22 mph). While a footballer typically runs less than 20 metres in a sprint (and Robben's speed is only the peak speed), the footballer also is running on grass with shin pads on. Now, players' speeds are often monitored in top European leagues. Below are the 15 fastest footballer sprints since recording (not necessarily today), according to official sources such as FIFA, the Premier League and Opta.[8]

---

[8] Not every league uses the same tracking systems in their stadiums to collect speed, distance metrics, etc. Therefore, comparing speeds across different leagues might prove to be not as straightforward as one might think.

15 Fastest Footballer Top Speeds in a Match

Rank	Player	Club	Top speed
1	Arjen Robben	Bayern Munich	37 km/h
2	Shane Long	Southampton	35.31 km/h
3	Antonio Valencia	Manchester United	35.2 km/h
4	Mathew Leckie	FC Ingolstadt	35.18 km/h
5	Lynden Gooch	Sunderland	35.16 km/h
6	Jamie Vardy	Leicester City	35.12 km/h
7	Kyle Walker	Tottenham	35.12 km/h
8	Gareth Bale	Real Madrid	34.9 km/h
9	Héctor Bellerín	Arsenal	34.77 km/h
10	Sadio Mane	Liverpool	34.7 km/h
11	Eric Bailly	Manchester United	34.5 km/h
12	Theo Walcott	Arsenal	34.3 km/h
13	Aaron Lennon	Everton	33.8 km/h
14	Cristiano Ronaldo	Real Madrid	33.6 km/h
15	Lionel Messi	Barcelona	32.5 km/h

Source: http://www.totalsportek.com/list/fastest-footballers/

CHAPTER FOUR

OTHER ISSUES ON THE PITCH

On-the-Pitch Issues: League

Perception of Relatively Defensive, Boring Games

Serie A was often branded as defensive, low-scoring, boring, old and slow by fans outside the league. The so-called 'catenaccio' (literally translated, 'door bolt') – a rather static, defensive-minded tactic that implies a highly organised and effective backline defence focused on nullifying opponents' attacks and preventing goalscoring opportunities – had been the hallmark of most Italian clubs and the national team. Some even believed that Italy had a defensive culture, not just in football, because for centuries, everyone was trying to invade Italy.[1] The league, and country, have been stigmatised for their style of play with the belief that often aesthetics were sacrificed in order to achieve a result.

Although pure catenaccio is no longer as commonplace in Italian football, the stereotypical association of ruthless defensive tactics with Serie A and the Italian national team continues to be perpetuated by foreign media, particularly with the predominantly Italian defences of

[1] http://bleacherreport.com/articles/1425160-great-team-tactics-breaking-down-how-arri-go-sacchis-ac-milan-took-down-europe

Inter (they invented catenaccio with coach Herrera) in the 1960s, Milan of the 1990s and Juventus from the 2010s onwards being in the spotlight. Rob Bagchi wrote in *The Guardian*: 'Italy has also produced defenders with a surplus of ability, composure and intelligence. For every Gentile there was an Alessandro Nesta.' In *Calcio: A History of Italian Football* historian John Foot also summed up the stereotypical tactics: ' . . .the tactics are a combination of subtlety and brutality. [. . .] The "tactical foul" is a way of life for Italian defenders.' (John Foot, 2010.)

It is interesting to see that the average goals per game in Serie A have increased each decade. It increased from 2.09 from the 1980/90 decade to 2.66 in the 2010/18 decade, a 27% increase.

Serie A Goals Per Game by Decade

2011–18		2001–10		1990–2000		1980–90	
Seasons	*GPG*	*Seasons*	*GPG*	*Seasons*	*GPG*	*Seasons*	*GPG*
2017/2018	2.63	2009/2010	2.61	1999/2000	2.50	1989/1990	2.24
2016/2017	2.96	2008/2009	2.60	1998/1999	2.76	1988/1989	2.11
2015/2016	2.58	2007/2008	2.55	1997/1998	2.77	1987/1988	2.10
2014/2015	2.69	2006/2007	2.55	1996/1997	2.64	1986/1987	1.93
2013/2014	2.72	2005/2006	2.61	1995/1996	2.63	1985/1986	2.06
2012/2013	2.64	2004/2005	2.53	1994/1995	2.53	1984/1985	2.10
2011/2012	2.56	2003/2004	2.67	1993/1994	2.42	1983/1984	2.39
2010/2011	2.51	2002/2003	2.58	1992/1993	2.80	1982/1983	2.10
10–18 Avg	**2.66**	2001/2002	2.63	1991/1992	2.27	1981/1982	1.98
		2000/2001	2.76	1990/1991	2.29	1980/1981	1.91
		01–10 Avg	**2.61**	**90–00 Avg**	**2.56**	**80–90 Avg**	**2.09**

Historically, Serie A has had consistently amongst the lowest average goals per game among the top five leagues, but it's not that much different than one might believe. It's interesting just how similar Serie A average goals per game is with the English Premier League. For example, the EPL is often considered a highly entertaining and fast-paced league yet is only slightly ahead of Serie A in goals scored per game. Researchers studied 17 seasons and found Serie A holds a 2.60 goal per game ratio from season 1999/2000 until 2015/16, with the EPL's figure not much different at 2.66.

Goals Per Game 1999/2000 to 2015/16

League	Goals Per Game
EPL	2.66
Serie A	2.60

Many would be surprised to learn that Serie A's 2.96 goals per game in 2016/17 was the highest among Europe's top five leagues. Roma and Napoli each broke the 90-goal mark while setting club record points tallies for a top-flight campaign.

Instead of just looking at average goals at the league level, researchers delved deeper and looked at the goals of the clubs that win the league titles. Researchers discovered through the data a difference in stylistic approach of the title-winning sides in Italy when compared with, for example, England and Spain.[2]

The notion that Serie A is a defensive-minded league holds truth when considering tactical styles that have brought success. Juventus's run of six league titles in a row did not once see them score more than 80 goals in the league, while goal tallies of 83 in 2014/15 for Manchester City, 89 for Manchester United in 2011/12 and 101 for Liverpool in 2013/14 were only enough to see them finish runners-up in the Premier League during those five years. The goal totals of the winners of the leagues show how the approach differs in Italy, with a style focused on keeping things tight at the back and playing at a lower tempo, making for more tactically astute battles between teams. In addition, Juventus, the league winners, are probably the most watched club in Serie A and re-emphasise a perception.

League Winner Goals for Each League 2010–17

League	Year	League Winner	Goals For	Goals Against	Comment
Serie A	2010	Inter	75	34	
Serie A	2011	Milan	65	24	
Serie A	2012	Juventus	68	20	
Serie A	2013	Juventus	71	24	
Serie A	2014	Juventus	80	23	
Serie A	2015	Juventus	72	24	
Serie A	2016	Juventus	75	20	
Serie A	2017	Juventus	77	27	
		Average	**73**	**25**	
EPL	2010	Chelsea	103	32	Italian coach, Ancelotti
EPL	2011	Man United	78	37	Sir Alex Ferguson
EPL	2012	Man City	93	29	Italian coach, Mancini
EPL	2013	Man United	86	43	Sir Alex Ferguson

2 http://www.fullmatchesandshows.com/2016/10/07/is-serie-a-a-defensive-low-scoring-league/

EPL	2014	Man City	102	37		Pellegrini
EPL	2015	Chelsea	73	32		Mourinho
EPL	2016	Leicester City	68	36		Italian coach, Ranieri
EPL	2017	Chelsea	85	33		Italian coach, Conte
		Average	**86**	**35**		
La Liga	2010	Barcelona	98	24		Real Madrid had 102 goals
La Liga	2011	Barcelona	95	21		Real Madrid had 102 goals
La Liga	2012	Real Madrid	121	32		Barcelona had 114 goals
La Liga	2013	Barcelona	115	40		Real Madrid had 103 goals
La Liga	2014	Atlético Madrid	77	26		Real Madrid had 104 goals
La Liga	2015	Barcelona	110	21		Real Madrid had 118 goals
La Liga	2016	Barcelona	112	29		Real Madrid had 110 goals
La Liga	2017	Real Madrid	106	41		Barcelona had 116 goals
		Average	**104**	**29**		

With eight of the past 17 champions not having to be top scorers to win Serie A, it shows a solid defence and more conservative style of play was decisive for teams who won the league. Teams who won Serie A but didn't top score often weren't far behind in the goals scored tally, but it was the goals conceded figure where a noticeable difference was found. The same doesn't apply in La Liga, as it's the quantity of goals that reflects the difference of Real Madrid and Barcelona from the rest of the league. There has not been a season in La Liga where Barcelona or Real Madrid have not scored 100 goals since 2007/08. The two clubs have 100+ goal tallies a total of 13 times over the course of the period studied, compared with four in total combining the EPL, Serie A, Bundesliga and Ligue 1. Real Madrid and Barcelona are also the most watched clubs globally in the Spanish league and the Champions League, helping brand La Liga's style.[3]

In an interview in the *Gazzetta* in January 2018, Arrigo Sacchi, who dominated European football by winning back-to-back European Cups with Milan in 1989 and 1990, was asked, 'This season, the games Juve-Napoli, Juve-Roma, Napoli-Inter and Juve-Inter should have been the best of Serie A, but instead these games were terrible . . . Why?'

At the time of Sacchi's appointment, Italy was rife with the influences of Helenio Herrera's catenaccio, so his obsession with creating an attacking side was widely regarded as odd. Sacchi famously revolutionised Italian

---

[3] Atlético Madrid's 2013/14 title-winning season was a big change for La Liga, where they won the league with an approach similar to the title winners in Serie A.

football with a complete team playing style with multi-purpose players, and even removed the 'libero' defender and replaced it with discipline and the use of tight and high defensive lines to utilise the offside rule as well as to ensure the distance between his defensive and forward lines was never more than 25 metres. His response was:

> *'Because we are still using the way of playing we had in the '70s . . . we only think about the results, without the way of playing, the emotions, etc. They asked Capello if he saw something new lately; he said yes, now they use a "sweeper" defender again [a very defensive tactic] and he's right . . . It's also related to history, Italy has always been conquered and occupied, and we always defended ourselves by escaping and being clever. We play football like we do war: when the enemy misses his try then we shoot back. Football is a reflection of history and society: we are an old country, in economic struggle, cultural struggle and moral struggle, without new ideas to change all that.'*

The reason that perception matters is that fans can only watch so many football games in an already saturated market. For example, on the weekend of 9 and 10 December 2017, football fans were treated to several top match-ups in Italy and Europe. The 'Derby d'Italia' between Inter (then-first place in Serie A) and Juventus (then-third place in Serie A) was the first time in years the match had top-of-the-table implications. The match finished 0-0, with Inter managing one shot on goal. Then-second place Napoli played then-seventh place Fiorentina, ending 0-0, with Fiorentina managing three shots on goal. Then-fourth place Roma played then-tenth place Chievo, with Chievo managing one shot on goal. The match had 10,000 spectators and ended 0-0. It is hard to have exciting TV highlights to capture audiences with short attention spans when the scores are 0-0. Meanwhile, on the same weekend, in La Liga, Real Madrid beat Sevilla 5-0, with Real Madrid scoring all five goals in the first half. Cristiano Ronaldo scored twice. Barcelona beat Villarreal 2-0, with goals from Messi and Suárez. In the EPL, in the Manchester Derby, Manchester City (then-first place in the EPL) beat Manchester United (then-second place) 2-1 in a thrilling game. However, while we have learned to never underestimate the capacity of Serie A fans to watch hours of highlights, replays and live discussions about a 0-0 match, the casual global football fans that Serie A needs to capture don't generally have the same capacity.

Also, today, global fans often consume sports via highlights clips. It is difficult to get fans excited about spectacular defensive tackles and organised defensive lines. Typically, fans want to see spectacular goals – and preferably scored by stars. This is what drives interest and growth, more often than winning itself. For example, Atlético Madrid have been to the Champions League final twice in the last four years and have certainly had increased revenues. However, Atlético Madrid have not grown their revenues to a level commensurate with their Champions League performances, and not as fast as one would expect if you believe there is a high correlation between winning and attracting fans. Atlético rank #13 in the Deloitte Football Revenues Rankings, only €10 million more in revenues than Roma, who didn't have a corporate shirt sponsor at the time or their own stadium. In addition, Atlético Madrid have had much more recent success on the pitch and in a league with higher TV exposure and revenues, including Champions League, than Roma. However, Atlético Madrid play a defensive-oriented style that gets results, which is a style that doesn't attract as many casual global fans.

League Winner Goals for Each League 2010-17

Rank	Club	Revenues	CL Finals	Last time won League title
#13	Atlético Madrid	€228.6 million	1974, 2014, 2016	2014
#15	Roma	€218.2	1984	2001

Atlético Madrid have signed world-class talent and have an incredible manager, but if a casual fan has the time to watch one football match during a weekend and has to choose between watching Real Madrid or Barcelona or Atlético Madrid play a bottom half La Liga club, most would not watch Atlético because they want excitement and goal scoring, plus the biggest stars. For example, on the 9 and 10 December 2017 weekend mentioned above, Atlético Madrid beat Real Betis 1-0 with only 26% of the possession and two shots on goal. The only goal was from a defensive midfielder. Atlético are extremely fun to watch as a contrasting style and an underdog against big clubs like Real Madrid or Barcelona or in Champions League match-ups.

This is relevant to Italian Serie A football because of how similar Juventus and Atlético Madrid are in scoring and defending goals. Imagine La Liga with Atlético Madrid being the undisputed league leader for six years, similar to the last six years of Serie A with Juventus.

Juventus and Atlético Madrid Goals For and Against 2014–17

2014	Goals For	Goals Against	Goal Difference	Notes
Juventus	80	23	+57	
Atlético Madrid	77	26	+51	Champions League final

2015	Goals For	Goals Against	Goal Difference	Notes
Juventus	72	24	+48	Champions League final
Atlético Madrid	67	29	+38	

2016	Goals For	Goals Against	Goal Difference	Notes
Juventus	75	20	+55	
Atlético Madrid	63	18	+45	Champions League final

2017	Goals For	Goals Against	Goal Difference	Notes
Juventus	77	27	+50	Champions League final
Atlético Madrid	70	27	+43	

Perception of Relatively Defensive, Boring Games

You don't have to know a lot about Italian football to understand that in Italy one team has recently dominated. Juventus have won the league title seven years in a row.[4]

Talent is getting concentrated at Juventus in Italy with their financial dominance over their Italian rivals. In the last few years Juventus have often taken some of their rivals' top players such as Napoli's Gonzalo Higuaín and Roma's Miralem Pjanic. In several, though admittedly not all, of these cases, the selling team were enjoying, or had just enjoyed a strong season. Juventus seem to be constantly under attack for buying the country's best talents, supposedly killing any competition that could have been developed in the process. While there's little doubt most

---

[4] Juventus have won the six Scudetti while many of its rivals have been relatively financially and talent-wise weaker than historically. However, Juventus did reach two Champions League finals during this period, beating Real Madrid in 2015 and Barcelona in 2017 to get to the finals, but also losing to Barcelona in 2015 and Real Madrid in 2017 in the finals.

players' skill justifies Juventus's interest, it's hard to escape the idea that their dominance of the league is inextricably linked to their dominance of the domestic transfer market which is related to their financial domestic domination. This is, of course, what football has become, and there's no suggestion Juventus are doing anything wrong – they need only look after their own interests, like any other club in Italy or Europe. Essentially every other Italian club has been involved in transfer dealings with direct rivals, but the same criticism was hardly heard. In addition, generally, Juventus can get outbid by a few clubs in Europe that have more financial resources for their own talent. As mentioned, Juventus only ranks #10 in the Deloitte Football Revenue Rankings. And in the last few years Juventus have done better in the Champions League than most clubs ahead of it in terms of revenues.

But is such concentration of talent a good thing for a league? Some experts point to this as one of the issues Serie A faces. However, Bayern is similar to Juventus in the German Bundesliga in domination and one could argue that Bayern has helped German football to grow globally over time.[5]

On the other hand, Bayern's dominance may be one of the reasons why international television revenue for German league football still falls well short of the English Premier League. Since Oryx Qatar Sports Investments (QSi)'s ownership, PSG of the French league are now increasingly similar to Bayern in domination. There are many factors that influence interest and isolating the effect of competitive balance and revenues is very difficult.

On any given weekend, overseas viewers have games in multiple countries to choose from. Matches in Italy frequently clash with those in Spain and England, where multiple teams have a good chance of challenging for the title. Bookmakers' odds typically suggest that six teams have at least a 10% chance of winning the English Premier League, and in Spain there are three legitimate contenders every year – Atlético Madrid, Real Madrid and Barcelona. While in Italy, for the last six years, the bookmakers have made Juventus the overwhelming favourite.[6]

---

5 http://bleacherreport.com/articles/2000345-is-bayern-munichs-dominance-good-or-bad-for-the-bundesliga
6 https://www.economist.com/blogs/gametheory/2016/05/boring-bundesliga

In 2016, James P. Curley and Oliver Roeder sought to test the claims that the English Premier League was more competitive than the other leagues in Europe by examining results and final standings data from six top European football leagues from 1995/96 to 2013/14.[7] When looking at the number of unique winners of the European leagues, they discovered that no one team has dominated. For instance, in these 20 complete seasons, Bayern Munich and Manchester United have won their domestic leagues 12 and 11 times respectively, and Juventus and Barcelona have won the Italian and Spanish leagues ten times each. Furthermore, England's EPL have only had four unique winners during that time, Spain's La Liga and Italy's Serie A have had five, and Germany's Bundesliga six.

Number of unique club winners of European leagues
20 complete seasons: 1995/96 to 2013/14

Club	#
Bayern Munich	12
Manchester United	11
Barcelona	10
Juventus	10

Title wins by most successful clubs in European leagues
20 complete seasons: 1995/96 to 2013/14

League	#
Germany	6
Spain	5
Italy	5
England	4

Examining winners may be too simplistic to come to any significant conclusion. Another way is to look at the diversity of teams in the top four places at the end of each season. Curley and Roeder discovered from 1995/96 to 2013/14, the same four teams account for an astonishing 80% of the EPL, 68% of La Liga, 65% of Bundesliga, and 65% of Serie A top-four finishes.

---

7 https://contexts.org/articles/english-soccers-mysterious-worldwide-popularity/

Percentage of top four clubs by European leagues
20 complete seasons: 1995/96 to 2013/14

League	%
England	80%
Spain	68%
Germany	65%
Italy	65%

In terms of unique top-four finishers, 15 different teams have finished in the top four in La Liga. Conversely, just ten unique teams have finished in the top four of the EPL. This analysis of the more successful sides in each league would actually suggest that the EPL is the least competitive league.

The researchers discovered that since the mid-1990s, more points are ending up in the hands of relatively fewer teams in England, Spain and Germany – the leagues are becoming more unbalanced. Among these, the EPL has surprisingly consistently been the most unbalanced.

They examined the success of the bottom four teams in each season when playing against the top four teams. They asked how many points the bottom four teams were able to accrue in games against the top four. In each season, the bottom four teams play a cumulative total of 32 games against top four opposition – a win is worth three points and a draw one, making 96 possible points available. In no year, in any league, did the bottom four achieve more than 28 points against the top four. Notably, in the EPL, Bundesliga and La Liga, the significant trend is towards the bottom four teams performing far worse against the top four. They concluded: 'The EPL may well be the most popular in terms of worldwide audience, but, from our analyses, this is not because of "competitive balance" or "upset likelihood." . . . In fact, there must be a sweet spot of upsets and competitive balance. In all sports, dominant dynasties are generally popular . . . Fans – particularly global fans – like to associate with winning teams. However, if games and leagues become too predictable it's possible that fans will lose interest.'

When Leicester City won the EPL in 2016, it was the first time any city outside Manchester or London had celebrated a Premier League title since

Blackburn won in 1994/95.[8] In addition, over the last 12 seasons ending with 2016 just five clubs have claimed 46 of the 49 Champions League berths in the EPL: Arsenal, Man United, Man City, Chelsea and Liverpool. (Everton in 2005, Tottenham in 2010 and Leicester in 2016 are the only exceptions.)

So far, there is limited evidence that the concentration of income has been directly related to a decline in competitive balance and limited evidence that it reduces interest in league football. Also, there is limited academic research to show there is a positive relationship between competitive balance and league revenues. Typically, many people believed that fans like to see high variability in winning percentage because it gives them faith that their team will be good the next season. Stefan Szymanski, now the Stephen J. Galetti Collegiate Professor of Sport Management at the University of Michigan, wrote about this in a 2001 academic paper in *The Economic Journal*. He examined the relationships between financial inequality, competitive balance and attendance at English professional league football.[9] He concluded 'that while financial inequality among the clubs has increased, competitive balance has remained relatively stable and match attendance appears unrelated to competitive balance'. However, he also studied FA Cup matches which have greater inequality. He concluded, 'Attendance at FA Cup matches relative to the corresponding league matches has fallen over the last 20 years.' But there are many factors that influence attendance and isolating the effect of competitive balance and revenues is very difficult. For example, in the book *Team Sports Marketing*, Baylor University professor Kirk Wakefield found that stadium quality is the first predictor and star players was the second-best predictor of sports attendance.

Jonathan Michie, a professor of management and director of Birmingham Business School, and Christine Oughton, a professor of management and director of the football governance research centre at Birkbeck, University of London, wrote a paper in 2009 for sportsnexus on competitive balance in football.[10] They concluded there has been a decline in competitive balance in all five top leagues; meanwhile, revenues have grown in all five leagues.

---

[8] London has Arsenal, Chelsea, Crystal Palace, Tottenham Hotspur, West Ham United, Fulham and Queens Park Rangers; Manchester has Manchester United and Manchester City.

[9] Szymanski, Stefan. 'Income Inequality, Competitive Balance and the Attractiveness of Team Sports: Some Evidence and a Natural Experiment from English Soccer', *Economic Journal* 111.469 (2000)

[10] Michie, Jonathan, and Christine Oughton. 'Competitive Balance in Football: Trends and Effects', sportsnexus (2004).

Fans Too Far and Attendance Too Poor
to Influence Referees

Most Italian football clubs play in old stadiums with a running track between the crowd and pitch. The running tracks are a legacy of stadiums being built for the World Cup in 1990. Besides impacting on the overall fan experience, the running tracks and poor attendance may actually be impacting the teams' on-the-pitch performance in European competitions. In 2003 Thomas Dohmen published a paper titled 'In Support of the Supporters? Do Social Forces Shape Decisions of the Impartial?' where he analysed the neutrality of referees during nine German Bundesliga seasons. He found that home ground advantage was less in stadiums with a running track surrounding the pitch than those without a running track. Why? Apparently, when the crowd sits closer to the pitch, the officials are more susceptible to getting caught up in the home crowd emotion. He wrote: 'The social atmosphere in the stadium leads referees into favouritism although being impartial is optimal for them to maximise their reappointment probability.' Referees are humans impacted by senses like sound and a desire to be liked. Referees tend to favour the home team as they systematically award more injury time in close matches when the home team is behind. Further evidence for similar home bias comes from referees' wrong, or at least disputable, decisions to award goals and penalties. The severity of social pressure, measured by the crowd's composition and proximity to the action, determines its effect.

This may not have been an issue in the 1990s with modernised stadiums for the 1990 World Cup, high attendances and a talent gap with other leagues. However, today, without such a large talent gap, Serie A clubs need all the help they can get. Juventus's stadium completed for the 2011/12 season does not have a running track.

Besides impacting the overall fan experience, racism and violence also can impact on a club's 'home ground advantage' by having clubs ordered to play matches behind closed doors. For example, Torino were banned from playing five matches in Serie A inside their stadium in 2003 due to the violence that occurred in February 2003 inside the stadium during a match with Milan. Tobias Moskowitz and L. Jon Wertheim, authors of *Scorecasting*, studied a series of matches played in Italy in 2007. Following several clashes between hooligans and police, clubs were ordered to play matches behind closed doors if they could not provide adequate security. This resulted in 21 matches being played with no crowd at all for the rest of the season. The results of their study were fascinating. Despite the absence of a crowd cheering them on, players essentially performed the same. They had the same shots on target percentages, the same passing accuracy and even the same amount of tackles were made as they normally would be. What do you suspect happened to the pattern of refereeing decisions once they were not subjected to the fans' verbal abuse and pressure typical at the homes of elite football clubs? Home ground advantage drops, drastically. The away team were penalised for fouls 23% less than they usually would be, were awarded 26% fewer yellow cards and 70% fewer red cards.

Quality Dilution with Too Many Clubs

For most of Serie A's history, there were 16 or 18 clubs competing at the top level. Since 2004/05, however, there have been 20 clubs altogether. One season (1947/48) was played with 21 teams for political reasons. Below is a complete record of how many teams played in each season throughout the league's history:

of Clubs in Serie A by Year

# of Clubs	Years
18 clubs:	1929–1934
16 clubs:	1934–1942
18 clubs:	1942–1946
20 clubs:	1946–1947
21 clubs:	1947–1948
20 clubs:	1948–1952
18 clubs:	1952–1967
16 clubs:	1967–1988
18 clubs:	1988–2004
20 clubs:	2004–present

In comparison, the English Premier League, Spanish La Liga and French Ligue 1 all have 20 sides too, the exception being the German Bundesliga which has 18. However, the revenues for EPL, La Liga and Bundesliga are higher, so the revenue per club for those leagues is higher.

On top of that, relegation used to claim four teams each summer instead of the current three. The increase was intended to generate fan interest in more towns in Italy. However, the unintended consequence was the technical level of the players in the teams was diluted, making the matches less interesting and attractive. This discrepancy increased as financial issues increased.

Some have suggested that it would make sense for Serie A to trim down and reinvent itself as a smaller league, but one packed with quality and competition in order to differentiate itself from other European leagues. Were that to happen, TV revenue would be distributed between fewer clubs, allowing for more stability, and greater investment in infrastructure and players. There'd be more quality, less quantity. In addition, fewer league games would make a multi-faceted season with many competitions easier to manage, especially as many Italian clubs can't afford to build deep, top-quality squads with backups which is necessary to compete in today's game. With European competitions an important driver of revenue and global brand identity (as well as coefficients for tournament spots), Italian teams could focus more on those tournament matches.[11] The players' union president said he would endorse a reduction in the number of clubs in Italy's league structure, from top to bottom, to provide better financial sustainability and improve the calendar.[12]

The standard of the teams coming up from Serie B is also being questioned, especially those teams reaching Serie A on the back of double promotions. Frosinone did it in 2015 and Benevento and SPAL in 2017. Benevento, who were founded in their current form in 2005, were promoted to Serie A for the first time in their history for 2017/18. SPAL was promoted to Serie A for the first time in 23 years before being promoted again to Serie A, in which they last participated in 1968. SPAL reportedly almost went bankrupt in 2013. Benevento and SPAL were among the bottom three of the Serie A standings in April 2018.

The most recent supporting argument for a reduction in the number of clubs is the performance of Benevento in the 2017/18 season with 13 defeats in 13 games, the worst start ever in the big five championships of

---

11 http://bleacherreport.com/articles/1639698-why-cutting-the-number-of-teams-in-serie-a-is-the-right-mov
12 https://fifpro.org/news/players-union-maps-out-italian-football-future/en/?highlight=WyJsZWd hbCIsImxlZ2FsJywiwiXQ==

Europe. It is interesting to note the previous record was held by Manchester United in 1930! Poor financial management has really hurt big or medium sized cities' clubs like Fiorentina, Napoli, Parma, Bari, Catania, Venezia and Modena and has led them to be relegated to lower levels at various times, providing an opportunity for well-managed clubs from very small towns like Empoli, Chievo, Sassuolo, Capri, Crotone, Frosinone and Benevento to rise to Serie A. The issue is these small clubs only can attract and have stadiums for a few thousand fans, and there is less interest from fans of bigger clubs (or casual global football fans) watching them play many of these small-town clubs that they do not immediately recognise.

One unintended consequence of reducing the number of clubs is that there would be fewer positions to develop local talent, especially since the big clubs can't have a B squad to play in Serie B. Serie A could introduce the notion of second teams/B teams into the league. This is something that is common in other countries like Spain and the Netherlands and this will help ensure a focus on improving talents in perfect harmony with the first team. Another unintended consequence is taking away a dream from smaller towns, and reducing the number of potential football fans in the long term; however, the economic viability of the league will most likely depend on its quality and attractiveness to a global audience.

Difficulty with Passports for Players

With fewer South American oriundi available, Italian clubs found it more difficult to find eligible talent. This led to false passport cheating. As previously discussed in the section titled Allegations of Cheating, in 2000/01, nine South American players were implicated in a scandal that centred on the provision of false passports to enable clubs to field non-European players as Europeans. This helped clubs overcome the limits on non-European Union talent.

In Spain, there has been migration from Latin America to Spain. Spain is the second destination of choice after the United States for Latin American migrants and the vast majority of Latin Americans in Europe are residents or nationals of this country. Following the 'Law of Historic Memory', Latin Americans with a Spanish parent or grandparent (and their descendants) have an automatic right to Spanish citizenship, even without residing in the country.

In La Liga a club can retain a maximum of three non-EU players. In La Liga, the players are allowed to claim citizenship from the land where their ancestors arrived from. A non-European player is entitled to apply for Spanish citizenship if he plays in Spain for at least five years. Furthermore, the players coming from the ACP countries referring to the Caribbean, Africa and the Pacific, which are signatory to the Cotonou Agreement, are not taken into account against the non-EU slots owing to the Kolpak ruling. In addition, players from South America get Spanish status after two years of playing in a Spanish division.

In France, there is a strong colonial connection to Africa and the Caribbean. Immigration from Africa to France started after World War II and so is more recent than Italians emigrating to South America. Footballers from former French colonies in Africa are more likely to have a French connection to gain French citizenship and most likely speak some French. French Caribbean islands (Martinique, Guadeloupe) footballers are French citizens and typically speak French. Italian emigrants to South America are now generationally on to great-grandparents, making obtaining a passport more difficult. In addition, football is the immigrant sport in France. In the same way that Italian-descent players in South America would then come to Europe, in France, African-descent players play in France as well as the French Caribbean Islands.

In Germany, of the 23 players representing Germany at the 2014 World Cup, 11 have foreign backgrounds. More than half of the players selected by Joachim Löw were either born outside Germany themselves, or have a non-German parent. The German squad had roots in eight different countries – nine when Germany is included. According to the most up-to-date figures from the Federal Statistics Office, one in five people living in Germany in 2008 was of foreign descent. From the total of 15.9 million with roots abroad, 2.9 million were from Turkey. Two likely starters for the national team at the World Cup – Serdar Tasci and Mesut Özil – both have Turkish parents. Lukas Podolski, Miroslav Klose and Piotr Trochowski were born in Poland, and moved across the border as children. All have been part of Germany's international set-up for years. Youngster Marko Marin was born in war-struck Bosnia-Herzegovina. His parents moved to

Frankfurt when he was two, and, when he came of age, Marin decided on a German passport. Mario Gomez was born in Baden-Württemberg, but his father comes from Spain. The German Football Association (DFB) is not afraid of celebrating its eclectic new generation of players. Since 2007, the DFB and its general sponsor Mercedes-Benz have given an integration prize under the label 'Football: Many Cultures – but a Single Passion'.

On-the-Pitch Issues: Management

Slow to Adapt to New Methods

Because of the issues discussed, Italy needs to change its football culture and mentality, especially at the club management level. Sacchi's four-year spell at Milan should have proved to the Italian coaches who valued defensive solidarity over aesthetics, that it was possible to be successful whilst playing beautiful football. However, most coaches and owners didn't want to betray long-held Italian football beliefs that, while not attractive, had a legacy of results and trophies.

In 1990, Juventus hired Luigi Maifredi on the back of a successful three-year period at Bologna and whose style of football was dubbed '*calcio champagne*'.[13] Having signed Roberto Baggio before Italia '90, it was hoped Maifredi, together with Baggio, would usher in an exciting new style of play for Juventus. Maifredi's tenure was disastrous and lasted one season before being fired. Juventus finished seventh in Serie A and wouldn't play in Europe for the first time in 28 years. Who replaced him? The ever-pragmatic Giovanni Trapattoni, so Juventus's experiment with eye-pleasing football lasted all of one season, and most likely, made a lasting memory.

The majority of coaches in calcio still believed in the philosophy of getting a result, which typically means defensive security first and foremost; the attitude is 'why change a mentality that had a history of success and was so deeply entrenched in the national psyche?' And as discussed previously, the data supports this view, especially with Juventus. Obtaining the result was all that mattered; 'if you wanted entertainment, go to the theatre' was the general assertion in Italy. Italian clubs wanting to

---

[13] Maifredi reportedly was also a former champagne salesman.

dictate play are rare because most of them are too focused on stopping the opposition from playing. This was a strategy that had worked in the past in Europe, but European clubs have gotten more talent and adapted tactics. Most teams in Europe know how to press, have speed and youth and can pass the ball with great fluidity. Italian football is slower, with slower and older players. However, the game has changed to faster, younger players with a high work rate. When Italian teams have the quality and a lead, the mentality is often to sit on the lead rather than add to the lead. This could also be because the players are older and slower. Italian clubs must learn to adapt to the current evolution of European football. The crux of the matter is that Italian coaches are caught between Italy's past and its future, between the traditionalists who felt threatened by change and the modernists who try to apply it. Unfortunately, in European football, with competing for European spots and the possibility of relegation, there is little patience. As previously discussed, fans care more than just about winning. The casual global fans who can increase the revenues want to be entertained and see goals scored. Without a change in philosophy, the commercial revenues will not appear. This then makes it more difficult to compete as revenues has the highest correlation to winning, especially with FFP.

In general, football has been slow to incorporate data analytics. In Italy, it has generally been even slower. With fewer resources, Italy needs to be on the cutting edge of innovation to compete. Most Italian football club management teams don't have the technological sophistication to adopt meaningful technology to capture data and analyse it. This is for both on and off the pitch. Data analytics is not an answer by itself, but it is a necessary tool for management teams to make better decisions and track performance. For example, in the Future of European Football there are analyses on goals per game and 'gravity scores' that reveal new ways of thinking about football.

Italian clubs have also been more short-term focused with regards to talent in comparison to other leagues. Serie A clubs change and transfer more players more often than any other league, which can have a negative impact on long-term development, on-the-pitch chemistry, familiarity and culture which can impact on results.

Number of Transfers by League from 2008 to 2016

League	Number of Transfers
Italy Serie A	1,156
Spain La Liga	928
France Ligue 1	832
England EPL	809
Germany Bundesliga	677

Drain of Top Coaching Talent

The decline in Serie A had led many of Italy's brightest coaching talents to work in other leagues. In 2016 Claudio Ranieri won the Premier League with Leicester City (after being fired the following year he joined French club Nantes instead of coming back to Serie A), and Antonio Conte won the EPL the following year with Chelsea. Carlo Ancelotti won the German Bundesliga in 2017 (after being fired the following year he reportedly refused to come back to work in Italy). In 2017 Roberto Mancini left Inter to go to Zenit St Petersburg. Christian Panucci is in charge of Albania and 2006 World Cup-winning coach Marcello Lippi is overseeing the China national team's drive to be a major power. In addition, in 2017, Fabio Capello and Fabio Cannavaro work in the Chinese Super League and Alberto Zaccheroni coaches the United Arab Emirates.

Of the top 20 highest paid coaches in Europe in 2016/17, as per financefootball.com, no Italian club is in the top ten. Roberto Mancini of Inter was 15th, Massimiliano Allegri of Juventus was 17th and Luciano Spalletti of Roma was 19th. Demonstrating the financial power of the English Premier League, nine of the top 20 paid coaches are in the English Premier League, three are in La Liga, three in Italy, two in Germany and one in each of Portugal, Russia and France.

Top 20 Highest Paid Coaches in Europe 2016-2017
as per financefootball.com € in millions

	Coach	Club	Annual Wage
1	Pep Guardiola	Manchester City	18.0
2	Carlo Ancelotti	Bayern Munich	15.0

3	José Mourinho	Manchester United	14.5
4	Arsène Wenger	Arsenal	10.5
5	Zinedine Zidane	Real Madrid	9.5
6	Luis Enrique	Barcelona	8.5
7	Jürgen Klopp	Liverpool	8.5
8	Antonio Conte	Chelsea	7.8
9	Ronald Koeman	Everton	7.0
10	Diego Simeone	Atl. Madrid	6.0
11	Jorge Jesus	Sporting	5.0
12	Unai Emery	PSG	5.0
13	Rafa Benitez	Newcastle	5.0
14	Roberto Mancini	Inter Milan	5.0
15	Thomas Tuchel	Borussia Dortmund	5.0
16	Mauricio Pochettino	Tottenham	4.5
17	Massimiliano Allegri	Juventus	4.0
18	Mircea Lucescu	Zenit St Petersburg	4.0
19	Luciano Spalletti	AS Roma	4.0
20	Claudio Ranieri	Leicester City	4.0

Source: Financefootball.com

Although change in some ways makes a team interesting and engaging, changing coaches can create some difficulties because the players have been selected for a particular coach and his system/formation. Many in the media focus on the number of recent coaching changes during a president's tenure, but big Italian and European clubs have a long tradition of quickly replacing coaches. The average stay for a coach in one of Europe's top five leagues was between nine and 16 months, according to a study by the Swedish-based International Centre for Sports Studies. We examined and compared Italian clubs' coaching changes versus selected other big European clubs over various time periods below. Italian clubs don't change any more frequently than their peers.

Number of Coaching Changes Since 2000

Club	Since 2000	1990–2000	2000–2010	2010–2018
Juventus	11	4	8	3
Milan	13	7	5	8
Inter	18	14	7	11
Roma	14	8	7	8
Napoli	15	15	13	3

Real Madrid	14	15	10	4
Barcelona	10	4	6	5
Bayern Munich	12	9	6	7
Atletico	15	21	13	3
Chelsea	15	6	8	8

Note: Excludes temporary or assistant coaches that transitioned to full-time coach.

Multiple studies found that there is no evidence that changing a coach helps a team win more games.[14] When the coach changes, then the new coach inherits players suited and trained for another system/formation. It can take time for the players to adjust to a new coach's system/ formation and then for the coach to sign the right players. During the transition, the team can lack balance. As discussed previously, the difficulty is that the coach has to be able to adapt to changes going on with players, even if the players aren't new, as well as competitive pressures. A football team is a complex, dynamic, living organisation that has to be nurtured on a daily basis. It takes a special coach to be flexible enough to adapt to an ever-changing group. During the transition, the coach is left with the difficult decisions of putting the players in positions to succeed, rather than implementing a system. With rotations being required and injuries impacting on the familiarity of players on the field, it seems that successful clubs will need to have a system from the first team through the academy.

On-the-Pitch Issues: Country

Relatively Worse Income Tax Rates

Related to attracting and retaining players are taxes, as players look to maximise after tax income. Typically, a club grosses up a player's wage to offset taxes (essentially paying the tax for the player), and the contracted amount is net of taxes. An academic study found taxes impact player decisions, and therefore impact the performance of football clubs across countries.[15]

---

[14] Dave Berri, 'Is Changing the Coach Really the Answer?' Freakonomics. http://freakonomics. com/2012/12/21/is-changing-the-coach-really-the-answer/.)
[15] http://eml.berkeley.edu//~saez/kleven-landais-saez09football.pdf

Each country in Europe has different tax rates as well as rules on how certain income (especially image rights) is treated and taxed. In Spain, football players that qualified used to take advantage of the 'Beckham Law' which had a flat tax rate of 24.75%, but this was repealed for football players in December 2014. In the UK, non-UK income and gains outside the UK are not taxed for qualifying non-domiciled football players. In addition, it was reported that EPL clubs were told that they can pay up to a fifth of their football total pay packages to 'image rights' companies rather than ordinary income. Such an arrangement means the player can avoid paying income tax on the money. It also allows football clubs to cut the amount of National Insurance contributions.[16]

In a 2013 report by Ernst & Young which investigated the tax rates and regulations in 30 countries for football players, Spain was ranked #2 (while the Beckham rule was still in effect), France #5, the United Kingdom #6, Germany #13 and Italy #16. This puts Italian clubs at a competitive disadvantage.

Favours Seniority

There is a 'brain drain' going on in Italy at the moment. Young people account for the bulk of Italian emigration. Over the last 20 years, roughly half a million Italians aged 18 to 39 have moved abroad, especially to more economically dynamic and progressive European Union countries such as Germany, France and the United Kingdom. Guido Tintori, research associate at Fieri, the International and European Forum on Migration Research, argues that skilled young Italian graduates 'not only are under-employed and underpaid, but are constantly frustrated by a society and a labour market that hinges on relationships and seniority over competence'. As discussed, this is the culture and mentality in Italian football that may be hindering development.

Not surprisingly, it is Italy's most qualified who are most likely to leave. This trend began in the late 1980s, with PhDs and researchers who could not find a place at local universities, which are hierarchically controlled, prone to corruption and starved of funding. Since then, many other

---

[16] http://www.dailymail.co.uk/news/article-4024326/Nearly-200-footballers-facing-HMRC-probe-using-image-rights-tax-dodge-cut-bills.html

professionals have joined them. As discussed, this culture and mentality is impacting Italian football.

In Italy, there is a strong cultural bias (familiar or patriarchal culture) not to move older, previously successful players. Essentially, in Italy if a player was once great almost nobody would ever ask the player to leave or retire. For example, the Agnelli family and Juventus management are still resented by some Juventus fans, some of whom signed petitions, for not renewing the contract of then 37-year-old 'Mr Juventus' Alessandro Del Piero. In another example, some Roma fans were upset that 40-year-old Francesco Totti was not provided more playing time and not offered a new contract. This puts clubs in a very awkward position in terms of moving on or developing talent. In other European countries, clubs have taken a more aggressive approach in the awkward situation of communicating to older players and legends that they must retire or move on. For example, Real Madrid let home-grown captain and legend goalkeeper Iker Casillas, who is three years younger than his historic rival Buffon, go to Porto in 2015; Casillas was also replaced as the Spanish national team's primary goalkeeper.[17] In contrast, Buffon has continued to play; and, in fairness, finished fourth in the Ballon d'Or voting in 2017.

On the Pitch Issues: Technology

Synthetic Ball Speeds Up the Game

Football has changed and evolved immeasurably in the last 20 years. One of the biggest changes has been the use of synthetic footballs (versus leather), which with each passing year have become more and more plastic.[18] The last ever leather ball used at a World Cup was the legendary adidas Tango. From 1986 onwards, with the introduction of the adidas Azteca – the World Cup's first ever fully synthetic football – every single passing year and World Cup has seen the footballs become more plastic. In addition, in 1970, the first adidas ball went black and

---

[17] Real Madrid has other examples such as home-grown Raúl who signed with Schalke 04 when he was 33 years old.

[18] *Goal's* Carlo Garganese has written on the numerous negative effects synthetic balls have had on the game.http://www.goal.com/en/news/1717/editorial/2010/07/19/2032331/goalcom-comment-for-the-good-of-the-game-stop-using-these

white for high visibility for the first World Cup ever televised in colour but needed 32 panels to do so. By 2006 adidas had the count down to 14 panels.

In 2014 FIFA announced that the ball was the most advanced and fastest ball ever created for the sport, supported by science. In addition to materials, science has allowed balls to have fewer pentagonal and hexagonal panels, which improves 'optimal aerodynamic continuity and flight speed'. Researchers used wind tunnels and kick robots to demonstrate this relationship between the number and shape of panels and materials to achieve better aerodynamic, speed and flight characteristics.[19] The dry weight of balls is approximately the same today as 50 years ago. However, the older leather balls would absorb more moisture throughout the game, and slow the ball.

Synthetic balls have led to the art of defending, one of Italian football's historic strengths, becoming more challenging and shifted an advantage to attacks, which can give Italian football clubs focused on defence a disadvantage in European and international competitions. In simple terms, synthetic balls help negate defence. There seems to be a deliberate effort by the footballing bodies to make the footballs more synthetic in order to make the game faster, allow for more spin, and to provide 'more excitement'. Fast balls make football more about youth, speed and athleticism and less about skill. The sport has become more reliant on younger players with speed, in part, because of faster balls.

Before the World Cup 2018, goalkeepers from Spain and Germany's national teams voiced concern over the adidas Telstar 18 ball to be used after the ball was used in an exhibition match. 'I bet you as much as you like that we'll see at least 35 goals from long range because it's impossible to work out . . .And it's covered in a plastic film that makes it difficult to hold on to. Goalkeepers are going to have a lot of problems with this ball,' Pepe Reina, who plays goalkeeper for the Spain national team and Italian club Napoli, said, per Spanish newspaper *AS*.

---

[19] https://io9.gizmodo.com/fifas-new-world-cup-ball-is-the-fastest-and-most-aeodyn-1584774348

On-the-Pitch Issues: Legal/Regulatory

Negative Football Rule Changes to Italian Tactics

Today's liberal interpretation of the offside rule hurts defence-oriented teams. Twenty years ago, any player standing between the goalkeeper and last defender when the ball was played was deemed offside – regardless of whether he was active or passive. This was very important to many Italian football clubs' defensive systems, which centred on a high defensive line and pushing up the backline on call as defenders anticipated a through ball. For example, Arrigo Sacchi, who coached the great Milan teams in 1989 and 1990, famously removed the 'libero' defender and replaced the position with a strict and efficient use of the off-side trap. Such was Italian football genius that would regularly catch an attacker offside. Today, the same strategy is severely handicapped by the rule change.

A second rule change is back-passes to the goalkeepers. Before 1992, goalkeepers were allowed to pick up back-passes from their own teammates. Since 1992, this has been outlawed. The option of slowing down the tempo in this way and giving defences an easier option when in trouble was eliminated. In terms of effects, the rule change has been credited with creating a foundation for the type of pressing that Pep Guardiola's great Barcelona side of 2008 to 2012 engaged in, as opposition teams can't just relieve pressure by passing the ball back into their goalkeeper's waiting arms.

In a third rule change prior to the 1998 World Cup, FIFA made the tackle from behind a red card offence. The wording emphasised that it was a tackle 'which endangers the safety of an opponent'. Players like Marco van Basten had to endure such tackles during their careers and it is said to have contributed to the introduction of zero tolerance for tackles from behind the player with the ball. The Dutch great's playing career ended prematurely at the age of just 28 in 1993 with the effect of dangerous tackles on him believed to be one of the reasons. In addition, zero tolerance against the two-footed challenge was also added. In fairness, these changes did not just impact on Italy and the Italian league, but hard tackles made Italian defences incredibly effective, and, when combined with a defensive duo as vertiginously talented as Maldini-Baresi, almost impenetrable.

A fourth rule change is that these days multiple balls are used during a game. Today, as soon as one ball goes out of play, a ball boy on the sidelines throws in another. This means there are no pauses in the action, unlike two decades ago when the same ball was retained and players would have to wait – sometimes 30 seconds to a minute – for spectators to return it. Generally, Italian sides used the time to regroup in defence more than others.

Lastly, another modification that is relevant is the strictness of the referees. Into the 1990s there was leniency that saw tough defenders like Claudio Gentile have an entire career without being sent off. Officials were far more tolerant of tough play decades ago. Dangerous tackles were still accepted as part of the game. Referees would allow a defender to accumulate more offences before being booked. Around the mid-1990s the emphasis changed to protect goal scoring, creative star players. For example, there was less protection for Diego Maradona than there is now for Lionel Messi. In comparing the two, Joe Bernstein for Mail Online wrote: 'In an era where defenders could kick lumps out of creative players and get away with it, particularly in Serie A, he [Maradona] never shirked . . . Messi is much better protected by referees.' Italian football was as physical as it was technical. Today, even if a referee misses a foul, the perpetrator could still face penalties after the event based on video evidence. In addition, if any players try to commit fouls which may cause injuries, they would face very stiff penalties in terms of long bans, fines, loss of endorsements and so on. Today, some of Italy's identity of tough defence is being regulated out.[20] Franco Baresi, one of the league's greatest defenders, explained to *Corriere della Sera*: 'Defenders' attitudes have changed,' he said. 'They now know that every little indiscretion will get picked up by the TV cameras, so they're more careful, more cautious. Defenders are more afraid. They don't get as tight and that's an advantage for strikers.'[21]

---

[20] http://www.goal.com/en/news/1717/editorial/2011/11/23/2767812/arrigo-sacchis-ac-milan-vs-pep-guardiolas-barcelona-the

[21] http://www.independent.co.uk/sport/football/european/serie-a-italian-football-lost-love-defending-catenaccio-highest-scoring-league-europe-a7956206.html

CHAPTER FIVE

OVERALL FAN EXPERIENCE OFF THE PITCH

Off-the-Pitch Issues: Overall Fan Experience

Not Global Entertainment Brands, No Community-Centric Culture

In the late 1990s and 2000s, two very important and fast-growing segments in European football became broadcasting and marketing (sponsorship and licensing) rights. The growth of these areas illustrates that professional European football is a global entertainment business, in which the big clubs of today (e.g. Barcelona, Bayern Munich, Manchester United and Real Madrid) have been leaders. These clubs realised that their matches and best players captivate live, global audiences, from which they generated marketing activities, sponsorships and licenses.

Today, fans care more about why a team exists, how their sports team wins, and whom it wins with versus just winning (what the result is). The how and why are critical parts and what inspire passion and loyalty. The big clubs mentioned previously have embraced this concept to commercial success. In contrast, most Italian football clubs assume the only thing that matters to fans are results.

Most owners assume if they give the fans trophies, then they will be adored and respected. This is conventional wisdom. However, we learned in our research that fans today are much more complex than sports owners, management and media believe. Attitudes have changed. What consumers of sports, media and entertainment expect and desire have changed. Sports owners wrongly believe that winning is the mission. However, winning is a result (a 'what'), which comes at the end of a process. The players, the fans, the entire community need a mission, a greater purpose, than just winning; they need a 'mission' or 'why' to create extraordinary loyalty and passion. Most owners and executives don't appreciate that to be successful their entire strategy, both on and off the field, needs to be based on the 'why', which essentially comes from the values and expectations of their fans and community, which is the core or centre of their culture. Once a sports organisation understands 'why', then they can focus on 'how' – the types of players the fans want, the style of play the fans want, the overall experience the fans want – then winning becomes a result versus the mission.

The order from club managements should be 'why', 'how' and lastly 'what'. Successful football clubs both on and off the pitch aren't just providing a 90-minute football match; they are providing a larger experience or entertainment that draws in global community members to care and actively participate and then continuously engages members so that the club is a part of their daily lives, and a part of their identity. This approach can forge extraordinary loyalty, inspiration, strength, passion and identity beyond local fans. This extraordinary loyalty and sense of identity leads to increases in global fan bases and revenues. This is important in today's football business world because these fans and their spending, plus the money from the global sponsors and broadcasters who want access to these loyal fans, are needed to pay for the talent and infrastructure required to compete at an elite level, especially with Financial Fair Play restrictions based on revenues. In part, this has been circular because without building commercial operations and global fan bases, qualifying for, and receiving money from, European competitions plays an extraordinary part of the financial models and viability of most clubs.

Professor Susan Fournier from Boston University and Lara Lee, former executive at Harley-Davidson, wrote an article titled 'Getting Brand Communities Right' in the April 2009 issue of *Harvard Business*

Review. According to them, 'A community-based brand builds loyalty not by driving sales transactions but by helping people meet their needs.' Management teams need to better understand their community members' values, give them what they want, and improve and inspire their lives. It is not just about status and winning. Fournier and Lee wrote, 'People participate in communities for a wide variety of reasons – to find emotional support and encouragement, to explore ways to contribute to the greater good, and to cultivate interests and skills, to name a few. For members, brand communities are a means to an end, not an end in themselves.' Community members want to be empowered, inspired, escape, enjoy, celebrate, connect, share and socialise. They want content to share and discuss. They want their sports team to unite them.

The internet and digital technology have allowed sophisticated, active community engagement. With reality TV culture, community members want to be as close to the players as possible, with video – at their practice, at the gym, in the tunnel, on the bus, in the press room and in the dressing room. The players in the team have to match what the fans want to see, root for and care about. With data analytics, they want access to, and the ability to manipulate data and analysis like the coach. The coach of the team has to employ a style of play the fans want to see. With more transparency and accountability in the world, the fans expect more management transparency in terms of financial information and decision-making. They want the club to be managed in a way they would expect. The game today is only a part of an entertainment story. With so many high quality branded products, fans expect high quality licensed sports products and services from their club. Generally, this is not the mentality of the owners and management of Italian clubs.

The sports clubs that do this bring together a global community with a sense of belonging felt so deeply by fans around the world that they are synonymous with its identity. The history, feelings, traditions, rituals and emotions are intertwined. It will be impossible to tell where the fans' identity and purpose start and stop, as they are one and the same. Respectful rivalries help define the identity of the community and are reasons for anticipation and discussion. As the community grows and is more easily identifiable, it leads to worldwide sponsors spending big money for association with and access to the community, as well as television broadcasters paying lots of money to distribute the games to a large, passionate audience. The passion and experience lead to increased stadium receipts.

Big global sponsors are attracted to a club's global community brand that they want to be affiliated with because the brand also represents their own brand and identity. Winning helps because of the exposure as well as supporting the brand identity of being a winner. In 2016, 15 clubs in Serie A had sponsors on the front of their shirts, while five clubs had an empty space, including Roma, Lazio and Palermo. Roma was the only club in the top 20 valuations in 2016 that did not have a shirt sponsor.[1] No English Premier League club had an empty shirt. To compare the business that clubs have done on their shirt deals, English clubs bring in a total of €220 million a year on shirts. In Italy, the figures are considerably worse. Serie A brought in €83 million, compared to €103 million in Ligue 1 and €105 million in La Liga.

The totals below include all signed deals for matchday shirt and kit sponsorships, and naming rights for stadiums and training grounds. The only Italian club is Juventus and it is less than 25% of Barcelona, Real Madrid and Manchester United and less than half of Bayern Munich.

Football's Most Valuable Sponsorships
(for 2015/16 season)
€ in millions

Rank	Team	Annual Average
1	Barcelona	€210
2	Real Madrid	195
3	Manchester United	193
4	Chelsea	133
5	Bayern Munich	98
6	Arsenal	80
7	Liverpool	74
8	Manchester City	69
9	Tottenham Hotspur	67
10	Juventus	47

Source: https://www.forbes.com/sites/mikeozanian/2017/06/06/the-worlds-most-valuable-soccer-teams-2017/

---

[1] Roma signed a shirt sponsorship with Qatar Airways in 2018.

Shirt sales tell a lot about identity, passion and loyalty. A fan can pay around €100 for a football shirt. The prices don't vary that much amongst the top clubs, so status isn't gained by price. To spend that money, the fan wants to make some sort of statement. The statement implicitly is that he/she identifies with and supports the club's values and is a part of the community. Although not widely known, clubs typically don't actually get money per shirt sold. Those revenues are typically sold to the shirt manufacturer (adidas, Nike, etc.), who takes the risk. Therefore, when a club buys a player and the shirt sales are reported, the club doesn't pocket those revenues directly. Increases in the profile of players can lead to renegotiations of a shirt contract. It is difficult to know precisely how many shirts a club sells because of reporting, as well as how many fake shirts are sold. While imperfect, the list below provides a sense of which clubs have a passionate and loyal global community.

2016 Estimated Number of Shirts Sold by Each Team (and player with best sales numbers):

1. Manchester United (approx. 2,850,000) – Paul Pogba
2. Real Madrid (approx. 2,290,000) – Cristiano Ronaldo
3. Barcelona (approx. 1,980,000) – Lionel Messi
4. Chelsea (approx. 1,650,000) – Eden Hazard
5. Bayern Munich (approx. 1,500,000) – Robert Lewandowski
6. Arsenal (approx. 1,125,000) – Mesut Özil
7. Juventus (approx. 850,000) – Gonzalo Higuaín
8. Liverpool (approx. 805,000) Philippe Coutinho
9. PSG (approx. 685,000) – Ángel Di María
10. AC Milan (approx. 650,000) – Keisuke Honda
11. Atlético Madrid (approx. 500,000) – Antoine Griezmann
12. Leicester City (approx. 350,000) – Jamie Vardy

Source: https://hypebeast.com/2016/11/football-club-players-with-most-shirt-sales-2016

The list above shows the commercial power of players with strong national followings like Keisuke Honda, a Japanese player for Milan in 2016. As of 2017, he plays in Mexico. Hailed as the 'Messi of the Pyramids' in the Italian media, the Egyptian winger Mohamed Salah played for Roma from 2015 to 2017. He was the only Serie A player in the 2017 ESPN

World Fame 100 Athletes (38 of the 100 are football players). Salah was sold to Liverpool for the 2017/18 season. Both Milan and Roma failed to take advantage of their respective player's star power, as neither had any meaningful sponsors from their home countries.

In 2016 Sassuolo had the biggest shirt sponsorship deal in Serie A worth €22 million with Mapei. The club is owned by Giorgio Squinzi, who controls Mapei adhesives and sealants, and he also named the stadium after his company. Juventus (with affiliated Fiat) and Milan (Emirates) followed with €17 million each for their shirt sponsors, while Inter (Milan-based car tyre company Pirelli, which has a long history with the club) get €12 million and Napoli (Lete, Italian spring water) €9.5 million. From there it's a big drop-off, as Atalanta gets €2.5 million.[2] The Premier League's top earners were Manchester United with €60 million, Chelsea €55 million, Arsenal €38 million, Manchester City and Liverpool €25 million and Tottenham €22 million.

There was speculation in 2016 that Milan-based Pirelli would not continue its long-time sponsorship of Inter, and that Inter scoured Europe in an extensive search to find a new sponsor. A Pirelli executive said: 'Without cups it does not make sense for Pirelli to continue the sponsorship. Pirelli-Inter? Football is a vehicle of great importance worldwide. If Inter are relegated to national football it makes no sense for Pirelli to continue.' In the end the parties signed a new agreement. In 2017, adidas ended its sponsorship deal with Milan, after almost two decades. The seven-time European champions have not finished higher than sixth in any of the last four seasons in Serie A which means they are missing international exposure in Champions League matches.

It is possible that the culture of being fan-centric can be better supported through ownership structure that forces the organisation to adopt and cater to fans. This is because the fans have a formal organisational way to engage and be active. They have a say. Real Madrid and Barcelona are owned by members. German clubs are also owned by members and Germany has a law, commonly referred to as the '50+1 Rule'.[3] Put simply, the rule requires that, in order to obtain a licence to compete in the

---

[2] http://www.totalsportek.com/money/inter-milan-etihad-airways-shirt-sponsorship-deal/

[3] The only exceptions to this rule were Bayer Leverkeusen and Wolfsburg, each of which had long been owned and operated by large corporations Bayer pharmaceutical company and Volkswagen, respectively. The Bundesliga is also reportedly thinking of changing the 50+1 rule.

Bundesliga, the members must own a majority of its voting rights (at least 50% plus one share). Despite some alterations to the rule over the years, the basic point remains: the members of a club retain overall control, thereby drastically limiting the ability for external ownership.

Owner-members play a key role in operational policy (such as electing the club president, as with Real Madrid and Barcelona). This in turn means that there is greater emphasis on the individual fans than in other leagues, where ownership models vary significantly. In an interview with *The Guardian,* current Bundesliga chief executive Christian Seifert explained this concept further: 'They are very fan orientated . . . Borussia Dortmund have the biggest stand in the world. The Yellow Wall holds 26,000, and the average ticket price is €15 because they know how valuable such a fan culture and supporter base is.'

Moving beyond the importance of developing a community-centric brand and a sustainable economic-sport model, the more tangible side of the matchday (and hence overall fan) experience is most affected by stadium quality and star players. In *Team Sports Marketing*, Baylor University professor Kirk Wakefield found that after stadium quality, the number two predictor of stadium attendance is star players. His research demonstrated that after signing a star player, even if the team had a worse record with the star player, attendance went up. Whether the additional revenue from attendance, as well as increased media coverage and merchandise sales, covers the cost of the star player is another matter, as it relates to being able to execute in marketing and monetise the interest and fan base of the player. Today, this is easier with the use of technology and social media. The research reinforces the circular nature of revenues and star players.

To his credit, Berlusconi was on to some of these very principles when he purchased AC Milan in 1986. He saw the fans as customers. He understood the importance of stars. He saw the importance of broadcast rights. Even after purchasing Milan, he spoke about building the club's own stadium. However, Berlusconi rapidly rose to the forefront of Italian politics in January 1994. He was elected to the Chamber of Deputies for the first time and appointed as prime minister following the 1994 parliamentary elections, when his party, Forza Italia (a cheer for the Italian national football team turned into a political party), gained a relative majority a mere three months after having been launched. After entering politics, he had other priorities and distractions to fully execute his vision of a cicular model. This was a crucial time in European football. He always had the money to buy talent when he wanted and when it served his purposes, and unfortunately the club seemed to rely on that as opposed to building a self-sustainable economic-sport model. Eventually, the necessary investments (transfer fees, salaries, stadiums) seem too large to just keep funding with no end in sight, especially if the synergies with other priorities and interests are not as valuable or necessary.

In a 2008 unpublished MBA thesis at Judge Business School in Cambridge, Francisco Cutio showed that winning games doesn't necessarily help football teams make profits. Rather, the effect works the other way. If a team finds new revenues, those revenues can help them win games because they can help buy/retain better players: 'But contrary to the common idea that good [on the pitch] performance will drive good financials, there is evidence that better revenue-generating structures can have a significant impact on the performance of the team . . . only with good financial results can clubs buy and retain good players and create good teams. Therefore, a team should develop a sustainable economic-sport model to make profits to buy/retain better players, which leads to better results.'

In a 9 February 2018 article for the *Financial Times*, Simon Kuper wrote: 'Certainly, over any one season, a club with small revenues can – if everything goes right – beat the big boys. Leicester City kicked off the 2015/16 season with €143m in revenues for the previous year; Manchester United had €544m, yet Leicester won the English title. In the Champions League, the knockout rounds are a randomising device that favour chance. But measured over ten seasons, the correlation between a club's revenues and its average league position is about 90%, as the sports economist Stefan Szymanski and I show in our book *Soccernomics* (2009).'[4]

It becomes very clear that talent on the pitch, which requires money, and overall fan experience and engagement (from stadium attendance to watching and communicating via a device) off the pitch, which leads to money, are two critical and interconnected issues.

---

[4] https://www.ft.com/content/19455408-0b96-11e8-839d-41ca06376bf2

In modern football, what separates the business models of the most profitable clubs from those of their rivals is not television or matchday revenues but rather 'commercial' income, chiefly from corporate sponsorships. And those contracts in turn depend on having global name recognition. At the turn of the century, Real Madrid successfully leveraged the signings of 'Galácticos' to become a worldwide sporting brand and one of football's highest-earning clubs. When they signed Neymar, PSG, which already receives a higher share of its revenues from commercial deals than any other club (although much of it is from affiliated entities), wanted to follow in Real Madrid's footsteps.

Although transfer fees have generally increased with the sport's revenues over time, their share of clubs' overall spending has remained more or less steady – big clubs are reluctant to surrender more than 25% of their annual revenue on a single player. Just four of the 19 major European transfers have exceeded this threshold. Neymar's deal is estimated to cost PSG around 40% of 2017/18's turnover (see chart below). No top team has spent such a large percentage of its income on a player since the signings of Figo and Zidane in 2000 and 2001, respectively. The only other player that was more than 25% of a club's revenues was Falcao. This is explained because he was bought shortly after AS Monaco won promotion from France's second division, where broadcasting and sponsorship revenue are much lower.

European football, Share of Revenue (from the following season) Spent on a Single Transfer Fee, Over €60 million

Player	Percentage Revenue	Buying Club	Transfer Fee
Zinedine Zidane	51%	Real Madrid	€78 million
Luís Figo	45%	Real Madrid	62
Neymar	41%	PSG	222
Radamel Falcao	35%	Monaco	60
Gonzalo Higuaín	24%	Juventus	90
Cristiano Ronaldo	23%	Real Madrid	94
Paul Pogba	20%	Man United	105
Álvaro Morata	20%	Chelsea	65
Ángel Di María	19%	Man United	76

Kevin De Bruyne	19%	Man City	74
Gareth Bale	18%	Real Madrid	100
Romelu Lukaku	17%	Man United	85
Raheem Sterling	17%	Man City	63
Zlatan Ibrahimović	16%	Barcelona	66
Kaká	15%	Real Madrid	65
James Rodríguez	14%	Real Madrid	80
Edinson Cavani	14%	PSG	65
Luis Suárez	14%	Barcelona	82
Ángel Di María	12%	PSG	64

Source: The Economist

PSG has likely chosen the right player to pursue this strategy. Next to Ronaldo, Neymar is perhaps the most marketable footballer in the world. They both transcend the sport. Neymar has more followers on Instagram (79 million) than Nike, his main sponsor (73 million). PSG's Instagram followers, 8.9 million, rose by 10% in the week after news of his transfer broke, according to Socialblade, an analytics firm. Prior to his latest pay rise, *Forbes* reported, he was the only active footballer to make more money off the pitch than on it. Starting in 2018/19, Nike will pay Barcelona €155 million a season to have its logo on their shirts; in contrast, Nike pays PSG just €24 million a year. With Neymar, and now Mbappé, PSG will likely try to renegotiate its Nike contract. Juventus were the only club to sign a star player on this list, and the player, Higuaín, was playing at Napoli in Serie A. Higuaín has 2.3 million Instagram followers.

Fans purchase shirts of players that they identify with. The fan is putting the name of another human being on their back as if he/she were him. The fan is essentially saying to the world he/she wants to be the player, play like the player, look like the player, etc. Commercially savvy clubs ideally want a player whose identity closely matches their own, while also satisfying on-the-pitch needs. Commercially savvy clubs also think about how the player can reach potential new fans. None of the top ten players with the highest shirt sales currently play in Serie A. Four of the ten players once played in Serie A: Pogba (Juventus 2012–16), Ibrahimović (Juventus 2004–06, Inter 2006–09, Milan 2010–12), Coutinho (Inter 2008–13) and Sánchez (Udinese 2006–11).

Top Ten Players with the Highest Shirt Sales in 2016:

1. Lionel Messi – Barcelona #10
2. Cristiano Ronaldo – Real Madrid #7
3. Paul Pogba – Manchester United #6
4. Zlatan Ibrahimović – Manchester United #9
5. Mesut Özil – Arsenal #11
6. Neymar Jr. – Barcelona #11
7. David De Gea – Manchester United #1
8. Philippe Coutinho – Liverpool #10 (moved to Barcelona in 2018)
9. Alexis Sánchez – Arsenal #17 (moved to Manchester United)
10. Sergio Agüero – Manchester City #10

Source: https://www.totalsportek.com/football/clubs-with-most-shirt-sales/

Poor Stadium Experience (Poor Facilities)

Milan legend and Ballon d'Or winner Marco van Basten said in an interview with *La Gazzetta dello Sport* in 2017, 'You know what makes me the saddest of all? To see the San Siro half empty . . . That was unimaginable in my day. Milan may be lacking big-name players, but they are also lacking a modern structure . . . Things are not going any better in Italy's other stadiums either, with almost all of them the same as they were in the 90s.'[5]

In *Team Sports Marketing*, Baylor University professor Kirk Wakefield found that stadium quality is the number one predictor of sports attendance. In his study he found that one of the main reasons that the stadium quality is so important is that season ticket holders spend a lot of time getting to and being in one place, so it needs to be inviting and comfortable. He quoted the famous movie line from Kevin Costner: 'Build it and they will come', and added 'of course, it never hurts to put good players and a good team on the field.' Just how many fans will go and sit in an old stadium with uncomfortable seats, no good access to Wi-Fi and a bad view? The data shows a lot less than local population, winning and post-season performance would predict. With lots of entertainment options and high-quality digital TV, fans expect to go to a game in a modern, comfortable stadium and have a fun and safe experience with

---

[5] http://www.gazzetta.it/Calcio/Serie-A/Milan/18-01-2017/van-basten-il-milan-cinese-non-mi-va-giu-che-tristezza-san-siro-vuoto-180473983565.shtm

positive memories. With lives connected to mobile devices and social media, fans expect to use these mediums to share, research and discuss before, during and after a game. Many fans feel that it is better to stay at home and have replays, Wi-Fi and be able to go online with a secondary screen and connect via social media with friends. As fan expectations and needs have changed, the stadiums have not. So, what was once an Italian habit of going to the game as the big family entertainment is no longer. New habits are being established and reinforced, which is to watch the game at home with all the conveniences.

Many stadiums that play host to Serie A matches today are from the Second World War era and are rented by the clubs from municipalities. They are old and uncomfortable. The average age of facilities is more than 60 years old, according to a study done by the FIGC, the Italian Football Federation. Prior to the 1990 World Cup in Italy, ten stadiums were upgraded to various extents and two, Turin's Stadio delle Alpi and Bari's Stadio San Nicola, were built from scratch. Within 20 years, the 71,000-seat 'Delle Empty' in Turin had already been demolished, replaced in 2011 by the modern, 41,500-seat and privately funded Juventus Stadium, commercially known as the Allianz Stadium since July 2017. The San Nicola still stands but is loved (for its famous 'flower' design) half as much as it is loathed (because it fails virtually every fan-friendly test imaginable).[6]

Only two of the original 1990 stadiums don't have a running track, which keeps fans further from the pitch experience. The running tracks are the result of a deal with the Italian Olympic Committee to help source extra funding in 1990. Yet in almost three decades, most of those tracks have never seen an athletics competition (some don't even meet official requirements). Most stadiums are old, dilapidated, badly located or poorly designed. Most stadiums have very few bathrooms and food and beverage stands. Currently, they don't have high-value-added, high-end customer services such as corporate boxes and banquet facilities that are such significant contributors to revenues. They are not covered or furbished for cold weather. There are no mega screens, no Wi-Fi, and no instant replay. It is widely accepted that with the exception of Juventus's new stadium, Italian stadiums are outdated with regards to accepted

6 http://theworldgame.sbs.com.au/blog/2017/03/27/where-italian-football-lost-its-way

comforts and technology. Lastly, many stadiums have poor parking infrastructure or are difficult to access. Often fans must park their cars far away, and there are multiple police checkpoints to pass to even get to the stadium, which results in long waits. Fans often complain they have to leave for the stadium several hours before the match.

In contrast to Italy, 16 out of 20 Premier League clubs, ten out of 18 Bundesliga clubs and seven out of 20 La Liga clubs own their own stadiums.[7] If the clubs were to build their own stadiums and leave, then the rent paid to the municipalities and other entities would cease; therefore, there is no incentive for government-related entities to aggressively be approving development plans to build new stadiums or pushing the clubs to leave. In fact, it took Juventus nine years to get approval to complete its new stadium. The project started in 2002 when Juventus got its first authorisation from the municipality of Turin. In Naples, the government refuses to renovate the stadium because of lack of budget or to authorise the club to build their own infrastructure, otherwise it will lose the rent, which hurts the budget. In 2011, Lazio president Claudio Lotito was banned from the club's Stadio Olimpico for two months for accusing the Italian Olympic Committee (CONI) of extortion over the price Lazio have to pay to rent the stadium – €2 million.[8]

Putting aside the stadium, the experience getting to park and into the stadium has been challenging. Because of clouds of fan violence and terrorism, metal detectors and barriers were adopted, but the queues to get in are much longer. Public transport in Italy is older and more limited than other European countries. In order to reach most of the stadiums in Italy, a fan typically needs to take a car or a scooter. This makes things bad on the way to the stadium but things are worse on the way back home at the end of the match. The roads around the stadiums connecting them to city centres are simply unsuitable for thousands and thousands of cars flooding back. Fans can easily remain stuck at the stadium for more than one or two hours after the match has ended. This is unacceptable for modern standards but the municipalities generally seem to have litte interest in fixing this. The result is that a casual fan pays to go to an old, uncomfortable stadium

---

7 http://www.insideworldfootball.com/2016/06/27/european-stadia-big-money-sticks-clubs-homes/
8 https://www.timesofmalta.com/articles/view/20110803/football/Lazio-president-Lotito-banned-from-the-Olimpico.378593

and spend a lot of time to get there and to park a car. In fairness, the San Siro got a dedicated underground station in 2015.

Some fans stopped going to matches because they were frustrated with the 'tessera del tifoso', a supporter ID scheme operated by football clubs in conjunction with law enforcement. Signing up is mandatory for anyone who wants to purchase season tickets and tickets for the home supporters' section of a given stadium. The only ways to get in without a tessera are either to sit in the more expensive neutral stands, or to get a friend who owns a tessera to buy your ticket for you, effectively vouching for your behaviour. In either case, your name must still be provided, and another form of identification furnished at the entry gate. Proponents of the tessera argue that it makes it easier for clubs to keep troublemakers out. Fans with stadium banning orders are unable to sign up. But opponents of the scheme contend that the tessera criminalises the innocent, subjecting all football spectators to Orwellian levels of surveillance. Ultras, in particular, feel persecuted, since they are the ones who traditionally pack out the relevant parts of the stadium.[9]

Some of the big clubs in Serie A shared or currently share a stadium with another club, something that limits the ability for both clubs and fans to fully identify with a place that isn't truly 'theirs' and limits the club from creating a unique experience. Milan and Inter share a stadium, as do Lazio and Roma (and before 2011 Torino and Juventus) and Chievo and Hellas in Verona, and Sampdoria and Genoa in Genoa; so basically ten out of 20 teams of Serie A before Juventus got its own, and still eight out of 20 today.[10] In order to support strong loyalty and emotions today, a club needs to have a cathedral of football that their fans can worship at and call their own. If improvements are required legally, to upgrade the toilets for instance, the three representatives from Inter and their three AC Milan counterparts on the board of the organisation that runs the stadium reach agreement relatively quickly. However, if general improvements are proposed, such as increasing the number of toilets, the decision gets mired in politics. Stadium sponsorship can only be agreed

---

[9] Some fans are happy with the tessera del tifoso. For example, for AC Milan fans since the late 2000s the card serves as a debit card with AC Milan colours and is named Carta Cuore Rossonero (Red Black Heart Card); it also provides a 15% discount at the store and online.

[10] Atalanta played all of their Europa League matches at the Mapei stadium of Sassuolo because their stadium did not meet UEFA rules.

if it does not conflict with the interests of either club. There are red seats for Milan and there are blue for Inter. But there are also green, yellow and orange. It is a spiritual home but, for fans of both clubs, it is not their stadium. They do not own it.

Italy has a compelling pay TV offering. In Italy with a basic pay TV subscription fans can see almost every Serie A game live. In England fewer matches have live broadcasting with basic pay TV subscription. Italian fan football culture has shifted so that it is much better, easier, cheaper, safer and more enjoyable to stay at home and watch the game. There isn't a compelling 'entertainment experience' to encourage fans to go to the stadium.

Matchday revenues account for 11% of total revenues in Serie A, compared with 23% in both the English Premier League and the German Bundesliga.[11] The Deloitte Money League Report for 2016, stated: 'Matchday revenue growth in Italian football is still constrained by lack of widespread investment in stadia, reflected by the fact that three of the four Italian clubs are in the bottom quartile of the top 20 for matchday revenue. Despite individual efforts to change this, there is a possibility that Internazionale or AC Milan, or even both, will drop out of the top 20 in the next edition, as the new broadcast deals in the Premier League take effect.' If you compare Milan's €24.9 million matchday income to that of Arsenal's €119.8 million per season, you can clearly see the gap between the two.[12]

The Stadio delle Alpi where Juventus used to play was very rarely sold out in its history. Finally, in the summer of 2003, Juventus purchased the delle Alpi from the council of Turin for a fee of around €25 million. The delle Alpi's design was widely criticised due to poor visibility. This was caused mainly by the distance between the stands and the pitch. Views from the lower tier were also restricted due to the positioning of advertising hoardings. The stadium's location on the outskirts of town made it difficult for fans to attend games and the stadium design left spectators exposed to the elements. These factors contributed to low attendances; in the 2005/06 season, for example, Juventus's average attendance was 35,880. The poor

---

11 https://www.economist.com/news/business/21640356-countrys-largest-clubs-are-belatedly-becoming-more-businesslike-more-just-trophy-assets
12 https://www.theguardian.com/football/the-gentleman-ultra/2015/oct/29/italian-clubs-serie-a-dominate-europe-modernise-stadiums

visibility led to very low attendances. For example, in the Coppa Italia home match against Sampdoria in the 2001/02 season, only 237 spectators showed up.

Juventus opened its new stadium, which cost around €150 million, in 2011. It was the first stadium in Italy to be owned by its club rather than by a local municipality. The modern stadium moved fans closer to the action, providing a universally unobstructed view, and the impact on TV is also obvious. Gate revenues increased by 183% in the stadium's first season, despite the fact that the new venue has a significantly smaller capacity than its predecessor, the Stadio delle Alpi.[13]

Naming rights and the sale of land adjacent to the Juventus Stadium have provided additional sources of income. Since moving into its new stadium, the club has won seven Scudetti and reached two Champions League finals. It is not directly correlated, but the additional revenues have helped attract and retain players. The new arena provided Juventus with €41 million in revenues in 2016/17. The environmentally sustainable stadium features a shopping centre, club museum and an array of corporate hospitality options that come under the umbrella of the Juventus Premium Club. Adam Digby, the author of *Juventus: A History in Black and White*, says the love for the Juventus Stadium among fans is unanimous. 'After years of sharing the Olimpico with Torino or playing in the soulless delle Alpi, the Juventus Stadium feels like home. It's given a sense of belonging and because it's small and full – therefore making tickets scarce – attending a game feels much more important than before when they were playing in front of a half-empty ground.'

Juventus, like most big clubs that own their own stadiums around Europe, have an impressive, interactive museum. During the tour of Allianz Stadium and Juventus Museum, which costs €22 per adult (€18 for a member of the Juventus Official Fan Club), a fan will have the chance to explore the dressing rooms, media area and many more exclusive parts of the stadium. The museums of big clubs that own their own stadiums go far beyond being a collection of memorabilia and another revenue source. They are places of pride, meeting points, branding experiences and commercial centres. Real Madrid's museum is the second most visited tourist site in Madrid after the Prado Museum.

---

13 http://swissramble.blogspot.ca/2012/01/juventus-black-night-white-light.html

If one reads the TripAdvisor comments about the stadium and museum tour of the iconic San Siro, for example, which has to host both Inter and Milan, one will find comments such as 'a little disappointing, especially when compared to Liverpool or Barcelona', 'compared to [Barcelona's] Camp Nou, this museum tour was ridiculously unprofessional', 'there are no trophies or cups' and 'not a popular touristic place probably due to the lack of magic, vision, etc . . . on branding'. In 2014, Milan created Casa Milan. According to the club, Casa Milan aims to stir the emotions and entertain and bring shared passion, togetherness and constant and continual engagement with the club. Unfortunately, Casa Milan is not located close to the stadium or training grounds.[14]

Infrastructure spending on stadiums by governments as it relates to hosting major international competitions is an important part of infrastructure for European football leagues. For example, in 2013, the European Commission found that French state support for the construction and renovation of nine stadiums in order to host the UEFA European Championship in 2016 was in line with EU state aid rules. France approved over €1 billion in state support for the construction of four new stadiums in Bordeaux, Lille, Lyon and Nice and the renovation of five existing stadiums. Obviously, this benefits the resident clubs but the Commission found that the project would not be viable without public support and the investment furthers a common EU objective. In addition, when the Olympics were held in London in 2012, West Ham secured a 99-year lease to move into the transformed Olympic Stadium. It was not ruled to be state aid.

Unfortunately, Italy has not hosted any recent major football competitions. The clubs and leagues either didn't fully appreciate or didn't have the vision to see how important modern stadiums are to revenues. For Euro 2012, Ukraine and Poland beat Italy for the right to host the Euros. When Italy did not get the Euros in 2012 a good part of Italy celebrated because they believed the construction would have been another scandal with the richest getting richer and the rest of the country picking up the bill. During the proposal process, there

---

[14] https://www.tripadvisor.com/Attraction_Review-g187849-d283702-Reviews-Stadio_Giuseppe_Meazza_San_Siro-Milan_Lombardy.html. http://casamilan.acmilan.com/en

were media reports that brought up hosting the World Cup in 1990 and how much alleged construction corruption there was and how much Italy went over budget. The lost opportunity to push for a government-funded overhaul of stadium infrastructure for Italian football/Serie A was probably underestimated. The Italian Football Federation bid for the 2016 tournament and lost to France. The 2020 Euros tournament will be hosted in several nations as a 'romantic' one-off event to celebrate the 60th 'birthday' of the European Championship competition. The Stadio Olimpico in Rome will host group stage and quarter-final matches.

FIFA World Cups in Europe Since 1990

Year	Country	Stadium for Final
1990	Italy	Stadio Olimpico, Rome
1998	France	Stade de France, Paris
2006	Germany	Olympiastadion, Berlin

UEFA European Championship

Year	Country	Stadium for Final
1992	Sweden	Ullevi, Gothenburg
1996	England	Wembley Stadium, London
2000	Netherlands	Feijenoord Stadion, Rotterdam
2004	Portugal	Estadio da Luz, Lisbon
2008	Austria	Ernst-Happel-Stadion, Vienna
2012	Ukraine	Olimpiyskiy National Sports Complex, Kiev
2016	France	Stade de France, Paris
2020	Multi	Multi Country

We investigated whether ticket prices were a part of poor overall fan experience. It doesn't seem like pricing is impacting attendance. Interestingly, the average price for the cheapest ticket in Serie A and the Bundesliga is €17.50 and €12.75, significantly below the Premier League and La Liga. While low ticket prices may help Bundesliga attendance, Bundesliga clubs are majority owned by the fans by German Law, and therefore Boards of Directors are sensitive to ticket prices. Serie A matchday ticket and season ticket prices are low to attract fans, but also probably reflect the quality of the stadium experience.

Season Ticket and Matchday Prices (€)

| League | Most Expensive Ticket | | Least Expensive Ticket | | Cheapest |
	Season	Matchday	Season	Matchday	% of Avg. Salary
Serie A	€2,043	€204	€115	€17.50	1.25%
La Liga	989	288	151	31	2%
Bundesliga	678	256	58	12.75	1.25%
EPL	1,068	578	72	35	2%

Source: https://www.theguardian.com/news/datablog/2013/jan/17/football-ticket-prices-premier-league-europe

We also analysed the cheapest season ticket to average annual salary by country to adjust for relative wealth. The analysis show that Serie A's cheapest ticket as a percentage of average salary is tied with the Bundesliga for the lowest; less than La Liga, while Spain has high unemployment and a challenging financial situation, especially a few years ago. (In 2012 Eurozone finance ministers agreed that Spanish banks would be provided with up to €100 billion of rescue loans.) The Bundesliga stadiums have high attendance and utilisation. The Premier League and La Liga are similar, although the EPL data may be skewed by clubs and salaries in London and Manchester, as Italian clubs would be in Rome and Milan.[15] Therefore, it is difficult to argue that poor attendance is related simply to ticket prices or the economy.

Poor Stadium Experience (Power of the Ultras)

'Ultras' are tight-knit groups of fanatical supporters, created not just to support a club but to promote the group's own brand and business interests. These groups began in Italy in the late 1960s, growing out of organised supporters' clubs that were established as meeting points for fans. The particular historical and political culture of Italy has had a huge influence on their development. In the 1960s and 1970s, Italian society was highly politicised. Protests in piazzas across the country challenged the political status quo. Political terrorism emerged. The Ultras grew in this climate. Fans took the banners and flags from the piazzas to the stadiums. They took similar names to political groups. More significantly, these groups reflected the traditional political climate and ideology (often far right or

---

[15] http://www.stadiumguide.com/ticket-prices-in-europe-our-analysis/

far left) of their region. Extreme localism also needs to be factored into the Ultras' culture. Historical local traditions remain strong in Italy and have not been superseded by national ones. This emotional attachment is called *campanilismo* and refers literally to the love of one's own local bell tower (*campanile*). These local and political factors help structure rivalries with other fans. Consequently, derby matches between cross-town rivals become hotly contested affairs for local pride.

By the mid-1970s, every major club in Italy had its own Ultra group and a decade later, most had dozens. The Ultra groups constantly splintered, regrouped, renamed and reinvented themselves. Their main goal is to take possession of the centre of the 'Curva'. The Curva is an area behind the goal and has traditionally been the place where a club's poorest, but most devoted, fans assemble. The Curva is highly territorial and Ultra groups stake out their turf with fights, stabbings, shootings and, sometimes, by making alliances and business deals. It is estimated that there are close to 400 Ultra groups in Italy.[16]

In Italy, the economic transformation of football was instigated by Silvio Berlusconi who saw the commercial aspect of football. This commercialisation of football re-politicised the Ultras in a different way. Ultras started to join together to resist the changes; they perceived that the commercialisation of football challenged their position as the authentic voice of football fandom. In the 1990s, Ultras started displaying banners declaring 'No al calcio moderno' ('No to modern football'). In a sport characterised by the perceived disloyalty and selfish interests of players and owners, the Ultras see themselves as the only authentic and faithful elements of a club. In today's often confusing and isolating world, they offer a sense of belonging. It is a double-edged sword – a club needs passionate fan groups who maintain the rituals and traditions as well as create an atmosphere but would prefer not to have the fans be quite so extreme. The passionate fans and the club have to find a balance where the passion is the same but the violence, inappropriateness, racism, etc. is not a part of it.

In their book *Football, Fascism and Fandom*, Alberto Testa and Gary Armstrong make a distinction between those Ultras who did put politics at the centre of their identity and those who did not. Testa, a researcher in deviance and crime at the Ealing Law School, University of West

16 https://www.theguardian.com/world/2016/dec/01/nside-talys-ultras-the-dangerous-fans-who-control-the-game

London, believes based on the last estimate in 2013 that those whose agenda is political 'were only 11% of the total nationally'. He believes, though, that this number is increasing. 'The extreme right is growing in all parts of Europe,' says Testa, 'and all over Europe, the extreme right is monopolising the terraces. You cannot speak about Ultras without underlining that there is a strong ideological component.'[17]

In this context, Italy has one of the highest rates of youth unemployment in Europe. The Italian youth unemployment rate started rising dramatically after the 2008 financial crisis, reaching its peak of 43% in 2014. In 2017, among the EU member states, the youth unemployment rate of Italy (35%) was exceeded by only Spain and Greece. This group of frustrated young people are susceptible to the sense of community provided by the Ultras and an ability to express their frustration.

Ultras have been at the centre of most of the violence and are involved in the illicit businesses of ticket touting (ticket touting is not a criminal offence under Italian law, only an 'illecito amministrativo' – administrative fraud, punishable with a fine) and counterfeit merchandise, or what are called in Italian 'gadget': badges, shirts, key rings, bumper stickers, scarves and so on. The illegal activities and protests brought them into conflict with the police and the authorities, often at matches. This started to impact on stadium attendance. Unlike fans in Germany who remain part-owners of their clubs, Italian fans have no ownership rights. Despite this, the Ultras have been incorporated into the patrimonial culture within Italian football. Owners realised that empty stadiums were bad for business. So the owners accepted the Ultras and negotiated with them.

The clubs provided Ultras with hundreds of matchday and season tickets to resell and free travel in return for a safe stadium with a passionate atmosphere. In addition, when a club wanted to remove a coach or player that they couldn't because of contractual obligations, the club allegedly would provide tickets and other things to the Ultras to start chanting against him. Even though the Ultras were supposed to provide a safe stadium, as the Ultras grew in influence, the number of people injured inside and outside football stadiums increased from 400 in the 1995/96 season to 1,200 in 1999/2000. As attendance continued to decline with a poor stadium experience, the Ultras became ever more powerful. There are

17 http://www.espn.com/soccer/blog/espn-fc-united/68/post/2512302/lazio-roma-rome-eternal-city-derby-paolo-bandini

allegations that they could block the purchase of players they didn't like, or the sale of those they did (especially if they were local), by threatening whole stadium boycotts that would cost clubs millions in lost revenues. They would also delay matches in displays of power to clubs' owners. As the Ultras' power grew, it became difficult to change. Lazio's Ultras had certain merchandising rights for the club, as well as receiving free tickets. Allegedly, when the owners attempted to remove these privileges, bombs were sent to the club's offices. Fabio Capello, the highly successful Italian coach, who was also in charge of the English national team, said Italian football was 'held hostage' by Ultras.

Mario Monti, Italy's prime minister in 2012, suggested that football be suspended for two or three years. Cesare Prandelli, Italy's national coach in 2012, said that he would not object if Italy withdrew from Euro 2012 in Poland and Ukraine for the good of the game. Neither happened.[18]

Ultras stand accused of making the stadium a less welcoming place for the average fan. Sensationalist media coverage has often portrayed Ultras with a broad brush as troublemakers and hooligans. Most Ultras do bring a lot to the grounds in terms of atmosphere. They make noise and sing songs. Most do care about and carry the rituals and traditions. They display this love through choreographed banners, flags, chants, and in some cases, pyrotechnics. There are a small minority of people that hurt the reputation of the 99% who are just unbelievably passionate fans. However, allowing the Ultras (or this minority) this much power may have worked in the short term but the clubs have not benefited in the long run. It costs the clubs money in the long run, especially with the focus on overall fan experience and the need to generate commercial revenues. The target audience needs to be the silent majority of the fans and families and must be provided an experience to attract global fans (who also visit as tourists).

Italian clubs are not the only clubs that suffer from Ultras. There are incidents at several clubs in the other top five leagues as well. However, in general, Italian clubs have been the least effective in dealing with the issue. In Italy, Ultras still have too much power, and it has got to the point that allegedly Ultras have made death threats against players and coaches and even their families. Owners face extreme pressure from the

---

[18] http://www.nytimes.com/2012/06/03/sports/soccer/stain-of-scandal-again-taints-italian-soccer. html

Ultras who are the most vocal group, who focus on short-term, on-the-pitch performance. Ultras are less focused on the quality of their stadium experience. Consequently, investment in a stadium is not seen as essential.

In September 2017, Juventus president Andrea Agnelli was banned for one year and both he and Juventus were fined by the Italian Football Federation (FIGC) for his role in allegedly selling tickets to Ultra fans that encouraged touting, also known as scalping. Agnelli allegedly authorised the sale of season passes and other tickets. He acknowledged meeting with a fan. Unfortunately for Agnelli, unbeknown to him at the time, the fan would later be linked to the Calabrian 'Ndrangheta crime mob and has since been sentenced to nearly eight years in prison for scalping. Anti-mafia prosecutors said the 'Ndrangheta had been involved in scalping among Juventus Ultra fans for at least 15 years, guaranteeing order in the stadium in exchange for open ticket access. However, Agnelli said the meetings with the fan came only with large numbers of other fans at celebratory occasions; he was unaware of any associations of the fan; and that the club never intended to engage in illegal activity. He and Juventus denied any wrongdoing and appealed the ruling. In December 2017, his one-year ban was lifted, but his and Juventus's fine was increased and Juventus will have to play a match with one of its main sections closed. The Juventus security director and ticketing director had their suspensions and fines cancelled. However, a former marketing director had his appeal rejected and was banned for one year and fined.

It is worth noting that of the 22 people who directly died from Ultra fights over the past 50 years: 1 died in the 1960s, 1 in the 1970s, 5 in the 1980s, 8 in the 1990s, 6 in the 2000s and 1 in the 2010s, so the 1980s and 1990s were definitely more violent than today.[19] However, it seems attitudes have changed. As previously mentioned in a 2016 survey, diehard fans complained about the organised crime and Ultras in the stadium and singled out these two issues as reasons behind a decline in interest.[20] This is reflected in declining and poor attendance.

In responding to the assault in the UK that left Liverpool fan Sean Cox in critical condition ahead of the first leg of the Champions League semi-final in April 2018, Jim Pallotta said, 'It's depressing though that all

[19] http://www.corriere.it/cronache/14_giugno_25/ciro-altre-vittime-calcio-ventidue-morti-50-an-ni-violenze-db153174-fc64-11e3-8e7c-9b5f094e2972.shtml

[20] https://www.google.com/amp/www.repubblica.it/sport/calcio/2016/10/02/news/atlante_tifo_italiani_in_fuga_dal_calcio-148926536/amp/

of the other fans at Roma get blamed for something that, going back to that saying that I had about a year and a half ago . . . a few people wrecking things for everyone else.' Pallotta praised the majority of fans for the support they give and said the efforts of the Stadio Olimpico's 'ultras' were part of their success this season. He said, 'The only reason we come back and win games like we did against Barcelona [overturning a 4-1 first-leg deficit to win on away goals] is because of the 99.9 percent of the fans in the Curva Sud [where the ultras congregate] who are great . . . Then, occasionally, you get a few, normally outside of the game, more than anything else . . . it's just absolutely ridiculous. But it's time now for things to change in Italy and in Rome because it is just happening too much . . . We have a long history at Roma and what's going on when you have a few stupid people is that they destroy our history and they attack our legacy and I'm tired of it . . . It's not just an issue for Roma. It's an issue for Italy and it's an issue for the authorities and it's an issue for all of [us] to band together and to finally wake up so that we don't have a reputation . . . that's not deserved around the rest of the world . . . that our fans are not good fans because our fans are the best fans in the world.'[21]

Poor Stadium Experience (Clouds of Racism and Violence)

When fans and families come to the stadium, the expectation is that they will have a fun and safe experience in a comfortable stadium with positive memories. Putting aside the poor quality of the stadiums, in Serie A there are clouds of racism and violence.

'I don't believe it is just an Italian problem; it's global,' Juventus defender Giorgio Chiellini said regarding racism and violence. He is right. The Italian league is not the only league that has dealt with clouds of racism and violence. However, for a league that has had many challenges and is not seen as 'modern', re-emphasised by its old stadiums and poor attendance, it has a more dramatic impact. The league overall may seem a little out of step with changing attitudes and could be more sensitive to the global audience and potential sponsors in an era of Italian football when there are already other clouds.[22]

[21] http://www.espn.com/soccer/as-roma/story/3475756/roma-owner-james-pallotta-condemns-actions-of-moron-roma-supporters
[22] http://www.sport24.co.za/Soccer/International/racism-clouds-new-era-for-italian-football-20170509

Serie A has sanctions procedures but the criteria for applying them are so specific (such as the whole stadium must be able to hear the abuse), they are hardly ever used. And when they are, the penalty is suspended, so fines only apply in the event of a second offence. Another problem is that although Italy has strong legislation covering racial abuse, the law requires positive identification of the individuals involved, and clubs cannot be held responsible for failing to identify perpetrators. The result is racism is never really consistently punished.

Anti-Southern and territorial discrimination are prevalent in Italy and in the stadiums. Southern Italians are described by these extremists as outside the nation, and have been disparaged with stereotypes of being poor, dirty, uneducated, uncultured and criminal, not unlike other immigrant groups in Italy. (Podaliri and Balestri, 'The Ultras, Racism and Football Culture in Italy', p. 90.)

Because few football stadiums in Italy are owned by the teams, clubs have not fully taken control of security issues. According to the Italian Interior Ministry, in the 2004/05 season, 272 professional football matches in Italy had some episode of violence, with a total of 1,219 people injured. In 2007, a police officer was killed during a riot at a game in Sicily, in part because the stadium did not adhere to the required safety measures. At the time, only six of the 18 stadiums used in Serie A met the security requirements – like having electronic entrance turnstiles, numbered seating, video surveillance and stewards to control seating. Smoke bombs and 'rescue' flares are regularly used at matches despite being banned by the Pisanu Law. As a result, stadium security was improved and the Interior Ministry in 2009 introduced identity cards (tessera del tifoso) for supporters. While the reported number of violent incidents has declined, the number of spectators has continued to decline as well, suggesting poor quality stadium experiences may be a larger factor than currently believed. Serie A clubs, in partnership with local and national governments, will need to do far, far more, including implementing desperately overdue stadium upgrades and helping to ensure fan safety in and around matches to get fans back into the stadiums. For example, most stadiums don't have high definition (HD) TV monitors pointing towards the crowds to clearly identify fans making racist comments or throwing things onto the pitch.

As previously discussed in the section titled Fans Too Far and Attendance Too Poor to Influence Referees, besides impacting on the overall fan experience, racism and violence can impact on a club's 'home ground advantage' by having clubs ordered to play matches behind closed doors. Tobias Moskowitz and L. Jon Wertheim, authors of *Scorecasting*, point to the case of a series of matches played in Italy in 2007 behind closed doors and concluded home ground advantage drops drastically, as the crowd is not influencing refereeing decisions. The away team were penalised for fouls 23% less than they usually would be, were awarded 26% fewer yellow cards and 70% fewer red cards.

Poor Online Engagement by Clubs

Sports media is being consumed in a dramatically different way than in the past. Watching sports is becoming a multiscreen and social media experience. While sports fans are watching a game on HDTV, they also want rich statistical information through the club's website, to watch a replay, and they may be tweeting and/or texting and/or posting about the match. Sports fans want to enjoy entertainment, including a wide range of content, especially data and video, and services on their devices that they can also share via social media. More than 80% of sports fans monitor social media sites while watching games on TV. More than 60% of fans will use their phone to check social media while at a game. Sports fans expect an audiovisual experience of games – summaries, multi-angle replays, special cameras and delayed recordings. Fans follow their team in a high-tech way, with all the statistics available, minute-to-minute commentary and postings in multiple languages.

In fact, sports fans don't even need a TV to watch sports. They want to choose the platform they prefer – mobile device, tablet, Xbox, etc. and chose the medium in which to interact – Facebook, Twitter, Instagram, etc. It is increasingly common for sports fans to watch the game with a 'second screen' up as they communicate with other fans via social media. They may want to call up replays themselves; they want to experience the game with more than one screen, but with the inputs that they choose, not the TV producer of the game. For example, sports fans may want to see a heat map of colours showing where each player or players have spent their time on the field. This technology is the same as the coaches and technical staff use to evaluate the squad. And then they want to post, share and comment on the information.

Technology enables the content for experiences and active fan engagement to be scalable around the world. The access fuels the connection and passion (active engagement), while the club's traditions and rituals reinforce the identity association. Social media is important because it is the preferred method of following clubs and players around the world. Therefore, as a growing number of sports fans are engaging on platforms like Twitter, Instagram and Facebook, clubs are increasingly relying upon social media. The first impact of social media in the sports world was immediate score updates. No longer would fans have to watch the game or search on the internet for the score of their favourite team because social media took care of it with live update notifications, which is incredibly useful for the fans who are too busy to watch the game. Then social media provided up-to-the-second data statistics. Fans can get any sort of information they desire by staying tuned in to social media. The best part is the data statistics that are typically shared on Twitter and Facebook are interesting facts not many people know about. Watching a live game with a team's Twitter feed nearby is guaranteed to give fans a different perspective. Reacting to a goal only to realise you're the only person in the room to see it happen is one of the worst feelings in the world. With social media, fans can react instantaneously with other fans. The reactions and celebrations are posted, shared and commented on.

Social media provides many aspects of marketing and engagement previously unavailable to teams – it changes how teams and their fans can interact and affects how often fans are exposed to content from the clubs they follow. Clubs are using social media to create opportunities for fans and keep them actively engaged and connected. In addition, clubs can receive feedback from fans immediately as well as respond to questions. Clubs can communicate with fans, fans can communicate with teams – the sports world is changing. Creating this social media following not only enables teams to enhance and grow their brand, but it can also energise existing fans and inform them of events.

Today, sports fans are as interested in the lives of the players and their behind the scenes, authentic moments. They want messages from the players. These daily interactions, which are becoming more and more like reality TV, are becoming as important, possibly more so, than the weekly league matches themselves. Generation X (aged 35–49) and Generation Y (aged 25–35) spend almost seven hours and six hours, respectively, on average on social media per week, more than TV. This will become increasingly important in attracting new fans who grew up with a device attached to their hand. The match is a reason to connect and experience once a week like a social club event and is the event to connect and discuss the rest of the week together. Sports and debate go hand-in-hand. In fact, it's one of the best parts about sports. Social media has brought the debate about players, clubs and leagues to an entirely new level. Opinions are expressed on a daily basis. What's even better is those opinions have the chance to go viral. Whether it's creating a blog and sharing ideas with the masses via social media or simply making a comment on Facebook, expressing an opinion has never been so easy. Beyond opinions, thanks to social media, fans have access to all of the latest transfer rumours and news at their fingertips. In addition, social media has dramatically improved interacting with other fans around the world of the same favourite club. While it's easy to make new friends while cheering for the same club at a live sporting event, it's even easier to do so on Twitter or Facebook. Even better, finding fans who meet at live games, at a supporters' club gathering, on the stadium museum tour or on social media means long-term friendships can be born.

Serie A and its clubs are well behind other clubs in online engagement. Blogmeter, a social media monitoring and analytics company, analysed the official Facebook profiles of 16 international football clubs involved in the main European competitions for two months: from December 2014 to January 2015. The results showed Italian football is chasing Spain, England and Germany when it comes to social media activity. Milan, the Italian leader, is in eighth place, having 'only' 30% of the fans that the top Spanish clubs have. Juventus is the next Italian club in the ranking at 11th place, with less than 16.3 million fans at the end of January. Inter, Roma and Napoli are standing at the bottom, 14th, 15th and 16th respectively with less than 6 million fans. The gap between the top European clubs is noteworthy. Furthermore, the distance within Europe is increasing day by day. On Facebook, Real Madrid is gaining popularity with an average of 50,000 fans a day against 19,000 by Juventus and 11,000 by Milan.[23]

Looking at this as at the beginning of 2017, the story is very much the same – there is still clearly a massive gap between the Serie A teams and the rest of the major European leagues. Even the Bundesliga and Ligue 1 have teams that are more popular with fans (at least from an online presence perspective) than Serie A.

Top 12 Teams with Highest Social Media Following

Team	Total # Followers (mm)	League
Barcelona	159.9	La Liga
Real Madrid	159.5	La Liga
Manchester United	97.9	EPL
Chelsea	63.5	EPL
Arsenal	55.3	EPL
Bayern Munich	52.8	Bundesliga
Liverpool	40.2	EPL
PSG	38.1	Ligue 1
Juventus	35.0	Serie A
Milan	32.1	Serie A
Manchester City	22.7	EPL
Borussia Dortmund	15.1	Bundesliga

Juventus, Milan and Roma (Roma comes in at #15 with 11 million total followers) are the three key leaders in social media in Serie A. Platforms such as Twitter, Facebook and Instagram have changed the game. Fans now feel closer and more engaged with their teams, and unfortunately for many Italian football fans, there isn't a lot being done overall to make fans feel closer to the clubs. Roma has made the most progress in social media. Paul Rogers, the person who spent 14 years managing Liverpool's digital and social content, was brought into the club by Pallotta to help turn Roma into the most modern and engaging club in Italy. Statistically speaking, since Rogers became head of Roma's digital media team, the club has more than doubled its global social media following – an increase of 145% in the first three years, accounting for more than seven million new followers, and picked up numerous digital awards around the world.[24]

23 http://promoovertime.com/serie-a-chasing-european-clubs-on-the-web/

24 http://www.italianfootballdaily.com/three-ways-serie-can-improve-marketing/

For example, when it was announced that Francesco Totti would play his final game for Roma after 25 years, Paul Rogers and his team began to work on a content plan that they hoped would pay a fitting tribute to the player himself, engage the club's supporters and also allow fans of other clubs to join the conversation. Although the team only had 8.8 million Facebook fans (and 11 million total social media followers), they were able to generate over 70 million video views in five days and broke every single digital record they measure (Facebook, Twitter, Instagram, Snapchat, YouTube and official team website). These videos were shared over 850,000 times and inspired over 170,000 comments, and for one month, Roma outperformed every other team in the world in terms of Facebook videos.[25] Clearly this was a 'once in a lifetime' type of event, but this example shows how with creativity, emotion, focus and a well-thought-out plan, there is a way for the Italian clubs to increase their presence on social media and have more of an impact, especially in terms of fan engagement.[26]

Poor Online Engagement by Players

Ever since Twitter started in 2006, professional players and coaches have been creating Twitter pages for themselves to connect with their fans. One of the biggest thrills about social media is the ability to interact with your favourite sports star. Whether your favourite player retweeted you, liked something of yours on Facebook or commented on your Instagram photo, fans connecting with players has never been easier. Social media isn't just a way for players to connect with their fans; they can easily express their opinions. Players often say whatever comes to mind. In addition, athletes use social media to raise awareness for their charities, as well as have fun with their fans by meeting them in public places.

Very few Italian or Serie A players are rated highly in total social media followers. Italy and Roma legend Francesco Totti joined Twitter in September 2016. He has approximately 225,000 Twitter followers as of 2017. Roma fans' favourite Radja Nainggolan (joined March 2012) has 544,000 followers as of 2017. Dries Mertens (joined November 2011) of

25 https://www.linkedin.com/pulse/how-roma-88m-facebook-fans-generated-over-70m-video-views-paul-rogers/
26 https://www.facebook.com/facebookmedia/success-stories/asroma

Napoli has 700,000 followers as of 2017. Compare this to Gerard Piqué (joined December 2010) of Barcelona, Marcelo (joined November 2012) of Real Madrid, and Toni Kroos (joined July 2011) of Real Madrid who have 19 million, 10 million and 7 million Twitter followers, respectively. Obviously, the players of Real Madrid and Barcelona and the clubs themselves mutually benefit from their exposure and promotion by their clubs. In fact, often the amount of money a player makes from corporate sponsorships is tied to the player being at a club like Real Madrid or Barcelona where they will get a high level of exposure and promotion. The value of the club is so much that in the case of Real Madrid, 50% of the money in a player's image rights and endorsement contracts goes to Real Madrid to compensate them for the exposure and promotion.

For individual players across a variety of social media platforms (Twitter, Instagram and Facebook), the result is perhaps even more staggering. Looking at the 12 most followed players, there isn't even a single Serie A player on the list.

Top 12 Players (and former players) with Highest Social Media Following

Player	Team	Total # Followers (mm)	League
Cristiano Ronaldo	Real Madrid	261.7	La Liga
Neymar	PSG	155	Ligue 1
Leo Messi	Barcelona	153.2	La Liga
David Beckham	N/A	88	N/A
Ronaldinho	N/A	69	N/A
Kaká	N/A	68.4	MLS
Gareth Bale	Real Madrid	66.3	La Liga
Andrés Iniesta	Barcelona	57.9	La Liga
Mesut Özil	Arsenal	56.9	EPL
Wayne Rooney	Manchester United	49.4	EPL
Luis Suárez	Barcelona	47	La Liga
Gerard Piqué	Barcelona	43.7	La Liga

Serie A Players with Highest Social Media Following

Player	Team	Total # Followers (mm)	League
Gianluigi Buffon	Juventus	12.6	Serie A
Leonardo Bonucci	Milan	5.7	Serie A
Mauro Icardi	Inter	4.3	Serie A
Francesco Totti	Roma	3.5	Serie A
Dries Mertens	Napoli	2.45	Serie A

When looking at the numbers for the top player from each of the most popular Serie A teams, the drop-off is tremendous and just goes to show how difficult it has been for Serie A teams to attract star players.

Decentralised Supporters' Clubs

Official supporters' clubs play an important role in football. They are often a community of fans that share their common support and passion for a club. Historically, supporters' clubs in Italy have been decentralised from the football club. Despite many Italian clubs having established ticket outlets, some supporters' clubs still operate as ticket outlets (especially for key matches), sell merchandise (sometimes forged), organise away travel for fans and arrange social events. Members of supporters' clubs pay fees to the supporters' club, not the club. Typically, there is no supervision by the Italian clubs and no quality control because the supporters' clubs are decentralised. Official supporters' clubs are often situated in bars and in the heart and social lives of the local geographic community they serve. They want some official affiliation with the club, while Ultras typically do not, including asking the club to make players available for social functions and dinners. The supporters' clubs typically provide a space to socialise and interact and associate with people away from the family and work colleagues which leads to a stronger attachment to the club. The supporters' clubs were created out of necessity because the clubs historically were not providing a way to connect and stay involved beyond just going to the matches.

In contrast to most sports clubs in Italy, a few big European sports clubs closely manage their supporters' clubs, as the fans are similar to 'subscribers' or 'members' of a club. Most have an official supporters' or fan card, like an identity card, so their fans officially feel a strong sense of belonging to the sports club. Typically, big European football clubs themselves receive the fees (like subscription revenue) and provide special merchandise, discounts on tickets and merchandise, personalised services, special privileges and other benefits. Most big European football clubs invest significant energy and resources in helping community members start and support official fan clubs. Supporters join to be brought together by the same feeling, the same passion, and the same source of pride of being a fan of their club. Most sports clubs expect their official fan clubs to register and even have their own distinctive name. These fans attend or watch games together. Some big European football clubs celebrate long-time community members.

Lastly, supporters' clubs in Italy have been used for political purposes. For example, Berlusconi allegedly used Milan supporters' clubs for his political campaigns. In addition, football clubs have allegedly used their supporters' clubs and Ultra groups to express messages to certain players and coaches in chants or banners. This behaviour may turn off potential global members not interested in local Italian politics or who don't agree with the behaviour.

It appears that anything that makes Italian football more organised, professional, 'official', transparent and commercially focused is an issue for Ultras and organised crime. The decentralisation of supporters' groups can negatively impact the consistent quality of the fan experience, and clubs are missing out on additional revenues. However, certain supporters' clubs are critically important as 'culture carriers'. Over time, they will need to be empowered with technology and social media to stay more relevant as a new generation has new attitudes and expectations.

CHAPTER SIX

OTHER ISSUES OFF THE PITCH

Off-the-Pitch Issues: League

Decisions Made for the Short Term,
Not for the Common Good

Milan legend and Ballon d'Or winner Marco van Basten said in an interview with *La Gazzetta dello Sport*: 'Italy had the richest, most beautiful league. Everybody wanted to play in Italy, but you did not know how to manage this advantage . . . with scandals, inadequate structures and arguments, you've fallen behind.' He added the Italian league had been 'thinking only of today and forgetting tomorrow, so you shouldn't be surprised to be behind now.'[1]

In the Serie A General Assembly there is often a deadlock due to a tug of war between the big and small football clubs. Since each club can cast one vote in the General Assembly, decisions are paralysed because qualified majorities are needed for each change in the regulations, from governance to television rights. With the current fragmentation, owners with influence over ministries or regulators can try to persuade the smaller clubs to vote one way.

---

[1] http://www.gazzetta.it/Calcio/Serie-A/Milan/18-01-2017/van-basten-il-milan-cinese-non-mi-va-giu-che-tristezza-san-siro-vuoto-180473983565.shtml

Most disputes revolve around money. For example, there was a disagreement about the 'parachute rule' which protects small clubs being relegated to Serie B by the club receiving a €12 million 'parachute' sum to offset lost TV revenues. However, in 2017, the dispute was around governance. Big clubs supported an amendment to the statute to provide a new, more managerial governance, with a CEO in charge of generating and increasing revenues and a managing director taking care of the sports part. In essence, the league would be managed more like a traditional business. In this model, the president would have a representative role. This model would strip the assembly – in which each of the 20 Serie A clubs has the same importance – of its powers.

Many of the club owners in Serie A have been short-sighted, which has led to poor decisions. To give some context it is helpful to understand what happened in English football, which overtook Serie A in league revenues in the 1990s. Despite significant European success in the 1970s and early 1980s, the late 1980s and early 1990s marked a low point for English football. Stadiums were crumbling, hooliganism was common, and English clubs were banned from European competition for five years following the Heysel Stadium disaster in 1985. The Football League First Division, the top level of English football since 1888, was behind leagues such as Italy's Serie A and Spain's La Liga in attendances and revenues, and several top English footballers had moved abroad.

By the turn of the 1990s, the downward trend was starting to reverse. At the 1990 FIFA World Cup, England reached the semi-finals and UEFA lifted the five-year ban on English clubs playing in European competitions in 1990. Clubs started to implement recommendations from the Taylor Report on stadium safety standards, which proposed significant and expensive stadium upgrades and also led to safer and more comfortable stadium experiences. As stadiums improved, match attendance and revenues rose.

Revenue from television also became more important. The Football League received €9.3 million for a two-year agreement in 1986, but by 1988, in a deal agreed with ITV, the price rose to €65.9 million over four years. In 1990, the 'Big Five' football clubs in England at the time (Manchester United, Liverpool, Tottenham, Everton and Arsenal) wanted to form a new league that would bring more money into the game overall, and, in particular to them, as the 'big' clubs. The argument given at the time was that the extra income would allow English clubs to compete with teams across Europe. The Big Five's approach was long-term greedy in that they were willing to share the TV rights' revenues with less globally recognised clubs in a more equal way in order to build a stronger and more competitive league overall. This was in contrast to each big club negotiating their own TV deal directly. BSkyB won the TV rights with a bid of €411 million over five years with the BBC awarded the highlights package broadcast on *Match of the Day*. The next contract, negotiated to start from the 1997/98 season, rose to €985 million over four seasons. The third contract was a €1.65 billion deal with BSkyB for the three seasons from 2001/02 to 2003/04.

The big clubs made a very good long-term decision in selling their television rights on a collective basis at that time. Today, EPL money is divided into three parts: half is split equally between the clubs; one quarter is awarded on a merit basis based on final league position, the top club getting 20 times as much as the bottom club, and equal steps all the way down the table; and the final quarter is paid out as facilities fees for games that are shown on television, with the top clubs generally receiving the largest shares of this. The income from overseas rights is currently divided equally between the 20 clubs. Providing money to the smaller clubs did provide them with greater opportunities to compete and a stronger league. The Big Five could have said that they wanted to negotiate their own individual contracts, which they individually would have benefited from in the short term. In the English Premier League 14 of the 20 teams must agree to major changes. The 'Big Six' of Manchester United, Manchester City, Liverpool, Arsenal, Chelsea and Tottenham Hotspur, the Premier League's six richest clubs, often face resistance against their efforts. For example, the 14 other clubs blocked the Big Six from receiving a greater share of income from the next multi-billion-pound round of TV deals and end the system by which money from international TV rights sales is shared equally by all 20. The Big Six wanted 35% of the next international TV money to be distributed according to 'merit' – in other words, where clubs finish in the league. This would be a major change to the arrangement which has operated by agreement since the original 1992 breakaway of the then First Division clubs to form the Premier League, which was itself motivated by the bigger clubs no longer wanting to share TV money with the Football League's other three divisions. Income from international TV rights 25 years ago was negligible, so the clubs agreed to share that money equally, while only a third of British TV income is divided equally, the other two-thirds shared according to where clubs finish in the league and how many times they are shown on television. Now, though, the Premier League's popularity has made it prime content for burgeoning pay TV operations around the world, delivering approximately €3.6 billion to the 20 clubs in the 2016–19 round of deals. That bonanza, added to the €6.2 billion from the competition between Sky and BT for British subscribers, plus other highlights deals, makes a total of €10.2 billion in the current three-year cycle. The distribution of TV money last season showed that the champions Chelsea received €184m in total while bottom-placed Sunderland were paid €113m, but the booming international income was shared equally, the 20 receiving €47.5 million apiece. The so-called 'Big Six' clubs argue that as the global revenue rises, as it is expected to again when the 2019–22 deals start to be negotiated, they should receive a larger share because they are the ones which international viewers tune in to watch. The other 14 clubs have been resisting these moves, in an effort to hold on to their equal share of the money. They are arguing that the sharing arrangement helps them to sign high-quality players and keep the league 'competitive and compelling' and therefore attractive on TV. A few of the smaller clubs are said to have been inclined to agree to the new 35% merit payment arrangement, but the agreement of 14 is needed to effect such a substantial change.

With the context of England, it is easier to understand what happened in Italy. In Italy, the revolutionary changes caused by the emergence of new broadcasting platforms in the 1990s (pay TV in 1993 and pay-per-view in 1996) were similar to England. In the period from 1993 to 1999 the TV broadcasting rights were managed collectively by the league. For the first time ever, Italian fans had the opportunity to watch matches on live television. At the beginning, from 1993 to 1996, only one or two matches, played in advance on Saturday night or postponed until Sunday or Monday night, were broadcast on a satellite platform. From 1996 onwards, the arrival of pay-per-view technology created the opportunity to watch all matches live. As a result, the annual TV rights of Serie A went from €50 million in 1992/93 to €1.13 billion in 2010/11.

In 1996/97, there was a critical turning point in Italian football because, for the first time ever, TV rights of €204 million exceeded revenues from stadium gate attendance of €176 million. However, the owners of Serie A spent almost all of the increase in TV rights money on transfer fees and salaries for players, and neglected to invest in improving stadium experiences and merchandising opportunities, which was starting to be exploited by rival clubs, such as Real Madrid and Manchester United who adapted, innovated and invested and looked for additional revenue streams. Media-related sources increased by 215% in Serie A whereas other sources decreased by 7% from 1998 to 2008 (Alessandro Baroncelli and Raul Caruso). Without additional sources of revenue, the big clubs were losing money and increasing debt.

Another issue was that there were two competing subscription TV providers. At the end of the 1990s in Italy, two platforms existed: Telepiu (a subsidiary of Canal+) and Stream (involving Telecom Italia). BSkyB entered the market in 2000, acquiring control of Stream. Because clubs could negotiate their own TV rights and some were on one platform as opposed to another, it was expensive for fans to subscribe to both. Experts have estimated that up to 60% of the public were illegally pirating the games from pay TV providers in Italy. In September 2002, the pay TV providers renegotiated downwards the football rights from the previous season because the uptake was not as high as expected. In 2003 BSkyB/Stream merged with Telepiu to create a single satellite platform called Sky Italia. The deal was authorised by the European Commission in 2004, with the restriction that since there was only one pay TV provider, no pay TV deal with a football club could run longer than two years (*Football in the New Media Age* by Raymond Boyle and Richard Haynes). This would limit both the value of any contract and the investment in the brand of Italian football. At the time, Prime Minister Silvio Berlusconi's family controlled Mediaset, a major player in the free-to-air media market in the country, which theoretically could have benefited from this restriction.

After lobbying from the big clubs in Italy, in 1999 the Italian Antitrust Authority (AGCM) forced the league to stop the collective bargaining of not free-to-air rights, including pay-per-view, pay TV and international rights to each single team. Pay TV companies applied strictly market-based system pricing, with the income clubs got being tied to subscriptions, viewers and other market indicators. This generated a huge boost to the big club owners but a strong imbalance in favour of the big teams, with a first place to last place ratio of about nine to one in 2002 versus less than two to one in England.

As a result, the small and medium teams complained. There was even a stoppage of play in 2002/03 as small and medium clubs boycotted matches because they were getting about 10% of what big clubs received, which put them under financial strain in trying to compete for talent. In the end, the major clubs agreed to pay out a small amount to help the other smaller clubs. Finally, the government intervened and in 2008 reintroduced the collective bargaining starting from the 2010/11 season onwards, in the hope of a more balanced distribution of TV resources among teams.

Based on the law, the revenues were supposed to be allocated with 40% equally distributed among the clubs, 30% allocated according to historical performance (with 5% depending on the previous season's standings, 15% depending on the last five seasons' standings, and 10% depending on 'sport tradition' and historical ranking), 25% allocated by the number of fans (as per surveys) and 5% based on the population of cities. As one can imagine the calculation of fan base has been very controversial. In 2007, according to AC Nielsen, Juventus had approximately 10 million fans, Inter and Milan 6 million fans, Napoli 3 million and Roma 2.5 million.[2] A new calculation was done in 2011 that had meaningfully different results. Therefore, a new agreement was reached in 2011 which cut the percentage allocated by the number of fans in half.

Besides Serie A, some other European leagues, including La Liga, allowed clubs to sell their rights individually, leading to the top clubs in Serie A and La Liga generating higher revenues in the short term, as they didn't have to share any amounts with smaller clubs. Therefore, at the beginning of the shift in football to media rights being the most important revenue driver, the top clubs in Serie A and La Liga at least were competitive with the big five English clubs because even though the big five had to share in the EPL, the EPL had the largest TV contract. There are more subscribers for pay TV in England than in Spain and Italy. The English Premier League TV rights went up in value faster than the other leagues. Therefore, even though the top five shared a percentage with other English clubs, the revenues grew

---

2 Il Sole 24 ore, 2 November 2009; Baroncelli and Caruso (2011)

so large that the top five may have actually made more in the long run than they would have had had they negotiated their rights individually, especially at that time. In order to compete with the English clubs' larger revenues, the big clubs in Serie A and La Liga did not want to share the revenues, as they now had to compete against top English clubs that were making as much or more, even with a collective division. It was a short-term decision that the big clubs most likely felt they were effectively forced into making in order to compete in terms of reve

nues to pay the most talented players. Top clubs in Serie A and La Liga could have made the decision to take less in the short term to build a stronger and more competitive league in the long term, but then this would have a short-term setback, and there is no guarantee that it would have worked. The reduction in revenue could have theoretically caused the Italian clubs to innovate to find new and more revenues sources, which is what Juventus did after being relegated in 2006. It seems likely that Italian culture, shaped by regional identity as well as historical, political and economic unpredictability, was also a backdrop for big Italian clubs to be more interested in themselves and the short term.

It is interesting to look at the size and growth of the media rights of the various leagues.

Estimated Football Media Rights Spend by Sports Business Previous Contract and 2018–21
€ in millions

League	Previous Amount	2018–21 Amount	Growth
English Premier League	2,070	3,800	71%
Spanish La Liga	1.200	1,500	25%
German Bundesliga	817	1,400	83%
Italian Serie A	961	1,130	17%
French Ligue 1	640	807	26%

Source: http://www.italy24.ilsole24ore.com/art/panorama/2016-06-27/football-112520.php?uuid=ADDQ0lj
http://en.calcioefinanza.com/2016/11/24/tv-broadcast-rights-serie-2018-21-challenge-earn-re-enhance-stadiums/

Italy's Serie A football media rights have the slowest growth among the top five leagues, and will rank fourth overall.

From 2016, clubs in La Liga were no longer permitted to negotiate their own TV rights. It is now split 50% equal share for all 20 clubs, 25% merit-based on where the club has finished in the table in the last three years, and 25% on the resource generation ability of the club. The new La Liga distribution system is similar to what the English Premier League installed, with the biggest difference being one major clause in the new legislation which states that no club should get less money with the new system than what they are getting previously. This means that Real Madrid and Barcelona will still be making somewhere around €140 million a year. This amount is actually less than what several top English clubs receive in an already competitive market for revenues to afford talent. The rest of La Liga will receive a significant increase. According to *Forbes*, for example, Sevilla could see revenue from TV rights doubling from around €26m per season (2014/15) to €52m per season due to the new agreement.[3]

Italian Serie A is in a different stage of development to a league such as the English Premier League. Serie A actually needs to invest for growth to catch up. Therefore, putting aside revenue splits, both big and small clubs must be willing to sacrifice short-term revenues for greater exposure and promotion to gain growth. This may be difficult because the smaller clubs typically don't know how long they will be in the top division before being relegated to a lower division (or go bankrupt or have a scandal). In Italy, many of the clubs that have been relegated have gone bankrupt, especially because foreign investment had been almost impossible without financial and regulatory transparency. Therefore, they are also more short-term focused. This has led to global TV contracts that maximise revenues but do not maximise viewers, exposure and packaging. Below is a list of major football competitions and the primary rights holders in the United States.

Primary TV Rights Holders in the United States

Competition	2005 Primary Rights	2015 Primary Rights	Expiry
FIFA World Cup	ESPN	Fox Sports	2026
European Championship	ESPN	ESPN	2020
Champions League	ESPN	Fox Sports	2018

[3] https://www.forbes.com/sites/bobbymcmahon/2015/12/05/1-6b-worth-of-tv-deals-good-news-for-real-madrid-barcelona-and-la-liga/#7816cec5166f

Premier League	Fox	NBC	2022
Bundesliga	Gol TV	Fox Sports	2020
La Liga	Gol TV	beIN	2018
Serie A	Fox	beIN	2018
Gold Cup	Fox	Fox	2016
Major League Soccer	ESPN/Fox	ESPN/Fox Sports	2022

Major football competitions are held by four networks: ESPN (estimated 97 million pay TV households), NBCSN (80 million), Fox Sports (88 million) and beIN Sports (17 million). Fox Sports and NBC have both free-to-air and pay TV channels and much broader reach than indicated, and also cross-promote games across many channels they control.

Before 2012, Spain's La Liga was on Gol TV and Italy's Serie A was on Fox. In 2012 Serie A matches essentially disappeared from the TV sets of many American fans because the rights switched from Gol TV to the newly launched beIN Sport, which made it available to about 8 million households. To make matters worse for Serie A, beIN Sport also purchased the rights to La Liga and France's Ligue 1. When Real Madrid or Barcelona are playing, they take precedence over any Serie A games, restricting access and prime times for Serie A clubs in a major market. In response to the move, Marc Ganis of the Chicago-based Sports Corp. Ltd consulting firm said, 'The ratings are going to be so low that they will be almost unmeasurable . . . Considering the push that European football is making in the United States, taking additional money and losing exposure becomes fools' gold. They need to have a long-term strategy, not short-term.'[4]

The EPL averaged 185,000 viewers for 118 live telecasts on Fox Soccer for the 2010/11 season, 321,000 for 48 broadcasts on ESPN2/ESPN and 58,000 for 54 games on ESPN Deportes, according to data from Nielsen Media Research and the networks. Serie A averaged 54,000 viewers for 96 live telecasts on Fox and Ligue 1 53,000 for four broadcasts on Fox.

Gol TV averaged just 29,000 viewers for 75 La Liga telecasts among its Hispanic audience, the only portion Nielsen measures. ESPN Deportes averaged 115,000 people in its Hispanic audience for La Liga, but viewers expanded to an average of 770,000 for the two league 'Clásicos' between Real Madrid and Barcelona.

---

[4] http://www.espn.com/soccer/news/story/_/id/1135765/la-liga,-serie-a-vanish-for-many-u.s.-viewers

Lino Garcia, general manager of ESPN Deportes said, 'It's going probably from a better distributed network to a lesser distributed network. Therein lies the real difference to the viewer. Some of this product is going to be unavailable to many fans to whom it was available before.' Fortunately for football fans, play-by-play man Phil Schoen and highly excitable, colourful commentator Ray Hudson moved from Gol TV to beIN Sport. However, when any league is competing directly against the Premier League juggernaut's start times, let alone Real Madrid and Barcelona, it's simply difficult, no matter how entertaining. It will take time. Even being with a network with wide distribution, it is important to still be jointly marketing and promoting compelling stories and rivalries, have league highlight shows supported by social media, and have start times that don't compete head to head while still being convenient in a saturated football TV market. People underestimate the importance of GMT, but when you're operating a business, it means you sit right in the middle globally. Greenwich Mean Time is very much in the EPL's favour. Leagues have to balance fans in their local market (who create the atmosphere for global fans, sponsors and broadcasters), the Far East and California in the same day.

The English Premier League, which has the biggest American following, sells its international rights directly. The EPL is more sophisticated than both Serie A and La Liga because they have been in the market as a collective selling entity far longer. Serie A and La Liga sell them through agents. In an interview with Die Zeit, Agnelli, the president of Juventus, said: 'I believe that Serie A in Italy, in similar fashion to the Premier League in England, should be represented by people who understand that the entire championship is a single product. It needs a business plan for the development and promotion of our game . . .In Italy nothing happens without the president's assembly.' The league is seen as weak and lacking decision-making powers (as was seen in the sale of TV rights). The sale of TV rights was assigned to a marketing company called Infront, which was also in charge of marketing for a number of clubs in Serie A and the national team. This inevitably can lead to a perception of a conflict of interest.

In the 2014/15 season, the EPL was carried by 80 broadcasters in 212 territories worldwide, and an average game is watched by over 12 million people. In comparison, its closest rival, Spain's La Liga, drew an average of just over 2 million fans per game. La Liga's top two teams, Real Madrid and Barcelona, at the time negotiated their own TV contracts since they are able to get more money from the global TV audiences than selling La Liga as a whole. Other top European national leagues' numbers are also much lower in comparison to the English league. Italy's Serie A drew 4.5 million viewers for an average game and Germany's Bundesliga was roughly 2 million viewers.[5] This exposure gives the Premier League unprecedented power to negotiate both its centralised television rights deal and the clubs' individual sponsorship deals.

In 2017, Serie A assigned its international TV rights predominantly to IMG for €371 million per season – nearly double the value of the previous deal. Even that deal did not have unanimous support. The new figure places Serie A third in Europe for international rights after the English Premier League (€1.3 billion) and the Spanish league (€636 million) and ahead of the Bundesliga (€240 million). This is discussed later.

One of the issues why Italian clubs seem not to work together as well as the UK, where the legal system – and much of civil society – operates on the basis of reciprocal trust, is that Italy's is based on 'una diffidenza reciproca' – essentially, mutual distrust. This is especially true when clubs see scarce resources and a zero-sum game combines with strong regional affiliation (A. Baroncelli and R. Caruso, 2011).[6]

Poor Global League Promotion, Poor Online Engagement

The lack of cooperation for the greater good extends beyond just TV contracts to investment and promotion of the league's clubs and key rivalries. While, for example, Spanish La Liga or Spanish clubs have offices outside of Spain (in 2016 La Liga set up its office in New Delhi, their third office in Asia) or German Bundesliga or German clubs have offices outside of Germany, Italian Serie A and Italian clubs do not have as much of a global physical presence. The Italian league's relatively weak presence in China is a good example. Even though in the 1980s, Serie A was the primary overseas league someone in China could watch,

---

[5] https://contexts.org/articles/english-soccers-mysterious-worldwide-popularity/

[6] A. Baroncelli and R. Caruso; https://core.ac.uk/download/pdf/6463357.pdf

today, the German Bundesliga is the most popular European league on China's digital media, according to analysis conducted by the Mailman Group. The Chinese technology and social media agency publishes 'The Red Card' study each year, which monitors the respective reputation and attention paid to each league on social media, e-commerce, apps and the open web. Among China's 500 million football fans, the German top division ranks first. The report itself suggests a number of reasons for the Bundesliga's success in Asia, including a 'comprehensive content strategy' of presenting all 18 clubs online in China, as well as genuine efforts to reach fans with viral marketing campaigns. Yet the real hard work seems to come off the back of a TV deal with broadcaster CCTV5, which has shown matches in China over the past 20 years. The report states that the channel gets the highest average viewing figures and the highest total number of viewers. The Bundesliga also couples this exposure well with a Chinese language website – a tactic its European counterparts have yet to catch on to. In 2017, six English Premier League clubs and four Bundesliga clubs visited greater China, compared to two from Serie A. In the study's Chinese rankings, Juventus is #17, Inter #19 and Roma #21, behind German clubs Wolfsburg #15 and Schalke 04 #16. Interestingly, Milan is #7, with little investment. This demonstrates nostalgia still exists for Serie A in China and can be capitalised on.[7]

Serie A needs to position itself as a global entertainment brand that provides unique experiences and entertainment. This means that the league needs to recognise that it is in the entertainment and brand businesses. Any entertainment or brand business needs a digital strategy that connects social media, YouTube, games, apps and the web. The league needs to recognise that the matches are only part of the story. To make the league compelling, it is what is going on when the matches are not on that differentiates. The league needs exclusive content, including data and statistics, for a digital brand platform that captures pre-match, the match and post-match. For example, during pre-match, the following could be better provided: historical Serie A highlights to give context to rivalries; access to warm-ups, dressing rooms and the tunnel; and interviews with ex-players and coaches. Instead of leaving it to clubs, the league must also have fan relationship engagement management, have localisation

---

7 http://www.mailmangroup.com/en/red-card-2016/

with different languages and have a physical presence in key markets. La Liga has ten offices around the world and a physical affiliated network office in 30 other countries. Serie A should tie together Italian cultural experiences and corporate events in parallel with football matches. Serie A should have numerous legends of the game as Serie A ambassadors to play legends matches, host football clinics and share Serie A with fans around the world.

Football clubs and leagues who want to reach Chinese football fans must have digital adeptness that can cope with the rapidly changing pace of digital innovation in China. The Bundesliga created their 'Dream' campaign which included the production of video content with players and clubs exclusively for the Chinese fans across most available digital channels. The campaign generated over 15 million video views, the largest online football campaign.

Since there is data that demonstrates that the disproportionate popularity of the EPL may not be due to competitive balance, upset likelihood, or high scoring, it may be that the EPL is easier for global fans to follow and track. It is the only top league in an English-speaking country, where English has become the global language. The language may not have mattered as much in the 1980s and 1990s as fans passively watched football as a sport. Today, interaction and engagement are critical to building and keeping fans. A common language helps, although over time, content will need to be more local to compete.

League	Twitter followers	Instagram followers	Facebook followers	Total
EPL	16.5	14.4	40.8	71.7
La Liga	3.25	5.1	31.5	39.85
Serie A	1.1	1.8	4.5	7.4
Bundesliga	2.1	1.2	3.2	6.5
Ligue 1	0.3	0.55	2.5	3.35

RESULT Sports analysed the community growth across the big five European leagues (Premier League, Serie A, La Liga, Bundesliga and Ligue 1). New followers on each club's social media platforms, as well as the league's official accounts were totalled, revealing some interesting trends across the leagues. La Liga had the highest increase in followers (20.8 million) among the leagues' official pages, leaving the Premier

League (12.1 million) trailing in its wake. The other big five leagues were even further behind; the Bundesliga added 4.9 million new followers, Serie A just 1.4 million, and Ligue 1 a mere 790,000.[8]

In Asia, La Liga charted out a road map that will include exhibition matches, player visits and development programmes at the grass-roots level in India and other countries. Competing with the English Premier League for viewership, which has a favourable time slot for matches in India, La Liga said matches will kick off at 4:30 IST to suit the Indian audience. Major matches must be played in prime time around the world, even if inconvenient sometimes locally. The growing market is global. Now, it is not unusual for a Serie A match to start around noon, a historically very unusual start time, in order to satisfy the hundreds of millions of Chinese viewers – where it is 6pm in Beijing. The advertising revenues for these foreign audiences go far beyond any European television channel. Global viewers expect the best audiovisual product including cameras with technology for 360-degree replay, spider cameras, HD and 4K cameras and steadycams and mini-cameras to increase the broadcast value. The other leagues started these initiatives earlier, but at least Serie A is now catching up.

In addition, the Supercoppa Italiana (Italian Super Cup) is an annual football competition usually held the week before the season begins in Italy. It is contested by the winners of Serie A and the Coppa Italia in the previous season, as a curtain-raiser to the new campaign. Since 2009, the Supercoppa Italiana has consistently been played outside of Italy, typically in China and Qatar. So, Serie A has been trying.

Italian clubs have taken it upon themselves also and clubs such as Juventus and Roma compete in the increasingly important International Champions Cup (ICC), a series of friendly football matches organised to simulate a global tournament, during the summer. The tournament allows fans from around the world to get access to the clubs they follow and support, and potentially new global fans exposure to the clubs. The ICC was founded by Relevent Sports, a division of RSE Ventures, a sports venture firm founded in 2012 by Stephen Ross and Matt Higgins. Charlie Stillitano serves as the executive chairman of Relevent Sports, as well as the host of *The Football Show* on SiriusXM. During the 2014

8 http://en.calcioefinanza.com/2017/07/18/nearly-100-million-new-fans-follow-football-clubs-across-social-media-channels-201617

tournament, a match between Manchester United and Real Madrid at the University of Michigan Stadium in Ann Arbor, Michigan set the all-time record for attendance at a football match in the United States with 109,318 spectators.

With the decline in performance on the pitch and fewer stars, the once eagerly anticipated derbies with storied histories have not attracted much natural attention outside of Italy to the casual football fan. Regardless of the standings, the rivalries are as heated as they once were locally in Italy, but outside of Italy (where the revenue growth is), they have lost the attention and imagination of the casual global fan. In addition, rivalries between Juventus, the clear leader in the last six years, and emerging Roma and Napoli, whilst getting more exciting, have been relatively limited to Italy and not aggressively marketed globally by the league or clubs. For example, neither game (Juventus vs. Napoli or Juventus vs. Roma) has a derby nickname that draws upon history to aggressively market and draw in casual spectators. Rivalries or derbies help define the identity of each club for casual fans. Rivalries with star players and compelling storylines that capture the imagination are incredibly important in an intensely competitive market with lots of games to choose from, especially when the matches have consequences in standings and Champions League spots.

Lastly, Serie A relies heavily on its national title sponsor, TIM, and has sponsorship with two others, Nike and Panini. Similarly, at one time, La Liga had 80% of league revenues from one sponsor (BBVA) and three others. Today, in contrast, La Liga has a title sponsor (Santander); three global sponsors (EA Sports, Nike and TAG); regional sponsors in China (3), Asia (1), the Middle East (2), Africa (2) and Mexico (1), national sponsors (13) and licences (2). Therefore, opportunities do exist for Serie A.

Clouds of Scandals

Italian football has had a long history of scandals, and the Italian media has given them nicknames, *doping amministrativo* (doping[-like] administration), *bilanciopoli* (balance sheet scandal), *plusvalenze fittizie* (fictitious capital gains), *calcio scommesse* (football bet) or *plusvalenze fai-da-te* (DIY profit). Therefore, it is difficult to prove a direct correlation to scandal and decline in Italian football. However, after Europe unified, there seemed to be a sense that Europeans wanted more professionalism, transparency and fairness to compete globally. Scandals may make fans, and most likely sponsors, look at Serie A with a bit of cynicism.

Arguably, the biggest recent football scandal in Italy was the Calciopoli scandal of 2006, and it did have an impact with regards to the teams involved, punishments and publicity, as well as player defections. The scandal was uncovered in May 2006 by Italian police, implicating league champions Juventus and other major clubs including Milan, Fiorentina, Lazio and Reggina. A number of illegal telephone interceptions showed a thick network of relationships between club management and referee organisations. Club managements allegedly influenced the appointments of favourable referees. Transcripts of recorded telephone conversations published in Italian newspapers suggested that, during the 2004/05 season, employees of the clubs implicated had conversations with several officials of Italian football to influence referee appointments. Juventus and the other clubs deny this suggestion.

In July 2006, the Italian Football Federation's prosecutor called for Juventus to be excluded from the Serie A championship and assigned to Serie B, while for Milan, Fiorentina and Lazio to be downgraded to last place in the 2005/06 championship and relegated to Serie B. The prosecutor also asked for point deductions to be imposed for the following season for all the clubs. Lastly, the prosecutor called for Juventus to be stripped of its 2005 and 2006 titles. The punishment was long disputed because of the severity of the punishment for Juventus compared to the other teams involved. According to the court, the conduct of club executives was considered in all cases. While not real match-fixing, it was viewed as a violation of sporting principles. In the case of Juventus, allegedly the evidence was considered stronger than the other clubs. Juventus's representatives considered this assumption totally arbitrary. Juventus believe the case was never proven. Carlo Porceddu, a federal prosecutor from 1998 to 2001 and current vice president of the Federal Court of Appeal, stated in an interview with *Unione Sarda*: 'Revoking the 2005/06 "Scudetto" (championship) from Juventus and assigning it to Inter was a serious mistake. The Calciopoli investigation should have been more thorough, so much so that we, as the Federal Court, had limited the penalty to Juventus not withdrawing the championship title due to insufficient evidence. In fact, that aspect had been neglected. Then, the special commissioner of the Federation of that period had appointed a group of his friends, one of whom was also on the board of directors of Inter, and that title was revoked from Juventus and given to Inter. That was a grave error in my view.' In all, the government formally investigated 41 people and looked into 19 Serie A matches from the 2004/05 season and 14 Serie A matches from the 2005/06 season. Juventus originally announced that they planned to appeal the punishment in the Italian civil courts. FIFA announced that it had the option to suspend the FIGC, thus barring all Italian clubs from international play if Juventus went to court. Under pressure, Juventus dropped its appeal. Juventus officials cited the 'willingness shown by the Italian Football Federation (FIGC) and the Italian National Olympic Committee (CONI) to review its case during (CONI's) arbitration'. An appeal reduced Lazio's, Juventus's and Fiorentina's points deductions. Milan were unsuccessful in their appeal and were still faced with their original points deduction. (Milan, originally disqualified from the 2006/07 Champions League due to the scandal, went on to win the competition in 2007.) On 9 September 2015, the Supreme Court released a 150-page document that explained its final ruling of the case, which stated that the unwarranted activities caused significant damage to Italian football, not only in sporting, but also in economic terms.

The relegation of Juventus also prompted a mass exodus of important players such as Fabio Cannavaro, Lilian Thuram and Zlatan Ibrahimović. Some 30 other Serie A players who participated at the 2006 FIFA World Cup opted to move to other European leagues in the wake of the scandal. In all, some 30 players who had played in the 2006 World Cup that summer, a World Cup that Italy won, left Serie A for other leagues. Such a mass exodus of talent, talent that went largely unreplaced, left Italian clubs scrambling to put together squads that could compete both domestically and in European competitions.[9]

That disruption set off a desperate spending spree from Inter and Roma to try and take advantage of the situation. While there would be some short-term gains from that strategy, with Inter winning four Scudetti in a row after 2005/06 (2006/07 Juventus was not in Serie A; Roma finished

9 https://www.sbnation.com/soccer/2016/7/15/12197194/calciopoli-scandal-anniversary-juventus-milan-fiorentina-napoli

#2 in 2007, 2008, and 2010) and the Champions League trophy in 2010, the long-term impact of the spending left the clubs in precarious financial situations because they didn't build commercial activities. Unfortunately for Serie A, the scandal happened during a time the business of European football was changing rapidly, and Serie A was already behind.

Calciopoli was followed by more speculation, investigations and scandals as well, including unpaid wages and taxes, match-fixing and doping. Further scandals have led to further allegations, investigations and raids of club offices. Since Calciopoli, there have only been a few seasons in Serie A where points deductions were not imposed on clubs for some sort of investigation or scandal. It only serves to make us better understand fans who look at Serie A with a bit of cynicism, and maybe why potential global sponsors could be hesitant to spend significant amounts. Only 20% of the fans in a 2016 poll think that Serie A is 'cleaner' than ten years ago (around Calciopoli times). Only a third of the fans trust the federation. Therefore, for these reasons (lack of trust in the referees and federations etc.) 90% of the fans supported the use of technology (VAR) to add transparency and accountability. In the poll, fans also complained about the organised crime in the stadium and the Ultras.[10]

As we can see in the charts overleaf, there was a clear decline in attendance in Serie A before 2006. Attendance peaked in the early 1980s and got a bump in the early 1990s after the World Cup in Italy, and improved stadiums. But clearly since the early 1990s, the trend has been a decline. Of course, in 2007 there is a big drop because of the scandal, but the trend towards decline was well under way. So, to place blame primarily on the scandal is way too simplistic. This becomes clearer when looking at the second chart which shows attendance in the other leagues increasing during the same time.

---

[10] https://www.google.com/amp/www.repubblica.it/sport/calcio/2016/10/02/news/atlante_tifo_italiani_in_fuga_dal_calcio-148926536/amp/

Attendance in Serie A

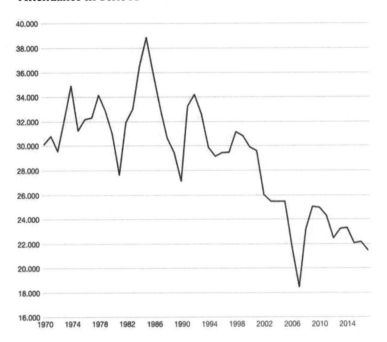

Fonte: European-Football-Statistics Scarica i dati

Attendance in Europe

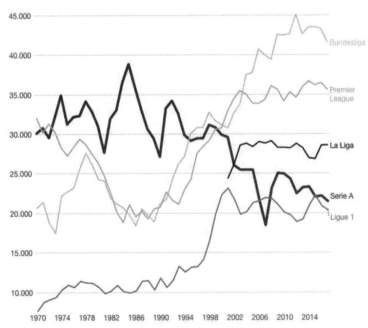

Fonte: European-Football-Statistics Scarica i dati

Parma were declared bankrupt in 2015, amid growing debts and a failure to pay wages or taxes since 2014. UEFA refused to give the club a licence to appear in the Europa League that season, but the club managed to obtain the required permit to participate in Serie A. But supposedly that would be unlikely to happen again under new league rules introduced in 2015/16. Italy's football association, the FIGC, says inclusion in its premier soccer league requires solid finances and transparency, with buyers having to disclose financial and banking qualifications within a month of purchase.

In March 2017, AC Milan announced its sale for €740 million, including €220 million of debt. The bidders were identified by Milan's owners as Sino-Europe Sports Investment Management Changxing Co Ltd. AC Milan announced the sale with no public signing or press conference. The club named only two individual investors, Li Yonghong and Han Li, along with state-linked Haixia Capital and other undisclosed 'state-controlled entities'.

Reuters reporters Adam Jourdan and Elvira Pollina followed a paper trail via Luxembourg, Hong Kong and a network of shell companies to the deserted 11th floor of the World Trade Centre in Changxing, two hours west of Shanghai and found that the offices of eight of the shell companies connected to the bid and registered there did not exist. They reported that 'guards and office workers said they had heard of Sino-Europe Sports, but had rarely, if ever, seen any employees'. Jourdan and Pollina reported that China Construction Bank (CCB), one of the highest-profile known backers, had pledged to invest around €150 million, but backed out of the consortium at the last minute, prompting the group to ask for more time to pay. Haixia Capital, which is owned by arms of the provincial Fujian government, State Development and Investment Corp (SDIC) and Taiwanese conglomerate Fubon Group were still on board, but only in a financing role, according to a Reuters source. Among the direct investors, only Li Yonghong remains, Reuters' source added. Li is not well known in China or in soccer. Reuters' China-based sources at CCB said that recent tighter capital controls would impact the investment, but they were not aware of how the deal would be finalised.

CCB, Haixia Capital and Fubon declined to comment. According to the Reuters article, a spokeswoman for SDIC said she wasn't aware of the deal and noted that Haixia Capital makes its own investment decisions. Reuters could not reach the Fujian government for comment. Neither Li nor Han could be contacted. The investment vehicle Sino-Europe Sports holds together a web of firms with names like Rossoneri Sport and Sino-Europe Milan. Most are also linked to Chen Huashan, the listed legal representative. Reuters could not independently reach Chen. The use of shell companies in deals is not unusual. However, it highlights the often obscure and complex network of investors and shell companies behind some Chinese overseas bids may be an attraction for those maybe seeking a quiet way to move money abroad.

US private equity fund Elliott provided Li's vehicle, Rossoneri Sport Investment Luxembourg, with a €180 million loan to complete the purchase of AC Milan. In September 2017, Reuters reported the Chinese owner was looking for one or more investors to share the financial burden, less than six months after buying the loss-making Italian club, which lost €75 million in 2016. In March 2018, according to Reuters, Elliott offered to provide additional financial support by extending liquidity to its Chinese owner. Li Yonghong has been making capital injections, under the terms of his acquisition, and must inject around €30–35 million by June 2018. In addition, in 2017, Elliott directly lent AC Milan €128 million to fund the acquisition of players and repay bank debt. All of Elliott's loans carry an average interest rate of just below 10%, repayable by October 2018. If Li defaults or misses payments to AC Milan, Elliott reportedly could take over the club. Elliott's latest offer to extend further financial support may be aimed at preserving the club's value. Reuters could not reach Li directly for comment and attempts to reach him through the club had been unsuccessful. The club did not respond to a request for a comment. In February, Li said his finances were sound and called recent press reports about financial difficulties irresponsible.

Obviously, Italy's football association, the FIGC, saying inclusion in its premier soccer league requires solid finances and transparency, with buyers having to disclose financial and banking qualifications within a month of purchase seems to be questioned by the media.

It is unclear if a potential buyer of a Serie A club needs to pass any meaningful financial net worth or background tests to acquire a Serie A club. Does a buyer really need to demonstrate that he/she/it has the liquidity to fund the club for the first few years? Are there any meaningful restrictions on the amount of debt a buyer can use to purchase the club? Does a buyer have to fully demonstrate where the capital came from and if it was reported and taxed? Does a buyer have to undergo a full criminal background check? All of these questions, especially with Milan being such a high-profile club, tarnishes the image of Serie A.

In July 2017, a company purchased Vicenza Calcio (Serie C), which is the club Roberto Baggio started his career with and has reached the semi-finals of the UEFA Cup Winners' Cup in 1998 before losing to Chelsea. In September 2017, there were reports about the club failing to pay wages. In January 2018, the club was declared bankrupt. In January 2018, the president of Foggia Calcio (Serie B) was arrested for money laundering related to organised crime.[11]

North American sports leagues have revenue sharing and no promotion and relegation. Because the owners are essentially tied together, they have several restrictions on ownership, the financial situation of clubs and ownership of other sporting entities or businesses that may pose conflicts of interest. Potential owners must go through comprehensive background checks (for example, they can't be involved in gambling) and demonstrate financial liquidity as well as agree that no more than a certain amount of debt may be obligated by a club. North American leagues have the power to fine owners and have even forced owners to sell clubs for scandals.

First introduced in 2004 for owners and directors of major British football clubs, the fit-and-proper-person test or director's test is a test aiming to prevent corrupt or untrustworthy businessmen from serving on the board of certain organisations. The first director known to have failed the test was Dennis Coleman, director of Rotherham United when they went into administration in 2006 and 2008. He claimed: 'I came in and in effect saved the club. It is totally unfair for me to be disqualified.' In November 2009, Stephen Vaughan, then owner of Chester City, became the first owner to fail the test, after he was legally disqualified from being

---

11 http://www.sportmediaset.mediaset.it/calcio/calcio/serie-b-arrestato-fedele-sannella-patron-del-foggia_1193528-201802a.shtml

a director of any company. This was a result of VAT fraud as owner of Widnes Vikings rugby club. In March 2012, Rangers owner Craig Whyte was found not to be a fit and proper person as the result of an independent inquiry. In June 2014, Louis Tomlinson, former member of the boy band One Direction, and John Ryan, businessman and previous chairman of Doncaster Rovers, launched a bid to buy Doncaster Rovers but one month later Ryan was found not to be a fit and proper person due to a lack of funding.

The Premier League has tighter restrictions than the rest of the Football League and Football Conference. In general, a businessman will fail the test if:

- They have power or influence over another Football League club
- They hold a significant interest in another Football League club
- They become prohibited by law from being a director
- They are filing for bankruptcy
- They have been a director of a club while it has suffered two or more unconnected events of insolvency
- They have been a director of two or more clubs of which, while they have been director, has suffered an event of insolvency

By having restrictions in Italy that may not exist in other countries, Italy may restrict potential buyers with resources, but it may also restrict those without the necessary resources or those with criminal backgrounds from potentially harming a club or engaging in unethical behaviour to keep the club afloat. Being able to fine owners (as opposed to deducting points from clubs which hurts the fans) and even being able to force owners to sell the club as a penalty for scandals, may help the league in the long run.

There are consistent challenges by clubs to the authority of various football bodies in Italy, which undermines their power and integrity. Powerful club presidents and directors also act as directors of the Italian Football Federation (FIGC) and Serie A. When there are investigations, all types of conflicts of interest arise.

Regarding the governance structure of Italian football, all Italian sports national governing bodies are recognised by CONI (the Italian Olympic Committee), which supervises, organises and promotes Italian sports through the National Governing Bodies ('Federations'). The Italian Football Federation (Federazione Italiana Giuoco Calcio; FIGC), also known as Federcalcio, is the governing body of football in Italy and is a founding member of UEFA and a member of FIFA. It organises the Italian football league, Coppa Italia, Italian national football team, and the Italian women's national football team. The headquarters is in Rome and technical department in Coverciano, Florence.

On 13 November 2017, after the Italian national team's 1-0 aggregate defeat to Sweden and failure to qualify for the 2018 FIFA World Cup, then-FIGC president, Carlo Tavecchio, resigned. An election of the new president took place on 29 January 2018. It is worth mentioning that Tavecchio was temporarily, at the same time, extraordinary commissioner of Lega Serie A, due to the inability of Lega Serie A to nominate a president in a very delicate period of time, including the sale of the Serie A TV rights. The three candidates for the FIGC presidency were the president of the National Amateur League (which League represents 34% of the total votes), the president of Lega Pro (which Lega represents 17% of the total votes), and the president of the Italian Players' Union (which Union represents 20% of the total votes). Each candidate was eager to win and, in four rounds of voting, no candidate reached the necessary majority, and consequently, no president was elected. At this point, CONI had valid legal grounds (it tried also as soon as Tavecchio resigned in November 2017, but the legal grounds seemed weak) to nominate and install an extraordinary commissioner in order to fix what FIGC had not been able to do by itself. Not being able to nominate the FIGC and Lega Serie A (which represent the top Italian football division) presidents represents a sporting and managerial failure for Italian football that demonstrates an inability to govern itself autonomously.

CONI secretary general Roberto Fabbricini has been appointed as extraordinary commissioner for the FIGC following its failed election process, while CONI president Giovanni Malago has elected to take a similar post at the Lega. Malago expressed his belief that it would have been wrong for him to take the helm at both the FIGC and Lega, adding that he also has CONI commitments ahead of the start of the 2018 winter Olympic Games in Pyeongchang. According to Italian newspaper *Gazzetta dello Sport*, he said: 'Let's say clearly, first you have to solve the problems in Lega Serie A, otherwise we will not solve anything, even in FIGC. That's why I decided to engage myself in the Lega. I have many friends and many people who recognise the gravity of the moment; the priorities are obviously TV rights and the renewal of governance.'

Lack of Collective Player Activism

The players in the league are aware of many of the issues and challenges first hand. For example, it has become too common in Italy that when a club loses a match, a select group of fans wait outside the stadium to criticise players and, sometimes, act violently. It's difficult to change that mentality. The Italian players' association, AIC, was founded around 50 years ago by 10 national team players. They have gotten involved in selected issues to try to help. For example, the government agreed to AIC's request to set up a commission to look into violence against players.

We are surprised that players have not become more active collectively in supporting one another and pushing more aggressively for change on key issues plaguing the league. For example, in spring 2017, Ghanaian Sulley Muntari, who played for Italian club Pescara at the time, was the subject of racial abuse by a section of Cagliari fans during an Italian league match. Muntari is an experienced player, helping Inter win the Champions League in 2009/10 and the Serie A title in 2008/09 and 2009/10. Muntari told the referee and his assistants several times about the chants from home fans in the final minute of Pescara's 1-0 loss. The official then showed a yellow card to Muntari for dissent, who was so angry with the booking that he walked off the pitch seconds before full-time, a decision that earned him a second yellow card, and then a red, from the referee. After the match, the Italian Football Federation (FIGC) announced that Muntari's yellow card would not be rescinded, and that he would have to serve a one-match ban. Incredibly, FIGC also decided not to punish Cagliari. Cagliari escaped punishment because

Serie A's disciplinary body said only 10 fans, less than 1%, were directly involved in the abuse of Muntari, raising further doubts about Italy's commitment to tackling racism in football. FIGC then-president Carlo Tavecchio told national news agency ANSA that he was 'satisfied' with the appeal ruling 'because roles and procedures which are guaranteed by our system were respected'. As background, Tavecchio was banned by UEFA for six months at the start of his Italian federation presidency in 2014 over a reference to bananas when discussing the presence of foreign players in Italy.

Receiving no support from Pescara, Muntari was forced to lodge an appeal himself with assistance from the players' union in Italy. The world football players' union, FIFPro, and even the head of the United Nations Commission on Human Rights, urged the Italian football powers to overturn the decision. Muntari's actions prompted a wave of support on social media, although football's ruling body FIFA, while applauding the player's principles, said it did not condone his decision to walk off. The Italian Football Federation's anti-racism advisor, meanwhile, hinted that other players should consider strike action in solidarity with Muntari if the decision was not overturned. Finally, after pressure from the players' union and others, the suspension was overturned by FIGC.

The players in Serie A could have been more vocal overall and more vocal about taking collective action on this and other issues that hurt the league. For example, in April 2014, NBA players threatened to collectively boycott play-off games in protest if they were dissatisfied with the league's response to the Los Angeles Clippers owner's racist comments. According to the players' union, the league's biggest star LeBron James threatened to boycott NBA games unless the owner was forced to sell the team before the next season.

In another example, in January 1965, 21 black players arrived in New Orleans for the American Football League's All-Star Game. Upon arriving at the airport, they couldn't find taxis willing to take them to their hotel. So, they decided to boycott the game. It brought national attention. Over the next two years, the racial climate began to change in New Orleans. Soon after, New Orleans desegregated its public facilities. The following year the city was able to convince pro football authorities to award New Orleans its own franchise.

Lastly, at an NBA game in December 2014 LeBron James and five other players wore 'I Can't Breathe' warm-up shirts in memory of a man who died while being arrested. The following night Kobe Bryant and all but one of his fellow Los Angeles Lakers wore the same shirt before a game.

Off-the-Pitch Issues: Management

Tolerated Unethical Behaviour, Unsustainable Business Models

Italian football was so successful on the pitch until the turn of the century, there was an arrogance that nothing needed to change, even as most clubs started to face serious financial and operational difficulties and challenges. Major scandals or rumours of mismanagement and unethical behaviour were dismissed as if expected in football. Similar to the discussion of TV rights, to give some context it is helpful to understand what happened in English football, which overtook Serie A in league revenues in the 1990s. Despite significant European success in the 1970s and early 1980s, the late 1980s marked a low point for English football. Stadiums were crumbling, hooliganism was common, and English clubs were banned from European competition for five years following the Heysel Stadium disaster in 1985. The Football League First Division, the top level of English football since 1888, was behind leagues such as Italy's Serie A and Spain's La Liga in attendances and revenues, and several top English footballers had moved abroad.

In the 1990s, after several chairmen and managers were allegedly taking or paying undisclosed money to facilitate player transfers, one of the first actions of the new Labour government on its election in 1997 was to establish the Football Task Force 'to investigate and recommend new measures to deal with the public's concerns', which resulted in four reports. The Labour Party asserted that it was 'widely recognised that there was a need for change'. Sir John Smith, who made his name as a Metropolitan Police deputy commissioner, analysed English football's corporate governance and values. Smith's final report in 1997 was highly critical of the English football industry for its weak governance, incompetence, political infighting and complacency. At the time, one manager explained that there were no principled professionals in executive management with the skills or expertise like in a typical company. Sir John Smith made the following conclusion: 'Since it is so successful, why should football bother about its occasional scandals? Why meddle with a success story? Does it matter if the world of football is tarnished by rumours of financial misbehaviour? There is a tendency for people within the game to dismiss this subject with a cursory statement: "That's football", as if it were the natural order of things for financial misconduct to be part of the game.'

The English clubs, whilst not perfect in producing their 'Football's Report to the Football Task Force', did start to slowly change, improve regulations and governance, professionalise and be held accountable, and revenues and attendance increased. For example, they established a Financial Advisory Unit for more regulation of clubs. The government stopped short of statutory regulation and instead urged the clubs to undertake a structural review of its 'constitutional structures, corporate governance and decision-making processes'. The English government did promote Supporters Direct, an umbrella organisation to provide support and assistance for its member trusts to secure a greater level of accountability and deliver democratic representation within football clubs and within football's governing structures. The government has also funded the Independent Football Commission (IFC), which operated from 2002 to 2008 in England as an independent body within football's regulatory framework to scrutinise and monitor the performance of the Football Association, the FA Premier League and the Football League and issue publicly available reports on its findings. (The IFC has been replaced by the Independent Football Ombudsman.)

In contrast, while the football industry was becoming a business and clubs in rival countries were being held accountable, Italian football clubs didn't change and Italy didn't have enough financial and regulatory transparency to raise outside capital. To make matters worse, Italian football clubs relied on financial tricks. Professors David Hassan and Sean Hamil wrote in their book *Who Owns Football?*, '. . . most top European football leagues tend to report losses after transfer activity is taken into account. However, the top league in England (€1,562 million), France (€337 million) and Germany (€1,038 million) all made combined operating profits over the 1996/97 to 2006/07 period. On the other hand, Italy made an operating loss of €1,355 million over the same period. In other words, by the standards of its peers, at the operational level Italian football is chronically loss-making before even taking into account any further deficit on transfer spending.'

Since 2000, at least 15 clubs that at one time participated in Serie A declared bankruptcy: in alphabetical order, Ancona (2004), Como (2004), Fiorentina (2002), Messina (2008), Monza (2004), Napoli (2004), Parma (2004), Perugia (2010), Piacenza (2012), Reggiana (2005), Salernitana (2005), Torino (2005), Treviso (2009), Venezia (2005) and Vicenza (2018). It was discovered that some of these clubs stayed financially afloat by cross-trading players using the football transfer market, wherein multiple players were exchanged between clubs, generally involving monetary consideration. This practice typically resulted in short-term financial benefit for the clubs. At various times, some of these clubs received points deductions for financial irregularities or failing to pay players, filed for bankruptcy more than once, were liquidated, or were banned from games in their stadiums with audiences for crowd violence.

Scandals also involved inaccurate dating of profits obtained via player transfers. For example, in July 2001, Roma sold their Japanese international midfielder Hidetoshi Nakata, but allegedly the club documented the profit in their accounts for the 2000/01 season, claiming that the deal was agreed to before the cut-off of the fiscal year, which was 30 June 2001 for most clubs.

Italian football journalist Luca Taidelli said: 'In 2010, when Inter won everything, they barely sold a cup in extra merchandise. There was no additional income. They didn't have a sophisticated commercial arm to take advantage of what the team did. At the stadium they also have this ridiculous situation where official shirts are being sold in the shop for €120, yet directly outside fake ones are being sold for €20 or €30. I can't imagine this happening anywhere else.' The temporary stalls selling fake merchandise popping up like mushrooms on matchday and disappearing immediately after the game, are oftentimes allegedly run by organised crime or local influential families reportedly able to blackmail or coerce the various municipality governments for decades in order to allow them to exist at the expense of the clubs' turnovers. That reduction in turnover has impacted the players clubs have been able to afford.

The amount of debt in Italian football is among the highest. The European Club Football Landscape report for 2015 by UEFA shows that of the top ten clubs with the most debt in European football, four are from Italy. It is important to analyse net debt in context against isolation, as the risk profile of debt to cash flow and assets needs to be taken into account. The big Italian clubs (with the exception of Juventus) do not own their own stadiums, so the multiple of long-term assets is generally higher since there are few fixed assets. The multiple of revenue gives some context of how much debt is to potential earnings. These financial numbers may not match audited numbers.[12]

UEFA Ranking of Clubs with Most Net Debt

Rank	Club	Country	FY15 Net Debt(€m)	YoY Growth (%)	Multiple of Rev.	Multiple of LT Assets
1	Man Utd	ENG	€536	11%	1.0x	0.8x
2	Benfica	POR	336	1	3.3	1.3
3	Inter	ITA	306	30	1.8	2.4
4	Valencia	ESP	285	13	3.5	0.8
5	QPR	ENG	279	n/a	2.5	4.8
6	AC Milan	ITA	249	-3	1.1	1.6
7	CSKA Mos	RUS	224	49	3.7	1.4
8	Galatasaray	TUR	222	47	1.5	4.2
9	Juventus	ITA	209	-4	0.6	0.8
10	AS Roma	ITA	208	43	1.1	1.5

Source: UEFA

Financial Fair Play has played a significant two-fold role in improving clubs' balance sheets, firstly by limiting major losses and secondly by requiring owners to permanently inject capital rather than allowing loans to build up year after year. According to UEFA, English clubs have enjoyed the most equity increases via earnings or capital contributions totalling €2.3 billion in the last five years ending 2015. Italian clubs are the next largest beneficiaries, totalling €1.1 billion. Since Italian clubs already have significant debt, with four of the top ten largest net debt amounts being Italian clubs, owners have had to inject capital. However, unlike the English clubs where the contributions have been in earnings, Italian club owners are injecting personal capital because of losses, which at some point is unsustainable. This is what has, and will, continue to cause ownership of Italian clubs to change or sustainable economic-sport models will have to be implemented.

---

[12] http://www.uefa.com/MultimediaFiles/Download/Tech/uefaorg/General-al/02/42/27/91/2422791_DOWNLOAD.pdf

In general, Italian clubs didn't invest in processes and procedures to run the clubs as real businesses. They are run on the whims of emotional owners. There are a few exceptions. The Agnellis have taken some of the things they have learned in global manufacturing at Fiat and applied them to Juventus to make them more global, process and data driven and accountable. Very few Italian professional football clubs have checks and balances like an independent internal audit committee. Even when the clubs do have them, they don't regularly review financial planning and risk assessment reports that would identify issues such as the over-reliance of revenues on a particular source. Most management teams don't have robust strategy and budgeting processes or the technology to gather and analyse the data in their businesses to make better decisions. Typically, management teams don't have club-wide meetings to help ensure a common mission and collaboration between groups or have training programmes to invest in improving their employees. Very few clubs have collaboration between marketing and commercial departments with sporting director departments. Sporting departments who scout and select players are seen as the most important area in the club, because it has a more visible direct impact on the pitch. It's not unusual for marketing and commercial areas to learn of player signings the same day as the media, losing out on marketing opportunities. Typically, coaches get hired by the owner, without interviews by others in, or consensus from, the organisation. Typically, players are signed and there is no formal onboarding process.

Increasingly, football clubs are competing with owners with transnational capital (Sklair 2001) as well as an international collaborative network of synergistic assets (Castells 1996, Millward 2011). The best examples of new versions of transnational owners with collaborative networks are owners in the English Premier League such as Stan Kroenke who controls the EPL's Arsenal, NBA's Denver Nuggets, NHL's Colorado Avalanche, MLS's Colorado Rapids and NFL's Los Angeles Rams. The Glazer family controls the EPL's Manchester United and NFL's Tampa Bay Buccaneers. Mansour bin Zayed Al Nahyan controls the EPL's Manchester City, which has investment in MLS's New York City FC and La Liga's Girona, as well as other clubs in Japan, Australia and Uruguay. Investments in several sports assets allows clubs to share best practices as well as provide potentially unique commercial opportunities for sponsors.

For those that have several football clubs, players can be developed and loaned out to controlled clubs.

Over-reliance on TV Revenues

Traditionally, Italian clubs have had a disproportionate amount of revenues from broadcasting. For example, in 2008 (before the collective TV contract took place) broadcasting revenues were around 66% of overall revenues, while matchday revenues were around 15%. For Real Madrid and Barcelona, which also did not have collective league TV rights, TV revenues represented around 38% and 37% of overall revenues, respectively. Per the information overleaf, in 2008, AC Milan, Inter and Roma collectively made more in broadcasting than Real Madrid, Manchester United and Barcelona combined, who were the top three overall revenue clubs. However, the matchday revenues of the three Italian clubs was a fraction of the top three overall clubs. In 2012, after the collective TV contract took effect, the absolute revenue decreased in broadcasting for the top Italian clubs. In fact, the matchday revenues of each of the top three clubs in the Deloitte Revenue Rankings in 2012 were more than any broadcasting revenues of an Italian club. The Italian clubs over-relied on broadcasting revenues and underinvested in stadiums and creating a matchday environment that would generate revenues as well as commercial arms. For those seeking to turn around a club's finances, one of the most important tasks is to boost matchday revenues, which account for 11% of total revenues in Serie A, compared with 23% in both the English Premier League and the German Bundesliga. That means improving the matchday experience. As previously mentioned, few Italian clubs own the stadiums they play in, and unlike in England and Germany, where official encouragement and incentives have led to stadiums being upgraded, Italian ones largely remain in a poor state.[13]

Ironically, for a country so expert in marketing brands, the owners of the football clubs never marketed the brands of their clubs. Therefore, they had to play catch-up with clubs like Real Madrid and Manchester United who cultivated global brands. The Italian football clubs didn't have the resources or know-how or desire to make investments for the long term like Real Madrid and Manchester United.

---

13 https://www.economist.com/news/business/21640356-countrys-largest-clubs-are-belatedly-becoming-more-businesslike-more-just-trophy-assets

2008 vs 2012 Deloitte Revenue Report Broadcasting and Matchday Revenues

Club	Overall Rank	Overall Revenues	Broadcasting	Matchday
2008				
AC Milan****	#6	227.2	153.6 (67%)	28.6 (13%)
Inter*	#9	195.0	128.0 (66%)	29.8 (15%)
Roma**	#10	157.6	104 (66%)	24.0 (15%)
Juventus***				
Real Madrid	#1	351.0	132.4 (38%)	82.2 (23%)
Man United	#2	315.2	91.3 (29%)	137.5 (44%)
Barcelona	#3	290.1	106.7 (37%)	88.6 (31%)
2012				
AC Milan	#7	235.1	107.7 (46%)	35.6 (15%)
Inter	#8	211.4	124.4 (58%)	32.9 (16%)
Roma	#15	143.5	91.1 (64%)	17.6 (12%)
Real Madrid	#1	479.5	183.5 (38%)	123.6 (26%)
Barcelona	#2	450.7	183.7 (41%)	110.7 (25%)
Man United	#3	367	132.2 (36%)	120.3 (33%)

Source: Deloitte

* 'For the two years from 2007/08, the Nerazzurri will benefit from a new broadcasting contract with Mediaset worth a reported €100m (GBP 67.3m) a year. The deal is a significant uplift on the club's previous contract with Sky Italia… The club's average home league match attendance of 48,300, was a drop of almost 9,000 on two years previously… like AC Milan, Inter needs to be at the forefront of urgently addressing the matchday issues that are currently afflicting Italian football in order to keep pace with its European peers off the pitch… The planned reintroduction of a collective broadcast rights selling regime in Italy will make this an even more important area of financial focus for Inter.'

** Around €30m increase in broadcasting was due to a quarter-final run in the Champions League. '… matchday attendance of 36,300 was similar to the preceding season but below previous seasons.'

*** Juventus were #12 with 145.2 million but they were relegated to Serie B as a punishment.

**** AC Milan won the Champions League. 'The club's average league attendance of 47,600 was a reduction of almost 12,000 per match on the previous season, highlighting the urgent need to address the quality of the facilities at the San Siro and security for supporters… the decision for Serie A to return to collective selling of broadcast rights from 2010 is likely to mean a reduction in the level of broadcast revenue for top Italian clubs going forward. This places greater urgency on the club to address revenue generation from its stadium and falling matchday income in order to challenge for a top five position in future years.'

Why are the revenues of Italian clubs so highly concentrated on TV rights? Professors Tito Boeri and Battista Devergnini think that, 'A possible explanation relates to the governance structure and ownership of the clubs . . . much of the energy of the Italian Lega Calcio is spent on negotiations over TV rights, rather than investing in public goods, such as campaigns promoting stadium attendance, and technologies reducing the forgery of football merchandise and the violation of trademarks . . . owners can be easily blackmailed by organised groups threatening . . .' They point out that non-violent supporters and local communities are not involved in the ownership structure, which reduces their incentives to go to stadiums and contribute to isolating violent groups of supporters. The member-owned clubs like Real Madrid, Barcelona and Bayern Munich have such an incentive.

Poor Corporate Governance

In Italy, regional industrial families used the operating cash flow of their industrial business interests to cover their football club losses. There was no external monitoring or scrutiny with a private ownership model or pressure to make the business self-sustaining. The decision-making is focused on maximising what the regional industrial family or owner wants, which typically is to win at all costs and to have power and prestige. Accepting this relationship, the typical fans focus on winning at all costs, which, in turn, pushes owners to spend as much as they possibly can. Then, fans only care if the owners are wealthier, and more willing, to outspend rivals and competitors for the best possible players. The fan has no vested interest in the sustainability either. Business models become unsustainable, rational financial management is de-emphasised and complacency exists as long as the result, which is winning, is being achieved.

As Italian clubs lost money and needed capital, in order to raise money (which was difficult to do and still maintain control as this would open the club to scrutiny from potentially sophisticated investors), a few Italian clubs listed on the stock exchanges. The first to list was SS Lazio in 1998, followed by Juventus in 2001 and AS Roma in 2002. It was easier to raise capital than to search for ways to diversify revenues or to sell stakes to parties that may require financial and regulatory transparency. Although publicly listed, the clubs were still controlled by Italian families.

At many English Premier League clubs there was a history where football clubs had some sort of advisory role as they were unofficial fundraisers for the owners to build or upgrade stadiums or purchase land. There was some sort of formal dialogue with ownership. In 2000, the UK government funded the creation of Supporters Direct, an organisation directed to enhancing the role of fans in the running of the football clubs they support. There are over 170 Supporter Trusts in the UK. Not all of them have representation on the board of their club, but they have influence and secure a greater level of accountability. Member-owned clubs, such as Real Madrid, Barcelona and Bayern Munich, have an interesting corporate governance mechanism in that the members vote every few years as to who the president should be. In Real Madrid's case, the socios/members of the club ousted the incumbent president that delivered two Champions League trophies in three years, and their first in 32 years, in part, because of concerns about management malpractice. The socios/members had a vested interest in self-regulating and had the ability to vote and take action.

Real Madrid and Barcelona are member-owned clubs with the right to vote for a president. German fans have a '50%+1' ownership model. In Italy this does not exist, which provides an environment for owners to make decisions or utilise the club in a manner that suits him/her. In general, the Italian clubs' relationships with the fans are poor. The idea of relinquishing some control to the values and expectations of fans to help build a brand and identity which leads to more loyalty and passion was (and is) unheard of in Italy. In some ways, this is the secret to the commercial success of member-owned clubs such as Real Madrid, Barcelona and Bayern Munich. It is also a key driver to the capacity-filled stadiums in Germany, where there is a sense of community and managing the club for the community. The stadium experience (from ticket prices to the quality of seats and views) in Germany meets the values and expectations of the owner-members versus an owner being more concerned with his/her and his/her friends' experiences. Interestingly, member-owned clubs like Real Madrid have their own member discipline committees to fine, suspend or expel members for not adhering to the proper code of conduct at home or away matches.

Real Madrid, Barcelona and Bayern Munich have incredibly passionate, loyal and supportive fan bases, and are financially sustainable. The clubs have to be self-sustaining because there is no billionaire owner to subsidise the losses. In North America there is only one club that has community-member, not-for-profit ownership – the 'American football' NFL's Green Bay Packers. Green Bay, Wisconsin has a population of 105,139. The Packers have an exceptionally loyal fan base. Regardless of team performance, every game played in Green Bay has been sold out since 1960 (and many of the games are played in freezing temperatures and snow). They also have one of the longest season ticket waiting lists in professional sport: 86,000 names long, more than there are seats at Lambeau Field. The average wait is said to be over 30 years and the Green Bay Packers' shirt is the highest selling shirt in the NFL. Perhaps, it's partly because the club is managed to meet the values and expectations of its 360,584 shareholders versus one billionaire owner. As a publicly held non-profit team, the Packers are also the only American major league sports franchise to release its financial balance sheet every year, similar to Real Madrid, Barcelona and Bayern Munich. Real Madrid, Barcelona and Bayern Munich's members review and approve financial budgets. This ownership and corporate governance structure may make fans feel more responsibility to and passionate about their club since they have some say in matters.

Interestingly, in 1998, Sir John Smith wrote in his report on English football the following recommendation: 'No person should own more than 10% of the shares in any football club – thereby defeating the possibility of a single person treating a club as his, or her, personal fiefdom.' The recommendation was probably a non-starter since the clubs are owned in the manner that they are, but the idea of ownership believing that the fans don't exist to serve the business or management; rather, the club exists to serve the fans may be the centre of a sustainable economic-sport model.

Lack of Global Vision

The former Netherlands star and Ballon d'Or winner while with Milan in 1988/89 Marco van Basten said in an interview with *La Gazzetta dello Sport* in 2017: 'I cannot even bear thinking about Inter and Milan being run by Chinese owners . . . Such glorious clubs must remain in Italian hands. It's not just about history, but also passion. That is priceless.' He went on to add: 'The mistake was in thinking of the money too much,' with 'everything being done for the armchair spectator but nothing for the fans.' Van Basten is expressing a common opinion amongst Italians who are Serie A fans. Many Italian football fans believe that one can only truly understand what 'calcio' is all about if one is Italian.

Their opinions may not be a realistic approach in today's global business of football. Football has become a global entertainment business with global brands and identities. In order to generate revenues and grow to afford the best players, the league and clubs do need to attract the incremental global 'armchair' fan, while balancing not to upset the local fans and authentic identity of the club. This is a very tricky management balance, especially with the football market saturated and other leagues and clubs' investments. In addition, one of the reasons Serie A did not have the resources to compete was the idea that Serie A clubs should stay in Italian hands. The attitude, in addition to other factors, may have limited foreign investment which was necessary to compete. The English Premier League was the easiest for and most open to foreign investment, and the league benefited tremendously from this advantage.

Most owners and managers of Serie A clubs, and the league itself, are very focused on not upsetting local or Italian supporters and what the Italian or local press says. The intense local obsession with the club actually distracts management from the real growth opportunity, which is global fans. The league and owners are afraid to crack down on even unruly fans because of potential boycotts of matches, resulting in immediate loss of revenues, even if it is out of step with the values and expectations of many global fans. Too much management time is spent addressing local media, as opposed to building relationships with the international media. Most clubs don't have a physical presence outside of Italy. Many football clubs don't have multilingual management teams with work experience outside of Italy. Most Italian football clubs do not have English or other language translations on social media or in their websites. They don't have employees developing content that appeals to fans in different countries. The attitude is most likely a result of the clubs being utilised for local business connections and social and political capital.

Italian clubs are going to have to compete against clubs that transcend their country by identity and ownership. The English Premier League (Chelsea, Manchester United, Manchester City, Liverpool) benefited by embracing foreign ownership with significant resources and new ideas. PSG benefited from foreign ownership with significant resources and new ideas. Staying 'Italian' with primarily Italian ownership has limited the resources and ideas in the league, as well as making it too local a fan base when the revenues require a large global fan base to compete for world-class talent and build world-class infrastructure.

Besides the Premier League's openness to foreign owners, the EPL has been accepting of foreign managers and players. When Arsène Wenger became Arsenal's manager in 1996 he was only the fourth appointee from outside Britain and Ireland in English history. In his final season in 2017/18, he was one of 13, making the Premier League the only big-five division with a majority of foreigners in the dugout. And whereas on its first weekend in 1992 only 13 of those players who appeared were foreign, in the 2015/16 season 69% of players were, much higher than any other European league.

English teams have also been quicker than others to market themselves abroad. Manchester United began making regular pre-season trips to Asia in 1995, whereas Real Madrid did so only in 2003. With its three African sponsors, Arsenal has as many as continental Europe's five richest teams put together.

Lack of Professional Development

European football was notorious for hiring family and friends of owners, managers and players. There was no training or professionalism. When Florentino Pérez was elected president of Real Madrid he found that they needed to develop talent into sports management professionals with the skills to adapt to changes. A professional career in sports management was a new idea. Various areas required expertise such as digital media, sports analytics and sports event management. Therefore, they started Universidad Europea – Escuela Universitaria Real Madrid. Barcelona also started their own. Clubs in Italy have been slow to recognise the changes and need to hire graduates from sports management or business schools or build their own schools to develop young talent. And give young people an opportunity.

Off-the-Pitch Issues: Country

Patrimonial Ownership

Professor Mark Doidge in *Football Italia – Italian Football in an Age of Globalization* concluded that Italy's political construction has led to a state evolving through cronyism, as individuals sought to maintain power through a patrimonial system of patronage and corruption. He argues that the continued practice of patrimonial networks undermines the state and institutions, reinforcing hegemonic positions of already powerful groups and individuals.[14]

An important part of Italian culture is that direct and indirect relationships that are through families and companies and politicians are an accepted part of the governance structure of Italian corporate culture. In Italy, football consists of powerful individuals connected with powerful families connected with popular clubs, political parties and the media, who are in prominent positions to 'influence' decisions regardless of potential conflicts of interest. Unlike in the UK or the US, there are limited concerns about objectivity.

You can start to get a sense of the oligarchical power structure in Italy with no separation of powers or sense of conflicts of interest. If anything, a conflict of interest can be viewed as a positive, not a negative. For example, Lazio were facing bankruptcy because they had too much debt and a substantial unpaid tax liability. Then Roman entrepreneur Claudio Lotito purchased control of Lazio. Lotito made most of his money in a cleaning, security and catering business to mostly government-related entities, including while Berlusconi was in government. In 2004, Berlusconi said, 'Lazio has many fans and we are scared about the social impact and consequences of a bankruptcy, so we help Lazio by rolling its debt with the government into the next 23 years.' Thanks to Berlusconi's government, Lazio were able to roll the €140 million taxes due over that time period.[15] Lazio obviously have a large number of supporters who vote. In Italy there is a word, 'lottizzazione', which means dividing the spoils.

---

14 Ramon Llopis-Goig, *European Journal for Sport and Society*, Volume 14, 2017 No 1, 82–84
15 http://www.ilsole24ore.com/art/SoleOnLine4/dossier/Italia/2009/commenti-sole-24-ore/11-novembre-2009/adr-lotito-appalto-impresa-pulizie_PRN.shtml; http://espresso.repubblica.it/archivio/appoggio/2010/01/29/news/lotito-al-tramonto-1.124433

Berlusconi not only owned AC Milan, he also owned three TV stations that broadcast football and the advertising agency that had the Italian national team as a client.[16] Berlusconi counted on voters being dazzled by AC Milan's success. His political party was called 'Forza Italia', which is the most common football cheer for the national team, as in 'Come On, Italy!' or 'Go Italy!'. Many of Forza Italia's regional offices were in the same places as current or former supporters' clubs for AC Milan. In May 1994 his government faced a no-confidence vote in parliament. The vote was held when Berlusconi's club was beating Barcelona 2-0 in the Champions League final (Milan would win 4-0). When asked about the disappointing results of Forza Italia at the March 2018 elections he responded, 'First we did poorly because I was not able to be elected, second because all the issues they gave me the past years, and third, and we looked at that with our polls people, because I sold Milan, because we had many Milanisti voting for us and they thought I sold Milan to make money and now every time they watch Milan they have a pain in their stomach.' It seems Berlusconi links politics with Milan.[17]

Tobias Jones in *The Dark Heart of Italy* (2003) wrote, 'I've tried to explain the situation to English friends: "Just imagine Prince Charles and Tony Blair both own football teams, a few newspapers, and probably the odd television channel, and you begin to get the idea."' Jones argues that the consequence of the power structure is that 'it feeds suspicion because many people perceive football as prey to obscure powers.'

The scale and significance of the Italian industrial oligarchies provided an initial advantage when salaries were affordable for them, but then as the business of football became big and global, the structure became a hindrance. The patrimonial system restricts Italian football's ability to implement radical necessary changes and has hindered Italian football from being a global player.

Nepotistic System that Promotes Family and Friends

Italian football was based on a few very powerful oligarchies. Family and friends were given titles and jobs, not just at the football club, but in politics and the media. Children, relatives, friends and loyal workers

---

16 http://www.myjuventus.net/all-the-truth-about-juventus-other-clubs-scandals.html

17 http://www.itasportpress.it/serie-a/clamoroso-berlusconi-andra-a-finire-che-ricomprero-il-milan/

got to become a part of the football entourage, which could be a stop on the way to parliament or working in the family's media empire or conglomerate. The really difficult point was the centralisation of all powers in one person or a few people with limited chances for others to grow. Sons and daughters of owners or important businessmen would become 'agents', which meant they took a percentage of club transfer fees.

In *Capello: Portrait Of A Winner*, sports journalist and author Gab Marcotti wrote: 'But Capello did not stop there. "There are conflicts of interest everywhere and, in ethical terms, it's not ideal," he added. "I'm not just talking about Moggi here . . . we have a company like GEA which is operating almost in a monopoly situation. They control six managers and 100 or so players. It's an obvious conflict of interest. And there could be obvious repercussions. But I'm not the one who should be thinking about this. The people who run football should be looking at this.' Because of his stature, Capello's words carry weight. He had said what many probably believed, but nobody would state for the record.

GEA World was a football agency founded in 2001 and run by Alessandro Moggi (son of Luciano of Juventus) with the help of a number of influential shareholders, all of them scions of powerful figures in the Italian game: Chiara Geronzi (daughter of Cesare, the then-head of Capitalia, Italy's second biggest bank, which provides lines of credit to a number of Italian clubs), Francesca Tanzi (daughter of Calisto, the then-head of Parmalat and then-Parma owner), Davide Lippi (son of Marcello, then head of Italy's national team), Riccardo Calleri (son of Sergio, the then-Lazio owner) and Giuseppe De Mita (a former Lazio executive and son of Ciriaco, a former Italian prime minister). It wasn't just the appearance of nepotism; it was, as Capello pointed out, that it could be at least the appearance of potential conflicts of interest. GEA was linked to a whole galaxy of clubs and managers, and its chief executive was the son of the sporting director of Italy's biggest and most powerful club. GEA had over 200 Italian players and coaches as clients. In the aftermath of the Calciopoli scandal, GEA would come under attack. GEA and its shareholders were thoroughly investigated, and no charges were filed directly related to the scandal.

A politically significant example of the nepotistic system is the link between Libya and Italian football. Libya was an Italian colony at one time. Fiat had close ties to Libya and now-deceased Libyan leader Colonel

Muammar Gaddafi. Libya came to the rescue of Fiat in 1977 when its founder, Giovanni Agnelli, invited Libya's main foreign investment arm, the Libyan Arab Foreign Investment Company (Lafico) to buy a stake of about 15% in the struggling carmaker.

Lafico sold that stake in 1986, but in 2002 it bought just over 2% of the company. Football was a space where the ties could be utilised and reinforced. In addition, in 2002 Lafico purchased a 7.5% stake in Juventus and Colonel Gaddafi's son Al-Saadi Gaddafi joined the board of Juventus. The Supercoppa Italiana was held in the Libyan capital Tripoli in 2002. From 2002 to 2007, the state-owned oil company of Libya, Tamoil, was an official sponsor of Juventus. In 2003, Al-Saadi Gaddafi resigned from the Juventus board and signed a two-year contract to play for Luciano Gaucci's Perugia football club in Serie A. He didn't play all season until he was sent on the pitch as a second-half substitute with Perugia leading Juventus 1-0 and 15 minutes left in the game. *La Gazzetta dello Sport* reported: '[He entered] the pitch one minute after the dismissal of [Ciro] Ferrara [the Juventus centre back] . . . effectively restoring numerical parity'. Gaucci stated that 'Berlusconi called me up and encouraged me. He told me that having Gaddafi in the team is helping us build a relationship with Libya. If he plays badly, he plays badly. So be it.' (Foot 2011). Perugia went bankrupt in 2005.

Accusations of nepotism continue today. For example, Gianluigi Donnarumma celebrated not only his lucrative new contract at AC Milan but also the club's move to re-sign his older brother, Antonio, who shares the same agent. Antonio's deal was confirmed a day after Gianluigi signed a new contract at the San Siro. The elder Donnarumma is a former Milan youth keeper, who left to move to Genoa in 2012, where he only made one Serie A appearance in four years. Milan sporting director Massimiliano Mirabelli insists he was not just signed to help keep Gianluigi happy. He said, 'The first thing we had to do was to renew Gigio's contract, but I immediately had the idea of bringing in his brother Antonio too . . . The technical evaluation comes first and I think Antonio can be a 12th man for Milan.'[18]

Milan, where Kaká won the Ballon d'Or and World Player of the Year award in 2007 (played from 2003 to 2009), signed Kaká's younger

---

18 https://www.fourfourtwo.com/us/news/ac-milan-re-sign-antonio-donnarumma-brother-gianluigi#EMkEBCKYcmWWlSf8.99

brother Digão, who played as a central defender (Kaká reportedly got his nickname after his younger brother, Digão, mispronounced his name, Ricardo). After Kaká left for Real Madrid in 2009, AC Milan announced that Digão would be loaned to a Serie B club. The New York Red Bulls signed Digão in 2012. After playing in only one match for the Red Bulls, they mutually terminated their arrangement, leading to reported speculation that the club had given up on its pursuit of Kaká and that the brother was added to the club in an effort to recruit Kaká. Kaká would play for Orlando City in the MLS from 2015 to 2017.

Harvey Esajas, a Dutch defender, played seven matches for a second level Dutch club in the 1998/99 season. He then decided to move abroad to try to make it in Italy or Spain. He didn't succeed. He disappeared from the world of football for several years and worked at a Spanish circus and as a dishwasher. He then visited his close friend Clarence Seedorf, who played at AC Milan. Seedorf is regarded by many as one of the best midfielders of his generation, and in 2004, he was chosen by Pelé as part of the FIFA 100 best players. Even though he weighed 100 kg and had not touched competitive professional football in years, Milan coach Carlo Ancelotti eventually put Esajas in the squad where he was given a few minutes of play in one Italian Cup match in 2004/05, and was part of the Milan squad that lost to Liverpool in the 2005 Champions League final (although he was not on the pitch or bench for the match). At the end of the season, he moved to a Serie C club.[19]

Favourable Regulatory Changes that Hid the Problems

Italian football clubs had not established sustainable economic-sport models, and player transfer fees and salaries were rising. However, the football clubs have tremendous social importance, so Italian government officials in power tried to intervene and help the Italian football clubs.

In 2001, one of Berlusconi's first legislative acts was the introduction of changes in 'falso in bilancio' or 'false accounting'. False accounting was changed from being a criminal offence of danger to a crime of 'damage', and a minor infringement with a fine. In addition, the statute of limitations of 15 years was halved. At the time, the Judicial Affairs

---

[19] http://www.punditarena.com/football/cheffernan/strange-story-harvey-esajas/

Committee, which was involved in the legislation, had members that had worked as lawyers for Berlusconi in the past. The legislative change could have helped owners of football clubs who were using false accounting.

In 2002, Silvio Berlusconi as prime minister introduced the Salva Calcio decree, literally 'save football'. The decree allowed player transfers to be written off over an arbitrary ten years rather than the actual length of the players' contracts. This would improve the financial performance of the clubs by spreading the losses over more years. The amounts are staggering. Before Salva Calcio, for example, reportedly, Inter claimed player assets of €357 million, and after the decree were reportedly left with assets of €38 million. (Reportedly, Juventus and Sampdoria did not make use of the law.) The decree was challenged by the EU Minister for Internal Markets and in 2005 a compromise was reached allowing the assets to be written off over five years. As a result, the clubs had to overcome yet another capital shortfall, which later led to another financial gimmick.

Clubs were allowed to re-evaluate the value of their brand and disguise debt. The sale of the brand to oneself reportedly allowed for example AC Milan to save €181 million, Inter €159 million and Lazio €95 million. Roma, Sampdoria and other clubs also used this accounting trick.[20] The money that the subsidiary company pays to the one selling the brand comes from a bank loan. This way the assignee (the selling club) pays every year the capital quota of the loan, plus the interest. The entire money circle is a bank loan in disguise, which allows financially troubled clubs to spread the debt over many more years. In 2006, CoViSoC (the Italian Professional Football Financial Control Committee) defined this operation as an accounting gimmick that is used as a substitute for recapitalisation. CoViSoC did not declare such transactions as illegitimate, but it cancelled the economic effects of this operation with regards to the minimum requirements that football clubs must fulfil in order to register in the Italian championships. Therefore, those clubs that did not meet said minimum requirements would have had to obtain a recapitalisation from their shareholders. For example, Inter and Milan were reportedly requested to increase capital by around €100 million.[21]

---

20 'Il Sole 24 Ore', 2006. From the article it appears Juventus did not use this trick.
21 For the description of each operation, see 'Stato dell'arte e prospettive dell'azienda calcio in Italia: un approccio economico aziendale', Mario Nicoliello, 2007.

In 2011, Professor of Business Management at the Catholic University of the Sacred Heart, Baroncelli and Raul Caruso, Senior Researcher, wrote '. . . even in the face of the enormous economic interests, the regulatory framework into which [Italian] football has entered . . . has been inspired by opaque principles and, notwithstanding the numerous scandals that have occurred . . . Politicians and football authorities, in particular, have demonstrated a clear opportunistic behaviour by exploiting the popular impact of football, tolerating widespread illegality in the management of clubs . . .'

Lack of Financial and Regulatory Transparency

Although patrimonial networks and TV rights gave Italian clubs an advantage in the early years of the Champions League, they were not able to capitalise on the globalised market. Being a part of the business networks of families didn't provide greater financial or management professionalism.

By the late 1990s, many Serie A and Serie B clubs began to regularly resort to various accounting gimmicks in order to create the perception of better corporate situations, including false guarantees, tax debts and fictitious profits on players' sales (*'financial doping'*). The Prosecutor of Rome, between 1999 and 2002, started investigating financial doping. This may have contributed to why so many clubs started to declare bankruptcy.

The excessive exchanges of players that occurred between Inter and AC Milan between 1999 and 2004 clearly explain how clubs booked fictitious profits on players' sales. Between the seasons 1999/2000 and 2001/02 the two clubs from Milan exchanged Paolo Ginestra and Matteo Bogani, Fabio Di Sauro and Davide Cordone, Andrea Polizzano and Marco Bonura: each transaction yielded a profit for each of the players of around €3.5 to €5 million, which was a lot of money considering the average prices for which their teammates had been transferred to other clubs. In the 2002/03 season, another exchange of two quartets of players happened between the clubs. Milan sold Simone Brunelli, Matteo Definite, Matteo Giordano and Ronny Toma in exchange for Inter's players Salvatore Ferraro, Alessandro Livi, Giuseppe Ticli and Marco

Varaldi. The total price of the transactions amounted to €14 million. Through these operations, Milan obtained a profit on the players' sales of €12 million and Inter's profit totalled €14 million.

Later on, Inter and Milan also exchanged more famous players, for example the trade involving Francesco Coco and Clarence Seedorf, where both clubs collected €29 million. Other players involved were Andrea Pirlo, Andres Guglielminpietro, Dario Simic, Cyril Domoraud, Christian Brocchi and Umit Davala. Examining the Hernan Crespo deal more closely, Inter bought the Argentinian player for €38 million in the 2002/03 season with the amount amortised over four years, therefore €9.5 million per year. The following year, 2003/04, Crespo was sold to Chelsea for €24 million; consequently the financial statement recorded a loss of €4.5 million, but it did not happen. Instead, Inter registered in its financial statement a profit on players' sales of €21 million. Essentially, the value of the player on 30 June 2003 dropped to €4 million and then rose to €24 million in two months. However, in accordance with article 2426 of the Italian Civil Code, the valuation of an asset must be recorded as the purchase cost. After three seasons on the Inter books, Pirlo was sold to rivals AC Milan for €17 million on 30 June 2001, the last day of the 2000/01 financial year. The transfer fee was partially funded by the movement of Dražen Brnčić in the opposite direction for an undisclosed fee. In the same window Inter swapped Cristian Brocchi for Guly and Matteo Bogani for Paolo Ginestra. The deals were later reported by the Italian press to have been undertaken to create 'false profit' by inflating the players' values in the transfer fees in the swap deal. The exchange involving Ginestra and Bogani created an approximate €3.5 million 'profit' for both clubs.

The fictitious profit on players' sales did not solve the problem, it just postponed and then exacerbated it. Then the Italian legislator decided to help the owners by letting them take advantage of a negative external factor, the decrease in TV rights revenue. TV broadcasters, in the season 2002/03, offered a lower amount of money to clubs compared with previous years. The government used this as an excuse to enact the law 23/2003 (called the 'save football' or 'spreads debts' decree). It was said that clubs, receiving less money from television broadcasters, could no longer bear the increasing costs of the recent past and so it was necessary to depreciate the excess value over ten years to bring it to the current market value. In this way, the evaluation surpluses were diluted over a long period versus taking a one-time hit and requiring more equity. Thanks to the rule, the ficticious values of players' contracts could be reduced over time. The amounts were staggering. Inter depreciated players for €319 million, Milan for €242 million, Roma for €234 million, Lazio for €213 million and Parma for €180 million.[22] Once again, this just postponed and then exacerbated problems.

In addition, stock market flotations of Lazio, Juventus and Roma didn't provide as much financial professionalism or transparency as expected. The significant drops in share prices since their IPOs for Lazio, Juventus and Roma are below. For initial investors, the investments have been a financial disaster.

Share price change for publicly listed clubs v. total return (including dividends) for selected stock indices.

	Lazio	*Roma*	*Juventus*
Date of IPO	6-May-982	3-May-00	20-Dec-01
Club Stock Price % Change Since IPO	-93.5%	-80.0%	-48.0%
FTSE MIB % Change Since IPO	5.3%	-17.4%	13.3%
Euro Stoxx 600 % Change Since IPO	91.8%	46.9%	84.0%

In 2017, then Inter Milan president Erick Thohir urged Serie A to be friendlier to improve financial and regulatory transparency. 'Look at Major League Soccer (MLS); a lot of foreign investors are in the US because the way the industry is structured is very transparent and for investors it is secure. They understand before coming to the game what to expect,' he said.

Regardless of the investment sector, global investors typically place a premium on investing in the US because of its relative transparent legal, institutional and economic framework; policy decisions and their rationale; availability and accessibility of understandable data and information; timely decision-making; reporting requirements and supervisory practices; and accountability placed on leadership. There is a higher degree of confidence versus many other countries. England and Germany also benefit from this sense of confidence. Transparency and confidence enhances the efficiency

---

[22] Bianchi F., 'Ue, bocciato il decreto salva calcio. Molte società a rischio fallimento', *La Repubblica*, 1 November 2003

and valuations. This contributed to English clubs getting new foreign investors with capital to invest into the league.

Italy is more challenging, not just from a language/translation perspective, but the opaqueness of financial reporting and regulations. In financial speak, Italian football has 'high risk premium' for investment. Thohir said, 'Serie A is not easy . . . it's a challenge for everyone in football in Italy to be more transparent and open.' Getting foreigners to invest is, and will continue to be, more challenging, let alone at the same valuations in England or Germany because of the risk premium. It also may be more difficult for sponsors to feel comfortable with marketing metrics and contracts.

Forgery of Football Merchandise

According to Professors Alessandro Baroncelli and Umberto Lago (2006), Italian supporters are less likely to buy official merchandise from their own team than most European fans. In addition, in Italy there is more widespread forgery of football merchandise due to a large black-market economy. According to a new study published by the Institute for Applied Economic Research at the University of Tübingen in Germany (IAW), the Greek shadow economy is estimated to average 21.5% of GDP. Its fellow southern European states of Italy and Spain have shadow economies of 19.8% and 17.2% of GDP respectively. Germany and the UK are 10.4% and 9.4% respectively. Fake football merchandise is surprisingly sold right in front of most major football stadiums. This is a major loss for the club and the shirt sponsor (also because they have no store like that in front of big stadiums to sell official shirts).

2017 Percentage of Shadow Economy

Country	Percentage
Italy	19.8%
Spain	17.2%
Germany	10.4%
UK	9.4%

Source: https://www.forbes.com/sites/niallmccarthy/2017/02/09/where-the-worlds-shadow-economies-are-firmly-established-infographic/#9db1e4b742cc

Besides investing in creating global community brands, there must be improvement in protecting their brands in order for the clubs to generate additional revenues. For example, in June 2017, hours before the start of the Champions League final, Italian police seized more than 250,000 counterfeit T-shirts and other merchandise bearing the logos of Champions League finalists Juventus and Real Madrid. Police said the fake items, produced near Juventus's Turin base, would have had an estimated sale value of around €2.5 million, half of what officially licensed merchandise would retail for.[23]

Strong Presence of Organised Crime

Aligi Pontani, the managing editor for sports at the Italian daily newspaper *La Repubblica*, identified a number of structural, cultural and managerial issues including a 'strong, pervasive presence of organised crime' in Italian football.[24] Sophisticated criminal enterprises have professionalised corruption in football, according to a blog by Declan Hill, a Canadian journalist and author of *The Fix: Soccer and Organized Crime*. In 2012, FIFPro issued a report after interviewing more than 3,000 players in southern and eastern Europe. About 12% said they had been approached about fixing a match. Nearly a quarter said they were aware of match-fixing in their domestic leagues. Particularly vulnerable, FIFPro said, are players who frequently go long periods without being paid and face threats of violence if they do not cooperate in manipulating matches. There are several instances in Italian football where players reportedly were not paid, even in Serie A.

In 2011, an Italian football scandal emerged after a number of football-related figures were arrested or were being investigated by Italian police for alleged match-fixing. The scandal is also known as Operation: Last Bet, *Calcio Scommesse* ('Football Bet') or Scommessopoli ('Bet City' or 'Betting-gate'). The origins of the scandal were in the summer of 2011. After a member of Serie B side Cremonese suffered a serious car crash, tests showed that he and other members of the team had been drugged with sleeping pills. The culprit was one of their own teammates, who

---

23 https://www.thelocal.it/20170603/football-italy-police-score-with-cl-counterfeit-swoop
24 https://www.nytimes.com/2012/06/03/sports/soccer/stain-of-scandal-again-taints-italian-soccer.html

had been attempting to pay off a mounting series of gambling debts by arranging a series of defeats for his bookies. Cremonese's unexpected winning streak had forced him to take desperate measures. It soon became clear that Cremonese was merely the tip of the iceberg. The Italian authorities discovered that players and coaches of several clubs were approached or approached others to fix matches.

In the *Financial Times* on 9 February 2018, Simon Kuper made the following observation about football club Olympique de Marseille (OM) who beat Milan in 1993 for the Champions League trophy but have since fallen behind big clubs: 'Marseille weren't well placed to lure a sugar daddy, partly because the city's powerful mafias have always tried to interfere with the club. Tapie [former owner of Marseille] says that when he bought OM [Marseille] for a symbolic single franc in 1986, mafiosi ran the club's snack bars and merchandise stands. He claims to have solved the security problem by bringing in martial arts athletes as guards. But as recently as 2013, Adrien Anigo, a jewel thief and the son of OM's then sporting director José Anigo, was gunned down in Marseille in a gangland killing.'[25]

Challenging Demographics

Fewer babies were born in Italy in 2014 than in any other year since the modern Italian state was formed in 1861, highlighting the challenging demographics. The number of babies born to both natives and foreigners living in Italy dropped as immigration, which used to support the overall birth rate, tumbled to its lowest level for five years. 'We are very close to the threshold of non-renewal where the people dying are not replaced by newborns. That means we are a dying country,' an Italian health minister said. This situation has enormous implications for every sector: the economy, society, health, pensions, just to give a few examples. Obviously, it affects the numbers of potential new fans in Italy. This highlights why Italian clubs need to be focused on global growth. The southern regions are expected to see a steady decrease in population over the next 50 years. The centre-north is already more populated than the south, and this trend is projected to become even

---

25 https://www.ft.com/content/19455408-0b96-11e8-839d-41ca06376bf2

more marked. Currently, 66% of people live in the centre-north. By 2065, that percentage is expected to shift to 71%.

The main factor that distinguishes Italian from Spanish demographics is migration. The immigration boom and bust that occurred in Spain, especially since the beginning of the 21st century, did not take place in Italy. The impact on population growth was substantial. Although the population aged over 65 increased at the same rate in both countries, the Spanish immigration boom helped rejuvenate the demographic base, which did not happen in Italy. These trends finally resulted in clearly different ageing rates. In other words, Italy has a worse demographic structure than Spain, a fact that could weigh heavily on the country's future. Germany has an even worse demographic issue. This information may also support reducing the number of clubs in Serie A.

2060 Estimated Population by Country from the European Union in millions

Country	2010	2060 (est.)
UK	62	78
France	64	73
Germany	81	66
Italy	60	64
Spain	45	52
EU27	501	517

* The British birth rate is now at its highest in a generation, while Germany has had below replacement fertility for 45 years. Germany already welcomes anywhere from 100,000 to 200,000 immigrants every year, but the German population is shrinking.

Source: europa.eu/rapid/press-release_STAT-11-80_en.doc

Challenging Economic Situation

While Italy is the world's ninth largest economy in GDP Purchasing Power Parity (PPP) terms (with Spain in 14th place), it has poor growth. Italy has consistently underperformed compared with the rest of the euro area during the past three decades, a trend which started long before the introduction of the euro and has deteriorated in the aftermath of the financial crisis. Italy's very low growth performance could jeopardise its global geo-economic position and become a heavy burden for future generations. Italy, once a manufacturing powerhouse, is also experiencing weaker external competitiveness and its exports are growing less than world trade, so Italy is losing global market share.

In comparing Spanish and Italian GDP growth, in annual terms the difference seems somewhat limited. However, the contrast between cumulative growths is significant, 50% since 1997 in Spain versus 10% in Italy. Moreover, according to EU forecasts, in 2018 Spain will surpass Italy in per capita GDP (in PPP terms) for the first time ever. In Spain there was a property bubble that caused big problems in the construction and real estate sector, but that was very concentrated. In Italy there is more of a long-term problem that is linked to the lack of economic growth over decades. Examining bankruptcies filed for both economies, it's clear that both countries had a relatively similar trend in bankruptcies until very recently. Bankruptcies in Italy have been increasing while bankruptcies in Spain have been decreasing. It is estimated that there are €360 billion of bad loans from Italian banks to borrowers weighed down with debts they cannot afford. Therefore, the banks are struggling to offer new credit to the households and firms that need them. The IMF projects the Italian economy will not get back to its pre-crisis size until 2025. Obviously, it has and will be more challenging for Italian clubs to borrow money from Italian banks. This will also cause more pressure for Italian football clubs to look for new equity capital, most likely outside of Italy.

Although Italy has significantly less unemployment than Spain (11.5% versus 19.7%), more Italians than Spaniards don't look for work. From 1990 to 2014, female participation has risen from 34% to 53% in Spain, in comparison, from 35% to only 40% in Italy. Hence, although there is a much lower unemployment rate in Italy, their inactivity rate is much higher than Spain's.

Dysfunctional Justice System

Italy has more laws on its statute books than any other European country, but in the media Italians have been portrayed as considering them to be 'mere suggestions, polite recommendations, and even paternalistic forms of advice', rather than binding rules.

Italy's justice system has long been one of the most dysfunctional in Europe. Prosecutors say it is all but impossible to reach a definitive verdict for a multitude of crimes within the prescribed time frame. That's partly because legal cases take so long in Italy. But it is also because Italy is unique in Europe. Its statute of limitations starts from the moment an alleged crime is committed rather than from the point it is discovered, and the time limit is not extended when a defendant is put under investigation or charged or sentenced. No other major European country has both rules. In addition, unlike most European countries, Italy counts the time when a first conviction is being appealed as part of the limitation period. As many cases take years to come to court in the first place, with suspects then allowed two appeals with hearings that can stretch over months, convicted criminals can often rely on running out the clock to avoid jail.

According to website *L'incredibile Parlamento Italiano*, more than 90 Italian parliamentarians – almost one in ten – have either already benefited from the statute of limitations or are currently on trial or under investigation for white-collar crimes and misdemeanours, many of which have a short judicial shelf life. Only 286 people are serving time in Italian jails for white-collar offences compared with 7,986 in Germany, according to the Council of Europe. To speed up the justice system, Italy could hire thousands more judges, but with the current challenging economic situation, the government most likely can't afford it.[26]

In June 2017, Italian lawmakers approved a new law extending a series of statutes of limitations for court cases, a move aimed at reducing the number of criminals who escape punishment because of Italy's slow judicial system.

The lack of transparency and dysfunctional justice system makes it difficult to punish unethical behaviour that is prevalent in Italian football. It also discourages potential investment in football clubs from foreign investors.

---

[26] https://www.reuters.com/investigates/special-report/italy-justice/

Italian Not a Global Language

Italians have a low percentage of English language speakers amongst European countries. With players and management not as familiar with English, it makes it more difficult to market globally. It also makes it more difficult to attract investment as many international business people with capital are comfortable speaking English, they see major cities in the UK like London as a safe and attractive place to spend time and are comfortable with English financial and legal transparency.

The language may not have mattered as much in the 1980s and 1990s as fans passively watched football as a sport with a commentator. Today, interaction and engagement are critical to building and keeping fans. A common language helps, although over time, content will need to be more local to compete. The English Premier League certainly benefited from having a more common language.

English Language Knowledge in European Countries

Country	Percentage
UK	95%
Greece	33%
Germany	32%
France	24%
Portugal	15%
Italy	14%
Spain	12%

Source: http://languageknowledge.eu/languages/english

Although Spain has lower English knowledge, Spanish is the world's second most spoken native language, after Mandarin Chinese. In the EU, Spanish is spoken as a second language by 8% of the EU population. Italian is spoken as a second language by 3% of the population. In the EU, Italian is the fourth most taught foreign language after Spanish, French and German, in that order. Although over 17 million Americans are of Italian descent, less than one million people in the United States speak Italian at home. In addition, there has been a decrease in the number of Italian speakers in the United States. The percentage change from 1980 to 2010 was a negative 55%.

US Census Bureau Number of Italian Speakers

Year	Number
1980	1,614,344
1990	1,308,648
2000	1,008,370
2010	725,223

In contrast there are 41 million native Spanish speakers in the US plus a further 11.6 million who are bilingual, mainly the children of Spanish-speaking immigrants. This puts the US ahead of Colombia (48 million) and Spain (46 million) and second only to Mexico (121 million).

On-the-Pitch Issues: Technology

Impact of Video Games

Juventus defender Andrea Barzagli described Cristiano Ronaldo's bicycle kick for Real Madrid against Juventus in the Champions League quarter-final as 'a PlayStation goal' that 'will go down in history'. There is a convergence of video games and the actual sport on the pitch.

For millions of football fans across the world, video games – primarily the record-high-selling FIFA series from Electronic Arts, but also its rival series Pro Evolution Soccer and the more cerebral Football Manager – act as both a gateway introduction to football and, later, another way of satisfying an established obsession.

According to an ESPN.com poll conducted by Richard Luker, 34% of FIFA players became big professional football fans after playing the video game and 50% of players gained at least some interest in professional football due to their love of playing FIFA. According to the EA Sports sales records, FIFA sold nearly 800,000 copies in the first nine months of 2014, meaning that approximately 400,000 more people in the US have gained an interest in watching professional football (soccer) than they would have without FIFA's influence. Per NBC viewership numbers, this would mean that approximately 57% of Americans watching the Premier League games on NBC are people that would probably not have had an interest in professional football before FIFA emerged. In the early 2000s in America, only truly committed fans would know top European football players. Historically, most casual fans in America would know European professional footballers from just watching the World Cup. Today, they know the players, not only from televised Champions League and league matches, but they know the players from playing FIFA video games. There is no doubt that the rise in popularity of the FIFA video game series in the US has coincided with a rise in popularity of pro soccer there. The percentage of Americans who identify themselves as avid pro football (soccer) fans has grown every year since 2009, according to ESPN.com. In this same period, the popularity of the video game series has expanded rapidly.[27] Often, the selection of star football players by video game players plays a role in the video game player's favourite team.

FIFA's various iterations alone have sold more than 150 million copies worldwide, according to *Forbes*. By some measures, it is the most successful sports video game franchise in history, even without including the latest instalment, FIFA 19, released in September 2018. Pro Evolution Soccer has more than 80 million copies in circulation, while the Football Manager series ranks as one of the best-selling on PC.[28]

Video games are not merely representations of the game, but influencers of it. Video game players spend hours trying to bring to life and master the tricks their video game idols could do only in virtual reality. In addition, the tricks and actions in the game influence not only how future generations want to play the game but how current fans want to consume the game. Fans want to see star players scoring incredible goals. As attention spans shorten and fans have less time, some fans don't fully watch the 90-minute game. They want to see short videos of highlights. This is why it is increasingly important to have an exciting, entertaining, attacking, beautiful style of play. This is what 'gamers' are trying to do when they play. They relate to this style of play.

---

27 https://www.huffingtonpost.com/andrei-markovits/fifa-the-video-game-a-maj_b_8085220.html
28 https://www.nytimes.com/2016/10/14/sports/soccer/the-scouting-tools-of-the-pros-a-controller-and-a-video.html

On occasions, the line between simulation and reality can almost become blurred, as Pirlo explained in his book. 'On 9 July 2006, I spent the afternoon sleeping and playing PlayStation in Berlin. Then, in the evening I went out and won the World Cup.' That was over a decade ago, and the excitement the game inspires in players has only grown since, with the realism of the virtual version getting closer and closer to reality. 'I don't notice the difference,' Brazil legend Ronaldo told FIFA.com during the final of the FIFA Interactive World Cup 2014. 'I think a genius made this video game. You can see they learn from us, the players on the field. So, I think we still have to improve on the real field to improve the video game even more.' An expert of the video game himself, the two-time FIFA World Cup winner added that he only ever chooses to play 'as Brazil and Real Madrid'. We're living in an age when the real and virtual influence each other.[29]

Former German Bayern Munich and Manchester United midfielder Bastian Schweinsteiger explained that he never plays himself in a video game: 'I never play as my player . . . Most of the time, I choose Premier League teams because I really like English football.' Players that play start to appreciate and understand the players, the clubs, the style of play and develop preferences. These are the casual fans clubs need to attract. Without many star players that 'gamers' want to select or leagues that they know because they are not on mainstream TV, these casual fans are not being introduced to Serie A.

In addition, esports is the world's fastest-growing spectator sport. Last year, esports tournaments and live streams drew 258 million unique viewers. Put another way, more people watched other people play video games in 2017 than all NFL regular-season games combined. Esports tournaments have sold out Madison Square Garden and World Cup stadiums. With a few exceptions, Serie A is behind incorporating esports with its league.

---

[29] http://www.fifa.com/news/y=2015/m=5/news=blurred-lines-footballers-and-video-games-2605031.html

On-the-Pitch Issues: Legal

Italian Owners with Limited Ways to Skirt Financial Fair Play (FFP) Limits

Revenues matter in European football. The owners and clubs that could and did spend prior to 2009 to jump-start their brands and fan experiences had a tremendous first mover competitive advantage, as long as they kept up the investments and created a sustainable economic-sport model. Revenues really matter since Financial Fair Play (FFP) was introduced in 2009. The Union of European Football Associations (UEFA) established rules to prevent professional football clubs from spending more than they earn in the pursuit of trophies. According to UEFA, about half of European clubs were losing money and it was an increasing trend. UEFA worried that financial problems would threaten European football's long-term survival. This makes sense, but there were a few criticisms of FFP. First, FFP solidifies the position of the big clubs that already generate the largest revenues and have the revenues to spend on the best players (this benefits clubs in leagues with large TV rights contracts). The best players not only increase the probability of winning, they also attract fans and sponsors. With the exception of Juventus at #10, the other Italian clubs that are not in the top ten are at a disadvantage.

In May 2015, ten teams (including Inter, Roma and Monaco) had to sign 'settlement agreements' to work towards achieving break-even for the 2018/19 season. Also, owners who control companies that could be sponsors of the club have an advantage of potentially artificially inflating revenues to give them financial flexibility with FFP. For example, Manchester City was purchased by Sheikh Mansour who heads the International Petroleum Investment Company (IPIC) which holds more than 18 major investments in over ten countries and on five different continents including Virgin Galactic and Daimler. (Sheikh Mansour is the deputy prime minister of the United Arab Emirates, minister of presidential affairs and a member of the ruling family of Abu Dhabi. He is the half-brother of the current president of the UAE, Khalifa bin Zayed Al Nahyan). In 2014, Manchester City and Paris Saint-Germain (PSG) were heavily sanctioned by UEFA for breaching

FFP rules. Sheikh Mansour had bought Manchester City in 2008 for €210 million and has since accumulated total losses of €535 million, excluding approximately €200 million on facility upgrades.

PSG was bought by Qatar's sovereign wealth fund, Qatar Investment Authority (QIA). In 2011/12, it spent massive sums on players. Although this spending at both clubs led to massive losses – especially excluding a related party sponsorship of up to €200 million a year by the Qatar Tourism Authority to PSG – it has led to success on the field. Paris Saint-Germain's deal with Qatar Sports Investments has raised questions as to how they relate to FFP because key sponsors are related or affiliated companies. In Italy, Jeep, the car company, is one of the main sponsors of Juventus. Jeep is owned by Fiat. Juventus and Fiat are both controlled by the Exor group, which is controlled by the Agnelli family. Bayern Munich is part-owned by three German companies – Allianz Insurance, adidas and Audi – and plays in the Allianz Arena.

FFP would restrict a new owner with capital investing in an Italian club to turn it around. However, new owners with related or affiliated companies for sponsorships can make a quicker impact, as seen with Manchester City and PSG. Without the synergies, generally, it will take clubs longer to improve their status as they balance player spending with commercial revenue growth. Owners who have other businesses that can be sponsors of their clubs are at an advantage. Although Juventus has some synergies (Jeep) and Inter has Suning sponsorship, few Italian club owners and clubs exist that today rival Manchester City and PSG's financial power and commitment. In addition, no Italian club has been able to tap into a loyal and passionate global community to the extent of Manchester United, Real Madrid and Barcelona, which will take time.

CHAPTER SEVEN

MILAN
THE RISE AND FALL
OF AN EMPIRE

Note to reader: The next five chapters are short case studies of five clubs: Milan, Inter, Juventus, Roma, and Napoli. The case studies apply the framework we developed to the specific clubs to shed more light on both the on the pitch and off-the-pitch (business) aspects of the clubs, and the league. A reader can decide to skip the case studies and continue to Part Four: The Future.

Overview

Associazione Calcio Milan, commonly referred to as AC Milan or simply Milan, was founded in 1899. The football club has spent its entire history, with the exception of the 1980/81 and 1982/83 seasons, in Serie A since the establishment of the league in 1929/30. Milan have won seven European Cup/Champions League titles (1963, 1969, 1989, 1990, 1994, 2003 and 2007; second behind Real Madrid) and 18 Serie A league titles (tied for second with Inter behind Juventus's 34 titles).

Since 1926, Milan have played their home games at Stadio Giuseppe Meazza, commonly referred to as the San Siro (also sometimes known as 'La Scala del Calcio', in reference to La Scala, the opera house in Milan). Ironically, the second president in the history of AC Milan was Pietro

Pirelli, whose presidency lasted 20 years. It is ironic because there is a strong bond linking Inter and Pirelli, since the two brands came together for the 1995/96 season. The San Siro has been the home of Milan since 1926, when it was privately built by funding from Milan's president at the time, Piero Pirelli. Based on the English model for stadiums, the San Siro was specifically designed for football matches, as opposed to many multi-purpose stadiums used in Serie A. The stadium was owned by AC Milan until it was sold to the city council in 1935. Since 1947, the stadium has been shared with city rivals Inter, and is the largest stadium in Italian football with a total capacity of 80,018.

Inter are considered Milan's biggest rivals and matches between the two teams are called 'Derby della Madonnina', which is one of the most followed derbies in football. The name of the derby refers to the Blessed Virgin Mary, whose statue atop the Milan Cathedral is one of the city's main attractions. Another big rivalry match is with Juventus, known as 'Derby d'Europa'.

The club's shirts are black and red stripes. The colour red was intended to evoke the fire of the players and make the connection to the devil, a symbol of the club, and black was to inspire fear in their opponents.

Rossoneri, the team's widely used nickname, literally means 'the red and blacks' in Italian, in reference to the colours of the stripes on their shirts. In honour of their English origins, the club have retained the English spelling of the city's name, as opposed to the Italian spelling Milano. The modern badge used today by the club represents the club colours and the flag of the Comune di Milano, with the acronym ACM at the top and the foundation year (1899) at the bottom.

Milan's anthem is 'Bet on the Final'.

Milan are one of the best-supported football clubs in Italy. Historically, Milan were supported by the city's working class, while cross-town rivals Inter were mainly supported by the more prosperous middle class. Former Italian Prime Minister Silvio Berlusconi owned the club for 31 years, between 1986 and 2017.

Milan Under the Berlusconi Era:
The Rise and Fall of an Empire

Milan are one of the best examples of the rise and fall of Italian football, not only because of their dominance in the late 1980s, 1990s and part of the 2000s, but also because of their decline as a result of the many issues previously discussed. Silvio Berlusconi had been a passionate fan of Milan since childhood, having grown up going to the San Siro with his father. Fittingly, he acquired Milan in 1986 and saved the club from bankruptcy. Berlusconi was an innovator and reinvented the business of European football in many ways. In contrast to old money regional industrial families who controlled the press and used football to build loyalties and increase regional pride, new money Berlusconi used his media properties to help create one of the first global brands in modern football. He saw Milan as a product to sell, with the content coming in many different forms. Berlusconi's channels were full of football discussion shows, highlights packages and news programmes. He was focused on the fan experience and cross-selling his other groups' products (and later, in 1994, politics). From a political and business perspective, taking a club from bankruptcy in 1986 and turning them into a European/world champion club in just three years demonstrated his ability to build something world class from the ground up and gave him a credible platform and notoriety from which to launch his political career in 1994.

Like the old money regional industrial families, Berlusconi invested vast amounts of his own money and supported the losses. These losses were perhaps more acceptable to Berlusconi as his wealth grew, but also because football helped his other businesses, political ambitions and national and European interests, while the other industrial families had relatively limited synergies and interests. Shortly after taking over, Berlusconi appointed an unknown rising manager, Arrigo Sacchi, and signed Dutch internationals Ruud Gullit, Marco van Basten and Frank Rijkaard. Before Berlusconi, Milan's last three Scudetti were in 1962, 1968 and 1979. With talented players and an innovative coach in the 1980s, 1990s and 2000s, Milan won the Serie A championship in 1988, 1992, 1993, 1994, 1996, 1999, 2004 and 2011. Milan also won the European Cup/Champions League in 1989, 1990, 1994, 2003 and

2007. Berlusconi was focused on a positive fan experience in a stadium that was renovated in 1990 for the World Cup; the salaries of the players and investments were affordable (especially as his wealth grew); he benefited from not sharing growing pay TV revenues; he pushed for greater exposure and revenues by helping start a new Champions League format; and there was an Italy 1990 World Cup excitement carry-over.

In the early 1990s, with Italian politics still reeling from a series of corruption scandals, the most well-known being 'Mani pulite' ('clean hands'), Berlusconi formed the Forza Italia party, thus filling a vacuum just as he had in 1986 when he took over Milan. Berlusconi choosing to name his party 'Forza Italia' was perhaps the most indicative example of how intertwined Berlusconi's political ambitions were with Milan and football, where the most well-known Italian football phrase became the official slogan of his political party. Berlusconi combined the patrimonial culture of Italy with football to reinvent national politics. Unfortunately, this was a distraction and instead of carrying out his vision for the club, he was more focused on using Milan for political purposes. The ambition for Milan transformed from a global entertainment brand and business into a political tool. Milan didn't capitalise on its first mover advantage to build a sustainable business, while Real Madrid and others did, and the results showed both on and off the pitch over time.

Player costs and required investments increased, but they were initially softened by a boost from TV revenues and his increasing wealth; this provided him with even less incentive to seek to expand revenues and make the business self-sustaining. Eventually, at the same time as the costs were steadily increasing to unsustainable levels, his political career was becoming more challenging, his businesses which were tied to the Italian economy were suffering, and both the political and business synergies slowly began to dissipate. Milan was over-reliant on TV revenues and had not invested in hiring and developing enough management professionals able to adapt and change to a new era. As a result, Berlusconi started to sell the star players who were responsible for the club's success during 2003–07 in order to raise capital, and replaced them with more affordable players to cut costs at the end of the 2000s/beginning of the 2010s. He did not make the investments necessary to have a global entertainment brand, such as a new stadium for a positive fan experience or to focus on online engagement. Many of the Italian elements that helped Berlusconi have a short-term advantage, eventually not only weakened Milan in the long run, but also weakened the league in the long run.

On the Pitch

Since Berlusconi acquired Milan in 1986, the club have won eight Serie A championships and five European Cup/Champions League trophies. They have also finished in second place in Italy four times and lost in the final of the European Cup/Champions League three times, arguably, making them the most successful European team on the pitch over this initial 20-year period. Spending on players was also relatively consistent from 1986 to 2007, with Milan paying both higher salaries and having larger transfer payments than their competitors. The success on the pitch certainly helped support Berlusconi's credibility in politics with the idea that he made Milan a power in Europe and the rest of the world and he could and was doing the same for Italy as prime minister.

Nevertheless, there was a gap in success on the pitch in Europe from 1996 to 2003, with the end of the Capello era and the construction of the Ancelotti era. It took some time to transition older players, rebuild and adapt to changes. Additionally, Milan suffered from a series of disappointing transfers during that period. Meanwhile, while the rest of Serie A generally had declining on-the-pitch performance, Milan experienced Italian and European success from 2003 to 2007 with a new talented generation of players and Berlusconi's willingness to spend more (and more signings working). Unfortunately, this could not last forever and while there was a decline for the next few years afterwards, Berlusconi made a last-ditch effort in the summer of 2010 to bring success to his club, which led to a Serie A championship the following season in 2011. During this time, Berlusconi was facing more vocal criticism as prime minister from political rivals, and in 2011 his party suffered big losses in local elections including the painful loss of Berlusconi's home town and party stronghold, Milan; Berlusconi would resign in 2011. After that, the decline on the pitch resumed, with Milan selling many of their top players in the summer of 2012. In the chart overleaf, one can see after 2012, there is blank space.

AC Milan Results 1987–2017

Year	Serie A	Champions League
1987		
1988	Winner	
1989	3rd	Winner
1990	2nd	Winner
1991	2nd	Quarter-finals
1992	Winner	
1993	Winner	2nd
1994	Winner	Winner
1995		2nd
1996	Winner	
1997		Group
1998		
1999	Winner	
2000	3rd	Group
2001		Group
2002		
2003	3rd	Winner
2004	Winner	Quarter-finals
2005	2nd	2nd
2006	3rd	Semi-finals
2007		Winner
2008		Round of 16
2009	3rd	
2010	3rd	Round of 16
2011	Winner	Round of 16
2012	2nd	Quarter-finals
2013	3rd	Round of 16
2014		Round of 16
2015		
2016		
2017		

Talent

During the first 20 years of success after purchasing the club in 1986, Berlusconi brought many of the best players to the club and was willing to spend what was necessary to do so, in both transfer fees and salaries. The strategy for talent was formulated/concentrated around three factors: buying the best players, buying the best younger generation of players (in their twenties), and developing great talent within the youth teams. For all three groups of players, Milan also focused on keeping them for a long time to make sure they were able to fully develop into a cohesive unit that shared Milan's values and culture. All of that worked well during the first 20 years of Berlusconi's presidency:

- Players recruited who were already top players included Gullit, Shevchenko, van Basten, Rijkaard, Papin, Savicevic, Baggio, Weah, Inzaghi, Seedorf, Nesta, Rui Costa and Cafu.
- Young players who were recruited in their twenties and became top players during their years at Milan included Kaká, Pirlo, Gattuso, Dida, and Boban.
- Top players from the youth team included Baresi, Maldini, Costacurta and Albertini.

Furthermore, between 1987 and 2007, ten of the 18 players that won the Ballon d'Or played for Milan at some point (Gullit, van Basten, Papin, Baggio, Weah, Rivaldo, Shevchenko, Ronaldo, Kaká, Ronaldinho), which was more than any other team. During Berlusconi's presidency alone, an AC Milan player was awarded with the Ballon d'Or seven times, making Milan number one for that ranking over that time period. However, the last Ballon d'Or winner was in 2007.

AC Milan Ballon d'Or Results Since 1986

1987 Ruud Gullit Winner
1988 Marco van Basten Winner
Ruud Gullit 2nd
Frank Rijkaard 3rd
1989 Marco van Basten Winner
Franco Baresi 2nd
Frank Rijkaard 3rd
1992 Marco van Basten Winner
1994 Paolo Maldini 3rd
1995 George Weah Winner
1999 Andriy Shevchenko 3rd
2000 Andriy Shevchenko 3rd
2003 Paolo Maldini 3rd
2004 Andriy Shevchenko Winner
2007 Kaká Winner

To complement the Ballon d'Or trophy, which is awarded to only one player (usually a striker), UEFA started the '11 d'Or', which recognises the top player in each position on the pitch. Since its creation in 2001 to 2007, Milan had players selected every year and no other team had more players selected than Milan over that period as well (defender Contra in 2001, defender Nesta and midfielder Seedorf in 2002, defenders Nesta and Maldini in 2003, defenders Cafu and Nesta and striker Shevchenko in 2004, defenders Maldini and Cafu and striker Shevchenko in 2005, forward Kaká in 2006, defender Nesta, forward Kaká and midfielder Seedorf in 2007). If you add up the numbers, Milan had 15 players out of 77 during these years, proving it was not just one superstar striker but the entire team that had exceptional talent. Equilibrium between attack and defence has always been a key to Milan's success in the '80s, '90s and 2000s, and talent on the field was therefore well distributed.

While clearly having the best and most complementary players over that 20-year period, Milan would probably not have been as successful without its three talented coaches: Sacchi, Capello and Ancelotti, who won almost all of Milan's trophies under Berlusconi's presidency. These three coaches were all young, and on the rise, when appointed by Berlusconi, and two of them were former Milan players. As a result, Milan combined talented players with talented and innovative managers who knew the history and values of the club. Consistent with the decline of the league, today none of them coach in Italy.

Decline in Talent: 2007–17

Many of the problems previously highlighted regarding Serie A are also true for Milan, with the decline in talent and subsequent reasons why perhaps the most important.

Golden Generation

Carlo Ancelotti's success as coach of Milan from 2001–09 was in large part due to the 'Senators', a group of similarly aged players who were very familiar with each other. This is great for a generation because it meant the players grew together and knew each other well, especially in

Milan where it was common for players to stay for a decade, and reach their peak at the same time. As success in football requires an enormous amount of teamwork to string together a series of passes to score or teamwork to keep a defensive shape to prevent opponents from scoring, this is incredibly important. Many of Milan's Senators, such as Pirlo, Gattuso, Nesta, Seedorf, Shevchenko, Ambrosini, Kaladze and Abbiati, were exactly in their 'peak period' between 2003 and 2007, implying that it was not a coincidence that this period was a great cycle for the club. While others like Maldini, Inzaghi and Dida were older, the first two were exceptions and relied on their mental skills and experience to be effective. Additionally, Kaká, who joined in 2003, was the only young one (25 in 2007), but he relied heavily on his speed, so it is likely that his peak was at a much younger age. After 2007, when all the Senators were over 30, it was inevitable that without any new investment in new young players the cycle would end. That factor, coupled with the lack of preparation for a successful transition, helps to explain the decline seen on the pitch.

Lack of Investment

During the first part of Ancelotti's era, Milan were investing every summer to keep talent at a high level without changing the team too much. One or two impactful players were brought in every summer, such as Kaká and Cafu in the summer of 2003, Stam and Crespo in 2004, and Jankulovski and Gilardino in 2005. The summer of 2006 was the first time Milan went against this strategy when they sold superstar and tifosi idol Shevchenko to Chelsea without replacing him. At the time there was an argument that Kaká needed more space to really become number one. And the next season Kaká was awarded the Ballon d'Or and Milan won the Champions League, partly thanks to his new position on the pitch as a real forward and not an attacking midfielder because of Shevchenko's presence. After 2006/07, Berlusconi became much more reluctant to invest and purchase star players from other teams and similarly stopped offering large salaries to keep the best players already in his squad. The amounts were just getting too large as football was changing. In addition, the team was ageing, therefore the overall level of talent was decreasing (departing stars were replaced by good but not great players). To make matters worse, during the summer of 2009, Ancelotti left after eight years, the club's major superstar Kaká was sold, and their captain Maldini retired after 25 years at Milan. From a financial perspective, the club was in a much better position after selling Shevchenko and Kaká due to both the proceeds from the sales and the amount of money it saved in terms of salaries. However, from a business and brand perspective, there was a lack of 'star power'. It started to show in the financials. In 2006, Milan ranked #6 in the Deloitte Football Money League.

After finally understanding how these changes were negatively impacting the performance on and off the pitch as well as the political implications, in 2010 Berlusconi started once again to make greater investments in talent and to acquire more high-profile players, including superstars Ibrahimović, Robinho, van Bommel and Boateng. These players brought talent and strength to Milan, and with the help of some of the ageing Senators, helped them to win Serie A right away in 2011. But the willingness to invest was again under discussion during the summer of 2011 when Pirlo left, due to the unwillingness of Milan to extend his contract. This subsequently led him to sign with Juve, where he led them to four Scudetti in a row. Still, the 2010/11 and 2011/12 seasons seemed to see the club back on track to be in the European top five if some investment was made to support this new rise. Unfortunately, Berlusconi probably knew that the team would need essentially prohibitive levels of investment for the future in order to be successful, including the purchase of a handful of top players, both to maintain the depth of the team and to replace the retiring Senators, a new stadium, better technology and merchandising investments. Each year, Milan dropped one spot in the Deloitte Football Money League and fell out of the top ten in 2013/14.

With his businesses still not fully recovered and having resigned in 2011, it seems the massive investments didn't make sense. During the summer of 2012, he sold his best players (Ibrahimović, Thiago Silva, van Bommel and even Pato the following winter) in order to raise capital from the transfers and also to save money on the high salaries they were being paid, but the problems didn't stop there. Almost the entire generation of Senators hung up their boots in the summer of 2012: Gattuso, Inzaghi,

Nesta, Seedorf and Zambrotta all retired, leaving only Ambrosini and Abbiati who were both 36 years old. To add to the obvious on-the-pitch effect, much of the talent and culture that had been so ingrained for so long left along with them. The club had not developed another group of stars. Since then, it has been almost impossible for Milan to attract superstar talent. Shortly after, Berlusconi started to look for buyers of the club and continued to cut investment.

Poor/Unlucky Investment Decisions

Even if the level of investment was clearly not sufficient to maintain a highly competitive team after 2007, it would be unfair to say that the club never tried to discover new talents and didn't invest anything in transfers.[1] The problem was that many of the young players that Milan took a chance on didn't do as well as expected. While the club focused on trying to develop new, younger talent, most of the players they identified as the stars of the future did not pan out, with players like Pato, Gilardino, Gourcuff, Balotelli, El Shaarawy, Huntelaar, Boateng, Flamini and de Jong all disappointing at Milan, resulting in poor performance on the pitch and a high turnover in the squad with eight to ten new players every year.

Although Milan had less money to spend than its competitors who developed commercial arms, there was still some prestige in the name. It seems Milan focused on bringing in older (over 30) players to the club during the late 2000s. It seems they hoped that since these players were past their performance peak, there would be low/no transfer fees, but the players would still perform at a relatively high level or bring some marketing exposure. This strategy was particularly problematic for fans, who did not appreciate players such as Emerson, Essien, Torres, Ronaldo, Amoroso, Vieri, Mancini, Cassano, etc. Additionally, many of these players that they added were of a similar age and appeared to be brought in for political (Ronaldinho) and marketing reasons (Beckham, Ronaldinho, Honda, Ronaldo, Onyewu and the returns of Shevchenko, Kaká and Balotelli).

---

[1] There were reports and allegations of an unusually close relationship between star agent Mino Raiola and Adriano Galliani.

Lack of Talent Development

Milan not only bought many of the best players during the late '80s and the '90s, but also excelled at talent development within the club's system. Legends like Baresi, Maldini, Costacurta and others came from the Milan youth teams, which was a clear advantage over their competitors because not only did they not have to pay large transfer fees to acquire the talent, but it also provided a lot of value in terms of culture, identity, stability and loyalty (these three players alone spent 20, 25 and 21 years as professional players for Milan respectively, as absolute protagonists). Over the years, however, the club focused less on talent development and Milan's advantage in this area began to erode, resulting in a succession of average players that they eventually sold. However, some things may be improving, for example Patrick Cutrone, Gianluigi Donnarumma, Davide Calabria and Manuel Locatelli came directly from the Primavera squad.

Favouring Seniority

Seniority is something that is deeply rooted in Italian culture and identity and is especially true in the case of Milan. It is understood that respect must be shown to the older and more experienced players, which is both a blessing and a curse, and becomes a major problem when the older players take for granted their position and assume they will play no matter what, even if they are not in top physical condition. In doing this, there is a compounding effect as it weakens the team by making it less aggressive and slower, and it also undermines and disenfranchises young players who know they are not going to play much anyway. This was a major problem for Milan in the late 2000s, and as good as the 'Senators' were, it has put the club in an impossible position of trying to replace all that talent at once – as highlighted by the major decline on the pitch seen in 2007, and then again more fully in 2012.

Off the Pitch

Business Model

Berlusconi had been able and willing to financially support Milan in the past, but then football became a much more substantial, global business in the early 2000s. Required investments in players and fan experiences sky-rocketed. Berlusconi invested less and less, and the results are evident in the revenues. According to the Football Money League published by Deloitte, Milan fell from fourth in the ranking in 2000 to 16th in 2015/16. In the 2016/17 Deloitte Revenues Ranking, for the first time since it has been published, Milan fell out of the top 20 to #22, which is even more remarkable given they had been in the top ten in every edition up to and including 2012/13. For the 2016/17 season, Milan brought in its lowest revenues since 2002.

2000/01–2016/17 Deloitte Revenues Ranking
€ in millions

Year	Revenues	Ranking
2000/01	164.4	4
2001/02	159.1	4
2002/03	200.4	3
2003/04	222.1	3
2004/05	234.0	3
2005/06	238.7	5
2006/07	227.7	6
2007/08	209.5	8
2008/09	196.5	8
2009/10	235.8	7
2010/11	235.1	7
2011/12	256.9	8
2012/13	263.5	10
2013/14	249.7	12
2014/15	199.1	14
2015/16	214.7	16
2016/17	191.7	22

Interestingly, Berlusconi's wealth declined from 2000 to 2003 and then again from €9.6 billion in 2005 to a low point of €4.6 billion in 2012 and €5.6 billion in 2016. Perhaps unsurprisingly, in 2012, Berlusconi sold or didn't re-sign several players. This decline in wealth can be explained by the fact that most of his businesses are tied to the Italian economy, as he never really focused on growing globally, whereas many other successful Italian business owners did. For example, from 2004 to 2007, Berlusconi was the wealthiest Italian (according to *Forbes* at least), but since 2012 he has ranked from fifth to seventh as other Italians with companies such as Luxottica, Giorgio Armani, Prada, Alliance Boots and Ferrero/Nutella expanded globally and exported products and were thus able to become much more financially successful.

Berlusconi's Wealth Published by *Forbes*
€ in billions

Year	Wealth	Rank in Italy	Prime Minister
2000	13.9	#1	
2001	11.5	#1	Yes
2002	7.6	#1	Yes
2003	5.2	#1	Yes
2004	8	#1	Yes
2005	9.6	#1	Yes
2006	8.8	#1	Yes
2007	8.6	#1	
2008	6.4	#3	Yes
2009	4.7	#2	Yes
2010	6.8	#3	Yes
2011	5.6	#3	Yes
2012	4.6	#6	
2013	4.7	#7	
2014	5.7	#5	
2015	6.7	#6	
2016	5.6	#5	
2017	6.2	#5	

Source: Forbes

The lack of financial and legal and regulatory transparency in Italy, and most likely at Milan, made it difficult to raise new capital, let alone sell the club. The business of football had changed and Milan was slow to recognise this and failed to adapt quickly enough once it did. As a result, the club had major difficulty attracting and keeping talent and investing in infrastructure for the fan experience.

Salaries

Looking at salaries alone, Milan had by far the largest drop-off over the ten-year period from 2006/07 to 2016/17. This coincides almost perfectly with Berlusconi's decline in wealth and lack of investment in the club more broadly. Given the magnitude of these numbers, it appears as though it would be impossible for Milan to catch up to the other top clubs under the Berlusconi/old school business model.

Total Payroll by Club 2006/07 and 2016/17
€ in millions

Club	2006/07	2016/17	% Increase
Real Madrid	170	289	70%
Barcelona	160	340	113%
PSG	32	255	697%
Manchester City	78	276	252%
Manchester United	124	266	115%
Chelsea	165	284	72%
Juventus	97	143	47%
Inter	110	105	-5%
AC Milan	120	77	-36%

Milan also still had the highest-paid player in terms of salary on their team in 2007, but the other teams quickly surpassed the club in the next couple of years (Messi with Barcelona in 2008, Ronaldo with Real Madrid in 2009 and Kaká with Real Madrid in 2009). By 2017, Milan didn't have a single player in the top 20.

Highest-Paid Player in European League (2006/07)
€ in millions

Player	Club	Salary	Ranking
Kaká	AC Milan	9.0	1
Ronaldinho	FC Barcelona	8.5	2
Lampard	Chelsea FC	8.0	3
Terry	Chelsea FC	8.0	4
Torres	Liverpool FC	7.9	5

Highest-Paid Player in European League (2016/17)
€ in millions

Player	Club	Salary	Ranking
Neymar	PSG	33.9	3
Ronaldo	Real Madrid	21.47	1
Messi	FC Barcelona	21.02	2
Bale	Real Madrid	19.21	4
Pogba	Manchester United	17.7	5

Source: http://financefootball.com/2017/02/13/top-worlds-highest-paid-football-players-2017/

Sponsorship

For the start of the 2017/18 season the shirts are supplied by German sportswear manufacturer adidas, a sponsorship deal between adidas and Milan that has run since 1998. The deal was scheduled to run until 2023 for €20 million a year, but an early termination of the deal was announced in 2017 when ownership of the club transferred, effective in 2018. Audi also ended its sponsorship agreement with the club at the beginning of 2017. The termination of these deals signify that Milan is not attractive enough anymore for sponsors and international investors and only Emirates seems to be willing to stay for now, with a €100 million contract from 2014 to 2019. AC Milan will be wearing PUMA kit (who also supply Arsenal and Borussia Dortmund) from the start of the 2018/19 season after signing a long-term deal with the German sportswear giant.

Medical Technology and Milan Lab

From an innovation perspective, Milan were actually at the forefront in the late '90s/early 2000s thanks to the Milan Lab. The Lab officially started in 2002 but its genesis probably had a lot to do with superstar Redondo being badly injured in 2000 (right after being transferred from Real Madrid to Milan in the summer of that year), which rendered him unable to play for two years and he struggled to fully recover thereafter. Jean-Pierre Meersseman, a Belgian chiropractor, started the Milan Lab with the innovative idea that data and ideas learned from all of the different fields of medicine could be combined to enhance the fitness of players. Kinesiology, psychology and neurology were all part of it and a team of engineers and mathematicians collected massive amounts of data which was an innovation for a football club in the early 2000s. For example, they would deeply analyse a player's jump by looking at the angle of the knee, how the muscles worked and the speed, pressure and explosiveness that resulted. They then added a player's biophysical data and physiological data to get more complete results. The impact of the Milan Lab was immediate after just one season – the use of medicine went down by 70%, total practice days lost decreased by 43% and players' injuries decreased by 67%. This innovation therefore became an integral part of Milan's vision and strategy. For example, Meersseman had a veto vote on any transfer and had to personally evaluate each potential new player for Milan. This was a collaborate check and balance system. The Lab also helps explain why Milan was still successful in the mid-2000s in spite of the older age of its players compared to the rest of the top European clubs.[2]

Nevertheless, the competitive advantage gained from being at the forefront of medical technology lasted for eight years and then the club started to struggle even more financially and cut the budget, including the Milan Lab. The impact of the cuts in the Milan Lab showed up on the pitch. During the following three years, the club suffered more injuries than during the previous eight years combined. Jean-Pierre Meersseman quit the club in 2013 as well. Other clubs copied the Milan Lab. The advantage was lost.

---

2 Maldini and Costacurta played at a high level until they turned 40 and Maldini is the oldest captain ever to win a Champions League.

TV Channel

Milan has a TV Channel, one of the first in Europe. Milan TV is a subscription-based television channel and it first broadcast in December 1999 as Milan Channel. The channel offers Milan fans exclusive interviews with players and staff, full matches, including replays of all Serie A, Coppa Italia and Champions League/UEFA Cup games, in addition to vintage matches, footballing news and other themed programming.

Culture and Identity

History

Since its inception, culture has always been very important to Milan. Founder Herbert Kilpin gave a speech at its founding, 'We are the team of this big city: the Milan! Red and black, flaming colours, will be our symbol. Italians, English and others will carry on this enterprise to make us famous and remembered through time and in every country, thanks to the strong and beautiful way we express our sportivity.' The Milan Cricket and Football Club was born in December 1899, and so was its culture. From his speech we can extract the idea of an Italian base of players surrounded by a group of foreign stars playing in a 'strong and beautiful way'. Kilpin also touches on the notion of having an impact beyond Italy ('in every country'), which has been a core value of Milan's.

When Berlusconi took over Milan in 1986, he felt that the culture had drifted over time, and so he tried to instil how he perceived things used to be before the drift. Berlusconi immediately set up the exact same objectives as Kilpin 87 years before him, by saying: 'We should aim to dominate nationally and internationally and be remembered not only for the success but also the positive way we play.' He achieved this on-the-pitch success almost immediately with Sacchi at the helm leading Milan to a European championship in just a few years.

In terms of playing style, Milan focused on bringing in the most elegant and attacking players, such as Maldini, Nesta, Pirlo, Kaká, Baggio, van Basten and Shevchenko. Most of these players were uncontroversial off the pitch as well, which helped with Berlusconi's image as a politician.

Even now, with Berlusconi no longer in charge of the club, he is still focused on Milan's playing style. He recently called the new coach to request that the team play with a specific formation (two strikers and one creative midfielder), which he had explicitly demanded from all the previous coaches while president.

Off the pitch, loyalty and family values were incredibly important. For example, Baresi and Maldini played for Milan for their entire 20- and 25-year careers respectively and were captains of Milan for a period spanning 27 years. Even when the club got relegated to Serie B in 1982, Baresi decided to stay, even though he could have gone anywhere else as part of Italy's World Cup-winning squad. For Maldini, his history with Milan goes back to his father, Cesare, who played for and was captain of the club in the '60s, and whose sons also played for Milan Juniors more recently.

Looking at the coaching history, it is clear how important loyalty was to Berlusconi and the rest of the club. Many of the coaches were former players (like Liedholm, Capello, Ancelotti, Inzaghi, Maldini's father, Seedorf, Brocchi and Gattuso) and also held previous jobs within the club or coached the youth teams.

Lastly, among the most successful teams in Italy, Milan historically have had a very high percentage of Italians on the pitch. From its founding, the composition of the club and its fan base has traditionally been from the industrial regional working class. Therefore, people were especially proud to have local Italians competing at the highest level with international stars. When Berlusconi took over, he tried to maintain this Italian base – globalising the team just enough as in the founder's speech.

Cultural Drift

Over time, Milan suffered from a series of events that built on each other to eventually create a noticeable cultural drift which culminated in 2012. Examples include:

- Summer 2009: Long-time captain Maldini left after 25 years; coach Ancelotti left after eight years; superstar Kaká left after six years
- Summer 2011: Superstar Pirlo left after 11 years
- Summer 2012: Most of the Senators retired at the same time,

including Gattuso (13 years), Inzaghi (12 years), Seedorf (10 years) and Nesta (10 years)

As Gattuso said when he retired: 'I've seen things happening in our players' room that I have never seen before . . . Things that would be impossible with the players we used to have here . . . It was time for me to leave,' and 'When I lost a match I broke down in frustration. Today players lose, take a selfie and put it on the Internet. They make me sick.' Another example of cultural drift is the way Milan handled retired legend Maldini. The legend never took a position in the club, which would have been a great way to pass on 25 years of Milan's culture to the next generation. Ten years after retiring, Milan's legendary captain is still not part of the club staff. With so many of these prominent culture carriers retiring at the same time and not being involved with the club, the subsequent drift was inevitable.

Milan also started to buy players that, while talented, were not representative of the club's identity and were not strong cultural fits. Some of these players even got in trouble off the pitch for various forms of bad behaviour. Even though Milan won the Scudetto in the midst of the decline (2010/11), they were (and still are) unable to ever fully recover their lost identity which impacted off-the-pitch revenues.

In a desperate move to try to bring back that lost culture and identity, Milan have hired six coaches since 2014, and out of those six coaches four were/are former players (Seedorf, Inzaghi, Brocchi and Gattuso, the current coach). Abbiati (one of the Senators) is now team manager as well. However, all of these moves have been unsuccessful so far; although it is difficult to judge because of the lack of relative investment.

Poor Fan Experience

Opposite is matchday attendance. The peak in attendance was in the early 1990s, but then generally attendance has declined. Even with stars attendance declined as the stadium got older. There was a recent pick-up with the enthusiasm of new signings. It is unclear if this is temporary.

Milan's Matchday Attendance and Rank

Stadium	Season	Avg Attendance	Max Capacity	Utilisation	League	Rank
San Siro	1979/80	40,660	85,000	47.8%	Serie A	4
San Siro	1980/81	31,282	85,000	36.8%	Serie B	1
San Siro	1981/82	45,781	85,000	53.9%	Serie A	2
San Siro	1982/83	35,111	85,000	41.3%	Serie B	1
San Siro	1983/84	53,136	85,000	62.5%	Serie A	2
San Siro	1984/85	60,941	85,000	71.7%	Serie A	2
San Siro	1985/86	56,782	85,000	66.8%	Serie A	2
San Siro	1986/87	66,210	85,000	77.9%	Serie A	1
San Siro	1987/88	73,284	85,000	86.2%	Serie A	1
San Siro	1988/89	72,309	85,000	85.1%	Serie A	1
San Siro	1989/90	59,054	85,700	68.9%	Serie A	1
San Siro	1990/91	77,488	85,700	90.4%	Serie A	1
San Siro	1991/92	77,868	85,700	90.9%	Serie A	1
San Siro	1992/93	75,830	85,700	88.5%	Serie A	1
San Siro	1993/94	65,708	85,700	76.7%	Serie A	1
San Siro	1994/95	56,659	85,700	66.1%	Serie A	1
San Siro	1995/96	60,973	85,700	71.1%	Serie A	1
San Siro	1996/97	55,894	85,700	65.2%	Serie A	1
San Siro	1997/98	54,432	85,700	63.5%	Serie A	1
San Siro	1998/99	57,760	85,700	67.4%	Serie A	2
San Siro	1999/00	58,522	85,700	68.3%	Serie A	3
San Siro	2000/01	52,304	85,700	61.0%	Serie A	2
San Siro	2001/02	58,616	85,700	68.4%	Serie A	3
San Siro	2002/03	61,354	85,700	71.6%	Serie A	2
San Siro	2003/04	63,245	85,700	73.8%	Serie A	1
San Siro	2004/05	63,595	85,700	74.2%	Serie A	1
San Siro	2005/06	59,993	85,700	70.0%	Serie A	1
San Siro	2006/07	47,117	85,700	55.0%	Serie A	2
San Siro	2007/08	56,642	85,700	66.1%	Serie A	1
San Siro	2008/09	59,731	80,018	74.6%	Serie A	1
San Siro	2009/10	42,809	80,018	53.5%	Serie A	3
San Siro	2010/11	53,916	80,018	67.4%	Serie A	2
San Siro	2011/12	49,020	80,018	61.3%	Serie A	1
San Siro	2012/13	43,651	80,018	54.6%	Serie A	2
San Siro	2013/14	39,874	80,018	49.8%	Serie A	4
San Siro	2014/15	36,661	80,018	45.8%	Serie A	4
San Siro	2015/16	37,816	80,018	47.3%	Serie A	4
San Siro	2016/17	40,326	80,018	50.4%	Serie A	2
San Siro	2017/18	52,928	80,018	66.1%	Serie A	6*

*April 2018.

Museum

The Casa Milan was opened in 2014 and is a must see for Milan fans. The amazing tall and angular futuristic glass structure houses many Milan treasures, including trophies, as well as touch screen displays and a room dedicated to the Champions League. The Casa Milan website states: 'Casa Milan aims to stir the emotions and entertain: a unique place that is the very essence of the concept of #weareacmilan. Shared passion, togetherness, constant and continuous engagement with the Club, with the aim of uniting the Club's employees, players, fans, sports lovers, the Milanese and tourists. This is the goal of Casa Milan. A place that can also satisfy the Club's new commercial growth, entertainment and development requirements.' Obviously, this is a positive step in the right direction of the club. Unfortunately, it is not near the centre of Milan or the San Siro.

Online Experience

Milan have struggled to develop their online presence and social media strategy, which at this point is relatively poor from both a club and player perspective. Almost everything is in Italian and it appears there is very little focus on capturing a broader global audience. Unfortunately, a lot of this can be traced back to timing and the generational cycle of players and success on the pitch. The rise of the internet and the importance of social media became much more prevalent just when Milan's performance started to decline and many of these great players either retired or were past their peak.

Nepotism

Nepotism has been a serious issue for Milan. Barbara Berlusconi served as a member of the board from 2011 to 2013 and later in a power-sharing agreement as co-CEO with the team vice president Adriano Galliani until the end of the 2016/17 season. She wanted to financially expand the club and handled the business side and was in charge of the potential new stadium project and Casa Milan while Galliani handled the on-the-pitch-related matters. She attended secondary school at the Institute Villoresi College of Monza before graduating with a first-class degree in philosophy at the renowned Vita-Salute San Raffaele University in Milan. She wanted to revolutionise the club, and has strategies regarding new kits, a new stadium, new museum and an extended range of souvenirs for fans. These types of things were not, and aren't, common in Italian football. She received criticism for dating a player on the team. Then the player that she was dating allegedly rejected a move to PSG, which would have financially benefited Milan, in order to stay closer to her. In addition, it was reported that when the player was not playing well he still kept getting selected to play, which rightly or wrongly, was linked to his relationship. She denied she had anything to do with the deal or his selection. The player was eventually sold, but for less money than the reported PSG offer. In addition, Berlusconi's brother Paolo was also directly involved, serving as a board member from 2013 to 2017. The prevalence of nepotism was also evident with the employment of many long-time Milan staff members being close Berlusconi friends.

Obviously, there is tolerance of nepotism beyond management. Accusations of nepotism continue today. For example, Gianluigi Donnarumma celebrated not only his lucrative new contract at AC Milan but also the club's move to re-sign his older brother, Antonio. Antonio's deal was confirmed a day after Gianluigi signed a new contract at the San Siro. Milan signed Kaká's younger brother Digão, who played as a central defender.

Final Remarks

After 31 years, Berlusconi sold Milan, stating that it needed very significant investment to be able to compete again with the top clubs. In 2016, a preliminary agreement was signed with Chinese investment management company Sino-Europe Sports Investment Management Changxing, to whom Berlusconi's Fininvest sold a 99.93% stake of Milan for about €520 million, plus the refurbishment of the club's financial debt of €220 million, a total of €740 million. In April 2017, the deal was completed and Rossoneri Sport Investment Lux became the new direct parent company of the club.

The new owners have invested heavily in the transfer market in the summer of 2017 (around €230 million), but it will take time and more consistent investment before Milan can get back to where it was before. However, things look better from a talent development perspective. Milan now have the youngest team in Serie A (as of 2017) and also have the most number of players in the first team from the youth academy (seven players). In addition, Milan have seen an increase in season ticket sales.

In December 2017, UEFA rejected AC Milan's request to waive Financial Fair Play (FFP) rules, because they remain unconvinced about the Italian club's Chinese backers and uncertainties in relation to the financial guarantees provided by the main shareholder. Milan have incurred losses of €255 million in the past three seasons – significantly more than the €30 million allowed. The club asked if they could strike a 'voluntary agreement' after a takeover by entrepreneur Li Yonghong in April 2017. UEFA said the situation will be assessed again in early 2018 and Milan will continue to be subject to the ongoing monitoring process. Under FFP, any club that spends more than it earns faces sanctions, which can range from a fine to a ban from European competition. There is also concern over whether or not the club will be able to repay loans to an American hedge fund. As reported by Sky Sports, hedge fund Elliott Management is thought to have loaned €178 million to the club's Chinese owners, as well as €128 million to the club itself. It has been reported that all those loans, combined with €50 million of interest, must be repaid by October 2018. If these loans are not repaid, it has been suggested that Milan could be excluded from future European competitions should they qualify. In February 2018, Li said his finances were sound and called recent press reports about financial difficulties irresponsible. AC Milan reportedly hired a bank to find lenders interested in refinancing both the club and Li's vehicle, but no deal has been signed yet.

In April 2018, AC Milan's general manager said he is optimistic there will be no repercussions on Milan's summer transfer activities, although he does expect some sanctions after his third meeting with UEFA to update them on the economic situation of the club and discuss a settlement agreement in view of potential financial fair play (FFP) restrictions.

CHAPTER EIGHT

INTER GETS INTERNATIONAL MONEY

Note to reader: We could have included Inter in a discussion of the revival of Italian football because they were purchased by Chinese owners in 2016 and seem to be in a more stable financial situation than AC Milan. However, we felt that it is still too early to draw any conclusions.

Overview

FC Internazionale Milano, commonly known as Inter, were founded in 1908 by a group of members of the Milan Cricket and Football Club (now AC Milan) that wanted the club to have an official or stronger position to defend the presence of foreigners on the team. (At the time foreigners on Italian teams were being questioned as nationalism flourished in Italy in 1908 in an uncertain and unstable international environment.) The club has spent its entire history in Serie A, won 18 Scudetti (tied for second with Milan behind Juventus's 34 titles) and three European Cup/Champions League trophies (1964, 1965 and 2010). From 2006 to 2010, the club won five successive league titles, equalling the all-time record at that time.

Since 1947, Inter have played at the Stadio Giuseppe Meazza (most often referred to as the San Siro), which is named after the national team and Inter superstar of the 1930s (who also played for AC Milan at the end of his career). The stadium is the largest in Italian football with a total capacity of 80,018. Inter's most vocal fans are known to gather in the Curva Nord, or north curve of the San Siro. This long-standing tradition has led to the Curva Nord being synonymous with the club's most diehard supporters, who unfold banners and wave flags in support of their team.

AC Milan are considered their biggest rivals and matches between the two teams are called 'Derby della Madonnina', which is one of the most followed derbies in football. The name of the derby refers to the Blessed Virgin Mary, whose statue atop Milan Cathedral is one of the city's main attractions. AC Milan and Inter Milan fans are commonly referred to as 'cugini' (cousins), due to their similar origins (before the split). The other most significant rivalry is with Juventus; the two participate in the 'Derby d'Italia'. Up until the 2006 Italian football scandal, which saw Juventus relegated, the two were the only Italian clubs to have never played below Serie A.

The club's shirts are black and blue striped. It is rumoured that black was chosen to represent night and blue was chosen to represent the sky. The colour blue was also intended to oppose rivals AC Milan's red. Nerazzurri, the team's widely used nickname, literally means 'the blacks and blues' in Italian, in reference to the colours of the stripes on their shirts. Another nickname is 'Il Biscione', which means the big non-venomous grass snake and is a symbol of the city of Milan. The biscione was the emblem of the House of Visconti which gained control of the city of Milan in 1277. The biscione symbol is also used by Alfa Romeo.

The modern badge used today by the club represents the club colours and its initials 'FCIM'. The star on the shirts on the top of the badge means Inter have won at least ten Scudetti (since 1966). Inter's official song is 'C'è solo l'Inter', meaning 'there is only Inter', which was created by Elio and Graziano Romani in 2002. 'Pazza Inter Amala' is another very popular song played at matches and is perhaps the most famous and beloved song among Inter fans.

Inter are one of the best-supported football clubs in Italy. Historically, Inter were supported by the city's middle and upper class, while cross-town rivals AC Milan were mainly supported by the working class.

The Moratti Family and Changing Ownership

Like the Agnellis for Juventus, the Morattis are a very important family for Inter. Italian oil mogul Angelo Moratti had been president of the club from 1955 to 1968, leading Inter to their most successful period (Herrera's Inter with club legends Mazzola, Facchetti and Suarez). He sold the club in 1968. His son, Massimo Moratti, bought the club in 1995 from Ernesto Pellegrini, and then owned the club until 2013. The Moratti family made a fortune in the oil business, which Massimo Moratti mostly relied on to build a talented team. Massimo has reportedly spent around €1.5 billion of his personal wealth on Inter, especially as oil prices were rising. His most spectacular player acquisitions were Ronaldo from Barcelona in 1997, Vieri from Lazio in 1999, Ibrahimović from Juventus in 2006 and Eto'o from Barcelona in 2009.

In 2012, the club announced that Moratti was to sell a minority interest to a Chinese consortium. On the same day, Inter announced an agreement was formed with China Railway Construction Corporation Limited for a new stadium project; however, the deal with the Chinese company eventually collapsed. In 2013, an Indonesian consortium (International Sports Capital HK Ltd) led by Erick Thohir, Handy Soetedjo and Rosan Roeslani, signed an agreement to acquire around 70% of Inter shares, while Moratti would maintain his 29.5% stake. Later that year, Thohir, who also co-owned Major League Soccer (MLS) club D.C. United and Indonesia Super League (ISL) club Persib Bandung, announced that Inter and D.C. United had formed a strategic partnership.

During the Thohir era, the club began to modify its financial structure from one reliant on continual owner investment to a more self-sustaining business model, although the club still breached UEFA Financial Fair Play Regulations in 2015. The club was fined and required to reduce their squad in UEFA competitions, with additional penalties suspended in the probation period. In 2016, Suning Holdings Group, a company controlled by Zhang Jindong, co-founder and chairman of Suning Commerce Group, acquired a majority stake in Inter Milan from Thohir's consortium and from the Moratti family's remaining shares. According to various filings, the total investment from Suning was around €270 million, representing a 68.55% stake in the club.

Reportedly, Thohir's consortium still has 31% and Pirelli has less than a 0.5% stake.

Culture and Identity

Talent

In 1984 Ernesto Pellegrini bought Inter from Ivanoe Fraizzoli. German superstars Rummenigge, Matthäus, Klinsmann and Brehme were bought under his management and Trapattoni was brought in as manager, after his legendary spell with Juventus, where he remained from 1986 to 1991. During this period, Sacchi's AC Milan and Maradona's Napoli were dominating nationally and internationally but Inter won the Scudetto in 1989 and the UEFA Cup in 1991.

1989–2006: Mixed Fortunes: Great Talent but a Curse

The 1990s was a period of disappointment. While Inter's rivals Milan and Juventus were achieving success both domestically and in Europe, Inter suffered from repeated mediocre results in the domestic league standings, with their worst coming in 1993/94, when they finished just one point out of the relegation zone. Whilst Inter achieved some European success with three UEFA Cup victories in 1991, 1994 and 1998 and had arguably one of the most talented squads, especially around the 2000s, in the 18-year period from 1989–2006, the club didn't win a single Scudetto or Champions League trophy.

With Massimo Moratti's takeover from Ernesto Pellegrini in 1995, Inter twice broke the transfer fee world record in this period (€23.2 million for Ronaldo from Barcelona in 1997 and €36.9 million for Christian Vieri from Lazio two years later). However, the 1990s remains the only decade in Inter's history in which they did not win a single Serie A championship. For Inter fans, it was difficult to pinpoint who or what was to blame for the troubled times and this led to some icy relations between them and the chairman, the managers and even some individual players. Nationally, they suffered from the successive successful cycles of AC Milan and Juventus, and internationally, some of their best attempts in the Champions League were also blocked by AC Milan (where they lost in the semi-finals in 2003 and the quarter-finals in 2005).

The number of top players over that time period was incredible and was better or at least on a par with any other club in Europe. These players include Brehme, Klinsmann, Matthäus (Ballon d'Or winner), Ronaldo (two-time Ballon d'Or winner), Baggio (Ballon d'Or winner), Vieri, Zanetti, Bergomi, Toldo, Recoba, Seedorf, Pirlo, Bergkamp, Adriano, Simeone, Djorkaeff, Blanc, Veron, Roberto Carlos and Zamorano.

Inter also had a reputation for spending extreme amounts on both transfers and salaries, having too many players and too high a turnover of both players and coaches. This resulted in instability and poor results, in spite of the individual talent level of each player. While Inter appeared to have the best team on paper, this did not translate into the ultimate success on the pitch. For example, on 5 May 2002, when Inter had been leading Serie A for most of the season and only needed to beat Lazio (in a stadium where even Lazio fans cheered for Inter) to win the Scudetto, after leading 1-0 and then 2-1, the curse struck again. Lazio scored three unanswered goals and Inter lost the Scudetto to Juve that day, who were just as shocked by winning as the Inter fans were. This day was one that went down in infamy, and soon after Brazilian Ronaldo (who cried on the bench during the match) left for Real Madrid.

At the time, Inter probably had some of the best strikers in the world (Ronaldo and Vieri), talented midfielders like Di Biagio, Seedorf and Recoba, tough defenders like Cordoba, Materazzi and Zanetti and goalkeeper Toldo. Newly appointed coach Hector Cuper was also touched by this losing curse; he had just made it to two consecutive Champions League finals with Valencia before taking over at Inter, and promptly lost the Scudetto during the last part of the last game of the season.

During the next few seasons, the curse remained. In 2003, Inter finished second behind Juve and were eliminated in the Champions League semi-finals by AC Milan. In 2005, Inter finished third in Serie A and were eliminated by AC Milan once again in the Champions League quarter-finals. After this loss, the fans had reached their breaking point – while Milan were leading 1-0 in the return game (after winning 2-0 in the first game) Inter fans turned against their own players and launched fireworks onto the pitch, injuring the AC Milan goalkeeper and resulting in the suspension of the game.

2006–2010: The Successful Cycle

Whilst the Calciopoli scandal, which was brought to light after the end of the 2005/06 season, hurt some of the big clubs, it also led to the start of one of the most successful cycles for Inter and rewarded them with an 'off-the-pitch' Scudetto because of some of the penalties and relegations (which was the first one since 1989). After Calciopoli, not only were Juventus relegated to Serie B, but Inter also managed to buy some of their best players, including superstar Ibrahimović. Inter became the new favourites to win the Scudetto, with Roma the only club that were able to seriously compete. Inter then won four Scudetti in a row from 2006/07 to 2009/10, which brought its total to 18 when including the post-Calciopoli win.

During this period, Inter invested heavily in reinforcing the team each year in spite of the dominance on the pitch, and acquired players such as Brazilians Julio Cesar, Maicon, Maxwell and Adriano, Argentinians Samuel, Cambiasso, captain Javier 'El Tractor' Zanetti (who played from 1995 to 2014 for Inter and whose shirt number four was retired out of respect), Cruz, Colombian Cordoba and other top players like Ibrahimović, Stankovic, Vieira, Chivu and Figo. The only top Italian player in the squad at that point was Materazzi. This led to an impressive team with lots of physical strength and experience and was Inter's best hope for finally winning the Champions League, which hadn't been done since the back-to-back wins of 1964 and 1965. In order to achieve this dream, in 2008 Moratti replaced Roberto Mancini with José Mourinho as manager. Whilst this didn't immediately result in a Champions League title, with the club losing in the Round of 16 to Manchester United, Inter still dominated nationally and won its third Scudetto in a row. The following season, however, Mourinho made some radical changes – Ibrahimović was traded for Barcelona striker Eto'o; Figo retired; Cruz, Crespo, Maxwell and Burdisso left; Brazilian defender Lucio was brought in along with Dutch superstar Sneijder; and Diego Milito and Thiago Motta were bought from Genoa. The success was immediate as Inter won the Champions League, the Scudetto and the Italian Cup, which was the first time an Italian team had ever achieved such a result (which is referred to as the 'treble').

In December 2010, Inter claimed the FIFA Club World Cup for the first time after a 3-0 win against TP Mazembe in the final. Inter thus completed the quintuple, becoming the third team in the world to do so, after Al-Ahly in 2006 and Barcelona in 2009.

2010–Present: The Decline

Mourinho left the club the same night after that historical success and many fans still remember him saying goodbye to Materazzi in a very emotional moment. Inter have not been able to recover since. Benitez was brought in to replace Mourinho (who referred to himself as 'the Special One'), but the first few months were a disappointment on the pitch. While most of the players were still the same, the team was not playing at the same level any more. Benitez was then fired in December and Leonardo (former player and coach of AC Milan) was brought in. Inter performed better under Leonardo's leadership, but ultimately lost the Serie A title to AC Milan that season and were knocked out of the Champions League by FC Schalke 04 (led by former Real Madrid star Raúl González) who beat Inter at the San Siro (5-2). Similar to what happened to Milan, many of Inter's best players were ageing and retiring all around the same time and could not be replaced fast enough. This led to a decline on the pitch. Inter have not finished in the top three in Serie A since that season (2010/11).

Inter experienced a cultural drift after 2010 that was very similar to that of its Milanese rivals. After a great period of success with a stable team and generation, Inter saw these players ageing and leaving the club one by one, which damaged the successful culture and team strength at the same time. The drift was mostly due to the end of the cycle, Mourinho leaving and some superstars retiring. The following replacement choices didn't have the same talent and their financial power wasn't substantial enough to compete at the same levels any more.

Inter's Ballon d'Or Top Three Finishers

Season	Ballon d'Or
1964/65	Giacinto Facchetti 2nd
1989/90	Matthäus Winner and Brehme 3rd
1990/91	Matthäus 2nd
1992/93	Bergkamp 2nd
1996/97	Ronaldo Winner
1997/98	Ronaldo 3rd
2001/02	Ronaldo Winner (half season at Inter before joining Real Madrid)

Inter's UEFA Top 11 Winners

2002	Seedorf and Ronaldo
2007	Ibrahimović
2009	Ibrahimović
2010	Maicon and Sneijder

Oil prices steadily climbed from 1998 to 2008, dropped in 2009 and 2010, then rebounded and were above $100 a barrel from 2011–2014, before dropping off significantly thereafter. Strong and steadily increasing oil prices helped Inter invest in talent over the years, which culminated in their treble season in 2010 and further success in 2011. Oil prices were high from 2011–2014, but at that point Moratti wasn't the owner.

Inter's Italian League and Champions League/UEFA Cup Results and Oil Prices 1988–2013

Year	Serie A	CL/UEFA Cup	Oil prices $
1988/89	Winners		
1989/90	3rd		
1990/91	3rd	Winners UEFA Cup	
1991/92			
1992/93	2nd		16.75
1993/94		Winners UEFA Cup	15.66
1994/95			16.75

1995/96			20.46
1996/97	3rd	Final UEFA Cup	18.64
1997/98	2nd	Winners UEFA Cup	11.91
1998/99		Quarter-finals	16.56
1999/00			27.39
2000/01			23.00
2001/02	3rd		22.81
2002/03	2nd	Semi-finals	27.69
2003/04		Group	37.66
2004/05	3rd	Quarter-finals	50.04
2005/06	3rd*	Quarter-finals	58.30
2006/07	Winners	Round of 16	64.20
2007/08	Winners	Round of 16	91.48
2008/09	Winners	Round of 16	53.48
2009/10	Winners	Winners	71.21
2010/11	2nd	Quarter-finals	87.04
2011/12		Round of 16	
2012/13			

Off the Pitch

Culture and Identity

Obviously, having 'International' in its name helps set an identity. The original 44 founding members split from AC Milan to have international players in the team and made the statement 'we are brothers of the world', and that has been at the heart of Inter's identity over the years. One of the biggest differences between Inter and their two main rivals, Juventus and AC Milan, is the amount of foreigners they have in the team, which was most pronounced during the last successful cycle (Materazzi was often the only Italian on the pitch). Many coaches were also foreigners, like legends Mourinho and Herrera.

Interestingly, while the club's fans have embraced foreign players and coaches, that acceptance does not seem to fully extend to ownership. In 2013, when it was announced that Indonesian sports investor Erick Thohir and his consortium would acquire a 70% stake, the news was met with mixed emotions from Italians. While this was clearly positive from a financial perspective, not everyone was on board. In an interview with *La Gazzetta dello Sport*, ex-Inter Milan president Ernesto Pellegrini was quoted as saying, 'The Indonesian is only interested in business. The club must stay Italian and be restructured; I can help find other entrepreneurs. I have nothing personal against Thohir, I don't know him and he has an enviable financial position. However, this situation saddens me because I would hate to see my favourite team end up in the hands of a stranger.' Furthermore, immediately after the announcement, the Italian media began to speculate more generally about whether or not Thohir had the 'passion' to lead the team to success on the pitch. 'Money, to be sure, won't be lacking,' read a piece in Italy's influential sports daily, *La Gazzetta dello Sport* about Thohir, 'but what's doubtful is whether the passion is there.' Given the club's founding was rooted in being 'international', these are certainly interesting statements to make and to call into question whether or not Inter is different from some of the other Italian teams in its acceptance of foreigners. In a country where loyalty is valued very highly, being Italian lends a certain amount of credibility to an owner because that deep sense of pride and appreciation of the passion surrounding the team is never questioned – or at least questioned much less. Coming in as a foreigner, fans will always be slightly sceptical of the reason for the purchase and whether or not it is purely for financial gain or personal reasons.

With the Suning acquisition in 2016, Inter fans were left with an even less clear situation. The company had said it wanted to create a global sporting 'ecosystem', including club ownership, sports media rights, player agencies, training institutions, broadcast platforms, content production and sports-related e-commerce – which is obviously a much broader focus than even Thohir's ambitions. Many view the deal positively because of the financial resources that will be available to the club, and as long as Inter win on the pitch, many fans will stop questioning the ownership structure. However, if the team continues to suffer, confidence will probably be further eroded.

'Crazy Inter'

Inter is known for having 'artists' – those who have incredible talent but are often misunderstood. Players who fall into this category include Baggio, Recoba, Adriano and Balotelli amongst many others. All of their talent did not get converted into trophies but no one questioned that

Inter often had one of the best squads in Europe. Part of that concept is also explained in their song 'Pazza Inter Amala'. The song says 'Crazy Inter: love her!', referring to Inter having been capable of everything, from the worst to the best, from incredible losses like that 2002 Scudetto to great victories like the 2010 treble. The 'crazy Inter' the song refers to reminds the fans that they should love her for that, like art.

Revenues

Over-reliance on Broadcasting Revenues

Even when Inter won the treble in 2010, the club ranked #9 in the Deloitte Football Money League Revenue rankings. With no real focus on commercial revenues, in five years, Inter dropped to #19. As revenues declined to 2002–05 levels in 2013–16, Inter's performance in Serie A declined as the club had less money to spend on talent.

Inter's Deloitte Football Money League Revenues and Rankings 2000/01 to 2016/17
€ in millions

Year	Revenue	DFML Rank	Serie A Rank
2000/01	112.8	10	5
2001/02	n/a	n/a	3
2002/03	162.5	6	2
2003/04	167.1	8	4
2004/05	177.2	9	3
2005/06	206.6	7	1
2006/07	195	9	1
2007/08	172.9	10	1
2008/09	196.5	9	1
2009/10	224.8	9	1
2010/11	211.4	8	2
2011/12	200.6	11	6
2012/13	168.8	15	9
2013/14	164.0	17	5
2014/15	164.8	19	8
2015/16	179.2	19	4
2016/17	262.1	15	7

Looking at Inter's revenues breakdown in more detail over the years, it is clear they are very similar to most of the other Italian teams. Revenues are heavily skewed to broadcasting and are very low for matchday. When Inter were successful on the pitch, matchday revenues were noticeably higher, but since the decline those have seen an obvious drop-off. Interestingly, broadcasting revenues made up a much larger percentage as well, given strong Champions League performance, but have been affected by the shift from individual to collective broadcasting contracts.

Up until the 2009/10 season, Inter, like many of the other big Italian clubs, relied very heavily on broadcasting revenues as they were able to individually negotiate the sale of broadcast rights to their home league matches (the only other league that allowed this at the time was La Liga). The 2005/06 season was the first of a new two-year live rights deal with Sky Italia, which contributed to well over half of Inter's broadcasting revenue total for that year and the following one as well.

For the 2007/08 season, the trend was similar, this time with a different partner. For the three years from 2007/08, Inter benefited from a new broadcasting contract with Mediaset that was worth a reported €100 million per year (the original contract was for two years and then was extended for an additional year). However, like Juventus and AC Milan, this revenue source was severely affected by a push from the Italian government for Serie A clubs to return to a collective league-wide sale of broadcast rights from 2010/11 onwards. Given Inter's over-reliance on broadcasting revenues from these individually negotiated contracts, the drop-off from 2009/10 to 2010/11 was expected, but concerning nonetheless.

Interestingly, while the 2009/10 season was the most successful in the club's history, with Inter winning the Scudetto, Coppa Italia and Champions League, they did not move up in the Deloitte rankings, despite a €28 million (14%) uplift in revenue. During this season, matchday revenues saw a noticeable improvement, increasing by €10.4 million (37%) from 2008/09, which was the highest of all the Italian clubs, yet still only the 12th highest overall and at 17% was still much less than the major European clubs. This was also the season when plans were announced to redevelop the San Siro as part of Italy's UEFA Euro 2016 bid, but as the bid was unsuccessful, the renovation plans were put on hold.

The 2010/11 season gave the first hints of the decline to come. As previously mentioned, a shift to collective broadcasting rights hurt the club the most, but matchday revenues suffered as well. The only bright spot was an increase in commercial revenues, but it was not that much higher than 2005/06 levels.

Breakdown of Inter's Revenues 2005/06 to 2010/11
€ in millions

| | 2005/06 | | 2006/07 | | 2007/08 | | 2008/09 | | 2009/10 | | 2010/11 | |
	Revenue	%	Revenue	%	Revenue	%	Revenue	%	Revenue	%	Revenue	%
Matchday	29.2	14%	29.8	15%	28.4	16%	28.2	14%	38.6	17%	32.9	16%
Broadcasting	130.4	63%	128	66%	107.7	62%	115.7	59%	137.9	61%	124.4	59%
Commercial	47	23%	37.2	19%	36.8	21%	52.6	27%	48.3	21%	54.1	26%
Total	206.6		195		172.9		196.5		224.8		211.4	
DFML Rank	7		9		10		9		9		8	
League (Rank)	3*		1		1		1		1		2	
UCL Result	Quarter-Finals		Round of 16		Round of 16		Round of 16		Champions		Quarter-Finals	

Source: Deloitte

Whilst the 2010/11 season showed some warning signs, the following year was when Inter's decline really became visible in full force. Inter's performance on the pitch (a sixth-place finish in Serie A after four Scudetti in a row followed by a second-place finish) combined with a stadium becoming more obsolete greatly impacted matchday revenues, which declined by €9.7 million (29%) to €23.2 million, less than 20% of the Money League club with the highest income from this source, and just 13% of Inter's total revenue. The Nerazzurri played two fewer home matches in 2011/12 than in 2010/11, and average home league match attendances fell by over 8,000 (16%) to 44,577. Additionally, broadcasting revenues continued to come under pressure from both the collective rights agreement as well as a less impressive Champions League run that season, but still represented 60% of the club's total revenues.

From 2012/13 to 2015/16, the trend was fairly similar. Matchday revenues represented a tiny proportion of overall revenues, primarily because of Inter's struggling performance on the pitch as well as no concrete signs that any improvements to the stadium would be made in the near future. During this time period, Inter's absence from Champions

League play put a major dent in total revenue figures as well, and broadcasting revenues suffered in kind.

Breakdown of Inter's Revenues 2011/12 to 2016/17
€ in millions

	2011/12		2012/13		2013/14		2014/15		2015/16		2016/17	
	Revenue	%	Revenue	%	Revenue	%	Revenue	%	Revenue	%	Revenue	%
Matchday	23.3	12%	19.4	11%	18.8	11%	22.2	13%	25.7	14%	28.4	11%
Broadcasting	112.4	60%	81.5	48%	84.8	52%	97.2	59%	98.6	55%	130.1	50%
Commercial	50.3	27%	67.9	40%	60.4	37%	45.4	28%	54.9	31%	103.6	40%
Total	185.9		168.8		164		164.8		179.2		262.1	
DFML Rank	12		15		17		19		19		15	
League (Rank)	6		9		5		8		4		7	
UCL Result	Round of 16		n/a		n/a		Europa R16		n/a		Europa Group	

Source: Deloitte

Commercial Revenues Provide Strong Growth

All hope is not lost, however, as the most recent DFML report for the 2016/17 season showed a noticeable improvement for Inter, driven primarily by increasing commercial revenues. Commercial revenues received a huge boost (increased by €75.2 million or 137%) following the club's acquisition by Suning in June 2016, which is very positive from a diversification perspective and this led them to jump four places to 15th in the rankings. Nevertheless, this increase masked Inter's continued faltering on-field efforts which resulted in a seventh-place finish in Serie A and no participation in UEFA competition in 2017/18. The impact of the increase in commercial revenue has significantly brightened the future Money League prospects of Inter, who had looked destined to drop out of the top 20 for the first time, especially as all three of the revenue categories of Serie A clubs have grown at the lowest rates of the 'big five' leagues over recent years. Hopefully the new ownership can continue to promote Inter in the way that it was founded – a club with international roots and appeal that can take advantage of the globalisation and commercialisation of football.

Breakdown of Inter's Revenues 2013 to 2017

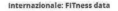

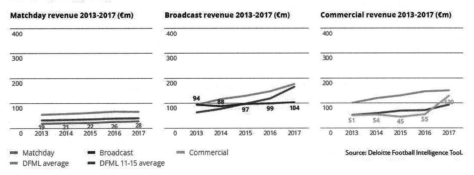

Source: Deloitte

When looking at Inter's revenue growth (or lack thereof) over time, it seems as though they have been suffering from an asymmetry problem – success on the pitch has not necessarily translated into success off the pitch in the form of higher revenues while a decline on the pitch has led to a huge drop-off in revenues. Basically, Inter need to better capitalise on their success, focus on stadium improvements, and continue to increase commercial revenue growth in order to improve their financial performance – which will hopefully then lead to improved performance on the pitch.

The agreements with Nike and Pirelli have kept commercial revenues fairly stable over the years, even during the decline on the pitch – but it wasn't until the Suning investment and their sponsorship that commercial revenues actually saw a significant boost. Granted the percentage of total revenue is about the same, but the magnitude of the absolute number is so much higher and has put Inter back on track to start to be competitive with the top clubs.

Poor Overall Fan Experience: Old Stadium

The San Siro used to be one of the best stadiums in Europe, not only for its high capacity (around 80,000 over time, with some changes due to security reasons), but also for the atmosphere during the games. Milan and Inter fans are both incredibly passionate and are known for great 'tifo' and singing.

The stadium was great for the '80s and '90s, but is now outdated, run-down, and generally provides a poor matchday experience in spite of the enthusiasm from the crowds. At this point, it needs to either undergo a massive renovation or the two teams need to move to different, more modern stadiums in order to keep up with the rest of the world.

Inter's Matchday Attendance and Rank

Stadium	Season	Avg Attendance	Capacity	Utilisation	League	Rank
San Siro	1996/97	46,715	80,018	58%	Serie A	3
San Siro	1997/98	78,000	80,018	97%	Serie A	2
San Siro	1998/99	62,576	80,018	78%	Serie A	8
San Siro	1999/00	63,796	80,018	80%	Serie A	4
San Siro	2000/01	50,677	80,018	63%	Serie A	5
San Siro	2001/02	62,434	80,018	78%	Serie A	3
San Siro	2002/03	61,943	80,018	77%	Serie A	2
San Siro	2003/04	56,141	80,018	70%	Serie A	4
San Siro	2004/05	55,225	80,018	69%	Serie A	3
San Siro	2005/06	51,501	80,018	64%	Serie A	1
San Siro	2006/07	48,423	80,018	61%	Serie A	1
San Siro	2007/08	52,299	80,018	65%	Serie A	1
San Siro	2008/09	55,520	80,018	69%	Serie A	1
San Siro	2009/10	56,368	80,018	70%	Serie A	1
San Siro	2010/11	58,764	80,018	73%	Serie A	2
San Siro	2011/12	44,778	80,018	56%	Serie A	6
San Siro	2012/13	45,796	80,018	57%	Serie A	9
San Siro	2013/14	46,088	80,018	58%	Serie A	5
San Siro	2014/15	37,270	80,018	47%	Serie A	8
San Siro	2015/16	45,538	80,018	57%	Serie A	4
San Siro	2016/17	46,620	80,018	58%	Serie A	7
San Siro	2017/18	58,283	80,018	73%	Serie A	5*

*As of 18-Apr-2018

*Source: http://www.transfermarkt.com/inter-mailand/besucherzahlenentwicklung/verein/46

For Milan and Inter, it used to be an advantage to play at the San Siro, but now this effect is largely gone. There is so much history rooted in those grounds, and if one team leaves, it is essentially conceding to the other side, which greatly upsets the diehard fans. Inter are struggling with the fact that they need to care enough about the locals to appease them, since they are the most passionate supporters, but at the end of the day, growth is going to come globally and from attracting casual fans. In order to have a self-sustaining business model, the new owners need to diversify revenues by improving the matchday experience. Inter have talked about the idea of a new stadium several times, but have never successfully completed the project, and they also seem to be waiting to see what Milan will do.

Online Engagement Catching Up

Inter's presence on social media is less developed than many of the other major clubs in Europe, and they rank fourth in Serie A in terms of total social media following on the major platforms, with 8.6 million followers across Facebook, Instagram and Twitter. As for the social media presence of individual players, Inter are struggling as well. Icardi, who has the highest following amongst Inter players, only has 4.3 million followers compared to Buffon from Juventus at the top of Serie A with 12.61 million. Considering there are players with 50+ million followers, Inter have a long way to go to gain international recognition on the same scale as the top teams in Europe. Unfortunately, and similar to many of Inter's rivals in Serie A, the rise and importance of social media coincided with the decline of Inter's results on the pitch. If social media had been as important in the 2000s as it is today, there is no doubt Inter would look better on this metric given the number of superstars in the squad. However, Inter do not currently have the same level of talent that they used to have during their previous successful cycle, and that has clearly hurt them from a branding and popularity perspective, especially on these platforms.

Needless to say, Inter have taken concrete steps to increase their online footprint. In 2014, Inter employed LMO Advertising with the purpose of growing engagement in the team's social media fan base in the US during its tour, with the bulk of the campaign taking place during the 2014 Guinness International Champions Cup tournament. The team of creators at LMO developed a social media effort that helped the Italian team appeal to American audiences while maintaining the club's European character. The goal of the campaign was to increase Inter's social media engagement with American audiences, build a stronger fan base and foster excitement among American fans.[1]

---

[1] https://capitolcommunicator.com/lmo-engaged-with-inter-a-soccer-club-in-milan-italy-to-grow-

In 2015, the club hired the Somethin' Else agency to develop a new fan engagement strategy. Somethin' Else will develop a coordinated approach to content distribution for the club, aimed at driving ticket sales in Italy and stimulating global interest online. The Italian content includes behind-the-scenes footage and video which is only available at the San Siro on matchdays. Internationally, the focus will be on shorter, mobile-friendly news pieces and updates which will be tailored to local markets and different time zones. The US, China, Japan, Indonesia and Australia are among the club's target markets. 'Inter have one of the biggest and most dedicated fan bases of any football club in the world,' said Somethin' Else's executive creative director. 'This is genuinely a radical move for them. By putting the marketing of the team at the heart of their business strategy, it will improve their ability to leverage the passion of the club into valuable new revenue going forward.'[2]

In 2017, Inter announced the Inter Media House project – a new way for fans to have exclusive access to the club. Content from the Inter Media House project provides fans with insights into the club. These insights are heightened with the use of virtual and augmented reality, which allow fans to peek in on the Nerazzurri's everyday life. The new Inter app helps distribute content in an even more interactive, faster and easier way. It also lets users customise and personalise their experience, and by setting the information setting to 'Always On', users receive real time notifications on their favourite players, details of training, matches and ticketing. With regards to this, Inter CEO Alessandro Antonello said in a statement: 'Football is changing and football clubs are becoming more and more like media and entertainment companies. Inter is a club with a long history – we celebrate our 110th birthday on 9 March next year – and we've enjoyed a great deal of success down the years. That's why we're one of the biggest football brands in the world. We want to ensure we remain at the forefront of the game in this time of great change by exporting our brand outside of Italy.'[3]

As a result of this concerted effort, Inter reached a major social media milestone in December 2017, hitting the 7 million follower mark on

engagement-by-the-teams-u-s-social-media-fan-base/

[2] http://www.sportspromedia.com/news/inter-opt-for-somethin-else

[3] https://www.sporttechie.com/fc-internazionale-milao-enables-new-media-approach-intel-media-house/

Facebook. Inter claim that more than 80% of their new followers come from outside Italy. Inter say that this growth shows that the club is becoming a 'modern entertainment company that puts fan experience at the heart of everything'. With video – including behind-the-scenes content, interviews and even live streaming of youth team games – at the heart of their Facebook strategy, and rich historical content including stories, images and old video footage on the website, Inter are changing.[4]

Inter TV

Inter also have a TV channel, which is one of the oldest of the big clubs. Inter TV is a subscription-based channel, entirely dedicated to the club and it is headquartered at Inter's training centre in Appiano Gentile. The channel offers Inter fans exclusive interviews with players and staff, full matches, including replays of all Serie A, Coppa Italia and Champions League/Europa League games, in addition to vintage matches, footballing news and other themed programming. It first broadcast on 20 September 2000 as Inter Channel, with the current name being adopted on 28 September 2017.

Power of the Ultras

The traditional Ultras group of Inter is *Boys San*; they hold a significant place in the history of the Ultras scene in general due to the fact that they are one of the oldest, being founded in 1969. Politically, the Ultras of Inter are usually considered right-wing and they have a good relationship with the Lazio Ultras. As well as the main group of *Boys San*, there are four more significant groups: *Viking, Irriducibili, Ultras* and *Brianza Alcoolica*.

While Inter have one of the best stadium attendances of Serie A and Europe, some of their Ultras have created problems over the years. As previously mentioned, many remember the AC Milan – Inter Milan derby in the quarter-finals of the Champions League in 2005, when AC Milan's qualification was clear (leading 3-0 on aggregate) and the Inter Ultras decided to launch fireworks onto the pitch to stop the game. AC

---

4 https://digitalsport.co/inter-milan-reach-social-media-milestone-as-ambitious-strategy-pays-off

Milan goalkeeper Dida was hit by one of them, the referee suspended the game for a while, and after realising that they wouldn't stop was forced to abandon the game entirely. Inter were heavily penalised later because of this and it is clear that the Ultras have too much power, but this is certainly not a unique problem to Inter.

Final Remarks

Sponsorships have been and will continue to be important to Inter in terms of revenues growth and branding power. Historically, Nike and Pirelli have been the most consistent sponsors and have provided stable commercial revenues. In March 2016, Inter and Pirelli announced that they were extending their long-time partnership for another five years. The new deal comprised a fixed amount and a variable figure based on the performance of the club on the pitch. The Pirelli brand has been a feature of Inter's shirts since 1995. The union is now into its 21st year and is one of the longest partnerships in the history of top European clubs. This solid and lasting relationship is built upon values which both brands have historically shared and which have defined their achievements over the years. Marco Tronchetti Provera, Pirelli's executive vice chairman and CEO was quoted as saying, 'Pirelli are a global player and the passion that a historic club like Inter generates in the hearts of fans all over the world is an important asset in maximising our brand.' It is clear that both sides value this relationship and see the commercial benefit from linking their brands together, which is rooted in passion and history.[5]

Shortly after this announcement, Suning purchased their majority 70% stake in the club. Given Inter's focus on expanding in the Chinese market, this was fortuitous in that Suning Commerce Group is one of the largest non-government retailers in China, has more than 1,600 stores covering over 700 cities in China (mainland China and Hong Kong S.A.R.) and Japan and its e-commerce platform, Suning.com, ranks in the top three Chinese B2C companies. In the 2016/17 season, Inter saw a large boost in commercial revenues as a result of this, which also bodes well for the future as further revenue diversification is a top priority.

After the change in ownership, Suning became the official training

---

[5] http://www.inter.it/en/news/51761

kit partner for the senior and junior teams and were granted naming rights to both the club's training ground and the club's youth training centre. The club's main training facility is now known as 'The Suning Training Centre in memory of Angelo Moratti', and the youth centre was renamed 'The Suning Training Centre in memory of Giacinto Facchetti', honouring two former Inter chairmen. Michael Gandler, Inter's chief revenue officer, said: 'This partnership is an important step for Inter as we continue to more effectively monetise the value of our assets. Through this partnership Suning can expect major branding opportunities, increased global media coverage and direct fan engagement on Inter's digital and media platforms. We also expect to further develop other core areas of our business through Suning, including e-commerce, retail and media.'

Suning have grand plans for Inter, but also recognise that it will take time to propel the club back to where it was during its former glory days. Steven Zhang, a vice president at Suning and founder Zhang Jindong's son said shortly after the acquisition, 'Have patience and trust in the club – I know fans love the club from their heart . . . Of course, the next game is important, especially if you own Inter, a club that has so much power and so much responsibility. But in order to succeed, I always think investing in . . . long-term strategies are what's most important for this club.' Some components of this strategy include focusing on the youth academy, upgrading training facilities and looking into cutting-edge technology to scout and analyse athletes. Suning have also talked about the need for more talent both from a player and coaching standpoint.

PART THREE

REVIVAL: NEW APPROACHES, OWNERS AND INNOVATORS

CHAPTER NINE

JUVENTUS – 'NEWVENTUS'

Note to reader: The next three chapters are short case studies of three clubs: Juventus, Roma, and Napoli. The case studies apply the framework we developed to the specific clubs to shed more light on both the on-the-pitch and off the pitch (business) aspects of the clubs, and the league. While there are signs of a revival with other clubs too, we highlight these three in particular to draw the reader's attention to specific changes, innovations and approaches. A reader can decide to skip the case studies and continue to Part Four: The Future.

Overview

Juventus FC, also informally known as 'Juve', were founded in 1897 as Sport-Club Juventus and are located in Torino (Turin). Juventus are the third oldest club in Italy, after Genoa (1893) and Udinese (1896). Juventus have won an Italian record 34 Serie A titles (Scudetti). On Juventus's shirt, they have three stars. One star equals ten Scudetti (Milan and Inter have one star because of 18 Scudetti). Juventus have won the last seven Serie A titles, an Italian record. They have been in the Champions League/European Cup final nine times, however, winning only twice. They have been in two finals in the last four years, losing in 2014/15 to Barcelona and in 2016/17 to Real Madrid.

Juventus means 'youth' in Latin. By choosing the Latin word for 'youth' as their name, inadvertently they opened the way for Juventus to attract supporters beyond Turin. As elsewhere, most other major Italian clubs are named after the place in which they are based. This feeds into the culture of *campanilismo* (literally 'bell-towerism') – your primary identity coming from your hometown or local area, rather than nation. Such parochial pride is particularly prominent in Italy, a country that was only unified in 1871 and still contains numerous local cultures, cuisines and dialects. By identifying themselves with an idea rather than a town, Juventus provide an alternative to the *campanilismo*. Indeed, the temptation they offer to stray away from home towns has led to them to be jokingly referred to as *la fidanzata d'Italia* ("Italy's girlfriend").[1]

Juventus have been controlled by the Agnelli family since 1923 when Fiat (Fabricca Italiana Automobili Torino) owner Edoardo Agnelli bought the club. His motto was 'everything can always be done better'. He implemented this saying by instilling the professionalism and will to win that is Juve's hallmark to this day. His sons Gianni, affectionately known as L'Avvocato, and Umberto became presidents in the 1950s and 1960s and now Umberto's son, Andrea, is the club's president. It makes the family the longest-lasting ownership in any sports franchise in the world. The Agnellis were generally popular employers. Many blue-collar workers adopted their football club as a weekend escape from factory life.

During its history, the club has acquired a number of nicknames, la Vecchia Signora (the 'Old Lady') being the best example. The other most popular nickname is 'i bianconeri' (the black and whites) in reference to Juventus's colours.

Juventus have played in black and white striped shirts, most often with white shorts, since 1903. Originally, they played in pink shirts with a black tie. According to legend, the father of one of the players made the earliest shirts, but continual washing faded the colour so much that in 1903 the club sought to replace them. Juventus asked one of their English team members if he had any contacts in England who could provide new shirts in a colour that would last longer. He had a friend who lived

1 http://www.theneweuropean.co.uk/culture/juventus-is-europe-s-most-colourful-football-club-1-5111889

in Nottingham, who, being a Notts County supporter, shipped out the black and white striped shirts to Turin.

The club has also been very successful throughout its history, which is why it is considered a symbol of the country's 'Italianness', locally known as Italianità. Juventus, in many ways, is the only Italian club that is considered a national club that transcends strong regional affiliations. For example, in Milan, Juventus have as many supporters as Milan or Inter. Many national Italian team players played at Juventus, and since a lot of the regions didn't have consistently competitive and financially viable clubs to support, many of those regional fans supported their national stars, who were playing at Juventus. In addition, many workers at factories throughout Italy that provide parts to Fiat historically supported Juventus because of the Agnelli/Fiat patrimonial connection. Also, since Juventus were consistently in European tournaments with many Italian national team members, many Italian fans considered Juventus at least their second favourite team to root for after their local club to beat other big European clubs. In Italy's 1982 World Cup-winning team, Juventus had six key players and on the 2006 World Cup-winning team, they had five. Two Juventus players have won the Golden Boot award at the World Cup with Italy: Paolo Rossi in 1982 and Salvatore Schillaci in 1990. Lastly, since most of the Italian emigration worldwide was from southern Italy, and Juventus was/is the most beloved in the south, many of the Italian émigrés across the world support Juventus as it reminds them of their country, again related to the national team. Therefore, Juventus have a large global fan base.

Juventus's official emblem has undergone a number of minor modifications since the 1920s. The previous modification of the Juventus badge took place in 2004, when the emblem of the team changed to a black and white oval shield of a type used by Italian ecclesiastics. A silhouette of a charging bull was a part of the emblem because the bull is a symbol of Turin. In January 2017, the Juventus badge changed, which was a big deal for some traditionalists. The new badge has the word Juventus on top, with two capital Js shown together in different fonts with a small opening between them to almost make a bigger J. The new logo represents three elements that make up the Juventus DNA: the 'J' of the name, the bianconere stripes of the shirt and the stylisation of the shield, the symbol of victory.

In 2015, Juventus officially announced a new project called JKids for its junior supporters on its website. Along with this project, Juventus also introduced a new mascot to all its fans which is called Jay, playing on another nickname for the club, 'le zebre' (the zebras). Jay is a cartoon-designed zebra, black and white stripes with golden edge piping on its body, golden shining eyes, and three golden stars on the front of its neck. The club's zebra mascot cheerleads in the home stadium before the game, at half-time, on the sidelines and online.[2]

Juventus have several significant rivalries. Their traditional rivals are fellow Turin club Torino and matches between the two sides are known as the 'Derby della Mole'. Their most high-profile rivalry is with Inter. Matches between these two clubs are referred to as the 'Derby d'Italia' (Derby of Italy) because at the time the derby nickname developed, the two regularly challenged each other at the top of the Italian league table, hence the intense rivalry. Juventus also have a rivalry with Milan, referred to as the 'Derby d'Europa' because both clubs have had so much European success. Juventus have rivalries with Roma and Napoli as well that revolve around regional pride as both teams have been towards the top of the league table more recently, although neither of the matches has a derby nickname.

Along with Lazio and Roma, Juventus are one of only three Italian clubs quoted on Borsa Italiana (the Italian stock exchange). Juventus went public on the Borsa Italiana in 2001. Today, EXOR, an Agnelli family holding company, owns around 60% of Juventus.

Calciopoli Scandal of 2006

Italian football has had a long history of scandals, and arguably the biggest recent scandal was the Calciopoli scandal of 2006. It had a major impact with regards to the teams involved and the punishments and publicity, as well as player defections.[3]

The relegation of Juventus prompted a mass exodus of important players who, most likely, didn't want to play in Serie B and, nevertheless, Juventus couldn't afford all of them with the loss of Serie A TV broadcasting revenues. Players that moved included Ibrahimović (moved to Inter); Vieira (moved to Inter); Cannavaro and Emerson (moved to

---

[2] http://www.juventus.com/en/kids/meet-j-mascotte.php
[3] See section and footnotes in 'Clouds of Scandals'

Real Madrid); Thuram and Zambrotta (moved to Barcelona); and Mutu (moved to Fiorentina). The coach Capello also left for Real Madrid. Some players stayed and their loyalty earned them endearing affection from Juventus fans and respect from rival fans. Superstars Buffon, Nedvěd, Del Piero and Trezeguet stayed, also helping establish a core nucleus for a rebuilding of culture and leadership on the pitch.

Most importantly off the pitch, the scandal caused Juventus the loss of domestic pay TV and European competition revenues, which were the most important parts of revenues in 2006. Juventus's revenues dropped over €100 million from €251 million to €145 million, and the club dropped from #3 in the Deloitte Football Revenues to #12. Juventus didn't fully recover to surpass the 2005/06 season's revenues until the 2012/13 season with revenues of €272 million, which placed them at #9.

Ironically, the scandal caused Juventus to recognise many of its own issues. Besides over-reliance on pay TV revenues, it caused the club to recognise that the business of football had changed and that Juventus were not sustainable as currently managed and structured. The club needed to find new revenues and the club needed professional management. Juventus had an advantage in that it could draw on lessons learned in its global manufacturing business and other investments. Fiat was a global brand with an identity and it controlled other car brands at the time including Ferrari, Maserati, Lancia and Alfa Romeo. Fiat's manufacturing businesses were utilising data and analytics to make informed decisions. The scandal was essentially a wake-up call for Juventus. While Juventus restructured, other clubs, especially Inter and Milan, used it as a short-term opportunity and went on a spending spree versus re-examining their industry and themselves and restructuring accordingly. While there would be some short-term gains from the opportunistic strategy of its rivals, with Milan winning the Champions League in 2007 and Inter winning five Scudetti in a row, the long-term impact of the spending left Milan and Inter in long-term precarious financial situations.

Culture and Identity

Every start of the season, in August, the first team plays the Primavera team in Villar Perosa, a village southwest of Turin where Edoardo had a stadium built. The village was built in the 1930s by Edoardo, the first family member to run Juve, and for a while was the team's training base. One might think that with the demands and money of modern football, the friendly match was no longer viable, but Juve has stuck with tradition. The first team taking on the best players from the youth sector is known as the 'Family Match' – which perfectly encapsulates the spirit of the event. As well as the Agnelli clan, who organise the day's events, the players' families also attend, and the game is never marred by poor behaviour from fans. With its unique and exciting atmosphere, the town of Villar Perosa comes alive for the occasion. The tiny pitch and quaint surroundings are reminiscent of proud parents watching their children play in the local park, with around 5,000 fans. A tradition of the Family Match is the pitch invasion before full time, with the supporters peacefully invading the pitch and the players literally taking off and giving fans their shirts, shorts and boots, as well as players signing autographs and taking photos with supporters.

The entire affair emphasises one of the key values of the club – family. Unusually for a club of its size, Juventus has a strong family philosophy. Players regularly remain part of the fold long after their playing days are over. It is sometimes said that Juventus's approach stems from the Italian tradition of close extended families. There may be some truth in this but it does not happen at all Italian football clubs. Czech star of the 2000s, Nedvěd, laughs about how Umberto Agnelli, Gianni's younger brother and by then the club president, used to drop by regularly at his place whilst out walking his dog. The president calling in unannounced for a coffee and a chat about how he was getting on was not something Nedvěd had experienced at his previous clubs.[4]

'Fino alla fine,' or 'until the end' in English, describes Juve well. The fantasisti (playmakers) make their fans dream, but grinta (the grit), the passion and fighting spirit until the game ends, makes Juve tick. Giampiero Boniperti (former superstar player of Juve and former president of Juve, and fan of the Juve style 'humble, labour and discretion') explained why: 'at Juve winning is not important, it's the only thing that matters'. The statement highlights how Juventus's culture and values are focused on results, no matter how they do it. This has led to successes on the pitch

[4] http://www.theneweuropean.co.uk/culture/juventus-is-europe-s-most-colourful-football-club-1-5111889

and even the national team's way of playing and winning is related to that philosophy.

'Humble, labour and discretion' is even reflected in their shirt colours – black and white – no flashy or eccentric colours. It is the same for their way of playing: defensive, no flashy game and no attacking imbalance. Just like Barcelona (tiki-taka) or Real Madrid (attacking, beautiful and improvised) are also focused on a way and style of playing, Juventus are focused on a style and way of playing that reflects their values – defensive and tough. Somehow, that is also related to the Agnelli family (in contrast to Berlusconi, for example). The Agnellis have always been more discreet and humble than Berlusconi, who identified himself as a TV/media personality. In contrast, the Agnellis are industrial people. Also, the city of Turin is different to Rome or Napoli or Milan. Turin is more industrial, less glamorous. Black and white are perfect to represent Turin, while one would expect Rome, Naples and Milan to have more colour and make more noise, etc. Just like their way of playing, the Juventus mentality has also become the one of the national team or vice versa because so many Juventus players have been on the national team. For example, even historical rival Materazzi from Inter would say after winning the World Cup that the base of the success was down to Juventus players – their mentality and culture. This would be similar to the core of Barcelona players trained in the tiki-taka style that led to Spain's World Cup victory in 2010. This link is also reinforced with the fans abroad – the way Juventus and the national team play and their identity are always mixed and represent the same Italianità around the world.

Another core value of Juventus is a sense of loyalty. Buffon accepted playing for Juventus in Serie B in 2006. At that time, Buffon was a superstar at the peak of his career, had just won the World Cup and had offers from every big club. Del Piero, Nedvěd and Trezeguet were also great players, and they stayed at Juventus during tough times too. The culture is also reinforced by the club maintaining a family spirit (Italianità again) and respect with many former legends being brought back in some capacity by the club.

Juventus has been known for its tough defence. Defender Claudio Gentile was nicknamed 'the dictator' due to his toughness and birthplace in Colonel Gaddafi's Libya. After being very physical with Diego Maradona in a 1982 World Cup game, Gentile said 'football is not for ballerinas'. Midfielder Romeo Benetti's toughness earned him notoriety. Benetti says he knew he had gone too far when he overheard a mother whispering to her small child in a restaurant one day, 'There's Romeo Benetti. Now, eat your lunch or I'm going to bring him over here to sort you out.'[5]

Juventus have an official mission statement on their website, which differentiates them from most sports clubs:

Juventus is a professional football club which is listed on the stock exchange and is one of the most famous and revered teams both in Italy and internationally.

The club's underlying purpose is to provide supporters with the highest level of enjoyment possible by continuing a winning tradition that has been established during a glorious history spanning over 100 years.

This aim is pursued by following a series of precise rules which are outlined in the club's code of ethics and followed by all employees and consultants.

Among the main principles is the desire to promote ethics in sport and bridge the gap between the professional and business side of football, while maintaining the utmost respect towards fans and all sport enthusiasts.

Juventus also strives to maintain stable relationships with its shareholders by creating profits through the development of the Juventus brand and enhancement of sporting organisation.

The company's core business model is based on participation in national and international competitions. The main sources of revenue emerge from the exploitation of sports events, the Juventus brand and the image of the first team. In fact, the most significant revenue stream comes from television and media licensing rights along with the sale of advertising space.

The mission statement recognises the importance of entertainment ('enjoyment') and the 'Juventus brand and the image'. Juventus also highlight the importance of shareholders, recognising that the business does need to generate returns to those investors.

5 http://www.theneweuropean.co.uk/culture/juventus-is-europe-s-most-colourful-football-club-1-5111889

As the record holders of Serie A titles, winning almost twice as many as any other Italian club, Juventus have been remarkably consistent, finishing in the top three in most years since the 1980s. Since Serie A was founded in 1898, they have won 34 times out of 116 official seasons (29%). Their seven titles in a row is an incredible record that is without precedent in Italy.

In the Champions League, in the late 1990s, Juventus were one of the top few clubs in Europe, but after 1999 there was a drop-off in performance. While Juventus were winning or placing high in Serie A in the early 2000s, they were having less success in Europe. After a semi-final appearance in 1999, Juventus only got past the quarter-finals once, in 2003, until 2015, reflecting the decline of the Italian league itself.

Juventus Performance in Serie A and the Champions League

Year	Serie A	Champions League
1981	Winner	
1982	Winner	
1983	2nd	2nd
1984	Winner	
1985		Winner
1986	Winner	
1987	2nd	Round of 16
1988		
1989		
1990		
1991		
1992	2nd	
1993		
1994	2nd	
1995	Winner	
1996	2nd	Winner
1997	Winner	2nd
1998	Winner	2nd
1999		Semi-finals
2000	2nd	
2001	2nd	Group
2002	Winner	Group
2003	Winner	2nd

2004	3rd	Round of 16
2005	Winner*	Quarter-finals
2006	Winner*	Quarter-finals
2007	Serie B	Winner
2008	3rd	
2009	2nd	Round of 16
2010		
2011		
2012	Winner	
2013	Winner	Quarter-finals
2014	Winner	Group
2015	Winner	2nd
2016	Winner	Round of 16
2017	Winner	2nd
2018	Winner	Quarter-finals

Talent

With financial support from the Agnellis, Juventus have had many superstar players. From 1981 to 2017, Juventus have had eight players finish in the top three 13 times for the Ballon d'Or, which is more than any other team. (Defender Fabio Cannavaro won in 2006 as a Real Madrid player, but had transferred from Juventus during the summer.) However, the last winning Juventus striker was Roberto Baggio in 1993; Zidane (1998) and Nedvěd (2003) were midfielders. While Juventus have had a remarkable number of players finish in the top three since 1981, with the exception of goalkeeper Buffon (who finished #9 in 2016 and #4 in 2017), no Juventus player has finished in the top ten since 2006.

Juventus Ballon d'Or Top 3 since 1982

1982	Paolo Rossi	Winner
1983	Michel Platini	Winner
1984	Michel Platini	Winner
1985	Michel Platini	Winner
1990	Salvatore Schillaci	2nd
1993	Roberto Baggio	Winner
1994	Roberto Baggio	2nd
1997	Zinedine Zidane	3rd
1998	Zinedine Zidane	Winner

2000	Zinedine Zidane	2nd
2003	Pavel Nedvěd	Winner
2006	Fabio Cannavaro	Winner
2006	Gianluigi Buffon	2nd

Juventus have consistently had talent, but as their revenues declined relative to their big club peers, especially after 2006 (Buffon was purchased in 2001), they could no longer consistently compete to sign Ballon d'Or contenders for world record transfer fees such as Baggio, Buffon, Cannavaro and Zidane. Juventus are now at #10 in revenues, placing them at a competitive financial disadvantage to sign talent. They have done an excellent job selecting players and taking advantage of their culture and leadership. Juventus rank tenth in overall salaries in Europe. When looking at salary growth, Juventus have grown, but since 2006/07 not at the same pace as the top five clubs. In addition, one of the biggest issues is new competitive spending from Manchester City and PSG, who have had explosive growth in salaries. Lastly, Inter and Milan have had negative salary growth since the 2006/07 season.

In the top ten teams' total wages in 2016/17, the only club in the top ten was Juventus at #10. AC Milan #12, Roma #15 and Inter #16 were the only other clubs from Italy. There were 15 clubs in the top 25 from the English Premier League.

2016/17 Top 25 Club Total Wages
€ in millions

Rank	Club	Total Wages	% Change Since 2006/07
1	Barcelona	€324 million	113%
2	Man United	308	115%
3	Chelsea	298	72%
4	Real Madrid	291	70%
5	Man City	288	252%
6	PSG	278	697%
7	Arsenal	272	
8	Bayern Munich	262	
9	Liverpool	233	
10	**Juventus**	**210**	**47%**
11	Tottenham	140	
12	**AC Milan**	**134**	**-36%**
13	Dortmund	131	

14	Everton	12	
15	**Roma**	**122**	
16	**Inter Milan**	**119**	**-5%**
17	West Ham	110	
18	Southampton	107	
19	Stoke	107	
20	Swansea	107	
21	Leicester	105	
22	Sunderland	105	
23	Atlético Madrid	100	
24	West Brom	98	
25	Crystal Palace	80	
NR	Napoli	77	
NR	Sevilla	51	

Source: http://www.dailymail.co.uk/sport/football/article-4564154/Hey-big-spenders-Palace-match-world-s-best.html

To compete, Juventus have developed good or very good players into elite players (e.g. Bonucci, Dybala and Pogba), but even so, Juventus have had a difficult time retaining players. Juventus have also consistently taken many top or promising players in Serie A from competing clubs (Pirlo from Milan, Higuaín from Napoli and Pjanić from Roma), as some of their biggest transfer spending was inter-league, because they do have relative financial strength in Italy. This not only improves Juventus but weakens their opponents and has contributed to their record seventh Scudetto in a row. When asked how he selects his signings, General Manager of Sports Area Giuseppe Marotta said: 'In two ways. We either take someone who is already an established champion: look at Dani Alves, [Mario] Mandzukic, [Sami] Khedira, [Gonzalo] Higuaín and so on. Or, we look for talent. But only a talent who can become a champion. That means someone who has not only the technical qualities but also the human values to turn into a champion, as happened with [Paulo] Dybala, for example.'

Juventus are not known for developing players from their academy. Juventus is not an easy club for a young player to make his breakthrough into the first team given the quality of the players. Of the recent squads, the only real regular first teamer to have worked his way up the hard way from the Bianconeri's youth sides is Claudio Marchisio, who has been with Juventus since the age of just seven. Marchisio is sometimes referred to as the 'De Rossi of Turin', in reference to his national teammate Daniele De Rossi of Roma, due to their similar playing style, as well as the fact that both are local born and bred youth products and are tipped to be future captains of their respective clubs. (After Totti retired, De Rossi did become Roma's captain.) Aside from Marchisio, Gianluigi Buffon and Giorgio Chiellini have become so synonymous with the club you would think they had been with the team since similar ages but that is not the case and a quick look at some of the names over the years who were expected to make the leap to the first team is disappointing.

Below is a list of the former Juventus academy graduates currently playing and have a market value of €10 million or more as per transfermarkt.com.

Market Value of Former Juventus Academy Graduates Currently Playing

Player	Year Born	Current Club	League Appearancesn	Market Value
Ciro Immobile	1990	Lazio	150	€45 million
Daniele Rugani	1994	Juventus	89	20
Iago Falque	1990	Torino	122	12
Leonardo Spinazzola	1993	Atalanta	50	12
Claudio Marchisio	1986	Juventus	293	10

Source: transfermarkt.com

Juventus's five former academy graduates currently playing and with a market value of €10 million or more as per transfermarkt.com is behind several big European clubs as well as behind Atalanta in Italy. It is also worth noting how few big academy graduates come from EPL clubs.

Selected Clubs Only
Number of Former Academy Graduates Currently Playing With Market Value of €10 million or More

Club	Number	Still at Home Club
Barcelona	19	6
Real Madrid	13	4
Olympique Lyon	10	3

Atlético Madrid	9	3
Bayern Munich	8	4
Atalanta	8	1
Manchester United	7	3
Juventus	5	2
Roma	5	3
AC Milan	5	2
Manchester City	5	0
Athletic Bilbao	5	3
Sevilla	4	0
Chelsea	4	1
Inter	3	0
Liverpool	2	0

Source: transfermarkt.com

Off the Pitch

Juventus ranked #10 in revenues in 2017, a decline from #2 in 2001. In 2007/08, Juventus dropped to #12, which may have felt like an aberration or temporary blip after the scandal, but the decline was under way and after 2003 (which was supported by a Champions League final appearance), Juventus never placed in the top two. Years after the scandal, and even with its own stadium, Juventus were #13 in 2011 and 2012.

Juventus Revenues as Reported by Deloitte
and Annual Reports
€ in millions

Season	Deloitte	Rank	Annual Report
2000/01	€173.5	2	
2001/02	177.9	2	€175
2002/03	218.8	2	215
2003/04	215.3	5	208
2004/05	229.4	4	229
2005/06	251.2	3	251
2006/07	145.2	12	186
2007/08	167.5	11	203
2008/09	203.2	8	240
2009/10	205.0	10	240
2010/11	153.9	13	172

2011/12	195.4	13	213
2012/13	272.4	9	283
2013/14	279.4	10	315
2014/15	323.9	10	348
2015/16	341.1	10	387
2016/17	405.7	10	562

Source: Deloitte. Juventus public filings. Figures may not match because public filings have to adhere to accounting standards.

Juventus's revenues have been supported recently by outstanding Champions League performances and have benefited by not having to share as much of the Champions League TV revenues because other Italian clubs have not gone far in the tournament.

For overall revenue growth, Juventus have been playing catch-up since 2010, and have grown faster than their peers, but their peers are also growing from larger numbers. PSG and Manchester City have grown their revenues at a much faster rate.

Club Revenue Growth from 2010/11 to 2015/16
€ in millions

Club	Growth	2010/11 Revenue	2015/16 Revenue
PSG	416%	€100.9	€520.9
Man City	209%	169.6	524.9
Juventus	122%	153.9	341.1
Man U	88%	367	689
Bayern Munich	84%	321.4	592
Real Madrid	29%	479.5	620.1
AC Milan	-9%	235.1	214.7

Source: Deloitte

As previously mentioned, Juventus's revenues have benefited from strong Champions League performances. However, Juventus's revenues are highly concentrated in broadcasting, and underweight in both matchday and commercial. This lack of diversification, while common to many of the other Italian teams, has made them less financially competitive from an international standpoint.

Juventus and Other Clubs' 2015/16 Revenue by Source
Per Deloitte
€ in millions

	Juventus	Manchester United	Barcelona	Real Madrid	Bayern Munich	PSG	Roma	Milan	Inter
Matchday	13%	20%	19%	21%	17%	18%	13%	12%	14%
Broadcast	57%	27%	33%	37%	25%	24%	71%	41%	55%
Commercial	30%	53%	48%	42%	58%	58%	16%	47%	31%
Total Revenue	341.1	689	620.2	620.1	592	520.9	218.2	214.7	179.2
DFML Rank	10	1	2	3	4	6	15	16	19

Additionally, when looking at growth in the various revenue components, while commercial revenues have grown in absolute dollars from 2010 to 2017 (€55.6 million v. €114.4 million), the percentage of total revenues has barely increased.

Juventus' Commercial Revenues
€ in millions

	Total Revenue	Commercial Revenue	%
Juventus - Commercial 2009/10	€205	€55.6	27%
Juventus - Commercial 2014/15	323.9	73.5	23%
Juventus - Commercial 2015/16	341.1	101.7	30%
Juventus - Commercial 2016/17	405.7	114.4	28%

Source: Deloitte

This lack of commercial revenue diversification is evidenced when comparing Juventus's sponsorship numbers to the other top European teams. Juventus ranks #10 in sponsorships and is roughly between a half and a fifth of the top five clubs, where the big amounts are concentrated.

Ranking of Clubs with the Highest Values of Sponsorships
(2015/16 Season)
€ in millions

Rank	Team	Annual Average
1	Barcelona	€210
2	Real Madrid	195
3	Manchester United	193

4	Chelsea	133
5	Bayern Munich	98
6	Arsenal	80
7	Liverpool	74
8	Manchester City	69
9	Tottenham Hotspur	67
10	Juventus	47

In the most recent Deloitte Money League Report for the 2016/17 season where Juve finished tenth once again, their performance in the Champions League, finishing as runners-up and earning them the highest ever UEFA distribution of €110.4 million, was the key factor in driving a €66.8 million (20%) increase in revenue. Sustaining a top ten Money League position may prove difficult for Juventus in the coming years, given the lower broadcast rights values for Serie A than in the Premier League. To maintain their position, they will need to reach the latter stages of the Champions League on a consistent basis. Tottenham Hotspur and Atlético Madrid's moves to new stadia are likely to further challenge their position.

Selected 2013–17 Financial Information Per Deloitte
Overall Fan Experience

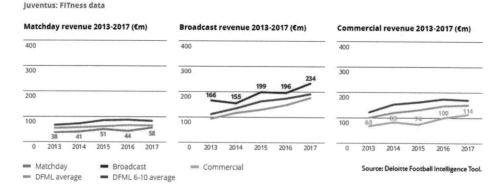

Juventus: FITness data

| Matchday revenue 2013-2017 (€m) | Broadcast revenue 2013-2017 (€m) | Commercial revenue 2013-2017 (€m) |

Matchday values: 38, 41, 51, 44, 58
Broadcast values: 166, 155, 199, 196, 234
Commercial values: 68, 100, 114

Legend: Matchday, Broadcast, Commercial, DFML average, DFML 6-10 average

Source: Deloitte Football Intelligence Tool.

Poor Stadium Experience, Before the New Stadium

One of the things the club recognised was that they needed to focus on overall fan experience to grow revenues, which meant they needed to own and control their own stadium. The 71,000-seat Stadio delle

Alpi, which was sometimes referred to as 'Delle Empty' in Turin was shared by Juventus and Torino and was very rarely sold out in its history. Juventus purchased the delle Alpi from the council of Turin for a fee of around €25 million. The delle Alpi's design was widely criticised due to the poor visibility. This was caused mainly by the distance between the stands and the pitch. Views from the lower tier were also restricted due to the positioning of advertising hoardings. The stadium's location on the outskirts of town made it difficult for fans to attend games, and the stadium design left spectators exposed to the elements. These factors contributed to low attendances; in the 2005/06 season, for example, Juventus's average occupancy rate was less than 50%. In 2006, the delle Alpi was closed and Juventus and Torino moved to the Stadio Olimpico. In 2008, Juventus presented the project of demolishing the existing Stadio delle Alpi and started to build a new stadium.

Good Stadium Experience, After New Stadium

Juventus opened its new, modern, 41,500-seat and privately funded Juventus Stadium in 2011, commercially known as the Allianz Stadium since June 2017, at a cost of around €150 million. It was the first stadium in Italy to be owned by its club rather than by a local municipality. The running track, which was widely blamed for ruining the atmosphere in the stadium, was removed with the fans moved closer to the action, providing a universally unobstructed view, and the impact on TV is obvious. Gate revenues increased by 183% in the stadium's first season, despite the fact that the new venue has a significantly smaller capacity than its predecessor.[1]

Naming rights and the sale of land adjacent to the stadium have provided additional sources of income. The environmentally sustainable stadium features a shopping centre, club museum, official club store, and an array of corporate hospitality options that come under the umbrella of the Juventus Premium Club. Adam Digby, the author of *Juventus: A History in Black and White*, says the love for the Juventus Stadium among fans is unanimous. 'After years of sharing the Olimpico with Torino or playing in the soulless delle Alpi, the Juventus Stadium feels like home.

---

[1] http://swissramble.blogspot.ca/2012/01/juventus-black-night-white-light.html

It's given a sense of belonging and because it's small and full – therefore making tickets scarce – attending a game feels much more important than before when they were playing in front of a half-empty ground.' The new arena made Juventus €41 million last year. The additional revenues and commercial opportunities have helped keep Juventus on track with other big clubs and have helped attract and retain players.

Juventus Matchday Attendance, Utilisation and Ranking

Stadium	Season	Avg Attendance	Max Capacity	Utilisation	League	Rank
Stadio delle Alpi	1990/91	43,114	67,229	64%	Serie A	7
Stadio delle Alpi	1991/92	51,832	67,229	77%	Serie A	2
Stadio delle Alpi	1992/93	45,868	67,229	68%	Serie A	4
Stadio delle Alpi	1993/94	44,670	67,229	66%	Serie A	2
Stadio delle Alpi	1994/95	50,524	67,229	75%	Serie A	1
Stadio delle Alpi	1995/96	41,946	67,229	62%	Serie A	2
Stadio delle Alpi	1996/97	33,144	67,229	49%	Serie A	1
Stadio delle Alpi	1997/98	48,106	67,229	72%	Serie A	1
Stadio delle Alpi	1998/99	47,311	67,229	70%	Serie A	7
Stadio delle Alpi	1999/00	43,941	67,229	65%	Serie A	2
Stadio delle Alpi	2000/01	38,623	67,229	57%	Serie A	2
Stadio delle Alpi	2001/02	40,550	67,229	60%	Serie A	1
Stadio delle Alpi	2002/03	39,771	67,229	59%	Serie A	1
Stadio delle Alpi	2003/04	34,373	67,229	51%	Serie A	3
Stadio delle Alpi	2004/05	28,107	67,229	42%	Serie A	1
Stadio delle Alpi	2005/06	30,734	67,229	46%	Serie A	1/20*
Stadio Olimpico	2006/07	18,085	25,500	71%	Serie B	1
Stadio Olimpico	2007/08	22,040	25,500	86%	Serie A	3
Stadio Olimpico	2008/09	22,407	27,500	81%	Serie A	2
Stadio Olimpico	2009/10	23,339	27,994	83%	Serie A	7
Stadio Olimpico	2010/11	21,966	27,994	78%	Serie A	7
Allianz Stadium	2011/12	37,674	41,475	91%	Serie A	1
Allianz Stadium	2012/13	38,711	41,475	93%	Serie A	1
Allianz Stadium	2013/14	38,342	41,475	92%	Serie A	1
Allianz Stadium	2014/15	38,553	41,475	93%	Serie A	1
Allianz Stadium	2015/16	38,690	41,475	93%	Serie A	1
Allianz Stadium	2016/17	39,925	41,475	96%	Serie A	1
Allianz Stadium	2017/18	39,623	41,475	96%	Serie A	1**

*Juventus was stripped of 1st place title in 2005/06
** As of 18 April 2018

In 2012, when the new stadium was finally opened, average attendance at home games jumped to approximately 38,000, the total occupancy rate increased from 78% at the Stadio Olimpico to 91% at the new Allianz Stadium, and matchday revenues increased by 174% year on year (while total revenues only increased by 27%) and made up 16% of the club's total revenues. Juventus also put together an impressive season, finishing first in Serie A. This trend of steadily increasing matchday revenues and occupancy rates has continued over the years, especially as the team has been so dominant on the pitch.

Juventus Matchday Revenues 2010/11 to 2016/17
€ in millions

	2010/11	*2011/12*	*2015/16*	*2016/17*
Average Attendance	21,966	37,674	38,690	39,925
Utilisation	78%	91%	93%	96%
Serie A Rank	7	1	1	1
Commercial Revenues €	53.6 (35%)	73 (37%)	101.7 (30%)	114.4 (28%)
Matchday Revenues €	11.6 (8%)	31.8 (16%)	43.7 (13%)	57.8 (14%)
Total Revenues €	153.9	195.4	341.1	405.7

Source: Deloitte

The new stadium has also greatly improved the overall atmosphere and fan experience and serves to reinforce the brand and value of the assets of the club. This has made Juventus more attractive as a club, to players as well as fans. Since Juventus made the move, they have won six Serie A titles in a row.

To improve the overall matchday experience, Juventus have 3,600 premium seats and 64 Sky Boxes. Boxes include reserved entrance to the stadium, luxury armchairs with personal LCD televisions, exclusive restaurants, bars, lounges, finger food at half-time and after the game, reserved parking and access to the museum.

To improve commercial revenue opportunities, Juventus started a corporate hospitality project, aimed at companies who wish to entertain their clients and partners to lunch or dinner at the Juventus Stadium before the match.

To diversify revenues, Juventus added a 34,000m² shopping complex with 60 shops, two bars and three restaurants open every day and a

70-minute guided tour of the stadium is offered every day. Guests are taken around to see the dressing rooms, facilities, museum and the pitch. By paying a visit to the Juventus Museum, fans can relive all the club's history and triumphs and enjoy a unique and memorable experience packed with technology, multimedia and memorabilia. In addition to the museum visit, fans have the chance to see the most exclusive areas of the Allianz Stadium. In 2017, the Juventus Museum ranked in the top 50 of Italian museums for visitors. In addition, Juventus introduced a new medical centre, J-Medical, as a result of a collaboration between the club and Santa Clara Group. The medical centre is situated in the stadium, next to the museum. The centre houses specialist clinics, operating theatres for outpatient surgery and a rehabilitation centre. In addition to providing affordable and efficient healthcare for the local community, the medical centre also serves as the club's in-house clinic for conducting players' medical check-ups.

Online Experience/Social Media: 2015 Champions League Final

Compared to most clubs in Serie A, Juventus has done a relatively good job with its online fan engagement and social media experience. However, compared to many of the other big European clubs, Juventus is still behind, in spite of its large global following. For social media specifically, Juventus is ranked #9 for the most popular teams on social media, with 35 million total followers (Facebook, Instagram and Twitter), which is a long way behind Barcelona with 160 million total followers.

The content team at Talkwalker analysed the social media story of the Champions League final in 2015 between Juventus and Barcelona. Both teams had world renowned stars such as Messi and Neymar for Barcelona and Pirlo and Pogba for Juventus. Talkwalker analysed over 20 million online posts in over 187 countries tracking more than 10 different written scripts (including the Roman Alphabet, Russian, Greek, Chinese (traditional, simplified), Korean, Arabic, Hindi, Persian and Thai) to create a truly global social story of the Champions League final and understand exactly what happens on social and online media. The build-up to the final was happening throughout the week before with the main Champions League Final hashtag (#UCLfinal) being used over 1 million times before a ball had even been kicked. And the buzz wasn't just in Europe where the final was being played; the biggest volume of usage actually came from North America. Barcelona scored after just four minutes and social media exploded with over 200,000 tweets posted within two minutes (1,700 tweets per second). Besides the goals scored, the other big event was the appearance of Xavi, the veteran Barcelona midfielder who was making his final appearance. The words most used on social media were (in order): perfect, brilliant, amazing and awesome. As the game drew to a close, online mentions reached their highest volume with the match ending with a goal from Barcelona's Brazilian sensation Neymar which produced 330,000 posts in two minutes (or around 2,750 posts per second).

While Neymar was the most discussed player overall, the conversation varied considerably depending on geography. For Europe, North America and Oceania it was Luis Suarez and his pivotal second goal for Barcelona that drove the most discussion, while in South America and Asia the focus was on Neymar and the final goal of the game. But one thing that was the same for every region was that the three most mentioned players were Barcelona's attacking trio of Messi, Neymar and Luis Suarez.

Barcelona came out on top on the pitch and they came out on top in online mentions too, with around two-thirds of the share of voice compared to Juventus. They also had much greater reach and engaged audiences more effectively than their Italian opponents:

Barcelona and Juventus Social Media Reach and Engagement During 2015 CL Final

	Barcelona	*Juventus*
Reach	1,844,872	839,526
Engagement	1,379,072	480,869

Source: Talkwalker

Barca dominated the owned social media conversation, with the official FC Barcelona Twitter channel driving around four times as much activity as Juventus's official channel. Even Barcelona's players, particularly

Neymar, used social media to connect with fans with Neymar's tweet featuring Luis Suarez, Neymar and Messi posing with the Champions League trophy the most shared tweet of the night.

For both teams the social conversation was truly global with the highest volumes of social discussion coming from countries on four different continents:

Barcelona and Juventus Social Media Top Countries During 2015 CL Final

Barcelona	*Juventus*
Spain	United States
United States	Spain
Brazil	Brazil
Indonesia	Indonesia
UK	Italy
France	France
Mexico	UK
Argentina	Argentina
Colombia	Mexico

Source: Talkwalker

The languages used to discuss the game were also varied with Spanish used more often than English and non-European languages such as Arabic and Indonesian also featuring in the top eight languages used to discuss the two teams:

Top Languages Used in Social Media During 2015 CL Final

Language	*Uses*
Spanish	820,000
English	785,000
Portuguese	190,000
French	150,000
Arabic	120,000
Italian	115,000
Indonesian	100,000
Turkish	75,000

Source: Talkwalker

Overall, the volume of discussion about the final was pretty astonishing with over 24 million mentions of the final and the players involved over the course of the week and around 5.5 million posts during the two hours of the final alone. The social conversation was truly global with large volumes of social conversation about the final coming from every continent. There was a particularly high volume of social discussion coming from Indonesia and the Middle East. Spanish and English are the preferred languages to communicate. Even with an Italian club, Italian was only the sixth most used language. Neymar was the most socially savvy football star with his Twitter handle and social activity driving far more engagement and attention than any other player involved in the match.

Online Experience/Netflix

There is an awareness that Juventus can make great strides in this area given their potential and international popularity. The best example of this to date is a Netflix documentary, which was released in February 2018. The three-part mini-series, entitled: *First Team: Juventus* offers behind-the-scenes access to the club and is Netflix's first foray into association football following the success of American football series *Last Chance U*. Erik Barmack, vice president of international original series at Netflix, is quoted as saying: 'Netflix is the home of passionate storytelling, and there are no more passionate fans than the tifosi of the bianconeri. We are excited to have unique, exclusive access to one of the most important squads in the world.' Federico Palomba, co-chief revenue officer at the club, said: 'It's a source of pride that Juventus are the first football club to be the subject of a Netflix original documentary. Collaborations of this kind confirm our passion for innovation and being, in every sense, a sport entertainment brand. In this way, we are determined to reach fans across the world and millions of Netflix users, who thanks to this docuseries can get to know Juventus from every angle.'

Juventus TV

Juventus have their own subscription-based TV channel (JTV). The channel offers Juventus fans exclusive interviews with players and staff, full matches, including all Lega Calcio Serie A, Italian Cup and games in the UEFA competitions (though not broadcast live), vintage matches, footballing news and other themed programming.

Power of the Ultras

As previously mentioned, Juventus have greatly improved the matchday fan experience with their vibrant but safe stadium. However, the club still struggles to deal with the Ultras and the amount of power they have. Juventus and its management recognise the Ultras are important to the success of the team, but with that aggressive fan base comes a host of problems including violence, illegal activity, pressures on management and lost ticket revenues. For example, some of the most powerful Ultra groups were involved in a scandal in which they were allegedly making illegal profits. Allegedly, Juventus management made a compromise with the Ultras whereby the club would sell hundreds of matchday tickets, on credit, to the leader of each Ultra group, in return for good behaviour. This was in clear contravention of the rules, which stated that no more than four tickets could be sold to any individual. Season tickets were also allegedly used.

Newventus

Newventus off the Pitch

In May 2010 Andrea Agnelli was appointed chairman of the board of directors of Juventus by his first cousin John Elkann, becoming the fourth member of the Agnelli family to run the football club after his father, his uncle and his grandfather. Not since his father Umberto's reign had ended in 1962 had a person with the last name Agnelli held the most prestigious position at the club. Andrea was disappointed in the state of the club, which was coming off the back of a dismal seventh-placed finish in Serie A. He saw not only a broken club but a broken system. Even today, he claims that in Italy there is 'a total absence of medium-to-long term vision. The Italian system thinks about earning one or two million today, rather than 10 million tomorrow.[2] Andrea Agnelli created a clearly defined club structure. One of his first acts as new chairman was to appoint Sampdoria duo Giuseppe Marotta as director of sport and then bringing former Ballon d'Or winner and fan favourite Pavel Nedvěd on the management team. By the time of the Czech's arrival in 2012, Agnelli had already started reinventing the Juventus brand. Andrea Agnelli is credited with overseeing the club's transition into the new stadium and balancing their finances. He and his management team rather impressively identified the problems with the old Italian model of clubs renting a stadium off the local council and took the rather bold decision to not only build their own, but also reduce the capacity from around 80,000 to 41,000. Agnelli has a vision of the future and the club's modernisation.

Juventus have done several things in the past few years to transform themselves into the Serie A powerhouse that it is today and to increase their local and global fan base. After Calciopoli, the club discovered they needed to make some changes to help rebuild. Juventus have focused on shedding their 'old lady' image and altering their business model in order to adapt to the new global football industry, whilst at the same time trying to maintain the history of success that is rooted in their humble culture, being a hard-working team focused on winning at all costs.

With financial support from the Agnellis, Juventus are still formidable. The Agnellis are still ranked in ninth position in terms of billionaire football owners, the first non-UK position. However, the last player they signed (which was inter-league) that was in the top 10 in the Ballon d'Or was Pirlo (ninth in 2006; fifth in the 2007 Ballon d'Or) in 2011. Pirlo finished seventh in Ballon d'Or voting at Juventus in 2012 (the top six were all in La Liga) and tenth in 2013 (Pirlo was the only player nominated for the 2013 Ballon d'Or). For a club that has recently competed in two Champions League finals and won seven Scudetti in a row, one might expect them to be able to buy more talent. Juventus don't have the revenues to compete for all of the world-class talent or keep it when they develop it. For example, in the 2015 Ballon d'Or, Juventus had two players in the top 20 – Paul Pogba at #15 and Arturo Vidal at #17. By 2016, both players were sold.

---

[2] *http://www.goal.com/en-us/news/the-juventus-guide-to-building-the-best-team-in-europe/1mu oiq4q697po1l37nhjzbpxjt*

After years of practising prudence in the transfer market, Juve enacted a €32 million buy-out clause in Miralem Pjanic's contract at Roma before doing the very same thing to get Gonzalo Higuaín from Napoli. This time, the fee was €90 million, the fourth-highest transfer fee in history at the time. Juve have decided to raise the bar. Still, in the 2017 Champions League final Juventus were playing a Real Madrid squad that cost €638 million, whole Juventus' cost €422 million (€216 million less).

As previously discussed, results only on the pitch do not necessarily translate to higher revenues, and there are FFP considerations as well. The culture, leadership and defensive orientation of Juventus has led to results on the pitch.

Newventus on the Pitch

Newventus: For a few years after being in Serie B, Juve had some difficulty competing with the top clubs until the 2011/12 season. The major catalyst for the turnaround on the pitch was the transfer of Pirlo from Milan to Juve during the summer of 2011. Pirlo was the attacking player of real quality that Juve needed to create attacking opportunities. Juve were already good defensively, but needed attacking and creative talent, and Pirlo brought that. They also added experienced and talented players like Barzagli (2011), Bonucci (2010), Vidal (2011), Tevez (2013), Pogba (2012) and Lichtsteiner (2011). The Newventus style was consistent with their historical culture and values – a tough team, humble and hard-working. It is an important part of why they made it to the Champions League final twice in the last few years, even though they rank around tenth in salaries and still have a noticeable difference in talent compared to bigger revenue clubs like Barcelona and Real Madrid.

Women's Team

In the most recent 2017/18 season, Juventus had a women's team competing in the Italian league (women's Serie A) for the first time in the club's history. Until this year, they only had women's youth teams. While there is still a very long way to go before they will be able to contribute financially to Juventus's overall bottom line, this represents a big step for the club in terms of promoting women and trying to reach a broader fanbase. This should help attract new female football fans.

New Logo

Juventus have sported an oval-shaped crest for the vast majority of their history, with only a brief change to that style occurring from the late 1970s until 1989. They wore two different badges designed around the famous bull on Turin's coat of arms during that period before switching back to the traditional design. Juventus decided to move away from the striped design, featuring the bull as part of a crest at the bottom of the logo, to a symbol based around the 'J' at the start of their name.

In January 2017, Juventus's new badge was revealed at a special ceremony led by president Andrea Agnelli at the Museum of Science & Technology in Milan. He said, 'We are here to present what will be the future of Juventus in the coming years… In order to grow we must keep winning and evolve our language to achieve new targets. The new logo defines a sense of belonging and a style that allows us to communicate our way of being.' Juventus are trying to transcend the sport aspect of the club to represent the philosophy behind the team. They want Juventus to be synonymous with ambition and excellence. The new visual identity was created to bring the signature and spirit of the club into new and unexpected fields.

The revolutionary change for the club is that for the first time in its history, there is no reference to the city of Turin in the logo, home of the bianconeri. Some of the local and most traditional Juventus fans did not fully appreciate that the new logo emphasised only the 'J' and the social colours (black and white) of the club, whilst completely ignoring the city where the club was born.

The club are trying to appeal to 'new' fans abroad which led to the change of the logo in the end. Roma and PSG also restyled their logos. Roma removed the historical 'ASR' denomination from the logo and the word 'Roma' and the 'Lupa' (female wolf) symbol of the Italian capital were updated. In the same manner, the French club emphasised the word 'Paris' while redesigning their new logo. PSG deleted the creation date of the club, because PSG is not older than most other big clubs, but the Parisian symbol, the Eiffel Tower, is emphasised. Obviously, some 'older, local' traditionalists complained, and this shows how complicated it is for clubs to develop a new marketing strategy without creating discontent from existing fans.

Final Remarks

Juventus have many signs of a revival and represent signs of optimism. They have long-term stable ownership, leadership, a distinctive identity and culture, are focused on branding, have a new stadium, have found a way to have consistent results on the pitch, have talent and are building a sustainable business model. They understand the changes and future of European football and are adapting. Juventus continues to renew and expand and sign new global sponsorships including with Swiss luxury watchmaker Hublot, Chinese tyre manufacturer Linglong Tire, and American candy brand M&M's. They renamed their stadium in a long-term sponsorship deal with Allianz. They were the first Italian club to partner with EA Sports. Starting in 2017/18, for the first time in the history of the club, the name of a sponsor, Cygames (Japanese video game producer), will be on the back of Juventus's game shirts.

In many ways Juventus do reflect a complicated Italy. While they have had many allegations made against them, in the end, the community have a sense of history, class and touches of human warmth. For example, when their new stadium was opened in 2011, many other big clubs would have invited another big club or rival to play the inaugural match. Juventus invited Notts County, who have not played in the top division of English football since 1990/91, because it was County who provided them with their first set of black and white striped shirts back in 1903. It is this blend of warmth, style and commitment to excellence that enables Juventus to rise above issues to which they, the league and the country are also prone.

CHAPTER TEN

ROMA
BUILDING A NEW REPUBLIC

Overview

Associazione Sportiva Roma, commonly referred to as simply Roma, were founded by a merger of several Roman football clubs in 1927 to give the Italian capital a stronger club to rival that of the more dominant northern Italian clubs of the time.

The club's home colours are the historic yellow and red tones of Rome, which gives Roma their nickname 'I Giallorossi' ('The Yellow and Reds'). Their club badge features a she-wolf, an allusion to the founding myth of Rome. The most known club anthem is 'Roma (non-si discute, si ama)', also known as 'Roma, Roma, Roma', by singer Antonello Venditti. The title roughly means 'Roma is not to be questioned, it is to be loved', and it is sung before each match. The official title of the song has also become the most known motto of the club. Renowned publication *France Football* have ranked 'Roma, Roma, Roma' #2 of the top ten best stadium anthems from around modern professional football. (#1 was Liverpool's 'You'll Never Walk Alone'. The song 'Grazie Roma', by the same singer, is played at the end of victorious home matches.)

For a club that has global football recognition, surprisingly Roma have won Serie A only three times, in 1942, 1983 and 2001. Remarkably, Roma have finished in second place in Serie A 12 times since 1980 (out of 37 seasons), or almost one in three. Roma were also runners-up in the 1984 European Cup and the 1991 UEFA Cup. Perhaps the reason the lack of trophies is overlooked is that the city that Roma shares their name with carries such strong emotions for those that have visited or dreamed of visiting. Rome's identity and Roma's identity are intertwined in so many ways.

Surprisingly, Roma have never had a player finish in the top three in the Ballon d'Or voting. Perhaps the reason this is overlooked is that Roma have a history of loyal, home-town heroes. Romans, and probably Athenians, have a special deep love, respect and worship for mythical legends and heroes, regardless of whether they win or not. The heroes are often legends precisely because of their love, loyalty and sacrifice. As was written once on a banner in the Curva Sud ahead of a derby: 'Sons of Roma are captains and icons; this is our advantage and something you will never have.' Recently, the home-grown captains have been Francesco Totti and Daniele De Rossi (with Florenzi and Pellegrini as young hopefuls).

One of the reasons why Roma attracts fans is the visual image of passionate fans in the Curva Sud proudly holding their club scarves or waving colourful club flags (and possibly red flares and smoke) and singing (and screaming) 'Roma, Roma, Roma' before each match. The tradition and ritual exemplify the unique emotional passion of not just Roma, but Italians and Serie A football. Because of the city, the history, the home-town legends and even the tragedies, Roma holds a unique place, something beautiful, in Italian and European football, beyond trophies.

Roma is the fifth most supported football club in Italy – behind Juventus, Inter, Milan and Napoli – with approximately 7% of Italian football fans supporting the club, according to the Doxa Institute-L'Espresso's research of April 2006. Historically, the largest section of Roma supporters in the city of Rome have come from the working class of the inner city.

Since 1953, Roma have played their home matches at the Stadio Olimpico, a venue they share with city rivals Lazio. With a capacity of over 72,000, it is the second largest of its kind in Italy, with only the San Siro able to seat more. The club received approval in 2017 to build a new stadium, with the 2020/21 season as the goal to start playing matches.

Roma's first and foremost rivalry is with Lazio, the club with whom they share the Stadio Olimpico. The derby between the two is called the 'Derby della Capitale', and it is amongst the most heated and emotional footballing rivalries in the world. While there are only five Scudetti between the two, the matches mean so much for local pride and bragging rights. The build-up is intense and almost as if nothing else matters. Many Roma and Lazio fans care more about winning the derby than where their clubs finish in the league; perhaps it has meant even more because of the league dominance of the northern teams. One element of the derby lost to the TV audience is the back-and-forth banter that goes on between each end over the course of a match. Fresh banners are unfurled at regular intervals once play has begun, creating the effect of a conversation at a distance. Against Napoli, Roma also compete in the 'Derby del Sole', meaning the 'Derby of the Sun'. Nowadays, fans also consider other Serie A giants like Juventus (a rivalry born especially in the 1980s) and Inter (a rivalry that picked up intensity in the mid-2000s as they competed in several Italian Cup finals), among their rivals, as they compete for the top of Serie A.

In 1993, then-Roma president Giuseppe Ciarrapico was on his way to prison and Roma were on the verge of bankruptcy. It was one of the worst moments in Roma's history. Franco Sensi, who grew up going to Roma matches as a boy and later controlled an Italian oil company, stepped in to help the club back on its feet with the help of Pietro Mezzaroma. Sensi became sole owner and president in November of that year. In 1999, he took Roma public on the stock exchange to raise capital and brought in Fabio Capello who had been a player at Roma 30 years prior (before playing at Juventus and Milan). Two years later, Roma won the one Scudetto under Sensi's chairmanship. In the next seven years from 2002 to 2008, Roma would finish second five times. When he died in 2008, his daughter Rosella took over (although due to Franco Sensi's health, she was named honorary president in 2004). In the four years from 2008 to 2011, Roma finished second twice and got to at least the round of 16 in the Champions League three times. But the club was heavily in debt. By 2011, Roma was de facto controlled by UniCredit, an Italian global banking company, due to a debt for equity swap restructuring, and the bank wanted to find a buyer. In 2011, a group of American investors including Thomas DiBenedetto, Jim Pallotta, Michael Ruane and Richard D'Amore reportedly paid around €70 million for the 67% of the club that was not owned by the public shareholders. The deal made the American group the first foreign majority owners of a Serie A club.

On the Pitch: 1980 to 2011, Before the Italian-American Purchase

Roma would reach heights in the league which they had not been to since the 1940s by narrowly and controversially finishing as runners-up to Juventus in 1980/81, with players such as Bruno Conti, Agostino Di Bartolomei, Roberto Pruzzo and Falcão. In 1982/83 Roma won their second Scudetto (the first one being 41 years prior). The following season, Roma finished as runners-up in Italy and finished as runners-up in the European Cup final of 1984. Roma's successful run in the 1980s would finish with a Serie A runners-up spot in 1985/86. In 1986, Berlusconi purchased Milan and raised the stakes and Roma began a relative decline, with two major highlights being a third-place finish in 1987/88 and an all-Italian UEFA Cup final, which they lost to Inter in 1991. The rest of the 1980s and the 1990s was largely sub-par compared to 1981–86, where the highest they could manage was fourth in 1997/98. The early 1990s saw the emergence of home-grown striker Francesco Totti. Roma improved in the 2000s, beginning the decade in great style by winning their third ever Scudetto in 2000/01. Totti led a group of talented players including Gabriel Batistuta, Aldair, Cafu, Walter Samuel, Emerson, Damiano Tommasi and Vincenzo Montella. The club attempted to defend the title in the following season but finished as runners-up to Juventus by one point. This would be the start of Roma finishing as runners-up several times in Serie A in the 2000s.

Roma's Serie A and Champions League Results
(and Oil Prices)

Year	Serie A	Champions League	Oil Prices ($)
1981	2nd		
1982	3rd		
1983	1st		
1984	2nd	2nd	
1985			
1986	2nd		
1987			
1988	3rd		
1989			
1990			
1991			
1992			
1993			16.75
1994			15.66
1995			16.75
1996			20.46
1997			18.64
1998			11.91
1999			16.56
2000			27.39
2001	1st		23.00
2002	2nd	Group Stage	22.81
2003		Group Stage	27.69
2004	2nd		37.66
2005		Group Stage	50.04
2006	2nd		58.30
2007	2nd	Quarter-finals	64.20
2008	2nd	Quarter-finals	91.48
2009		Round of 16	53.48
2010	2nd		71.21
2011		Round of 16	87.04

As previously mentioned, Franco Sensi was in the oil business. Although it was primarily an Italian business related to the Italian economy, oil prices are related to global markets. When Franco Sensi bought the club in 1993 and until 1999, oil prices were relatively constant, with the exception of the collapse of oil prices from $18.64 in 1997 to $11.91 in 1998, which may have influenced the decision to take Roma public.

During that time of flat oil prices, the club didn't finish in the top three in Serie A. As oil prices rose in the 2000s, spending on talent increased as well as most companies' borrowings for investments. Roma's results on the pitch benefited from not being implicated in the 2006 Calciopoli scandal. The oil price collapse from $91.48 in 2008 to $53.48 in 2009 left many oil-related companies and sports-related companies that were highly leveraged vulnerable.

Talent: 1980 to 2011, Before the Italian-American Purchase

In the 1980s and 1990s, Roma did have a few exceptional players, but none finished in the top three for the Ballon d'Or. Bruno Conti finished fifth in 1982 and Zbigniew Boniek finished sixth in 1985.

Obviously, Francesco Totti, the symbolic and beloved Roma hero and legend, who made his debut for the club as a 16-year-old in 1993 and played for Roma until 2017, is considered Roma's greatest player ever. Totti finished fifth for the 2001 Ballon d'Or and tenth in 2007, after he won the goalscoring title in Serie A. Many believe Totti paid the price of not winning the Ballon d'Or for a lifetime of loyalty to one club. Had he moved to one of the very top clubs consistently in the final stages of the Champions League, many believe Totti would surely have won the Ballon d'Or. In 2016, Ballon d'Or winner Luis Figo sent a 40th birthday apology to Francesco Totti. 'Sorry for stealing the Ballon d'Or in 2000 – you deserved it.' (Totti finished 14th in 2000.)

To think of Roma without Totti is unthinkable. His nicknames say it all: Er Bimbo de Oro (The Golden Boy), L'Ottavo Re di Roma (The Eighth King of Rome), Er Pupone (The Big Baby), Il Capitano (The Captain), and Il Gladiatore (The Gladiator) by the Italian sports media. Totti is the Giallorossi's record appearance maker and all-time highest goalscorer.

Before Francesco Totti, the symbol of Roma was Giuseppe Giannini (1982–96), nicknamed 'Il Principe' (The Prince). Like Totti, this midfielder turned down the big-money advances of the big clubs to stay with his beloved home town club. The same tradition was with great winger Bruno Conti (1973–90) who, aside from two loan spells at Genoa, spent his entire career with Roma.

After the Scudetto in 2001, key players left Roma during the following seasons. Walter Samuel went to Real Madrid (2004), Gabriel Batistuta to Inter (2003), Emerson to Juve (2004), Cafu to Milan (2003), Aldair to Genoa (2003) and Zago to Besiktas (2002). Most of the team was gone after two or three years, with only Totti remaining.

Fan Experience: 1980 to 2011, Before the Italian-American Purchase

The Stadio Olimpico in Rome currently has a capacity of around 72,000. In the 1982/83 season, Roma averaged almost 69,000 fans per game (although the stadium had a larger capacity then, but it has since been reduced for safety). Since then, the average stadium attendance has essentially declined with the exception of the 2000/01 season when Roma won the Scudetto, and then it continued its decline to around 35,000 in 2010/11. Even when the club was finishing second in the league in the 2000s or reaching the quarter-finals of the Champions League, attendance was generally declining.

Roma Home Stadium Attendance Season Averages and Ranking

Season	Average	Rank
1982/83	68,909	#1
1983/84	63,498	#2
1984/85	55,240	#4
1985/86	60,111	#2
1986/87	50,317	#4
1987/88	43,696	#4
1988/89	36,851	#4
1989/90	23,768	#9
1990/91	48,119	#4
1991/92	52,475	#2
1998/99	55,043	#3
1999/00	59,006	#2
2000/01	64,469	#1
2001/02	61,241	#2
2002/03	57,426	#3
2003/04	48,813	#3
2004/05	46,495	#3
2005/06	39,158	#3

2006/07	37,338	#3
2007/08	37,896	#4
2008/09	39,179	#4
2009/10	41,113	#4
2010/11	34, 649	#4

Source: WorldFootball.net

Poor Stadium Experience (Clouds of Racism and Violence)

In 1979 a Lazio supporter was hit in the eye with a flare thrown by a Roma fan and became the first fatality due to violence in the history of Italian football. Roma Ultras also forced the suspension of a game in 2004 when false rumours of a child being killed by police before the match caused chaos. As recently as 2009 the referee was forced to abandon play for over seven minutes because of fireworks being thrown onto the pitch. Roma players of a black or other ethnic origin have also come under attack from their own and their opponents' supporters in the stadium with banners and racist chanting. Once again, it is a very small minority of fans, but it does continue to happen.

Decentralised Supporters' Clubs

Roma believes it has over 200 fan clubs. They are not sure because traditionally in Italy there is no official or meaningful connection with the clubs. One club, UTR, has around 87,000 members with around 25,000 outside of Italy. They have their own headquarters in Rome filled with pictures, shirts and match memorabilia. They see themselves as the 'unofficial' caretakers of the traditions, history and culture. They make banners for the games and travel to away matches. They have monthly meetings and dinners with one player per month provided by the club. They organise charity dinners as well. The membership fee is €10 per year. They are an extremely nice group of people and have an incredible amount of passion, loyalty and love for the club. Another well-known Roma club is AIRC, founded in 1971, which has an estimated 120 affiliated clubs as members.

In April 2004, *Forbes* ranked the most valuable football clubs.[1] Of the top 15 clubs, Roma at #14 was losing the most money, even more than Chelsea which was purchased by multi-billionaire Roman Abramovich in the summer of 2003 and would have significantly higher future revenue growth. It is amazing to see that in the top six clubs in 2004 were Juventus #2, AC Milan #3 and Inter #6.

The 2006 Deloitte Football Money League was titled 'Changing of the Guard'. The big news was that after eight consecutive seasons at the top of the Money League, Manchester United were overtaken by Real Madrid. Real had transformed its revenues, doubling them in only four years. Real's revenue growth was not matchday revenues, as many of the UK clubs experienced, or broadcasting revenues, which many of the Italian clubs experienced, but strong progress in realising their commercial potential with sponsorships. Recruiting players such as Beckham, Zidane and Ronaldo had been the catalyst for substantial growth in merchandising and licensing revenues from Real Madrid's worldwide fan base. Recruiting world-class 'Galáctico' players had not necessarily always delivered the anticipated results on the pitch, but their presence has facilitated a transformation in the club's financial performance. This was helped in both 2004 and 2005 with pre-season tours of Asia, building their support base and receiving lucrative appearance fees for matches in China, Japan and Thailand. Other key contributors to the club's commercial success are its shirt sponsorship, a kit supply deal with adidas, and a lucrative band of official sponsors including Audi and Pepsi. Real also renegotiated an improved shirt sponsorship deal because of their improved global presence and appeal.

The changing of the guard was not just happening between Real Madrid and Manchester United, but it was happening to Italian clubs. In the 2004/05 season, Roma ranked #11 and had €132 million in revenues, the same as 2003 but less than 2002. Commercial revenues were €27.4 million in 2005 representing 21%, versus broadcasting at 58%. Commercial revenues were actually declining, but 2004/05 was the first season of a new, improved domestic broadcast contract with pay TV operator Sky Italia. In 2004/05, Deloitte wrote: 'Although the club attracted an average

---

[1] https://www.forbes.com/forbes/2004/0412/126tab.html#547f058c3425

home attendance of over 44,000 . . . Significant improvements in stadium facilities are necessary to grow matchday revenues.'[2]

In the 2007 report for the 2005/06 season, revenues declined to €127 million, primarily because of matchday revenues declining. Deloitte wrote: 'Again, in common with many Italian clubs, Roma's attendances fell in 2005/06. The average attendance of 39,700 at their Serie A home matches was 11% lower than the previous season and they used less than half of the Stadio Olimpico's 85,000 capacity. Going forward, more consistent performance on the pitch with regular qualification for the Champions League, coupled with improved matchday and commercial performance, is essential for revenue growth.' Deloitte also identified a big problem: 'Talks are ongoing between the clubs and Lega Calcio about how broadcast revenue will be marketed in future, with a return to central selling a possibility. In common with all the bigger Italian clubs, such a change would result in Roma needing to improve its revenue in other areas, to maintain its current Money League position.'

In the 2012 Deloitte report, Roma (ranked #15 overall) had the highest percentage of revenue coming from broadcasting in the top 20 at 64%, with Inter (ranked #8 overall) the second highest at 58%. Broadcast revenue contributed the second highest relative proportion of total revenue (58%) of any Money League club behind Roma (64%). Despite participation in the Champions League in 2010/11, Roma's matchday revenue decreased by €1.4 million (7%) to €17.6 million as average attendance levels fell by 15% to 34,665.

Revenues for Roma peaked in 2008 at €175.4 million. Roma would not surpass that revenue high-water mark until 2015, with the help of Champions League broadcasting revenues.

Deloitte Football Money League Amounts and Rankings 2000/01 to 2010/11
€ in millions

Season	Revenue	DFML Rank	Serie A Rank
2000/01	123.8	8	1
2001/02	136.8	10	2
2002/03	n/a	n/a	8

---

[2] https://www2.deloitte.com/content/dam/Deloitte/global/Documents/Audit/gx-deloitte-football-money-league-2006.pdf

2003/04	n/a	n/a	2
2004/05	131.8	11	8
2005/06	127.0	12	2
2006/07	157.6	10	2
2007/08	175.4	9	2
2008/09	146.4	12	6
2009/10	122.7	18	2
2010/11	143.5	15	6

The Italian-American Takeover

Roma being located in the city of Rome and their passionate fan base are two key assets of Roma. Roma have extremely passionate local fans who often can't separate the club's identity from their own, but Roma also have fans around the world, most often because the fans have Italian or Roman heritage or have visited or dream about visiting Rome and identify with Roman history, values and traditions. Rome's beauty and history make it the third most visited capital in Europe, after London and Paris.

The club had relatively decent success on the pitch in the 2000s, but it came at a big cost. The *Gazzetta dello Sport* estimated Roma's deficit in 2011 was €40 million. The losses were unsustainable and the club has significant debt. Revenues and relative revenue position compared to their peers were declining. In 2008 Roma were ranked #9 and had €175 million in revenues. By 2012, Roma's revenues had declined to €116 million and they were ranked #19. Roma dropped four places to 19th position in the Deloitte Football Money League, with total revenue decreasing to €115.9 million in 2011/12, a €27.6 million (19%) decrease. This is largely due to the club's failure to qualify for the UEFA Champions League. Roma's broadcast revenue decreased by €26.7 million (29%) to €64.4 million as a result of failing to qualify for Champions League football. Matchday revenue decreased by €2.9 million (16%) to €14.7 million. DiBenedetto acknowledged that his first order of business with Roma will be 'getting the budget in order and bringing the club under the Financial Fair Play parameters, considering that currently we're not'.[3]

Initially DiBenedetto was chairman but then Jim Pallotta became chairman in 2012. To get the budget in order, the club had to qualify for Champions League football. The change in revenues in any other area is

---

[3] https://www.theguardian.com/football/2011/mar/28/roma-takeover-us-businessman-dibenedetto

not nearly as significant. Therefore, Jim's focus was performance on the pitch. Because of coefficient rankings, Italy's Serie A only had the top two guaranteed for the group stage of the Champions League in 2012, with the third position going to the play-off round. The focus was to finish in the top two. Jim brought his passion and quantitative and data analytics approach in investing to all aspects of the club, but in particular player selection and training. After two seasons, the impact was felt, and by 2013/14, Roma had finished second three times and third once, while maintaining a much better financial situation than in the past.

No Nepotistic System

Jim has spent years assembling a world-class management team. He doesn't have any friends or relatives working at the club day to day. Mauro Baldissoni, a former top corporate and financial lawyer in Rome, is the general director running day-to-day operations. A Roma fan since childhood, he in many ways is the heart and soul of the club. He is extremely smart, diligent, hard-working, respected and is searching for excellence. Once established on the pitch, Jim added Umberto Gandini who was a senior executive at AC Milan for over 20 years when Milan went to six finals in the UEFA Champions League. Umberto added gravitas and European football connections. In 2017, Jim brought in 'Monchi' from Sevilla to be the football sporting director and to develop the club's youth system and implement a vast scouting policy inside and outside Italy. Monchi reportedly made over €200 million for Sevilla buying and selling players while Sevilla won multiple Europa League trophies over much richer clubs. Monchi adds experience and judgement to the data analytics. In addition, Monchi was a 'one club man' having graduated from Sevilla's youth academy and having played the rest of his professional football career at Sevilla. Guido Fienga was recently promoted to chief operating officer of Roma, in addition to his previous responsibilities in managing the club's media operations, including Roma Radio and Roma TV. He is a seasoned executive with an entrepreneur spirit. His background is as an investor in credit, sport and media sectors. Recently, he sold a majority stake of his credit servicing business to KKR, a leading global investment firm.

Lastly, Roma added Luca Danovaro as chief marketing officer to handle marketing, strategy and commercial responsibilities. Luca had worked at Nike and Samsung.

Pallotta seeks the best people he can find. Almost the entire executive group Pallotta did not know before he took over the club. With the exception of Mauro, the others were not diehard Roma fans before joining. The director of football, Monchi, being Spanish, is highly unusual in Italy. In addition, on the management staff, unlike most Serie A clubs, Roma have brought in experts from around the world including Spain (technical director), Canada and the United States (performance) and Germany (medical).

No Problem That Italian is Not a Global Language

With American owners and a meaningful presence of executives in Boston and London, English is often utilised for communication internally as well as with the fans. The top management team speak fluent English and that proficiency in English means that Roma has the most English content available for global fan engagement.

On the Pitch

Roma's Serie A and Champions League Results

Year	Serie A	Champions League
Pre-		
2011	6th	
Post		
2012	7th	
2013	6th	
2014	2nd	
2015	2nd	Group Stage
2016	3rd	Round of 16
2017	2nd	Play-off Round
2018	3rd	Semi-finals

The club's director of performance Darcy Norman and head performance coach Ed Lippie are not your everyday sports scientists. They apply a supply chain management and systems thinking approach to football inspired by the world of big business. It's an approach based on the idea that every action sets off a chain of events that will impact on performance. Roma only have the players for two or three hours a day, but they also focus on what the players are doing in the other 21 or 22 hours because those hours can either improve or hinder performance. There's an ecosystem at Roma dedicated to improving performance, but then each of those players will have an ecosystem outside of the training complex with family, friends and agents, and they impact on a player's lifestyle. Roma has adopted a 'motivation through education' methodology to preach habits that are performance-enhancing and injury-shielding that the club hopes players will adhere to away from the team. They include ideally refraining from alcohol, sleeping eight to ten hours a night, setting daily goals in the morning and even meditation sessions before bedtime or after waking up. The performance group tracks all types of data on the players, from quality of sleep to hours of training to heart rates while training and analyses it to help the coaches to make decisions and the players to reach peak performance.

Off the Pitch

Roma has been able to grow revenues primarily because of its improved league position, giving them an opportunity to earn Champions League revenues. For the most recent DFML report from the 2016/17 season, Roma's revenues dropped by €46 million (21%) and the club fell outside the top 20 for only the third time after failing to reach the Champions League group stage in that season. However, it is likely they will make a quick return to the top 20, having already won their group and progressed to the knockout stages in 2017/18.

Roma's Deloitte Football Money League Amounts and Rankings
2012 to 2017
€ in millions

Season	Revenue	DFML Rank	Serie A Rank
2011/12	€115.9	21	7
2012/13	124.4	19	6
2013/14	127.4	24	2
2014/15	180.4	16	2
2015/16	218.2	15	3
2016/17	171.8	24	2

Over-reliance on TV Revenues

Broadcasting revenue grew from €64 million in 2012 to €154 million in 2016, 140% growth. Roma's issue is that broadcasting represents 71% of revenues, the highest percentage in the top 20 clubs in overall revenues. Roma was able to increase matchday revenues from €15 million to €28.4 million (90% growth), even with an outdated stadium. While the growth is impressive, it is much less than the €51 million that Juventus had in matchday revenues in 2015. Management have worked hard to create a better overall fan experience in the stadium. For example, when the Italian-Americans bought the club, they discovered the best 2,000 VIP seats were actually given away for free to important people as favours. After the purchase, the free seats were taken back and sold as packages to fans with special privileges and access to food. They even did basic things like set up Wi-Fi access for fans to improve fan experience. The club also benefited from more home matches due to playing in the Champions League.

Breakdown of Roma's Revenue Sources 2011/12 to 2015/16
€ in millions

	2011/12		2012/13		2013/14		2014/15		2015/16	
	Revenue	%	Revenue	%	Revenue	%	Revenue	%	Revenue	%
Match Day	14.7	13	20.1	16	21.2	17	30.4	17	28.4	13
Broadcasting	64.4	56	66.0	53	69.0	54	114.0	63	154.0	71
Commercial	36.8	32	38.3	31	36.8	29	36.0	20	35.8	16
Total	115.9		124.4		127.0		180.4		218.2	
DFML Rank	19		19		24		16		15	
League (Rank)	7		6		2		2		3	

Source: Deloitte

The biggest issue for Roma has been commercial revenues which were €36.8 million in 2012 and €35.8 million in 2016. In comparison, Juventus, to whom Roma have finished second for three of the last four years, with third place the other time, have €101.7 million in commercial revenues. Part of this can be explained because sponsors may have been waiting to see if and when Roma would be approved for a new stadium and when it would be completed as commercial opportunities are often tied to corporate entertaining at a stadium. The stadium was approved in December 2017 and projected to be opened in 2020. In addition, Roma have been reluctant to sign a shirt sponsor unless they received an amount they felt was commensurate with their new position, which was also historically difficult to assess without the stadium approval. In 2018, Roma announced a multi-deal global partnership with Qatar Airways ahead of their Champions League semi-final match against Liverpool. In 2013, Roma signed a ten-year kit supply deal with Nike to start in 2014/15. A Nike executive stated at the time: 'We're proud to partner with AS Roma, a club with great heritage. It's a club that embodies strong characteristics, is recognised across the world and represents one of Europe's greatest cities.' Unfortunately, the deal with Nike does not take into account Roma's current improved position, so on a relative basis to comparable clubs, the revenues are lower.

Talent

As for talent, when the Italian-American group took over, Totti was 35 years old (born in 1976). Since 2011, Roma has had one player receive votes for the Ballon d'Or. Edin Džeko finished 28th for the 2017 Ballon d'Or after he became the first Roma player ever to reach 33 goals in a season in all competitions, surpassing the previous record of 32 goals jointly held by Rodolfo Volk and Francesco Totti, and ending the season with a tally of 39 goals in all competitions. Daniele De Rossi inherited the captaincy of Roma at the start of the 2017/18 season following the retirement of Totti. De Rossi was promoted from the Roma youth system to the first team when he was 18 years old. In February 2012, De Rossi signed a new five-year contract with Roma. Under new club ownership, he became the highest-paid Italian footballer in Serie A at €10 million (gross) per annum.

Roma's previous record for an Italian player was Totti (€8.9 million in the 2009/10 season).

In player selection there is a scoring system to evaluate hundreds of potential players by ranking 39 factors among four categories for the player: (1) principles of the game/tactics, (2) technical skills, (3) motor skills/ physical and (4) psychological. All training is videoed with players wearing a GPS tracker and both the player and coaches have access to the data and analytics. For physical conditioning, Roma tracks the time of training, results, diet and even sleep. With regards to player development, there is a focus on developing an 'intelligent player' that plays the 'Roma way' which is 'smart'. All of the academy players from ten to 17 are taught in the same system. Roma believes that skills like awareness, confidence and problem-solving are important to be successful, and that interactive technology offering data and analytics after the game and off the pitch are incredibly important. Roma have built up some incredible data analytics and are moving on to the next level of analytics, including machine-learning. The academy, which is already highly rated, continues to get better. Since 2003 at least three youth academy graduates have played at least ten games during a season, an achievement most clubs can't claim. As previously mentioned, Roma have invested in their player development academy and were the only Italian club in the top ten in Europe of having graduates playing in the top five leagues.

Upon reflection, Roma believes that they have sometimes given up too early on their youth in the academies. The club is reconsidering loaning out players like Lorenzo Pellegrini too early. (On 30 June 2015, Pellegrini signed for fellow Serie A side Sassuolo for a fee of €1.25 million. In terms of the transfer agreement, Roma retained a buy-back clause which affords the club the opportunity to re-purchase Pellegrini for a reported fee of €8–10m at a future stage. On 30 June 2017, Roma exercised the €10 million buy-back clause.)

Roma believe that maybe they will have to give a young player more playing time because players like Pellegrini will be extremely important to Roma over the next decade, not just talent-wise but culture-wise and in maintaining traditions of home-grown players that is a part of the core of what most Roma fans believe. Roma want to make sure that players like Pellegrini, young players, stay with Roma and understand that Roma want them. Roma have a bunch of other players in their youth programmes that they are pretty keen on, all the way down to some 15- and 16-year-olds.

In 2016, according to the Global Sports Salary Survey (GSSS), Juventus paid their players an average of €4.84 million per year – the eighth highest average salary in European football behind only Manchester United, Barcelona, Manchester City, Real Madrid, Chelsea, Paris Saint-Germain and Bayern Munich. Roma were in 11th place with an average of €3.6 million (Inter were 14th with €3.01 million.)

Roma compete against clubs with more financial resources and have to comply with Financial Fair Play rules. Many of their best players are targeted by bigger clubs and if a player wants to move, it is difficult to prevent it. Also, similar to many clubs, Roma often need the profits from transfer fees to comply with FFP. For example, Miralem Pjanic was sold to Juventus for €32 million after the player had joined Roma from Lyon in 2011 for €11 million. These profits helped Roma remain compliant with FFP.

In another example, Mohamed Salah was sold to Liverpool in 2017 for an initial €42 million fee that could rise to up to €50 million. In 2015, Salah joined Roma on a season-long loan for €5 million, with the option to make the deal permanent for a reported €15 million. Pallotta said Roma had 'no choice' but to sell Mohamed Salah after the Egyptian winger told the club he wanted to return to the Premier League. Pallotta said, 'He had one year left on his contract and what were we going to do? Either keep him for that year and then get zero or sell him . . . not many teams other than Liverpool were banging down the door to buy Salah…We don't have the revenues those other teams have so you have to buy and sell smarter, but when we look at the players that we've sold like Salah, we had no choice . . .'[4]

Perception of Relatively Defensive, Boring Games

With eight of the past 17 champions not having to be top scorers to win Serie A, it shows a solid defence and more conservative style of play was decisive for teams who won the league. Teams who won Serie A but didn't

---

[4] http://www.bbc.com/sport/football/43744526

top score often weren't far behind in the goals scored tally, but it was the goals conceded figure where a noticeable difference was found.

Roma scored the same or fewer goals than defensive-oriented Juventus from 2013 to 2015. In 2016 and 2017, Roma scored more goals than Juventus. In 2017, Roma scored the most goals they had ever scored (90), had the club's and the league's leading goalscorer in history (Džeko with 39) and accumulated their most points ever in the league (87) and finished in second place. The season with their second most goals scored ever (83) led to a third place finish in the league.

Roma's Goals and Goal Scorers from 2012/13 to 2016/17
Roma's focus is on a more attacking and exciting style of play.

Season	Roma Goals For	Goals Against	Place	Roma Lead Scorer	Goals	Juventus Goals For	Goals Against
2016/17	90	38	2	Dzeko	39	77	27
2015/16	83	41	3	Salah	15	75	20
2014/15	54	31	2	Totti	10	72	24
2013/14	71	25	2	Destro	13	80	23
2012/13	71	56	6	Osvaldo	17	71	24

Overall Fan Experience: Old Stadium

When American-educated Manolo Zubiria first joined Roma in 2013, he noticed there was no advertising in Rome about upcoming Roma matches – nothing. One couldn't even easily find a place where tickets were sold for matches. At the time, Roma only had one small store in a poor location – one could walk by it and not even notice it. So, he thought to himself, Roma should go into the streets and find tourists that would be interested in experiencing a Roma match. Italian laws make it hard to sell tickets to Italians from regions outside of the Lazio region, but there were no restrictions on selling tickets to foreign tourists. So, the opportunity was there, but Roma just needed to find an economical and efficient way to be able to sell tickets to foreign tourists near many major tourist sites, making it convenient for them. However, Roma needed permission from the authorities. There was a lot of resistance at first because 'it had never been done'. After repeated requests for approval, Roma's persistence paid off.

Roma developed 'mobile scooter ticket sales centres' ('Apette' in Italian), that could move to various historical sites and sell tickets from anywhere in the city. They trained a group of salespeople, fluent in at least four languages, on selling tactics, the layout of the stadium, and the different price points. The trained salespeople were dressed in full Roma outfits and equipped with iPads showing videos and photos of the stadium experience. The project was a big success.

While Roma are waiting for their new stadium, they have had to improve the overall fan experience at the Stadio Olimpico. One of the improvements was the AS Roma Fan Zone, an entertainment area designed for families and children at Giallorossi home games. For every home game, children, parents and fans can play each other at table football. Activities include 'Inflatable Penalties', where one can fly through the air to save a shot without getting hurt. There's also music and hostesses to entertain the kids, face painting and the skills of Roma's football freestylers. They entertain fans but above all kids, who can also challenge them. It's great fun and the club's staff are there throughout to assist supporters, children and families from when the gates open until kick-off. The club also created 'La Magic Land' – a new fan village for all Roma supporters looking to make the most of matchday at the Stadio Olimpico. 'La Magicaa Land' offers interactive, innovative and multi-sensory attractions for all Roma fans. It is designed to be more than just a site for pre-match fun and games, but a true experience for fans. The Fan Zone offers a virtual reality experience, which takes one inside the club's training ground at Trigoria. Luca Danovaro, the club's chief marketing officer, said: 'It's based on the twin aims of innovation and fun – and we hope it becomes a real attraction for our fans on the day of home games.'

Overall Fan Experience: New Stadium

In 2014, Roma first announced plans to build a new 52,000-seater stadium in the Tor di Valle area of the city, which they hope to have completed for 2021. They wanted to leave the over-utilised Stadio Olimpico, which they share with Lazio, to relocate to a new ground modelled on the Colosseum, connecting the identity of the club to iconic Rome. Roma chairman Pallotta said the club needed a new home if they are to keep up with the other giant clubs in Europe. 'If we are going to consistently compete as a top club in the world we need a new stadium, a stadium that is privately owned by AS Roma.' It was later hoped the construction could actually begin in 2015, 2016 and 2017, but all three years passed in bureaucratic deadlock. In June 2017, the Rome City Council approved a resolution that the new project was in the public interest. A second Conferenza dei Servizi began in September and concluded in December 2017 with all the institutions involved granting their approval.

The approval was particularly satisfying after the tireless work behind the scenes by Roma staff to finally secure the football club its very own home. Pallotta said, 'The city and fans deserve a world-class stadium. We are confident the Stadio della Roma will be among the best in the world and a key driver for the club's continued success.' The club says the stadium will contain the 'finest premium seating in world football, including private luxury suites, loge boxes and club seats'. In a bid to satisfy the Roma Ultras and keep their historical enthusiastic atmosphere, Roma will include a 14,000-capacity section that replicates the old Curva Sud. It also includes an interactive museum. Privately funded at the cost of nearly €833 million, the new complex is expected to more than double Roma's revenue models.

Roma Home Stadium Attendance Season Averages

Season	Average	Rank
2011/12	35,757	5
2012/13	39,748	3
2013/14	40,083	3
2014/15	40,118	1
2015/16	40,190	2
2016/17	32,638	5
2017/18	37,284	5

Roma's average attendance dropped from 40,190 in 2015/16 to 32,638 in 2016/17. On 2 September 2015, it was reported that construction was beginning on barriers in the Curva Sud. Not knowing what to expect of the barriers, the season ticket holders had little choice but to keep their prepaid seating, as they had done for countless seasons before. Rome's prefect commissioned the barriers for supposed safety reasons, which cost Roma and Lazio €600,000 each. No barriers were built at other teams' stadia; there weren't even any warnings about crowd control. There wasn't one violent incident reported during the entire year in Rome's Stadio Olimpico. Just two weeks after the barriers were erected, and the day after the Champions League group stage match against world champions Barcelona, the Curva Sud released an official statement on the internet via the capi-ultrà:

'None of us want to be away from our Curva, but we will stay out as long as it is not liberated! We will stay out until we can cheer freely and not as trained dogs. We spent money, some of us made sacrifices, but this is not what we bought. There is no difference between us, we are all fans and in love with the club and we show it in our different ways . . . We thank those who came out on Wednesday to sing with us, refusing entry into the stadium . . . Now more than ever, we unite to retake our dear Curva Sud. They can put in as many barriers as they want, but they'll never manage to divide our ideals . . . Avanti Curva Sud!'

The Curva Sud remained unified, maintaining their stance that none of them would be returning to their section of the stadium. Those who entered the stadium were greeted with banners reminding them that they were accomplices to the enemy – the authority. Several former Roma players shared their sentiment on the restrictions. Vincent Candela, a member of the 2001/02 Scudetto-winning Roma team stated, 'They are doing everything to divide the fans, not just in the Curva. The Curva is a group and they will reason together. They must not give up . . . I hope they come back to the stadium to cheer because the team needs the Curva.' Musical artist Antonello Venditti, who wrote 'Roma, Roma, Roma' after their 1982/83 championship-winning season shared, 'Do not split up the fans, just divide those who betray the values!' Venditti was referring to the select few violent Ultras betraying Roma's values and ruining the experience for over 99% of the fans. This is precisely the issue that Italian authorities and club owners have to contend with. In trying to protect the fan experience, drastic and draconian measures can also ruin the fan experience.

People wrongly claimed on the radio and on social media that Roma's management had somehow approved and shared the decision of the division, despite all the Giallorossi management's public declarations that they shared their fans' unhappiness. General director Mauro Baldissoni expressed his own disapproval on more than one occasion. On 26 October 2015, he said on Roma Radio: 'We believe the time to return to normality has come; there's no sense in football without fans. Even if we win, it wouldn't be the same. When politicians believe it's necessary to introduce extreme measures – such as I believe the Daspo is, which I think is at the limit of constitutional legality – they must do so by justifying it with a real and contingent necessity, while offering a solution that would re-establish normality. We often hear that we should aim to bring families, children and joy back to the stadium. It's hard to do that if the journey to the stadium is like entering a military compound. It's clear that this isn't tolerable for anything other than a very short period of time, and it has probably already been too long. We all have to work together to try and get back to what I would call normality, which is the joy of going to the stadium without any particular restrictions.'

After Roma's management's many meetings with government officials to try and resolve the situation over two seasons, finally in April 2017 the barriers were removed. The pulsating heart was back in the stadium.

Overall Fan Experience: The Bus

In 2014, Roma had never had its own team bus. Roma used to use a regular bus with a side panel decal of the club when travelling to matches. There was no sponsor presence or branding. It did not present the image the club was striving for. When Manolo Zubiria met with one of the bus vendors, the vendor explained under the previous owners someone at the club had met with them already three or four times to try to get a team bus, but in the end the club didn't have the €500,000 to pay for it. The vendor said that they had been through the process, and wasted their resources, too many times before. Roma convinced him they had a plan to get the money (which wasn't in the budget as the club tried to be FFP compliant). They developed a plan to help pay for the bus over five years by incorporating a social media initiative which would engage fans on the design of the bus. The side of the bus would have a large Roma logo, which would be a mosaic made up of fan photos. The project was called 'Ride with Us' and through an online platform, fans could pay €19.27 (Roma was founded in 1927) and they could upload their photo on the mosaic. The fan response was great, and Roma purchased their bus. The bus was then used in all Champions League away games, as far as Portugal and the UK. It was a great, innovative way to get fans more involved, who wanted to support the club in a unique way, and upgrade the brand image.

Global Entertainment Brand with Community-Centric Culture

Jim is an extraordinary owner because he truly believes the fans are the reason the club exists. He strives to make them proud, under the constraints the club has. He realises that the club needs to attract and engage new supporters wherever they are in the world to generate revenues while balancing the passion of the local fans, which is a core part of the identity. To Jim, Roma is more than a club; Roma is a mindset and Roma should inspire passion and emotion through football and the city of Rome.

With on-the-pitch performance being addressed, Roma's objective has been to increase their brand value by transforming the club into a truly global sports-entertainment company in order to generate revenues and compete with bigger revenue clubs. This starts with Roma's mission statement:

AS Roma is more than a club – it is an attitude, a way of life powered by the love, passion and loyalty of our fans. It is a symbol of the city, the red shirt its beating heart. It embodies Roman values, traditions and achievements. We live and breathe our history, and let innovation guide us to further our rich legacy. Roma creates legends.

Roma identified five core values that define who they are and which is the foundation of everything they do:

ROMAN: WE ARE ROMA: Our character defines us, not our reputation. It makes us who we are. What you see is what you get. AS Roma is authentic and real. Confident and passionate, we take pride in our city, its heritage and our team.

FAMILY: WE'RE LOYAL: Loyal, passionate and united, the bond between Roma and our fans is unwavering, unconditional. Love for the club is steeped in the city's culture and is passed down through the generations. We are selfless — working together for the common good.

ACCESSIBLE: WE'RE CARING: The smallest gestures can make the biggest difference and we look for ways to show we care. We are humble and put our fans first. Honest and transparent, we open our doors and invite our supporters in. We are part of the community and reach out to our fans wherever they are in the world.

DIFFERENT: WE'RE BRAVE: We dare to be different and are always open to new ideas. We explore ways to capture the imagination and make our mark. We are innovative. We take risks, embrace change and are constantly evolving. Failure is not fatal, but failure to change might be.

EXCELLENCE: WE'RE AMBITIOUS: We have the ability and drive to reach the top and the character to stay there, both on and off the pitch. We strive to be the best we can be, reaping the rewards of hard work and preparation. We are ambitious and always aspire to excellence.

What makes Roma unique is there is a passion, emotion, loyalty, pride and devotion that can only come from intertwining the history and traditions of a city like Rome with the club Roma, which is essentially an ambassador of the city that transcends the match on the pitch. In the end, Roma is the beating heart, the pulse, the rhythm and vital energy rushing through the city. Roma is a culture, a style, a passion, a flair that is passed down through the generations, a link, a bond. It's a family, a community, a sense of belonging. Built from the streets up, ingrained in the city's fabric, Roma is about the legends of its past handing on the torch to the stars and heroes of tomorrow.

Fans are often attracted to a club because of players they like or want to be. Francesco Totti is the representation of the values of the club. In 2011, Totti was recognised by the International Federation of Football History & Statistics as the most popular footballer in Europe. His shirt was the most popular seller for years for Roma. When Totti finished his career in 2017, Roma added him to the management team to work with Monchi because for Roma the key to shaping its future is not forgetting its past.

When comparing Roma's mission to Juventus (in the Juventus section titled 'Newventus'), one can see some differences in the clubs' approaches. Besides capitalising on their connection to Rome, Roma are trying to be different from the big clubs by being more approachable and not taking themselves too seriously. This self-effacing humour was also a loveable trait of Totti, who famously took a selfie with fans in the background after a goal and published a joke book poking fun at himself. For Roma, this includes big transfer signing videos that are inventive and humorous in contrast to over the top serious ones from bigger clubs trying to outdo each other or Roma players conducting funny interviews of other Roma players on Roma TV.

Lastly, Roma have the advantage that they can leverage everything that is Rome. Rome is a capital city like London, Paris and Madrid, which can help attract world-class players and their families. In addition, Rome attracts many tourists who might be casual football fans interested in going to see a European football match and then after a positive and special experience at the match could make Roma one of their favourite clubs; Rome attracts many foreign exchange students who might go to a match and go back to their home countries as a Roma fan; and Rome attracts people who identify with and admire the history, ideals and culture of the city and when thinking about a European or Italian club to support would by association, even never having visited the city, be a Roma fan.

A Higher Purpose

For a few years before 2018, the club has had 'Roma Cares' on the front of their shirt. Founded in 2014 with the aim of promoting education and positive values in sport, Roma Cares is a public charity tied to AS Roma's wider commitment to respect and corporate social responsibility. The charity carries out activities with the local community through projects and campaigns that principally aim to support and develop the growth of children and youth in disadvantaged situations. For this purpose, Roma Cares is involved in planning, implementing and organising free sports initiatives for disadvantaged children, guaranteeing them their right to sports and making sport accessible to the needy – recognising its primary and irreplaceable educational, social and protective function. Roma Cares' activities are aimed at benefitting those with physical, psychological, economic, social or family disadvantages. Roma coaches are used in the project to help them further develop emphathy which should help them become better leaders.

Overcoming a Lack of Global Vision

The Roman edition of *Corriere dello Sport* churns out Roma-related content at an incredible rate per day, while the city's more than half a dozen sports radio stations talk of little else. It can be understandably very difficult for management to be focused on global opportunities when there is such intense scrutiny locally. However, this focus locally takes energy away from global initiatives emanating from Rome. Therefore, many of the global initiatives with regards to sponsorship are handled outside of Rome.

Excellent Online Engagement: Club

Now the focus is on technology and innovation off the pitch. Roma were ranked 13th out of the top 25 most tech-savvy sports teams in 2016. Only three European football clubs made the list (Roma, Bayern Munich and Manchester City). After being voted one of the worst websites in the top five leagues in Europe at the end of 2015, Roma totally revamped its old website inspired by fans' feedback via Reddit, Twitter and fan forums. This is Jim's attitude. He sees himself as a caretaker of the club and is willing to cede control to the fans to improve and get better. He is not one for pomp and circumstance. He is a self-made person from a working-class area in Boston and will treat everyone with the same respect, regardless of wealth or class or position. Pallotta has made no secret of the fact that one of his many goals for Roma is to become the most digitally connected sports team in the world, and to do that the team needed to create something its fans would want to engage with.

Paul Rogers, the person who was head of content at Liverpool FC and first launched the club on social media, helped turn Roma into the most modern and engaging club in Italy. Statistically speaking, since Rogers became the director of Roma's digital media team, the club has become one of the fastest growing and most engaged club on social media in Europe.[5]

This digital generation do not want to be passive consumers of content. They don't want to be broadcast to or told what they can and can't consume. And it's not just on social media, either. Every football club has some pretty sophisticated fan-produced sites, blogs, podcasts and social media accounts operating alongside them, and they exist because these fans saw a gap in the market that wasn't being serviced by the clubs themselves. Roma didn't want to fall into that trap, so they really use and integrate fan feedback to make the club's digital platform better. Roma is trying to take the passion of its supporters that is already out there and help curate that content and give it an official stamp of approval.[6]

For example, when it was announced that Francesco Totti would play his final game for AS Roma after 25 years, Paul Rogers and his team began to work on a content plan that they hoped would pay a fitting tribute to the player himself, engage the club's supporters and also allow fans of other clubs to join the conversation. Although the team only has 8.8 million Facebook fans (and 11 million total social media followers), they were able to generate over 70 million video views in five days and broke every single digital record they measure (Facebook, Twitter, Instagram, Snapchat, YouTube and official team website). These videos were shared over 850,000 times and inspired over 170,000 comments, and for one month, Roma outperformed every other team in the world in terms of Facebook videos.[7]

Clearly this was a 'once in a lifetime' type of event, but this example shows how with resources, focus and a well-thought-out plan, there is a way for the Italian clubs to increase their presence on social media and have more of an impact, especially in terms of fan engagement.

[5] http://www.italianfootballdaily.com/three-ways-serie-can-improve-marketing/
[6] https://www.fastcompany.com/3054522/how-soccer-club-as-roma-is-becoming-the-most-fan-connected-sports-team-in-t
[7] https://www.linkedin.com/pulse/how-roma-88m-facebook-fans-generated-over-70m-video-views-paul-rogers/

Social Media Followers (As of February 2017)
(Deloitte Revenue Rank in parentheses)
Followers in Millions

Serie A Club	Twitter Followers	Instagram Followers	Facebook Followers	Total Followers
Juventus (9)	3.9	5.8	25.3	35
Milan (10)	4.4	2.9	24.8	32.1
Roma (15)	1.3	0.9	8.5	10.7
Inter (17)	1.2	1.3	6.1	8.6
Napoli (18)	1.3	0.7	3.9	5.9

Source: http://www.businessinsider.com/the-20-most-popular-rich-list-football-teams-on-social-media-2017-1

While Roma may be the fifth most popular club in Italy, they rank third overall in social media followers in Italy. It is impressive that they are ahead of Inter, who have won many more trophies, providing them with more opportunities to attract the attention of global fans. Roma still do not have the global scale and reach of Juventus and Milan. While the top 10 most followed clubs in social media appear in the Top 10 Deloitte Revenues list, Juventus being 10th on the list and also the 10th most followed on social media, Roma actually bucks the trend, appearing higher on the followed list (18th) than its revenues (24th).[8]

Poor Online Engagement: Players

Very few Italian or Serie A players are rated highly in total social media followers. Totti is the most popular Roma player and one of the most well known in the league, despite the fact that he is now retired. With that being said, his social media presence is less than some of the other notable players from the top teams in Serie A and is tiny compared to the bigger global stars such as Ronaldo and Messi. Italian and Roma legend Francesco Totti joined Twitter in September 2016. He has approximately 200,000 Twitter followers (225,000 as of 2017). Roma fan favourite Radja Nainggolan (joined March 2012) has 500,000 followers (544,000 as of 2017). Compare this to similar players in La Liga or the English Premier League and there are staggering differences. In addition, most

---

[8] http://digitale-sport-medien.com/tabellen-2/top-25/fussball/

of the time, Roma players do not message in English. This issue is not unique to Roma. Buffon is the player in Serie A with the most social media followers, approximately 13 million. Totti rated fourth at 3.5 million. The numbers are a fraction of the top five active players in the world.

As per the table below, the gap between the top five players in the world with the highest followings versus the top players in Italy is staggering.

Top Players for Serie A with Highest Social Media Following
Followers in millions

Player	Club	Total Followers
Gianluigi Buffon	Juventus	12.6
Leonardo Bonucci	Milan	5.7
Mauro Icardi	Inter	4.3
Francesco Totti	Roma	3.5
Dries Mertens	Napoli	2.45

As of November 2017, includes followers on Facebook, Instagram and Twitter

Top 5 Active Players with Highest Social Media Following (Jan 2018)
Followers in millions

Player	Club	Total Followers	League
Cristano Ronaldo	Real Madrid	307.7	La Liga
Neymar	PSG	185	Ligue 1
Leo Messi	Barcelona	174.4	La Liga
James Rodriguez	Bayern Munich	82.7	Bundesliga
Gareth Bale	Real Madrid	77.1	La Liga

Source: http://www.90min.com/posts/4632444-the-12-footballers-with-the-biggest-social-media-followings

Roma TV and Roma Radio

To Pallotta, to become a sustainable economic-sport entity, on the business side, Roma must be a multimedia entertainment company. Fans can watch the game on Roma TV. They can listen to it on Roma Radio.

They can follow along through Roma's website, social media channels and mobile app. Well after the final whistle, the game will provide content for Roma's enthusiasts to consume. 'The 24/7 around it is how you build out your global brand,' Pallotta said. 'That was the rationale in the first place for Rome more than any other city. It's Rome.' Pallotta and his investors refer to a triangle of business verticals which are sports, media and entertainment, and technology and distribution. The trick is to build robustness in all three.

One of the brilliant management moves by Roma was to have all media and communication operations centralised and placed near where the players train and practise. It allows the communications team to more effectively work together and have one consistent message. It also gives them more access to work in collaboration with the star content, which is the players, and get that content to the fans.

No matter what a fan is looking for, if it concerns the club, Roma TV has it. With live updates on training sessions, exclusive interviews with players and management, press conferences with the head coach and much more besides, Roma TV – the only official Giallorossi television channel – offers information, insight and entertainment around the clock. With studios located inside the club's training ground in Trigoria on the outskirts of Rome, Roma TV is on air every day of the week – with live news updates coming directly from the training pitches and dressing rooms. Ahead of every first team game, there's in-depth analysis on the opposition, an insight into tactics and interviews with the club's former players. Then, on the day of the match, Roma TV's reporters are at the stadium to guide you through what's happening on and off the pitch, conducting live interviews with players, coaches and fans and constantly interacting with the hosts back in the studio. Roma TV isn't just about the first team though. The channel pays its respects to Roma's past with shows featuring in-depth interviews with former Giallorossi legends and documentary pieces on the characters who wrote themselves into the history books of the club. At the same time, Roma TV always keeps one eye on the future, thanks to live match coverage of the Primavera side and updates on the Under-17s and Under-15s.

No football club in the world has more radio programmes dedicated to discussing its every move than AS Roma Radio. In a city where football talk shows provide the soundtrack to every journey across the city, Roma Radio is unique. By broadcasting daily from within the very heart of the club, Roma Radio is able to break down the barriers between the supporters and Roma's players and management – providing fans with a station that offers exclusive access to the people who matter most. As well as offering exclusive interviews with the management, coaches, players and club legends, Roma Radio offers round-the-clock information, entertainment, debate and in-depth analysis of every talking point surrounding the club. Launched in August 2014, Roma Radio has been providing unfiltered coverage of the club on a daily basis and with more shows than ever, including live commentary of every game Roma play. Roma Radio can be streamed online on the club's official website, on 100.7 FM and also via the Roma Radio app – available from Apple Store and Google Play – as well as Tune In; the station broadcasts live seven days a week. The scheduling switches between pure entertainment and a focus on players and the first team, with technical and tactical analysis as well as interviews and news. Roma Radio's unique vantage point allows the station to establish an extraordinary platform to exchange opinions and overcome the usual limitations between the fan and the club as well as introducing listeners to the thoughts and opinions of others within Italian football.

Centralising Supporters' Clubs

Roma is in the process of starting an official AS Roma Fan Club Network which is a group of Roma fan clubs around the world officially recognised by the club. The fan clubs provide a way for Roma's most loyal and avid fans to unite around their love and passion for the club. Recognising the importance of these fans, the Fan Club Network is to serve as a platform through which the club can demonstrate its appreciation for their support by enhancing their community experience and providing exclusive benefits. The fan clubs can apply for official status via the Roma website. Roma will provide some technology guidance and support for the social media the fan clubs choose. Once approved, the members receive a welcome pack with a fan club ID, gifts and benefits. It gives the fans direct and dedicated contact with Roma. Roma don't intend to make the AIRC or UTR unofficial fan clubs obsolete, but rather work with them to achieve a common goal.

Understanding the Impact of Video Games

As one of the most digitally connected sports teams in the world, Roma have strived to create an organisation that engages its fans through all digital channels. With the tremendous growth of esports and continued attention placed on games like FIFA, Roma partnered with Fnatic, the world's leading esports organisation, to launch their esports team. This joint venture will enable Roma to start building a strong legacy in esports and engage their fans in exciting new ways. Fnatic powers the club's esports division, offers support for training and events, and provides all esports-related logistical knowledge to nurture the club's players.

Italian Owners with Limited Ways to Skirt FFP Limits

Financial Fair Play dictates that clubs can spend up to €5 million more than they earn within a three-year assessment period. They can, however, exceed that limit by €30 million (previously €45 million), if it is entirely covered by a direct contribution from either the club's owner or a related party. Investment in stadiums, training facilities, youth development and women's football are excluded from what UEFA describe as 'the break-even calculation'.

In 2015, Roma were among ten European clubs punished for not being compliant with FFP rules. Roma agreed to pay a fine and to limit the number of new players they could register in European competition. Roma were allowed only 22 players, instead of 25, in their squad if they qualified for European competition the following season. Roma had to pay a fine of up to €6 million and must not report combined losses of more than €30 million for 2015 and 2016 combined. The agreement was necessary due to a historical deviation from UEFA's break-even requirement stemming from past economic losses and the challenging financial situation of the club before the current ownership's takeover. For Roma, the 2018/19 season is targeted as the date by which breaking even has to be accomplished. These financial constraints limit player acquisitions and put pressure on the club to sell players to generate profits in order to be compliant. This is why data analytics combined with experience, like Monchi's, are incredibly important to navigate profitability requirements. It also re-emphasises why consistency in the Champions League is important in terms of revenues and shows the importance of a new stadium for matchday revenues, which is highly correlated with commercial revenues.

Roma's ownership do not control many affiliated entities that it can use to easily increase commercial sponsorship revenues (e.g. like PSG and Manchester City), so it will take time for Roma to increase commercial sponsorships and commensurate spending on players and investments.

Final Remarks

When asked in an interview in *Gazzetta* in January 2018 about Roma, Arrigo Sacchi, who won back-to-back European Cups with Milan in 1989 and 1990, said: 'I told you before: football reflects society. Roma is the most beautiful city in the world but suffers a lot from problems and contradictions, a dispersive city. It's very complicated to win with Roma,' Capello said, 'One Scudetto in Rome is worth ten Scudetti in Turin.'

Roma believe that with its flexible and unique digital approach – combining sport, technology, and entertainment – and now with 15 million followers on Facebook, Instagram and Twitter, their sponsorship dollars should be higher, highlighting the impact, in particular, of social media. Today, it's about viewership and engagement on social media which can drive commercial sponsorship in many ways plus regular TV broadcasting revenues. Roma want more eyeballs and more opportunities to tell their story, to attract fans and keep them engaged. Pallotta believes that Roma can become a global sports and media conglomerate on the business side, which is important for generating money to spend on the sporting side in an FFP world. For healthy and competitive European football clubs, Pallotta does not believe that ceilings exist.

Roma's incredible come-from-behind win over Barcelona in 2018 to advance to the Champions League semi-final will be discussed later. One result from that win was that Roma united an entire country. Another result is that Roma was given a platform to showcase why they should be the 'second favourite team' of fans. Perhaps, Roma will be able to capitalise on some casual fans being tired with the traditional powers or wanting to also root for an underdog or a club that is different. The charismatic owner jumping into a fountain to celebrate (discussed later) or Francesco Totti taking a selfie with fans after a goal or Alessandro Florenzi running into the stands and hugging his grandmother in a goal celebration all reinforce that Roma is a friendly, fun and family oriented community. These powerful images help define Roma's identity.

On 23 April 2018, AS Roma agreed to a multi-year partnership with Qatar Airways which will make the airline the team's official shirt sponsor until 2021. Roma had been without a main jersey sponsor since 2014. Pallotta said, 'With a new stadium due to begin construction late this year and the team in the Champions League semi-final for the first time for 34 years, it's an exciting time to be a Roma fan.'

CHAPTER ELEVEN

NAPOLI – NEAPOLITAN RENAISSANCE

Overview

SSC Napoli (in full Societa Sportiva Calcio Napoli), known commonly as just Napoli, is the football club of Naples, in the south of Italy. The club was formed in 1926. Napoli broke the world transfer fee record in 1984 by acquiring Diego Maradona. Maradona played at Napoli from 1984 to 1991 and gave the club immediate global credibility and recognition. Maradona helped Napoli win their only two Scudetti in 1987 and 1990 and a European tournament, the 1988/89 UEFA Cup. Napoli are the only club in the south of Italy to have won Serie A.

Napoli's home colour is sky blue which leads to the nickname 'Gli Azzurri' ('The Light Blues'). The colour is representative of the blue waters of the Gulf of Naples. One of Napoli's nicknames is 'Partenopei'. The nickname apparently stems from Greek mythology, from the tale of Parthenope, a siren that attempted to lure Odysseus to his death on the rocks of Capri, the island near Naples. In the story, Odysseus had his men tie him to the ship's mast so he was able to resist the song of the siren. Consequently, Parthenope, unable to live with the rejection of her love, drowned herself and her body was washed up on the shore of Naples. Another nickname of Napoli is 'I Ciucciarelli', which means 'the little donkeys' in the local dialect. Napoli were given this name after a particularly poor performance during the 1926/27 season. It was originally meant to be derogatory, as the Neapolitan symbol is a rampant black horse, but the club embraced the name, and the club uses a donkey named 'O Ciuccio' as a mascot.

The city of Naples has a population of around 1 million people, which is the third largest in the country. Napoli is the fourth most supported football club in Italy with around 13% of Italian football fans supporting the club. Napoli's fans are known to be extremely passionate. Even with Napoli in Serie C1 during the 2005/06 season, Napoli had the third highest average home attendance in Italy for the season with only two Serie A clubs, Milan and Inter, having higher attendances. Napoli's final game of the season drew a crowd of 51,000 which now stands as a Serie C record. Napoli's foreign fan base has been growing exponentially during the last few seasons. This rising fan base recognises the effort of the club in implementing an expansion strategy in foreign markets. Owner Aurelio De Laurentiis stated, 'according to Nielsen's research, Napoli's fan base has drastically grown to 35 million in the last few years, with a huge presence in the United States, which accounts for 20% of the total. The number of followers (people that like watching Napoli play, even if they support other teams) reaches up to 120 million'. According to Nielsen's report, among the 35 million supporters, 4.6 million are located in Italy, 7.2 million in the United States, 5.1 million in Brazil and 1.4 million in Argentina. More than 15% of the 120 million followers come from the United States. Support in China is also dramatically growing, estimated at about 18 million. In 2017, Napoli created a department of five people specifically for international marketing development.

Napoli have many rivalries, particularly with the northern teams. The 'Derby del Sole', (Derby of the Sun) is a heated Italian football derby between Napoli and Roma, especially fierce during the 1970s and 1980s. The two clubs are considered the most followed and successful clubs outside of northern Italy (the heart of Italian football); Roma being from central Italy and Napoli from southern Italy.

Since 1959, the club have played their home games at Stadio San Paolo in the suburbs of Naples, which is the third largest football stadium in Italy after the San Siro and the Stadio Olimpico. The current capacity is 60,240.

The Naples city council asked the Italian government for permission to rename the stadium after Diego Maradona, but one stumbling block is an Italian law prohibiting public buildings to be named after any person who has not been dead for at least ten years.

The official anthem of the club is 'O surdato nnammurato'.

Notable former Napoli players include Diego Maradona, Gianfranco Zola, Fabio Cannavaro, Edinson Cavani and Gonzalo Higuaín.

On the Pitch

Before Maradona arrived in 1984, Napoli had finished second twice in Serie A (1968 and 1975). The club had a very loyal and passionate fan base, but were not able to compete and win at the highest level.

The Maradona Era

In the summer of 1984, Napoli bought Argentinian superstar Diego Maradona from Barcelona for a record transfer fee of €12 million and Napoli and the rest of Italy went crazy with his arrival. Maradona arrived in Naples in July 1984, where he was welcomed by 75,000 fans at his presentation at the Stadio San Paolo. Sports writer David Goldblatt commented, 'They [the fans] were convinced that the saviour had arrived.' A local newspaper stated that despite the lack of a 'mayor, houses, schools, buses, employment and sanitation, none of this matters because we have Maradona'. Prior to Maradona's arrival, Italian football was dominated by teams from the north of the country, and no team in the south of the Italian peninsula had ever won a league title.

Surrounded by other great players such as Careca, Ferrara, Bagni and De Napoli, Maradona and Napoli were able to win two Scudetti, in 1987 (versus Sacchi's Milan) and in 1990 (versus Trapattoni's Inter), as well as a UEFA Cup in 1989.

Napoli Record Post-Maradona Arrival 1984/95 to 1989/90

Season	Serie A	European Competitions
1984/85	8th	

1985/86	3rd	
1986/87	1st	
1987/88	2nd	Round of 32 (European Cup)
1988/89	2nd	Winner (UEFA Cup)
1989/90	1st	Group (European Cup)

Napoli's stadium is probably most famous for hosting the 1990 World Cup semi-final between Italy and Argentina. Considered to be the most intriguing match of that World Cup, Maradona, who played for Napoli at the time, asked for the Napoli fans to cheer for Argentina. The Napoli tifosi responded by hanging a flag in their 'Curva' of the stadium saying 'Maradona, Naples loves you, but Italy is our homeland'. The match finished 1-1 after extra time. A penalty shoot-out ensued with Maradona fittingly scoring the winning penalty for Argentina.

While Maradona was successful on the field during his time in Italy, his personal problems increased. His alleged drug use continued and he received fines from the club for missing games and practices, ostensibly because of 'stress'. Maradona would leave the club in 1992. Later on, in honour of Maradona and his achievements during his career at Napoli, his number ten shirt was officially retired at Napoli.

In the following years, Napoli would lose other important star players such as Careca and Gianfranco Zola. Maradona's departure also coincided with some disastrous financial mismanagement and Napoli slowly crumbled, with a relegation to Serie B in 1998. Eventually, financial disaster caught up with the company, and in 2004 Napoli were declared bankrupt with a debt of €79 million. According to the rules and regulations, it could not now participate in Serie B, so the only alternative was to try for Serie C1 – under new management and with a massive injection of funds.

The De Laurentiis era

At the time, the fate of Napoli was a major story in Italy and created endless conflict, even at a political level. Then suddenly movie producer Aurelio De Laurentiis appeared on the scene. He had previously offered €50 million for the club, which had been met with a refusal, but now he was back, resolute and ready to go. Time was of the essence, however.

He met in Switzerland with Pier Paolo Marino, managing director of the Udinese team, and together they made a pact to bring Napoli back to the fore – and to make it great. Marino was met by applause on his return to Naples – after all, he had been there for Napoli's first Scudetto. He left a well-placed and solvent Udinese team to try his luck again with Napoli. Aurelio De Laurentiis was new to the football world and was facing a huge challenge. Born in the Campania region to a prestigious film family, in 1975 he founded the FilmAuro Company, which has over 300 films to its credit in terms of production and distribution. De Laurentiis is behind a number of blockbuster film series that are among the top five box-office hits each year. A shareholder in Cinecittà and president of the Italian Film Producers' Association, his appearance on the scene was a real act of love. In a matter of days, he resolved a situation that had been festering for months. He paid the courts €30 million, founded Napoli Soccer, presented an ambitious project, put Pier Paolo Marino in charge of it, signed the team in Serie C1, and engaged Edy Reja as coach. It was the beginning of a new era. Napoli were back. The first year they almost won the final play-off against Avellino and promotion to Serie B. The next year, with an improved line-up, they made it.

De Laurentiis further beefed up the team by signing even better players, and was more than ready for the 2006/07 season, this time under their former name of Società Sportiva Calcio Napoli and with the much more ambitious goal of getting into Serie A. In June 2007, Napoli drew with Genoa on the last day of the season and thus won promotion back to the top division together with the 'grifoni cousins'. The exciting promotion brought back the enthusiasm of the golden age to the town of Napoli. The team was welcomed by a crowd of fans pouring onto the streets, which was reminiscent of Napoli during the Maradona age. This also led to the official start of the Neapolitan Renaissance, after 14 seasons and almost 5,000 days of waiting.

De Laurentiis was able to turn things around in an astoundingly short period of time. Moreover, he was able to accomplish this very impressive renaissance while having the team play a very attacking and pleasant-to-watch style of football. De Laurentiis is a unique owner given his background, and for him, performance on the pitch is similar to a show, which has allowed him to be an innovator within the defensive mindset of Serie A. He wants and expects the games to be entertaining, and he has made sure his team plays according to this vision. Every year since bankruptcy, Napoli have continued to improve on the pitch, signing players such as Cavani, Lavezzi, Hamsik, Higuaín, Callejon, Mertens, Insigne, Paolo Cannavaro and Christian Maggio. The hiring of Maurizio Sarri as manager in 2015 was also an important development in recent years, as he is considered to be a tactical mastermind in the greater football community. Just as importantly, De Laurentiis also focused on improving results off the pitch, especially in terms of revenues and financial performance. Under De Laurentiis' ownership, Napoli have finished second in 2013 and 2016, and third in 2011, 2014 and 2017. The club have also done well in recent Champions League seasons (including two Round of 16 appearances, in 2012 and 2017).

Napoli's Serie A and Champions League Performance from 2010/11 to 2016/17

Season	Serie A	Champions League
2010/11	3rd	
2011/12	5th	Round of 16
2012/13	2nd	
2013/14	3rd	Group
2014/15	5th	Play-off
2015/16	2nd	
2016/17	3rd	Round of 16

Talent

Maradona won the FIFA World Cup Golden Ball and Silver Shoe in 1986 and the Bronze Ball in 1990. Edinson Cavani finished 20th for the 2013 Ballon d'Or and Gonzalo Higuaín finished 20th for the 2016 Ballon d'Or. Napoli have been successful at signing players and giving them a platform to shine but then selling them for a lot more money. The three best examples are Ezequiel Lavezzi, Cavani and Higuaín. In July 2007, Napoli bought Lavezzi for a deal reported to be around €6 million. In July 2012, Napoli sold Lavezzi to PSG for a reported €26.5 million transfer fee. In July 2010, Napoli bought Cavani for a total fee of €17 million, and sold him in July 2013 to PSG for a fee believed to be around €64 million. In July 2013 Napoli bought Higuaín for €40 million and he was sold to rivals Juventus for a fee of €90 million in July 2016. Even while selling off players, Napoli have been able to use the money to bring in more talent, including the likes of Mertens, Insigne and Callejón. In June 2013, Napoli bought Dries Mertens for a reported fee of €9.5 million, and he finished the 2016/17 season as the number two goalscorer in Serie A. Lorenzo Insigne was a member of the Napoli youth academy and made the first team in the 2012/13 season. In July 2013, Napoli purchased Real Madrid youth academy graduate José Callejón for a €10 million fee.

De Laurentiis has spent money, made money and reinvested in players. This strategy has clearly paid off on the pitch, as Napoli have finished in the top three five times in the last seven years since the 2010/11 season. In line with keeping costs under control and carefully planning for the future, De Laurentiis has also concentrated on upgrading Napoli's academy, so that home-grown youth players can progress to the first team instead of the club continually having to gamble on bringing in new players at exorbitant prices. In the past, De Laurentiis has spoken of a desire to emulate Barcelona (as indeed have many other owners), but this project will take years to fully develop.

Attacking Style of Play

Since Sarri took over in 2015, Napoli have had prolific goalscorers and an attacking style of play. In the past two seasons, they have scored more goals than Juventus. Additionally, Napoli's leading goalscorer has significantly outperformed that of Juventus every year by a wide margin.

Napoli and Juventus Goals and Goal Scorers 2008/09 to 2016/17

Napoli

Season	Goals For	Goals Against	Place	Lead Scorer	Goals
2016/17	94	39	3	Dries Mertens	28
2015/16	80	32	2	Gonzalo Higuain	36
2014/15	70	54	5	Gonzalo Higuain	18
2013/14	77	39	3	Gonzalo Higuain	17
2012/13	73	36	2	Edinson Cavani	29
2011/12	66	46	5	Edinson Cavani	33
2010/11	59	39	3	Edinson Cavani	23
2009/10	50	43	6	Marek Hamsik	12
2008/09	43	45	12	Marek Hamsik	12

Juventus

Season	Goals For	Goals Against	Place	Lead Scorer	Goals
2016/17	77	27	1	Gonzalo Higuain	24
2015/16	75	20	1	Paulo Dybala	19
2014/15	72	24	1	Carloz Tevez	20
2013/14	80	23	1	Carloz Tevez	19
2012/13	71	24	1	Vidal/ Vučinić	10
2011/12	68	20	1	Alessandro Matri	10
2010/11	57	47	7	Matri/Quagliarella	9
2009/10	55	56	7	Alessandro Del Piero	9
2008/09	69	37	2	Alessandro Del Piero	13

Likened to Barcelona for its beauty and Bayern Munich for its efficiency, Napoli's style of play under Sarri is centred on intelligent movement and involves playing a high defensive line, with lots of possession and constant ball movement through the use of both triangle and vertical passing. With quick and precise passing, Sarri's 3-5-2 (that often seems like a 4-3-3 with an unorthodox attacking approach) formation is a blend of styles never seen before in Italy or elsewhere around the world. It's a hybrid of several already established tactical formations.[1]

What is most impressive is that Sarri has been so successful with a good team with many good players, but not one full of superstars. Many compare him to Sacchi, who transformed the mentality of Italian football in the 1980s and early 1990s and won back-to-back European Cups with Milan in 1989 and 1990. However, Sacchi always had the best players to draw from, whether it be with Milan or with the Italian national team, while Sarri does not. Sacchi himself validated this in an interview in *Gazzetta* in January 2018 when asked about Napoli's style of play. His

---

[1] https://fansided.com/2017/10/13/sarris-tactical-revolution-napoli-will-lead-new-era-winning/

response was: 'Sarri put Napoli in the future already. He doesn't have top players but still plays great football with quality and real values. Many players improved a lot with that way of playing like Koulibaly, Ghoulam, Mertens, Insigne . . . The Scudetto would be the right reward for that, for this generosity and beauty. But Napoli don't have the resources of Juve...'

Off the Pitch

Culture and Identity

Naples is a unique and highly colourful place, with a different culture from the other big Italian cities, just like Maradona is a unique person. He was very different from most of the other top players and therefore was a perfect fit for the club and the city. Maradona represented both sides of the coin: he was good and bad, successful but scandalous, talented yet undisciplined, toed the legal line, was passionate and had a taste for the show and the drama. For all of these reasons, no other top player would ever represent Napoli and its people better than him, and for many years, Napoli's culture and identity were deeply intertwined with Maradona as a person and a player. Over the years, however, after Maradona's departure, the club started to drift and lost a big part of its identity. The people of Naples were searching for a saviour and it took until 2004 to see any signs of hope.

Since 2004, De Laurentiis has developed the business and sports plan that Napoli had been missing since 1990. He has a clear idea of how the team should play (attacking and spectacular), is skilful at detecting, buying and selling talent (from Cavani to Higuaín to Lavezzi), has greatly improved the business model and increased revenues, and has a clear willingness to maintain Napoli's culture. Similar to Maradona, De Laurentiis is a very colourful person and so is perfect to manage the club of the most colourful city in Italy. What De Laurentiis has done with Napoli so far is impressive – taking the club from the third division to the Champions League in a matter of years. They are also currently playing a very attacking and ambitious style of football. The De Laurentiis era has brought back the passion and pride among Napoli fans and has allowed for the re-emergence of how things used to be when the entire city was deeply immersed in the (mostly) ups and downs of the club.

The Mission Statement of
Società Sportiva Calcio Napoli SpA

'The new Napoli, now owned by Aurelio De Laurentiis, is a company with modern and ambitious goals. In just three years it reasserted its sporting credentials by regaining its classification in the Italian Serie A and is now raising its sights to an international audience more suited to its size and geographical reach. Napoli is also pressing ahead with plans to evolve into a diversified entertainment business, offering its fans and partners more than just a football game by adding high quality shows and entertainment to its sporting events. From a corporate standpoint, its mission is to consolidate international partnerships by creating brand equity, that is, increasing the perceived value of the brand by promoting its notoriety, loyalty and differentiation in the reference market. [2]

Napoli differs from many of the other teams in Serie A and the rest of the football world in their stated mission – while most teams' mission statements focus on performance and core values, Napoli includes other metrics that are representative of De Laurentiis' vision. The club is not only focused on building a world-class football team, but also wants to create a unique fan experience that leverages other entertainment opportunities and increases the value of the club through brand equity.

Revenues

Napoli consistently competed in Serie A until 1998, when they were demoted back down to Serie B after their 18th place finish in the 1997/98 season. The club spent two years in the lower league, made it back to Serie A for the 2000/01 season, and were then demoted once again and ultimately went bankrupt in 2004 after languishing in Serie B for several years. Napoli's revenues have tracked the roller-coaster performance on the pitch over time, and it was only in 2008 when the team were promoted back into Serie A that they saw a noticeable increase.

---

[2] http://www.sscnapoli.it/static/content/Mission-77.aspx

Napoli Revenues and Ranking Per Deloitte
€ in millions

Season	DFML Revenue	DFML Rank	League	Rank
1999/00	€25		Serie B	4
2000/01	55		Serie A	17
2001/02	21		Serie B	5
2002/03	20		Serie B	16
2003/04	Bankrupt*		Serie B	13
2004/05	11		Serie C	3
2005/06	12		Serie C	1
2006/07	38.0		Serie B	2
2007/08	78.0		Serie A	8
2008/09	88.0	n/a	Serie A	12
2009/10	95.1	29	Serie A	6
2010/11	114.9	20	Serie A	3
2011/12	148.4	15	Serie A	5
2012/13	116.4	22	Serie A	2
2013/14	164.8	16	Serie A	3
2014/15	125.5	30	Serie A	5
2015/16	142.7	30	Serie A	2
2016/17	200.7	19	Serie A	3

Coming out of bankruptcy, Napoli were in Serie C1 (2004/05 and 2005/06), then got promoted to Serie B (2006/07), then finally made it into Serie A in the 2007/08 season. One can see the disparity in revenues by league, primarily because of TV broadcast and commercial revenues.

Breakdown of Napoli's Revenue Mix 2004/05 to 2007/08
€ in millions

	2004/5		2005/06		2006/07		2007/08	
	Revenue	%	Revenue	%	Revenue	%	Revenue	%
Matchday	6.2	56	4.3	36	8.4	22	12.5	16
Broadcasting	1.2	11	2.2	18	6.5	17	35.1	45
Commercial	3.5	32	5.5	46	6.1	16	29.6	38
Player Trading	0.1	1	0.0	0	0.0	0	0.8	1
Other								
Total	11		12		38		78	
League (Rank)	Serie C (3)		Serie C (1)		Serie B (2)		Serie A (8)	

Source Deloitte

With heightened focus and attention paid to turning Napoli into a successful business that more closely followed the economic-sport model, De Laurentiis miraculously managed to turn the club's finances around as quickly as he did their performance on the pitch (the team has even been dubbed the 'queen of the balance sheet' by the press). For the eight seasons between 2006/07 to 2013/14, Napoli were profitable, which is an incredible achievement given where the team was when he took over.

In the 2010/11 season, Napoli made their first appearance in the Deloitte Money League's top 20, with revenues of €114.9 million primarily due to improved performances on the pitch, resulting in third place in Serie A in 2010/11, their highest placed finish since the Diego Maradona-inspired team won the Scudetto in 1989/90. The club also reached the knockout stages of the Europa League. Unlike some of the Italian clubs higher up the Money League, Napoli benefited from the new Serie A broadcast rights deals, which helped drive an €18.6 million (47%) increase in broadcast revenue to €58 million, 51% of the club's overall total. Napoli also received €2.3 million in UEFA distributions for reaching the Round of 32 in the Europa League. Matchday revenue increased by €7.5 million (52%) to €22 million, with Europa League participation meaning five more home fixtures (26 in total) compared with the previous season, whilst the average home league match attendance continued to be strong at over 41,000. Commercial revenue totalled €34.9 million, underpinned by a long-term shirt sponsorship agreement with bottled water company Lete and a kit supplier agreement with Macron. Deloitte noted that the resurrection of plans to renovate the Stadio San Paolo, which following Italy's failed Euro 2016 bid, appear to have been shelved, but may be required to secure a Money League position in the longer term.

The 2011/12 season was a year to remember for Napoli fans. Not only did the club win the Coppa Italia, their first trophy for more than 20 years, but the Azzurri made a debut appearance in the UEFA Champions League, where they surprised many by qualifying from their group at the expense of Manchester City, before losing to eventual winners Chelsea in the last 16. This success saw Napoli move up five places in the Money League to 15th, with total revenues growing €33.5 million (29%) to €148.4m. A €27.8 million (48%) increase in broadcast revenues to €85.8 million was the largest contributor to Napoli's climb up the Money League. Commercial revenue rose as Napoli benefited from the dual shirt sponsorship between long-term shirt sponsor Lete and new joint-sponsor MSC Cruises.

However, a fifth-place Serie A finish in 2011/12 meant that Napoli missed out on Champions League football in 2012/13, which led to Napoli dropping out of the Money League top 20 in 2012/13.

In the 2013/14 season, Napoli returned to the top 20 (#16), due largely to a successful Champions League campaign, placing them just ahead of Inter, who fell two places to 17th, their lowest ever ranking. It was their participation in the group stage of the Champions League and subsequently Europa League that generated €40.2 million in UEFA distributions and drove the substantial 59% (€39.7 million) increase in broadcast revenues that has propelled them back into the Money League. Reflecting their outdated stadium experience, like most Italian clubs, Inter were the only Money League club to make less revenue from matchday sources. However, change was on the way. Following the payment of outstanding rent, an agreement was reportedly reached in April 2014 with the city council to secure the club's future at the Stadio San Paolo, with significant renovation of the stadium being supported by the Italian Olympic Committee.

Unfortunately, the club ended its record run of profitability and experienced a minor setback in the 2014/15 season. Prior to the season starting, a record low 6,500 season tickets were sold, which was just over 10% of the 60,240 stadium capacity, and was a foreshadowing of things to come. While Napoli's return to the red that season was primarily due to failing to qualify for the Champions League and lower than expected revenues from player sales, all areas suffered: matchday revenues fell by 32% from the previous year, broadcasting revenues fell by 28% and commercial revenues fell by 40%. Interestingly, although perhaps not surprisingly, in line with De Laurentiis' focus on keeping the team finances in order, as soon as it was clear that revenues were not where they needed to be, he made the decision to cut costs, starting with a sharp reduction in compensation to the Administrative Board of SSC Napoli, which includes, in addition to president De Laurentiis, his wife, two of their three children and the CEO, Andrea Chiavelli (total compensation was reduced to €1.025 million compared to €5.55 million in the previous year). This seems to be in direct contrast with how some of the other major team owners would respond in such a situation and clearly demonstrates how Napoli have a different, more responsible and less nepotistic, self-aggrandising business model than their competitors.

Since Napoli's emergence from bankruptcy, the revenue mix has shifted to being heavily dependent on broadcasting revenues, peaking at almost 75% in the 2011/12 season. Since then, however, diversification has been improving (albeit very slowly), but Napoli is still too dependent on broadcasting as well as player sales and incoming transfer fees. Given that Napoli frontloads amortisation costs in their accounting as well, this has the potential to create chunky imbalances and forces them to make difficult personnel decisions to avoid violating FFP.

Matchday revenues are also clearly not where they could be, especially considering Napoli's loyal fan base. However, while turnout has generally been declining since 2010, this season (2018) is showing signs of hope with average attendance figures for the year so far of 45,871 (76% of capacity) compared to 36,605 (61% of capacity) last season. This is obviously helped by Napoli's current performance in the league, but is something that can and needs to be leveraged in the future if Napoli wants to have any hope of keeping its best players and not be so dependent on Champions League revenues in order to stay profitable.

There have also been several external factors that have impacted Napoli's finances since their return to Serie A. In the years they have participated in the Champions League, Italy's UEFA country coefficient was high enough that Serie A was guaranteed spots for at least three teams. However, in the years Napoli missed qualifying, Serie A was ranked fourth (behind the EPL, La Liga and the Bundesliga), and thus was only guaranteed two spots. This resulted in bigger revenue disparities between Napoli and the top teams (i.e. Juventus) because for the years where they benefited from the revenue boost, more teams were involved thus their stake was diluted. Conversely, in the years they did not participate, fewer teams were involved and so those teams' revenues (and therefore transfer possibilities) increased disproportionately.

Breakdown of Napoli's Revenue Sources 2012 to 2016

	2012/13		2013/14		2014/15		2015/16		2016/17	
	Revenue	*%*	*Revenue*	*%*	*Revenue*	*%*	*Revenue*	*%*	*Revenue*	*%*
Matchday	15	13	20.9	13	14.14	10	15.35	10	19.4	10
Broadcasting	67	58	107.1	65	77.4	56	92.7	60	147	73
Commercial	24	29	36.8	22	22.26	16	29.78	19	34.3	17
Player Trading					17.57	13	12.19	8		
Other					6.29	5	5.34	3		
Total	116.4		164.8		173.66		155.35		200.7	
League (Rank)	Serie A (2)		Serie A (3)		Serie A (5)		Serie A (2)		Serie A (3)	

Source: http://swissramble.blogspot.com/2011/04/napolis-success-story.html for 2005–2010
Source: DFML for 2010–2014, 2017
Source: http://en.calcioefinanza.com/2017/06/03/napoli-2017-revenues-e300-million-player-trading-champions-league/ for 2015/16

Revenue Breakdown 2013 to 2017

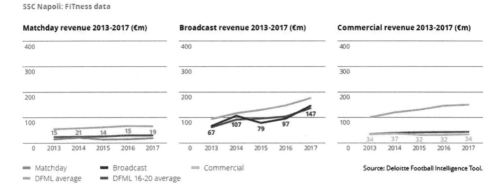

Overall, the story has been positive for Napoli and the outlook for the future is bright. In the last season where complete financial information is available (2016/17), the club posted record revenues of €200.7 million, moved back into the Deloitte Money League top 20 (#19) and have a slightly more balanced revenue mix, although as noted above, they are still too reliant on broadcasting and player sales (e.g. Higuaín to Juventus). More specifically, their return to the Champions League Round of 16 saw broadcast revenues increase by 51% to €147m, more than their entire revenue in 2015/16. On-field success also saw matchday revenue increase by 28% to €19.4m and further highlights the importance of UEFA competitions to Italian clubs' positions in the Money League. Commercially, Napoli's main sponsor, Acqua Lete, renewed its sponsorship in a record partnership ahead of the 2016/17 season. Whilst Napoli's prospects of moving up the Deloitte Money League Rankings next year are weakened by their group stage exit from the Champions League, their current title challenge, which is unfolding alongside Juventus, is providing excitement.

Fan Experience/Stadium

Napoli play their home matches in the Stadio San Paolo, which was built in 1959 and has been home to the club ever since. Stadio San Paolo is currently the third largest football stadium in Italy with a capacity of 60,240. Like many of the other stadiums in Italy, the San Paolo is old and outdated and is much in need of extensive renovations. De Laurentiis has been working on getting approval to make upgrades, which were scheduled to begin in the 2016/17 season, including things like improvements to players' facilities under the main stands, the instalment of 12,000 new seats, new catering and sanitary facilities for fans, a new press section, amenities for media members and improved hospitality. The ultimate goal was for the city of Naples to spend €25 million by 2019, in time for the 2019 Universiade, which it is hosting. However, these long overdue improvements have not been progressing as planned and De Laurentiis has been critical of the local government, saying, 'I want to work at the stadium but I also want to have skyscrapers built around it and I'm not going to have that. [. . .] If I wait for them, I'll be 350 years old. I'll buy land myself and build as I want.'

De Laurentiis' eventual plan would see Napoli only play crucial games at the San Paolo, leaving any and all upgrade works up to the local authorities. Meanwhile on regular terms, the club would have a private 25,000-seat stadium with an intimate auditorium that would be sold out week after week. He believes the reduced stadium size will create a more luxurious experience and make the stadium more appealing for television. In 2010, when the plans were getting started, he said: 'Napoli were well known to have the best fans, but now people come less and less to the stadium; they'd rather watch the game at home with their slippers on and with friends. It's also clear that our stadiums don't help to improve the perception of people . . . because they are old and not of high standards. But still, with the modern virtual stadium (TV, internet) even countries like England and Germany will lose stadium attendance at some point. We need smaller stadiums that offer a real show, where people live the show in a very different way than they would do at home. The 70- to 80,000-people stadiums are done. I would say in four years I would be able to say something about a new stadium for Napoli, but that will also depend on the city's ideas and the possibility. We should think about football globally, not only about the Italian football.'[3]

The problem is that allegedly De Laurentiis does not want to invest his own money because the stadium is owned by the city. Additionally, the local government is not in favour of this plan because they believe the stadium is for the people, and they fear a smaller stadium will put up economic barriers to stop people from accessing it. De Laurentiis has also been reticent to take outside money to carry out his vision or give up any share of the team. For example, in 2016 when a group of American investors wanted to take a 49% stake in Napoli and help with stadium renovations, De Laurentiis promptly turned them down.

Attendance

During the peak of the Maradona years, Napoli's attendance figures for home matches were impressive. From 1986–91, turnout for games was at least in the top three for Serie A, and in the 1986/87 and 1987/88 seasons, Napoli had the highest turnout, even beating Milan who were playing in a much bigger stadium.

Napoli Attendance During Maradona 1986/87 to 1990/91

Season	Attendance	Rank	Serie A Place	Top Team	Attendance
1990/91	54,032	3	8	Milan	77,054
1989/90	56,607	2	1	Milan	57,890
1988/89	59,965	2	2	Milan	72,437
1987/88	73,745	1	2	n/a	n/a
1986/87	65,450	1	1	n/a	n/a

For 1987/88, Milan were #2 with an average 72,177; for 1986/87, Milan were #2 with an average 58,812.
Note: Rank = attendance rank

---

[3] http://www.napolitoday.it/sport/ssc-napoli/de-laurentiis-voglio-costruire-il-mio-napoli-sul-modello-barcellona.html

By the 1993/94 season, attendances had started to slip, in line with Napoli's declining performance on the pitch. Interestingly, when De Laurentiis took over in 2004, the first year under his ownership saw a noticeable increase from an average of 18,660 in the 2003/04 season to 37,080 in the 2004/05 season, even though the team were playing in the Serie C1 league – only to reverse back the following year. However, by 2007/08, things finally started to turn around from the depths of the late '90s and early 2000s, with attendances finally reaching back above 40,000 and remaining close to that level all the way to the present day.

Napoli Attendance and Rank in Serie A 2007/08 to 2017/18

Season	Attendance	Rank	Serie A Place	Top Team	Attendance
2017/18	45,498	3	2*	Inter	58,283
2016/17	36,605	4	3	Inter	46,620
2015/16	39,099	3	2	Inter	45,538
2014/15	32,266	6	5	Roma	40,118
2013/14	40,918	2	3	Inter	46,246
2012/13	39,636	4	2	Inter	46,654
2011/12	40,632	3	5	Milan	49,359
2010/11	45,247	3	3	Inter	59,484
2009/10	45,647	2	6	Inter	56,195
2008/09	39,981	3	12	Milan	59,731
2007/08	40,754	3	8	Milan	56,906

Note: Rank = attendance rank
*As of 18 April 2018

In what would be considered a resurgence under De Laurentiis where Napoli's performance on the pitch has been much more consistent, attendance figures have responded in kind. In nine of the past ten seasons (and in the current season as well), Napoli's average attendance figures at home games have been in the top four of Serie A and are generally reflective of the club's standing in the league.

Napoli Attendance and Rank in Serie A 1990/91 to 2017/18

Stadium	Season	Avg Attendance	Capacity	Utilization	League	Rank
Stadio San Paolo	1991	54,032	60,240	90%	Serie A	8
Stadio San Paolo	1992	48,845	60,240	81%	Serie A	4
Stadio San Paolo	1993	53,127	60,240	88%	Serie A	11
Stadio San Paolo	1994	46,355	60,240	77%	Serie A	6
Stadio San Paolo	1995	36,235	60,240	60%	Serie A	7
Stadio San Paolo	1996	43,498	60,240	72%	Serie A	12
Stadio San Paolo	1997	48,824	60,240	81%	Serie A	13
Stadio San Paolo	1998	41,000	60,240	68%	Serie A	18
Stadio San Paolo	1999		60,240		Serie B	9
Stadio San Paolo	2000		60,240		Serie B	4
Stadio San Paolo	2001	40,176	60,240	67%	Serie A	17
Stadio San Paolo	2002	14,075	60,240	23%	Serie B	5
Stadio San Paolo	2003	28,599	60,240	47%	Serie B	16
Stadio San Paolo	2004	18,660	60,240	31%	Serie B	13
Stadio San Paolo	2005	37,080	60,240	62%	Serie C	3
Stadio San Paolo	2006	24,411	60,240	41%	Serie C	1
Stadio San Paolo	2007	34,140	60,240	57%	Serie B	2
Stadio San Paolo	2008	40,754	60,240	68%	Serie A	8
Stadio San Paolo	2009	39,981	60,240	66%	Serie A	12
Stadio San Paolo	2010	45,647	60,240	76%	Serie A	6
Stadio San Paolo	2011	45,247	60,240	75%	Serie A	3
Stadio San Paolo	2012	40,623	60,240	67%	Serie A	5
Stadio San Paolo	2013	39,636	60,240	66%	Serie A	2
Stadio San Paolo	2014	40,918	60,240	68%	Serie A	3
Stadio San Paolo	2015	32,266	60,240	54%	Serie A	5
Stadio San Paolo	2016	39,099	60,240	65%	Serie A	2
Stadio San Paolo	2017	36,605	60,240	61%	Serie A	3
Stadio San Paolo	2018	45,871	60,240	76%	Serie A	2*

Rank = League Rank in standings, NOT attendance rank
Source: http://www.transfermarkt.com/serie-a/besucherzahlen/wettbewerb/IT1; http://www.worldfootball.net/attendance/ita-serie-a-1991-1992/1/

Online Presence/Social Media

Napoli's presence on social media is still small relative to many of the major clubs – they are ranked 18th in terms of the total number of Facebook, Instagram and Twitter followers. They also have the smallest following amongst the five most popular teams in Serie A. This is primarily due to Napoli having a strong, but highly concentrated local following, rather than an expansive global fan base like some of the other major clubs.

Napoli also have yet to win Serie A or the Champions League since the rise of social media, and so the club's ability to generate awareness on a larger scale has historically been more restricted.

Napoli Social Media Followers

Serie A Club	Twitter Followers	Instagram Followers	Facebook Followers	Total
Juventus (9)	3.9	5.8	25.3	35
Milan (10)	4.4	2.9	24.8	32.1
Roma (15)	1.3	0.9	8.5	10.7
Inter (17)	1.2	1.3	6.1	8.6
Napoli (18)	1.3	0.7	3.9	5.9

From an individual player perspective, Napoli are lagging there too. Napoli's most popular player, Dries Mertens, has 2.45 million total followers compared to first place Juventus's Buffon with 12.6 million total followers. That number is also tiny compared to the major international stars with 100+ million followers.

In spite of this relatively small following, Napoli have introduced social media accounts in English, Spanish and Chinese, and plans are being made to include additional languages. In China, Napoli opened accounts on WeChat and Weibo, and when it comes to content, Napoli is not just translating from Italian but also creating original content in different languages.

More recently, Napoli have also started to experiment with more creative social media initiatives. For example, in May 2017, the club struck a partnership with Tinder where fans could swipe right on striker Arek Milik and welcome him back to the pitch following a serious knee injury in 2016. Milik then personally messaged fans for two weeks on Tinder and then chose four individuals to meet him in person.

Final Remarks

Under De Laurentiis' ownership with Sarri's coaching skills and vision for how the team should play, Napoli look to be in a great place, both financially and from a talent perspective, and the outlook is bright. However, in spite of good performances on the pitch and sound financial management, the club has still not reached the level in terms of revenues and operations that would put it on an even footing with the likes of the top global teams. When comparing Napoli to Juventus, in the period between 2008 and 2015, Juventus generated twice as much revenue. Juventus's average revenue per year came to €230 million compared to €120 million generated by Napoli, excluding non-recurring items (capital gains). While Juventus employed 155 workers, Napoli only had a staff of 36 people. From a talent perspective, the two teams' strategies have differed as well. Juventus have targeted more mature players who also had a higher impact on the balance sheet. Napoli instead aimed more towards potential younger stars (according to CAPEX to OPEX logic).[4]

This is reaffirmed in an interview De Laurentiis did in December 2015 when he was quoted as saying: 'We are looking at young players, because when a person is 27–28 years old it is more complicated to teach them a new way of playing. And then, it's not like I can put a gun to the head of some players to force them to join Napoli. We are currently negotiating to try to make our squad better, but it's not easy.'[5]

De Laurentiis spent more than any other Serie A club in the four years post-bankruptcy (€118 million – just ahead of Juventus).[6] This trend has slowed. However, De Laurentiis is focused on building a global brand: 'You are trivial, you always talk about the Scudetto, but in life there is not only the Scudetto. There is also the satisfaction of the jealousy of others who say we are the team playing the most attractive football in Europe. Today we are leading Serie A and fighting for Naples and southern Italy. This is more important than winning a Scudetto, which we will win anyway at some point, even if sooner is better than later. When we win the championship we should also keep the same organisation and structure that we have now; we bother many people in Italy, because the south has always bothered the north. Now that they have put in place VAR (Video Assistant Referee), I don't know what they can invent to cheat against us and put up more obstacles, especially now that we play great football that is not easy to replicate. Napoli this season has 3 B: Badass, Badass and Badass. Today at the stadium we had 53,600 fans. I'm expecting a full stadium this Wednesday versus City, and it would help us. We hope to keep giving to our fans this pleasing and serious football.' From this interview, he is identifying their beautiful, attractive playing style and defining his club to global fans as an underdog to richer clubs.

4 http://en.calcioefinanza.com/2017/02/28/juventus-vs-napoli-comparison-two-business-models/
5 http://napoli.repubblica.it/cronaca/2015/12/31/news/de-laurentiis-per-il-napoli-prendero-un-giocatore-importante-130431684/
6 http://swissramble.blogspot.com/2011/04/napolis-success-story.html

PART FOUR

THE FUTURE

CHAPTER TWELVE

THE REVIVAL OF
ITALIAN FOOTBALL

'The report of my death was an exaggeration.'

Mark Twain, in 1897 after his obituary had
been mistakenly published

'FINE' ('the end'), was the front-page headline of *La Gazzetta dello Sport*, Italy's most popular sporting newspaper. 'Apocalisse, disastro' ('Apocalypse, disaster') was the headline of *Corriere dello Sport*, one of its rivals.

After an embarrassing 0-0 draw against Sweden in Milan's San Siro stadium on 13 November 2017, following a 1-0 defeat in Stockholm three days before, the Azzurri failed to qualify for the 2018 FIFA World Cup – their first absence in 60 years.[1] In a country where *calcio* is interpreted as an element of identity and pride, not qualifying is an occasion for national mourning. Gianluigi Buffon, the team's beloved goalkeeper, understood the deep meaning when he tearfully apologised for having 'failed at something which also means something on a social level'. For many Italians, the disaster

---

[1] Italy had nearly 70% of possession across the two matches, and 37 shots to Sweden's 12, metrics that are strongly correlated with winning. But a long-range volley in the first leg, which deflected into Buffon's net via the leg of De Rossi, was enough to give Italy an embarrassing 1-0 aggregate defeat.

seemed representative of a broader national crisis. Italy's economy has struggled to recover after two deep economic recessions in the past decade. One day after the defeat, a sign of economic revival was overshadowed by the Azzurri's football failure – Italy's GDP growth had risen to 1.8% annually, beating expectations and reaching the highest mark since 2011.

The Revival of Italian Football

The good news is that when Italy failed to qualify for the World Cup it was a wake-up call and opportunity for change. It is yet to be seen how aggressively the league and decision makers seize the opportunity. There were so many signs that significant issues were, and still are, challenging Italian football and Serie A before 2017. However, just like how a World Cup win for Italy in 2006 obscured structural issues and a decline that was already underway in Serie A, we believe the failure to qualify for the World Cup is overshadowing some signs of a revival. Although many challenges still exist, there are signs of optimism for Serie A.[2] Hopefully, recognising those signs will encourage fans and decision makers that Italy's World Cup exit is far from an apocalypse or the end and at the same time won't take away from the urgency that serious changes are required to be more competitive.

Generally unnoticed in the last few years, certain Italian clubs (notably Juventus, Roma and Napoli) led by innovative owners are adapting and developing new ways to compete on and off the pitch. Foreigners with new ideas and more capital are buying clubs (Roma 2011; Inter 2013 and then 2016; Milan 2017). The takeover of Roma by American investors in 2011 was a new, positive development. Inter can also be expected to improve, thanks to its new Chinese owners. If the pattern of foreign investment grows, more Serie A clubs will have more resources and fresh approaches to compete and make the league more competitive and compelling. The influx of foreign capital to the English Premier League was a critical part of its success.

New foreign capital is not just required, but also more new ideas, strategies and professional management. Ironically, the 2006 Italian football scandal caused Juventus to reflect on its own issues and the

---

[2] https://www.economist.com/blogs/gametheory/2017/11/teary-azzurri

changes in the industry. In response, Juventus seized the opportunity to restructure, reposition and expand. They adapted and became 'Newventus', which has helped them advance to the Champions League finals in 2015 and 2017.

On the pitch, in recent years, there has been a shift in Italian football overall. Italy has gone from the land of catenaccio to the highest scoring league in Europe. The league has been trending away from its catenaccio heritage for some time. In the 2016/17 season, Serie A averaged more goals per game, 2.96, than any of Europe's top five leagues, even La Liga's 2.94. In the 2015/16 season, Gonzalo Higuaín broke Gunnar Nordahl's single season scoring record in Serie A, set in the 1949/50 season, which had stood for 66 years. In the same season, five players (Higuaín, Dybala, Mertens, Icadri and Immobile) scored more than 20 goals for only the fourth time in the history of the league. Edin Džeko has ended the season as Serie A's most prolific striker and equalled Roma's club record of 29 goals scored in a single league campaign, set by Rodolfo Volk in 1930–31.

Serie A is challenging perceptions. It has transformed into a league with more competitive, exciting and entertaining football. This may be masked by defensively-oriented Juventus being the Italian club watched more often globally, especially in the Champions League, as well as the Italian national team's style of play. However, Napoli have found ways to be fresh, young and exciting and they play dynamic, eye-catching football. They have yet to win Serie A this century, but they've performed well in the Champions League. Napoli have been leaders in making fans reconsider their perceptions of Italian football. However, Napoli are not the only team in Serie A trying to change the league's image – 'Derby del Sole' rivals Roma are on a similar path, doing everything they can to take the game to their rivals. Recently, Roma finished first in a 2017/18 Champions League group that included Chelsea and Atlético Madrid. Then, Roma shocked the world when they scored three goals at home to defeat Barcelona and advance to the semi-finals. In addition, there are a few other smaller clubs in Serie A who don't get global attention that are also playing attacking football. Maurizio Sarri of Napoli, Eusebio Di Francesco of Roma, Simone Inzaghi of Lazio and Gian Piero Gasperini of Atalanta, because of their faith in young talent as well as their attacking philosophies, want their teams to seize the initiative.

Juventus, the benchmark for great defending, not just in Italy but the world over, are appearing to recognise change. After the defeat to Real Madrid in Cardiff in 2017, manager Massimiliano Allegri's assessment of what the team needs to make another breakthrough in Europe is 'more goals'. Juventus have scored more goals to start the 2017/18 season than in any other season since 1959. But Allegri doesn't look entirely comfortable with it. Juventus have conceded more goals than in previous years. The number of chances created against them is also up, and this is their worst start to a season, from a defensive point of view, in a long time. In a press conference, Allegri reminded everyone that the team with the best defence usually wins the Scudetto. It's been that way for a decade. But maybe we'll see that change.

Wins for Roma, Napoli and Juventus in the Champions League in September 2017 have seen Italy move above Germany in UEFA's five-year rankings for the first time in seven years. Although Champions League reforms mean the top-four ranked nations receive four guaranteed group stage places from next season (as well as the associated revenue boost), promotion to a position that, ahead of the changes, would have also earned four berths and reduced the Bundesliga to three is nevertheless a psychological boost for Italian football. In the 2017/18 season, Roma and Juventus both made it to the quarter-finals in which there were two Italian clubs (Juventus and Roma), three Spanish clubs (Real Madrid, Barcelona, Sevilla), two English clubs (Liverpool and Manchester City) and one German club (Bayern Munich).

In the 2017/18 season Italy's league was the most open of the major European divisions. In November 2017, Napoli were the favourites, according to FiveThirtyEight, which gives five sides at least a 5% chance of winning – three more than for any other 'big-five' competition (those in England, Spain, Germany and France).[3] As the 2017/18 season progressed, Manchester City dominated the EPL, Barcelona dominated La Liga, PSG dominated Ligue 1 and Bayern Munich dominated the Bundesliga. Serie A, therefore, actually stood out as the most competitive league with Juventus and Napoli fighting it out at the top of the league.

In fact, the average strength of Italy's Serie A has now caught up with Germany's according to ClubElo.com, a website that rates clubs by the

---

[3] https://projects.fivethirtyeight.com/soccer-predictions

Elo formula, a ranking algorithm used in many sports which awards points based on the strength of a team's opponents and the importance of their matches. ClubElo.com also estimates that Serie A includes four of the world's top 20 teams (Spain's La Liga and England's Premier League each have five).

Also, after not qualifying for the FIFA Under-20 World Cup in 2011, 2013 and 2015, Italy's youth team beat Uruguay 4-1 on penalties following a goalless draw to place third in 2017 in South Korea. Third represents Italy's best-ever finish at an Under-20 World Cup. A total of 24 teams from around the world, with the stars of tomorrow, competed against one another for the ultimate youth-level prize. Riccardo Orsolini (born 1997), a physically strong and fast-paced winger who plays for Serie A club Bologna, on loan from Juventus, was the tournament's leading goalscorer with five.

After the Italian national team failed to qualify for the 2018 World Cup, interim manager Luigi Di Biagio called up Alessio Romagnoli (23 years old), Bryan Cristante (23), Lorenzo Pellegrini (21), Federico Chiesa (20) and Patrick Cutrone (19) and started Donnarumma over Buffon for friendly matches against Argentina and England in 2018, which is a change in attitudes towards youth development.[4]

In many ways, the Calciopoli scandal forced Serie A to move to adopt VAR (Video Assistant Referee) earlier than most other leagues to add more transparency and avoid match-fixing suspicions. Serie A is among the first European leagues (with the German Bundesliga and the Portuguese Primeira Liga) to use video technology to help the referee for all league games. The use of VAR demonstrates a willingness to embrace change and prove that it is both modern and focused on fairness and transparency. The Italian Football Federation and the Italian Referees' Association even held a masterclass by showing footage of incidents to managers and the media, including the audio track between the referee and VAR, to improve understanding of how they come to a decision. According to the Italian Football Federation and the Italian Referees' Association, of the 1,078 VAR decisions made in the first half of the 2017/18 season, 60 corrections were made by the VAR with 49 of those being the right decision. So only 11 mistakes were made using VAR from 1,078 decisions, or 1%. Stoppage time is up only by 19 seconds on

---

[4] Buffon actually started versus Argentina and Donnarumma started versus England.

average, while the time of review since matchday one has declined from 1 minute, 22 seconds to just 40 seconds. Greater transparency, on the whole, may be changing things for the better. Players know they are being watched. The number of fouls is down by 22%, from 260 to 203 over the same number of matches. Yellow and red cards have decreased and there is a feeling that player protests to the referees have been shorter.

Off the pitch, there have been a few encouraging signs.

In 2017, Serie A assigned its international TV rights predominantly to IMG for €371 million per season – nearly double the value of the previous deal. The agreement covers the next three Serie A seasons through 2020/21, and represents a step forward for the league from the previous deal with MP and Silva that was worth €190 million per season. The new figure places Serie A third in Europe for international rights after the English Premier League (€1.3 billion) and the Spanish league (€636 million) and ahead of the Bundesliga (€240 million). IMG will pay €352 million for global rights and a betting package, Rai International will provide €4 million for Italian language rights abroad and the remaining funds will be covered by signal providers and league promotions. 'The awareness of the Italian league's potential is growing… The clubs have chosen a partner that convinced everyone, not just for the economic terms but above all for the development plan,' said the CEO of Serie A advisor Infront.[5]

A four-part documentary on Juventus is to be streamed by Netflix in 2018. The four one-hour-long episodes hope to give Juventus and other football fans a behind-the-scenes look at the club, the players and its history. The content of Juventus's series promises to be mostly player-focused, offering viewers 'behind-the-scenes stories… and more intimate scenes of the players' lives'. Reports have not surfaced regarding how much money Juventus will make for the collaboration. Speaking about the news, Juve's co-chief revenue officer Federico Palomba said: 'It's a source of pride that Juventus are the first football club to be the subject of a Netflix original docuseries. Collaborations of this kind confirm our passion for innovation and being, in every sense, a sport entertainment brand. In this way, we are determined to reach Bianconeri fans across the world and millions of Netflix users, who, thanks to this docuseries, can get to know Juventus from every angle.' Netflix currently boasts

---

5 http://www.espn.com/soccer/italian-serie-a/story/3226980/serie-a-nearly-doubles-international-tv-revenue-with-new-img-deal

over 100 million users in 190 countries across the globe. This follows an announcement that Amazon Prime is close to signing an agreement with Manchester City for a similar series of shows that promises a 'unique and authentic inside view' of Manchester City and will pay the club around €11 million. The 'fly on the wall' series promises access from in the dugout and in the dressing room to on and off the training pitch. Sky UK, the major domestic TV rights holder who pays the Premier League €1.5 billion per season, is adamant that Amazon should not be allowed to use any matchday action. Sports documentaries certainly aren't new for either Amazon or Netflix, but they seemed focused on American sports until recently. The relatively quick international expansion shows just how cut-throat the competition between these streaming giants has become. We should expect many more sports shows on Amazon and Netflix, not to mention other emerging technology companies.

The overall fan experience is crucial to increasing revenues. In a survey to determine what percentage of Italian people define themselves as football fans, the low point was 2013 with 36% (the percentage was 52% in 2009). However, in 2016, the percentage increased to 38%.[6] Although it was a small rise, at least it is a step in the right direction. Juventus's success in reaching a Champions League final in 2017 combined with Roma's success in reaching the 2018 semi-final may renew and improve the interest. Demonstrating an interest in the fan experience in attending matches, the San Siro got a dedicated underground station in 2015.

The government also agreed that, from the 2017/18 season, clubs can throw fans out of stadiums and suspend their ability to attend matches. They have not been able to do this until the 2017/18 season because Italian legislation did not permit this.

Serie A has sold over 30,000 more season tickets compared to 2016/17. Between the 20 clubs in Italy's top league, 282,683 season tickets have been sold for the 2017/18 season, which is a 12% increase from the 251,895 sold during last year. Roma saw an increase of 1,000 to 20,000, and other Serie A clubs who saw an increase this year include Atalanta, Benevento, Crotone, SPAL, Torino, Lazio, Udinese and Verona.

Roma got its stadium approval in 2017. In addition to being a compelling social-economic-sport project, it feels as if, in the aftermath of Italy's failure to qualify for the World Cup, there was a little more

6 https://www.google.com/amp/www.repubblica.it/sport/calcio/2016/10/02/news/atlante_tifo_italiani_in_fuga_dal_calcio-148926536/amp/

recognition and urgency not just in Roma's stadium approval, but in re-examining stadiums in general.

Serie A has started to adopt a more global vision. For example, to the chagrin of local fans, but excitement of global fans, Serie A has started to arrange start times to key matches to coincide with more convenient hours in large global markets. The encouraging thing is that management, coaches and players are starting to recognise the historical lack of global vision and the need for longer-term thinking. AC Milan's former CEO Adriano Galliani said in a January 2017 interview: 'I am in favour of playing a few rounds of Serie A abroad. We have to push Serie A awareness around the world and we also have to be more careful when selling TV rights… it's not only about the money, rather the visibility… Even though Italian football is no longer ranked first, it's still an Italian excellence. It must be known. Some matches need to be played abroad, just like what happens in the NBA. TV rights agreements will be of fundamental importance in order to massively increase visibility.'

In 2017/18, for a competition that has always held holidays as sacrosanct, Serie A was willing to experiment for the first time in the week after 25 December 2017. 'The concept is simple. Professional football is an entertainment product and offering it during the holiday period is a great opportunity for those in charge…The Premier League has shown that it works to offer this product during the holidays – both in terms of stadium attendance and international TV viewership,' Roma general manager Mauro Baldissoni told the Associated Press. Following the successful example of the Premier League, the Italian league will play Serie A and Italian Cup matches over four of the next five days after Christmas. In the past, Serie A's winter break began before Christmas and lasted until after 6 January, which is Epiphany, a major Catholic feast day and the end of the holiday period in Italy. In the 2017/18 season, the break will be from 7–20 January. Serie A is providing an opportunity for families to go to the stadium while school is on break. The German, Spanish, and French leagues still won't play during the last week of the year. But other sports like the NBA and NFL do. 'Not taking advantage of this period and leaving it to other leagues means losing competitively in the international market so we've decided to get involved during this period,' Baldissoni said.[7]

7 https://www.independent.co.uk/sport/football/european/serie-a-coppa-italia-milan-inter-juven-tus-lazio-roma-a8127951.html

Vincenzo Montella, Milan's then head coach, agreed: 'Galliani's words spark curiosity. I am totally in favour of playing one match abroad, although I am not an expert on its feasibility.' Regarding playing the Italian Super Cup final in Doha, he said, 'It's a great opportunity to be known in and to get to know foreign countries. Serie A is very well known in the Arabic world. It's a main event and their facilities allow the perfect outcome of the event.' Gianluigi Buffon, goalkeeper and captain of Juventus and the national team said, 'Playing matches abroad? This seems to be the direction the whole sport world is taking . . . We are going towards the direction of sport-business, sport-show. I think this is the common direction sport is taking, not just football. Just like the NBA have been playing two matches per year in London over the last three or four years. Sport is changing its structure... but it is also true that this new system is bringing together worlds that seemed very distant.'[8]

There has been a growing audience for the country's football in China, resulting in Chinese investors buying two of its best-known clubs, AC Milan and Inter Milan. Italian football's largest foreign audiences came from Germany and China in 2016 with more than 86 million people in each of those countries having watched an Italian national team match on a cumulative basis, according to a report from Federcalcio prepared by auditors PwC. There are immense opportunities for Serie A clubs. For example, even without consistent significant investment, Milan are ranked sixth in China in terms of online presence in the Mailman 2018 report; Juventus are tenth and Inter are 13th; all higher than their Deloitte revenue rankings, demonstrating potential. However, those fans are being bombarded with other leagues and clubs, and the fan base that remembers Milan is now older. For example, Milan have 0.76 million Weibo followers, compared to 3 million for Real Madrid and 3.5 million for Bayern Munich. Juventus, along with Bayern and Real Madrid, were the only football clubs with Chinese apps in the top 15. Juventus also created the #ItsTimeToPromise campaign, which had impressive results. Fans made a promise to a club legend that they would stop at nothing to be in Cardiff during the Champions League final for a chance to win tickets to the match. Also highlighting a 'Newventus' approach, the Juventus VR app offers both 360 video and images of the club's facilities

8 http://en.calcioefinanza.com/2017/01/21/galliani-pushes-serie-abroad-playing-abroad-serie-will-gain-money-visibility/

in Turin, events and player appearances. Juventus launched a specific Chinese version with a club legend and broadcasted live on Yizhibo and Weibo, gaining over 1.5 million views. Today, China represents the largest country in terms of downloads for the Juventus app, behind the United States and South Korea.

In an encouraging sign that things are changing, two Serie A clubs are taking the impact of video games seriously. On 9 September 2017 the plan was for two professional esports players to go head to head on the pitch prior to the Serie A game between Roma and Sampdoria. This would have been a first in Italian football history, but heavy rain caused the event to be postponed until a later date. The FIFA 17 match was to be between Sampdoria's Lonewolf92 (Mattia Guarracino) and Roma's FIFA pro player Insa (Nicolo Mirra). Prior to the decision to postpone the match, Colin Johnson, head of FIFA at Roma and Fnatic told Esports Insider: 'Having the esports players being placed front and centre during a match day is a huge step for the two teams, as well as for FIFA esports in Italy in general. 'It shows how seriously both organisations take esports and pride will definitely be on the line for Nicolo and Mattia. And hopefully with more and more clubs entering the scene every week, this won't be the last time we'll have a FIFA competition mirroring a real-life match.'[9]

Demonstrating that players can take collective action, in April 2018, the entire Serie A took part in an initiative one weekend that had players wear a red stripe painted on their cheek like a stripe of lipstick to promote a campaign that seeks awareness of violence against women. The idea behind the campaign came from Italian organisation WeWorld Onlus, who teamed up with the players' association and Serie A to promote an end to domestic violence. Players and officials across the entire country took part in the campaign, with some of Serie A's biggest stars promoting the campaign even further on social media.

Another example is Roma who ranked #15 in revenues in 2015/16 without their own stadium or shirt sponsor, yet they are only €10 million behind #13 Atlético Madrid in revenues, who have been to the final of the Champions League twice in the last four years. With their own stadium, Roma can start to maximise commercial revenue and sponsorship opportunities.

9 http://www.esportsinsider.com/2017/09/sampdoria-roma-compete-esports-first-serie-showdown/

Encouragingly, the share prices of Juventus, Roma and Lazio have been up substantially in the last year. While down significantly from their initial public offering era highs, over the last 12 months Roma's, Juventus's and Lazio's share prices were up.

Stock Price Performance Since IPO and 1 Year April 2017–April 2018

Club	IPO Date	Since IPO	% Change 4/17-4/18
Lazio	May 1998	-93%	115%
Juventus	May 2000	-80%	27%
Roma	Dec 2001	-48%	14%

Lastly, depressed fans of the Italian national team should look at the last of the 'big-five' countries to miss a World Cup, France. Les Bleus failed to reach the 1994 World Cup, which also seemed like an apocalypse. The headline for *L'Équipe* was "Inqualifiable!" ('Unspeakable!'). *France-Soir* commented, 'Rocked by scandals and cowardice, undermined by crooks and buried under mounds of money, football is being dragged into disgrace.' France hosted the next tournament in 1998, showing up with a squad of young, attack-minded players known as the 'génération black, blanc, beur' ('black, white, Arab') because of the seamless mix of French-born and dual-nationality players. They beat Brazil 3-0 in the final.

In conclusion, there are some signs of optimism for Serie A, both on and off the pitch, although many challenges still exist. Complicating matters, changes in technology and tastes are happening at an alarmingly fast pace in the entertainment content, community brand and football industries.

THE FUTURE FOR EUROPEAN FOOTBALL

We make a few observations and predictions about the future of European football both on and off the pitch. We are not making any recommendations or judgements. We recognise the inclusion and importance of each observation and prediction is debatable, but after reading the analysis each one should provoke at least some thought.

The On-the-Pitch and Off-the-Pitch Observations and Predictions About the Future for European Football

On the Pitch

Talent
Recognition of Talent Compression and Luck
Recognition of Rotations, Depth and Systems
Speed, Youth and Work Ethic
Leadership
Understanding a Problem with Moneyball
A Search for Gravity

Off the Pitch

Overall Fan Experience
Global Brand Image for a Global Fan Base
The Raiders, Steelers or Cubs of European Football
The Reality TV Takeover of Football
I Want to be Him (Player Incorporated)
Smaller New Stadiums with More Unique Experiences
More International Matches and Match Times During
Convenient International Prime TV Time
Sports Theme Parks
Club Memberships

League
Financial Gap
English Premier League Develops into the NBA of Football
Clubs and Fans Will Start to Care Less About the Domestic League
More Women's Teams

Management
Owners That Control Other Entities for Sponsorship Synergies
Multinational Football Companies

Technology
Move from Traditional Broadcasting to Social Media/Technology Companies
VAR and TV Commercials

On the Pitch

On the Pitch: Talent
Recognition of Talent Compression and Luck

The difference between the winner of the 1932 Olympic Men's Marathon and the 20th place finisher was 39 minutes. The difference in the 2016 Olympics was 6 minutes. Absolute skill has never been higher, and relative skills difference has never been lower. Players are grinding to a physiological limit and performance is getting clustered. There is a greater pool of athletes playing and the amounts of identification, coaching, training methods and training facilities available continues to increase. Big clubs are paying significantly more money for players who are slightly better than most players because the difference between winning and losing in football is so small. With this difference being so small two things become more important: luck and culture (why, motivation).

In 2013, David Sally and Chris Anderson, who are professors at Cornell and Dartmouth, respectively, published a book titled *The Numbers Game: Everything You Know About Soccer Is Wrong* (London: Penguin Books, 2013). The authors attempt to dismiss common football beliefs through analysis. One of the most interesting statements they wrote is that football results are 50% luck. They claim that winning in football is 50% skill/strategy and 50% chance. One of the key analyses they use to support this argument is analysing the winning percentage of teams that are favoured to win:

Winning Percentage of Team Favoured by Bettors by *The Numbers Game*. Sport Winning Percentage of Favourite

Sport	Winning Percentage
Football/Soccer	50%
Baseball	60%
Basketball	66%

In football, the team favoured by the bettors won 50% of the time, compared to basketball's 66%. In basketball there is a shot clock and many opportunities for attack and defence. Therefore the better team has a higher probability of winning. In football, the underdog can 'park the bus' and waste time. In addition, the study concluded that 50% of all goals developed out of some sort of lucky incident such as ball redirections, lucky bounces, and blocks from a goalkeeper, defender, or post that return the ball right to a goal scorer. Jan Vecer, a former professor in the department of statistics at Columbia University who is working on an upcoming book titled *Soccermetrics: Science of Soccer Statistics*, explains, 'By the nature of the game, most of the goals happen in situations that cannot be easily replicated even when the players are in exactly the same position. If the situation cannot be easily replicated in terms of scoring, it adds randomness and there is no statistical explanation to it other than luck.' Randomness favours the underdog, which is why football is so compelling to watch for so many people. There will be players that underperform and others that overperform, plus injuries, distractions, near misses, and other elements that can't be anticipated. Football has a low scoring rate, which means that the entire result can be influenced by a single goal. Vecer explains, 'In this sense, soccer is one of the most unfair sports in terms that the probability of the weaker team winning (or not losing) to the better team is quite large.'

Impacting 'luck' in football are the interconnectedness and complexity of football. The analysis demonstrates a strong connection in football between teamwork and scoring goals. Combine that connection with the limited scoring opportunities in football, and it is self-evident that teamwork becomes vital to winning in football, similar to most businesses.

On average, Ronaldo and Messi possess the ball 20 times a game, three seconds each time, for a total of merely one minute per 90-minute game. You read that right! Ronaldo and Messi touch the ball for around 60 seconds per game, around 1 percent of the game time. With those 20 possessions, Ronaldo and Messi typically attempt four to six shots per game. Two of those shots will be on goal and one will go in the net as a goal. The statistics are that simple, as Ronaldo and Messi average one goal per match.

Goals mean a lot more in soccer than points do in most sports. Quality shot opportunities in soccer are very scarce, so making the most of them is critical. If Ronaldo or Messi are not 100% (slightly tired or slightly injured or have issues at home that are distracting them) or they play with players they are less familiar with, then they will just miss on their very few chances to score. Their teammates have to understand where they will be positioned on experience and how high they can/will jump or how far in front to place the ball and at what speed. If the teammates are off by only fractions, the very few chances are missed. This helps explain the paradox of why players need to play together often yet why they need rest and rotation to stay close to 100% over a long season. It also explains why favoured teams can lose even if they have a talent advantage. To be successful, players like Messi and Ronaldo need the ball at the right time, at the right place from a teammate willing to give up the ball. Every organisation and team need players who do all the little things and sacrifice for the betterment of the team and stars to score and everyone in between. They need to know how to behave, what the goals are, and what their roles are. This is why culture is important.

Culture, values and 'higher purpose' matter to fans and the players. One of the best football examples is SD Eibar in Spain. Eibar has 27,000 inhabitants in remote Basque Country. They were promoted up to La Liga from the Segunda Division in 2013/14, for the first time ever. They play in a 6,000-capacity stadium, had a €3.9 million budget, and market value of players at €6.9 million. The club had to utilise crowdfunding to raise €1.7 million to meet minimum capital requirements to be allowed into La Liga from the Segunda Division. Thousands of people from 50 countries participated in the crowdfunding. A player commented, 'For a small city and a small club to receive such support from across the world is something that makes me very proud – it feels like we're part of a family . . . The spirit is the most important thing that will help us overcome all the challenges we will have . . . We're going to have the lowest budget with no big names in our team but we will make it with the players and all of us pushing in the same direction – this is in our spirit.' With a culture and mission/purpose, the results are better than expected: 2014/15: 18th, 2015/16: 14th, 2016/17: 10th (20 clubs in La Liga, with the bottom two relegated).

Recognition of Rotations, Depth and Systems

Football players play long domestic seasons that are filled with domestic and European trophy competitions. In addition, during the seasons, top players have to play for their national teams for friendlies or qualifications for regional tournaments or the World Cup. When playing for their national teams some players have to travel long distances to and from the match. It is only natural that players get physically, mentally and emotionally more tired and can be more prone to injury or not performing at 100%. For example, Real Madrid had a slight competitive advantage over Barcelona after international breaks because Real Madrid's BBC (Bale, Benzema and Cristiano) from Europe typically had shorter distances for national team commitments than Barcelona's MSN (Messi, Suarez and Neymar) from South America.[10]

---

[10] Karim Benzema has not recently played for the French national team.

Rotating players and having a deeper bench will become more important, along with having younger players that recover from matches more quickly. Playing the same star players every match will lead to fatigue at the end of the season, which typically is when the critical tournament matches are. Rotating players means that the players on the pitch together may have less familiarity with each other. This, combined with few chances to score, can lead to upsets, especially at the beginning of seasons as teammates become familiar with one another. However, it also adds to long-term development of the players. To increase familiarity and performance and reduce upsets, more clubs will adopt systems where players have more defined roles and understanding of where teammates should be to reduce the potential negative impact of rotations. It will be difficult to have teams that play an improvisational style with the same star players, especially in winning domestic season-long titles. The system will need to be consistent through the organisation from the youngest academy players to the first team. The best example of this is Barcelona's tiki taka system and rotation policy (especially under Luis Enrique). So many talented Spanish players being familiar with a system (Barcelona players, especially academy players, and tiki taka) also benefited the Spanish national team that often played against collections of stars of other national teams who played in many different systems for many different coaches.

Speed, Youth and Work Ethic

As previously discussed, a higher and higher value will be placed on speed and youth. The game is faster, and speed is a differentiator. The game is more physically demanding and younger players can recover more quickly.

While the technical gap between football players is shrinking, they are looking to use their speed, size and strength as a competitive advantage. Squads consisting primarily of smaller, slighter and primarily technical players by modern standards will be at a disadvantage. It's one thing when your skill is that much better than everyone else's, but when other teams are close in skill the advantage will go to teams that are faster, bigger and stronger. Teams with slightly less technical talent can turn a match into a physical, street fight type of battle that the other teams are not used to nor comfortable with.

Professional athletes were asked, 'What qualities do you most appreciate in a teammate?' 26% responded 'work ethic'. More than honesty, loyalty and respect combined. The willingness of the players to sacrifice themselves on the pitch for the greater good of the team will become more important. In sports the money and fame support the attitude of 'what about me'. This is why it is important to have a good character group with leadership supported by a culture with values and a mission.

Leadership

Most world class organisations spend a lot of time thinking about, identifying and developing leaders. This will start to apply to football clubs on the pitch. At Real Madrid, they believe in four pillars of leadership on the pitch. The first pillar is the coach. The coach needs to be someone that the players relate to and respect. Because of the elite talent at Real Madrid, this probably has to be a former elite player and winner versus a coach that is excellent at maximising very good talent. Ideally, the coach has some association with and familiarity with the club and its culture. As for the three other pillars of leadership on the pitch, they are players. The second pillar is the captains. Real Madrid believes that the captains of the club must be the two most senior members of the club. The captains are not elected by the players or appointed by the coach. Real Madrid believes that the captains must know the history, traditions and values of the club the best. The third pillar of leadership is the academy graduates who grew up with the history, traditions and values, and can help assimilate new players. Historically 25% of the squad are academy graduates. The fourth pillar is the best player. Real Madrid believes that the best player must be recognised as one of the hardest working players. A player like Ronaldo sets the example for work ethic, professionalism and dedication. His example helps teach and drive the others in a way a coach can't. It is not as simple as trying to find the best 11 players. The players need to work together, understand the culture and values and take their cues from leadership.

Understanding a Problem with Moneyball

Moneyball and data analytics assumes that a player will perform exactly the same in the play-offs as he will during the regular season. However, Real Madrid looks for elite, proven players who perform when the pressure and level of competition is the greatest. Data scientists don't believe in players performing worse under pressure, but the idea of taking the level of competition into account in averages is new. This is critically important when scoring opportunities are at a premium and Real Madrid is focusing on winning championships against the best competition in pressure situations, not just getting to the final stages. A statistical average over long seasons, which includes playing weaker teams in less-important games, may lead to certain beliefs about a player. However, upon closer examination of only high-profile, pressure games, where trophies are on the line or the competition is very high quality, the statistics may lead to another belief and the willingness, deservedly, to pay more.

Real Madrid knows that luck and randomness play a major part in football, especially in play-off formats with one or two games, but the club tries to identify any statistical competitive advantage going into the Champions League. The value of that advantage may be more to Real Madrid and its economic-sport model than it may be for other teams; therefore, it is difficult to compare a player's value to Real Madrid versus another team, especially considering the value both on and off the field. In addition, it is difficult to argue that Real Madrid overpaid for a player when the club has an economic-sport model based on community values to maximise the economics of the player relative to his absolute cost, as well as the cost as a percentage of revenues.

Examining selected Real Madrid player performances during their time in La Liga and the Champions League illuminates the types of players the team values on the field. We selected players that played at least 50 games for Real Madrid. We did not examine players' statistics before or after they played at Real Madrid because they could have played in a different system with a different calibre of players. The Champions League games should have higher quality opponents than a typical La Liga game since teams must qualify. The analysis shows that Di Stéfano, Gento, Figo, Raúl and Benzema averaged more goals per game in the Champions League than in La Liga.

Goals per Game in La Liga and Champions League

Goals per Game*

	La Liga	Champions League	% Change
Di Stéfano	0.77	0.84	+10%
Gento	0.30	0.35	+19%
Figo	0.23	0.27	+15%
Raúl	0.41	0.50	+21%
Benzema	0.46	0.56	+20%

* Puskás and Zidane didn't have more than 50 games in the European Cup/Champions League for Real Madrid.

Examining Cristiano Ronaldo and Lionel Messi, since Ronaldo has been at Real Madrid, illustrates how dominant both players really are, averaging around one goal per game, which is absolutely remarkable. Comparing their goal-per-game numbers with the Real Madrid legends highlights how amazing they both are to average that rate. This is especially true if one considers that the average goals per game have gone from around 3.5 overall during the time of Di Stéfano to just above 2.5 over the last several decades.

Both of their Champions League goals averages are slightly lower than in La Liga, but that can be attributed somewhat to moving from simply ridiculous to merely obscene (and moving closer to the mean).

Goals per Game in La Liga and Champions League

Goals per Game*

	La Liga	Champions League	% Change
Ronaldo	1.07	1.06	-1%
Messi	1.07	0.90	-16%

* Since Ronaldo joined Real Madrid. Data from http://messi-vs-cristiano.com

We also examined the goals per game in the Champions League knockout rounds because these goals are typically against even greater competition (final-16 teams) versus the larger group stages. Obviously, there are fewer data points, but we see Ronaldo still manages one goal per game.

Goals per Game in Champions League Knockout Rounds

Goals per Game*

	Appearances KO Round	Goals	Assists	Goals Per Game
Ronaldo	50	50	11	1.00
Messi	62	40	10	0.65

Since Ronaldo joined Real Madrid. Data from http://messi-vs-cristiano.com

Examining the last three years with Zidane as coach, Ronaldo has picked up his Champions League average goals per game. His average is higher than his La Liga average, obviously, with less data points.

Goals per Game in Champions League Knockout Rounds from 2015/16 to 2017/18

Goals per Game*

	Champions League Appearances KO Round	Goals	Assists	Goals Per Game
Ronaldo	18	21	1	1.17
Messi	12	7	4	0.58

Data from http://messi-vs-cristiano.com

Examining the median for the top 50 scorers in Champions League history in the tournament, we find what we expected: on average most players, even the best ones, have slightly lower performance in the Champions League, probably due to more competitive teams and/ or teams playing more conservatively. Ronaldo's and Messi's goals per game in the Champions League are much higher than the average of the top 50 players, demonstrating how truly incredible they are. The percentage change in goals per game is -5% for the best players in the Champions League, while Real Madrid's best players over history are 10 to 20% higher.

Median Goals per Game for Top 50 Scorers
in Champions League History

Reg. Season	Champions	% Change
0.48	0.46	-5%

Taking what we learned from Real Madrid, we applied the same approach to some of the best players in Serie A over time. We calculated their average goal-per-game numbers in Serie A and in the Champions League to determine if there was a difference. The results were very interesting. The Italian clubs of the best players that had higher average goal-per-game numbers in the Champions League typically won the Champions League. There were only a few select exceptions.

Players Who Averaged More Goals per Game (GPG) in Champions League (CL) Compared to their Serie A Average Goals per Game (or were near statistical average of drop off) *

	CL GPG	Serie A GPG	Change %	Period	Club	Won CL?
Adriano	0.60	0.41	47%	2001-2009	Inter	No
Kakà	0.47	0.34	38%	2003-2009	AC Milan	2007
Platini	0.61	0.46	31%	1982-1987	Juventus	1984
Van Basten	0.78	0.61	28%	1987-1995	AC Milan	1989, 1990, 1994
Gullit	0.37	0.30	23%	1987-1993	AC Milan	1989, 1990
Del Piero	0.48	0.41	19%	1993-2012	Juventus	1996
Shevchenko	0.53	0.57	-6%	1999-2006	AC Milan	2003
Trezeguet	0.54	0.56	-3%	2000-2010	Juventus	No

*The Italian clubs of the best players that had lower average goal-per-game numbers in the Champions League typically did not win the Champions League.

Players Who Averaged Less Goals per Game (GPG) in Champions League (CL) Compared to their Serie A Average Goals per Game *

	CL GPG	Serie A GPG	Change %	Period	Club	Won CL?
Crespo	0.44	0.49	-11%	1997-2009	Int/Laz/Par/Mil	No
Eto'o	0.43	0.49	-12%	2009-2011	Inter	2010
Milito	0.41	0.48	-14%	2009-2014	Inter	2010
Dzeko	0.42	0.51	-17%	2015-actual	AS Roma	No

Higuain	0.45	0.57	-21%	2016-actual	Juventus	No
Totti	0.30	0.40	-26%	1992-2017	AS Roma	No
Tevez	0.37	0.59	-38%	2013-2015	Juventus	No
Ibrahimovic	0.32	0.56	-43%	2004-2009/2010-2012	Juv/Int/Mil	No
Dybala	0.23	0.55	-58%	2015-actual	Juventus	No
Vieri	0.26	0.71	-63%	1999-2005	Inter	No
Montella	0.10	0.47	-79%	1999-2006	AS Roma	No

We didn't include some of the best players in Serie A over time for various reasons. For example, Baggio (not enough Champions League matches), Batistuta (only played CL once with Fiorentina, and then twice with Roma but was also at the end of his career), Chiesa (played twice in CL with two different clubs), Signori (no CL games), Ronaldo (most of his CL matches were with Real Madrid as he only played in CL one season with Inter, only six games), Zola (didn't play CL while in Italy), Vialli (played CL one season with Juventus), Ravanelli (even if won the CL in 96 with Juve, only played one season in CL with them), and Icardi (no CL matches).

The data indicates that to help win the Champions League, a club needs one of their best players to perform at least as well or even better against elite competition. As we previously discussed, luck is an important element in football, but the fact that the data is consistent over time, even with very different styles of playing and different clubs, shows that there is a meaningful difference. All the players examined were also typically surrounded by other great players. As we previously discussed, goal scorers are highly dependent on their teammates, so their statistics also rely on others.

We studied Higuaín's and Dybala's average goal-per-game numbers in more detail. We examined their goals during what we classified as the most important games of the season including 'important matches' in Serie A and all Champions League matches for the last two seasons. The details are in the Appendix, but the summary is below.

Goals per Game in Serie A and Champions League

Goals per Game*

Season 2016/17:

	Less Important	*More Important*	*% Change*
Higuaín	0.72	0.27	-63%
Dybala	0.77	0.23	-70%

Season 2017/18:

	Less Important	More Important	% Change
Higuaín	0.62	0.40	-35%
Dybala	1.14	0.25	-78%

* Less important are Serie A matches against lower competition. More important matches are Champions League matches and selected Serie A matches and the Italian Super Cup finals.

Obviously, Higuaín and Dybala are great players. For example, Dybala scored two goals as Juventus recorded a 3-0 win over Barcelona in the first leg of the Champions League quarter-final in Turin in April 2017. It is interesting to see that they score less frequently in 'more important' matches or matches against 'better competition' than 'less important matches' or matches against 'weaker competition'. As we discussed there can be many reasons for this from luck to interconnectedness to game plan to limited data. We are not suggesting in any way that this is their fault or they are worse in big matches. We just thought the data was interesting, and it is analysis that more clubs will focus on.

A Search for Gravity

Ronaldo has scored goals in prolific amounts throughout his career, averaging more than a goal per game since joining Real Madrid. But the way he scores has changed over time. Age has forced him to adapt, but Ronaldo has improved his movement and his game understanding to compensate so that his average goals per game has not been impacted.

However, it is what Ronaldo does that is not covered in the typical statistics of goals and assists per game that matters when he is not at elite performance. Whether or not he is scoring goals and at peak performance, Ronaldo creates space for his teammates because he draws defenders like gravity. There is actually a gravity score to measure this. It is an actual number. Gravity in this context is defined as the tendency of defenders to be pulled to certain parts of the pitch. The gravity score measures how closely the primary defender defends a player off the ball at any given time. The higher an attacker's gravity score, the better they are at drawing players away from the ball when out of possession.

More than anything else, the primary factor determining a player's gravity score is their scoring ability. Defenders cannot stray from elite scorers like Ronaldo or Messi, to risk giving up a high probability of a goal. Against less efficient shooters, however, defenders can cheat an extra step toward the ball or the goal, making it easier for them to offer defensive help to teammates.

The best attacking teams account for all of these factors and put their forward players in positions where they have the most gravity to open space and create difficult decisions for defenders.

Quantifying gravity to understand its impact on the pitch is complicated. While it might be reflected in plus-minus data, nothing in the traditional 'stat sheet' reflects a player's true gravitational pull. But now that cameras in every stadium are capturing where players and the ball are at any given moment, we can determine the way defenses respond to different offensive players.

I was provided proprietary confidential information from various sources for my book *The Real Madrid Way*. The conclusion I can share is that Ronaldo and Messi's gravity scores are outliers, just like their scoring. So even in a game in which they don't score, it is likely that Ronaldo and Messi led the team in gravity score, meaning they provided more space and opportunities for teammates to score.

One can also look at heat maps and see how defenders have to respect Ronaldo's scoring. This is a simpler, and less quantitative, way to analyse Ronaldo's impact. One can take the heat maps of defenders and where they are positioned in a game and then compare that to when Ronaldo is not on the pitch or versus another team. By doing this you will see a much higher concentration and overlap over where Ronaldo is. You will see two defenders playing closer to Ronaldo than their typical positioning.

The smart tactical decision from Real Madrid was to add speed to complement Ronaldo. When fast footballers are on the pitch with Ronaldo, defenders have to respect their speed. This causes all types of frustration for opposing coaches and defenders. Because often, players are caught if they stick close to the fast players or Ronaldo or help their teammates. This causes defensive organisation to stretch and break down.

What makes Karim Benzema interesting is that through familiarity and skill, Benzema is effective in finding the open space left by Ronaldo and a fast player. In Champions League games Benzema's goal per game average is around 20 per cent higher than in La Liga. My hypothesis is this is because more teams focus a lot more on trying to shut down Ronaldo with such high stakes, providing more space and opportunities for Benzema. But this contribution from Ronaldo doesn't show up in the stat sheet.

Off the Pitch

Off the Pitch: Overall Fan Experience
Global Brand Image for a Global Fan Base

Experts estimate that over 70% of European football fans typically follow more than one European club, typically from multiple leagues. Most fans don't have a geographical connection and most fans spread the risk of losing or not winning a title across a number of clubs. This idea challenges the traditional belief that leagues and clubs must only be successful on the pitch to attract fans.

As respected football journalist Gab Marcotti wrote for ESPN.com: 'The real secret to the clubs' dominance is that they are massive universal brands that have learned to monetise their fan bases at a time when the game is as globalised as it ever was and as new money is flowing into it.'[11]

What are the drivers of brand image for a sport club? As discussed, there are many factors involved both on the pitch (e.g. performance, style of play, the stars and other players and their stories) and off the pitch (e.g. stadium experience, community culture, values and online engagement).

The football clubs who believe that only results on the pitch matter and don't appreciate that off the pitch and on the pitch are co-dependent will not be able to build sustainable economic-sport models and generate the revenues from a global fan base to buy the necessary talent and make the necessary infrastructure investments to consistently compete for European trophies. The football clubs and ownership who believe that fans simply want to see their favourite club win, don't understand that a real fundamental shift has happened in football. The rising player and infrastructure costs require loyal and passionate fans that support their clubs and their sponsors. Football clubs need to turn casual fans into true

---

[11] http://www.espn.com/soccer/blog/marcottis-musings/62/post/3351563/uefa-report-shows-gap-is-growing-between-superclubs-and-the-rest

believers and members, and use technology to do so. To turn a casual fan into a true believer requires a clear and identifiable set of values and mission statement. This may cause a casual fan to pay attention. Winning on the pitch can certainly help provide the platform to tell the club's story and demonstrate their values. However, winning is not enough. In addition, fans expect easy and accessible constant contact, engagement and responsiveness. Conventional broadcast media and TV do not create a feeling of membership and loyalty in a society that now predisposes people to have short attention spans and change quickly. A fan or follower is not the same as being a true believer or member of a community.

Membership delivers an entirely higher degree of loyalty.[12] It demands a whole other level of engagement from participants and, consequently, a deeper appreciation by the football club of their responsibilities. The deeper the connection goes and the more the member understands the club and vice versa in what values they have or what goals they share, then the closer you get to a true community. The connection must be centred around a strong identification and rich experiences that are based on being fan-centric in decision-making both on and off the pitch. Every winning culture has its own authentic personality and soul that can't be invented or imposed. A football club just need to be genuinely interested in getting what it is from their community and then be focused on aligning the community's values and expectations with their strategy, which can be powerful in generating extraordinary loyalty and passion. When that loyalty and passion are carefully, actively and frequently supported, they can lead to extraordinary commercial performance. This loyalty and passion can be sustained for a long time, even without winning. Keep in mind that the vast majority of the time a sports team won't win a championship, so a strategy is flawed if it relies on winning as the reason why the community will support the team. Also, it takes time to establish a culture and identity; it doesn't happen overnight. In a January 2018 article on ESPN.com, Gab Marcotti captured the idea that fans care more than about just winning: 'Consider Manchester United. They haven't won the Champions League since 2007/08 or the Premier League since 2012/13; they've generally been underwhelming since the departure of Sir Alex Ferguson. Yet guess what? They have the highest

---

12 *The Culting of Brands: Turn Your Customers into True Believers,* Douglas Atkin

revenues in football and the second highest wage bill. They built up a heck of a lot of credit with their success in the previous 25 years and those fans aren't going away any time soon. Being a universal brand generates a virtuous cycle of success: because you're rich, famous and successful, folks will flock to you. Sponsors and money soon follow. And, unless you're a fool who squanders it (and there have been cases…) that will only increase your wealth, fame and success.'[13]

The Raiders, Steelers or Cubs of European Football

The three top three shirt sellers in the NFL are the small market teams, the Green Bay Packers, the Pittsburgh Steelers and the Oakland Raiders. They all have very distinctive brands appealing to niche communities.

Top-Four Selling NFL Shirts (2015) by NFL Sales

Rank	Team
1	Green Bay Packers
2	Pittsburgh Steelers
3	Oakland Raiders
4	Dallas Cowboys

The Oakland Raiders recruited players who were perceived as rebels, misfits and outcasts who thumbed their noses at convention. Many of the players would not be welcome in most NFL teams. Raiders players relished bone-crushing hits, clothes-line tackles and knocking their opponents out of games. While they might have been a wild, fun-loving bunch, they worked hard and played to win, and the Raiders' fan base loved them. The Raiders' black and silver uniforms and pirate-like logo reflected an outlaw image. Al Davis created a counterculture image for his franchise that to this day is still among the most recognisable in all of sport. The team didn't just appeal to a local fan base but also to a national 'Raider Nation' that identified with the team's values and culture and bought lots of black and silver Raider merchandise. The nickname 'Raider Nation' refers to diehard fans of the team who attend home games, arriving at the stadium early and dressing up in facemasks and black outfits. The

[13] http://www.espn.com/soccer/blog/marcottis-musings/62/post/3351563/uefa-report-shows-gap-is-growing-between-superclubs-and-the-rest

Oakland Raiders have not won the Super Bowl since 1983, but if you are a fan of the NFL that doesn't like the establishment, you probably root for the Raiders, even if they are not your first or local team.

The NFL's Pittsburgh Steelers' notoriously hard-working, hard-nosed, blue-collar front four defensive line in the 1970s, nicknamed 'The Steel Curtain', reflected and took on the identity of the hard-working steelworkers of Pittsburgh. The players identified with the town and the town identified with them, and the town's fans loved it. So many people, within Pittsburgh and beyond, identified with being hard-working, hard-nosed, and blue collar that the Steelers developed a national following. If you are a fan of the NFL who has a blue-collar or tough labour job, you probably root for the Steelers, even if they are not your first or local team.

There is probably room in European football for 'counterculture' or 'blue-collar' clubs that transcend their local market identities. However, so far no club has been able to properly market their identity this way. The biggest and richest clubs, for the most part, have traditional values or represent some sort of establishment in football. In addition, in European football there may also be room for ethnic/geographic associated clubs – such as a club that had primarily African players or Brazilian players that fans with some sort of affiliation to or admiration for Africa or Brazil or their players or styles of play would root for. This strategy would capitalise on feelings of national pride, culture, traditions, player personalities and styles of play.

Before the Chicago Cubs won the 2016 Major League Baseball World Series, the Cubs had not won their league pennant trophy in 71 years and the World Series in 108 years. Yet the Cubs were consistently among the top attendance rankings in Major League Baseball (even though their stadium ranks #16 in capacity). The reason why fans flocked to see the Cubs is that going to a baseball game at Wrigley Field baseball park is an experience in itself. Fans even pay big money to watch Cubs games from the rooftops of nearby buildings. It didn't matter if the Cubs lost. In some ways, the identity of supporting a perennial loser said something about the fans' loyalty, not just supporting winning clubs. It was like a badge of honour. (The Boston Red Sox had something similar until they started winning, especially in contrast to the Yankees.)

Wrigley Field is known for its ivy-covered brick outfield wall, the unusual wind patterns off Lake Michigan, the iconic red marquee over the main entrance, the hand-turned scoreboard, its location in a primarily residential neighbourhood with no car parks, views from the rooftops behind the outfield and for being the last Major League park to have lights installed for play after dark, in 1988. Wrigley Field (1914) is the second-oldest baseball park in the majors after the Boston Red Sox's Fenway Park (1912). The Cubs have many traditions and rituals that make the entire experience fun. The ballpark is in a very accessible and safe location. Many of the Cubs' games are during the day and it is seen as a wonderful way for families or those looking for a break from work or school to spend an idyllic afternoon. When tourists visit Chicago, many want to experience a Cubs game at Wrigley Field – it is considered a 'must see'. There is probably room for a 'Cubs' club or two in European football who know how to create a unique fan experience, especially for families, and market the club and its identity around it. In many ways, going to a Cubs game feels non-corporate, authentic and nostalgic, while at the same time it is a commercial success.

Simon Kuper wrote, '. . . firstly, that most football fans aren't hunting glory. They don't go to the stadium because they expect trophies. They go because they like football, and because it's a way to spend time with parents, children or friends, to be together, to remember their own childhood in the same stadium. If going to the stadium is a safe and comfortable experience, they will go even if the team aren't good any more. For most people, being a supporter is about nostalgia, localism, togetherness and leisure entertainment, not about glory. In fact, many fans, especially those who support fallen clubs, disdain glory. They find identity partly in opposing today's big-spending winners, who can seem more like companies than like clubs. Losing against a big club can feel like proof of moral superiority.'[14]

The Reality TV Takeover of Football

The traditional TV broadcasting companies are definitely worried about losing a younger audience. There is global recognition that fewer are watching a full 90-minute game, and instead prefer to watch while on other devices as well as doing other things on other devices. Younger audiences are now watching more 15-minute highlights, challenging the idea that sports have to be consumed live, choosing to use their time to do other

---

[14] https://www.ft.com/content/19455408-0b96-11e8-839d-41ca06376bf2

activities. Younger audiences are also more focused on following star players that transcend the sport on social media. This audience considers the match itself just a part of what they do and who they are. They want to know about and follow the players' professional and personal lives. They want to watch the players drive to practice (see what car they have), walk to the dressing room (see what clothes they wear or headphones they use), getting ready in the dressing room (see what they do), and train (see what methods they are using). They want to see where they go, what they wear, what they listen to, who they date, where they eat and what their lives are like.

Popular entertainment TV shows like *The Bachelor* in America where an eligible bachelor selects a bride from dozens of potential women have been converted into sports equivalents like the NFL's *Hardknocks* where coaches select players for the final squad. Cristiano Ronaldo and Kobe Bryant have their own movies/documentaries. Sports and entertainment and reality TV are starting to mix at an increasing rate.

Short video clips on a regular basis can be better aligned to some emerging technology companies' and clubs' own technology strategies than traditional broadcasting. The clubs that can afford global superstars will be able to control and monetise content, away from traditional broadcasting and leagues. Clubs with large global fan bases that can feed them with content will create valuable entertainment media companies/ brands, shifting more value and control from broadcasters and leagues to themselves. The value of sponsorships at practice, in the dressing room and on the bus will become more valuable. One day it is possible that the number of minutes of social media video views of practices could exceed the actual minutes of the live games so that shirt sponsorship of practice could exceed sponsorship of matchday shirts. Or at the very least the top clubs will start to demand more money for the value of those views on their social media platforms. One of the best examples of this is because, in part, of the social media video views of the players on Real Madrid TV and Real Madrid App and social media. In 2017, Real Madrid extended their sponsorship agreement with Fly Emirates by signing a world-record kit deal, surpassing the previous record held by Manchester United and General Motors (Chevrolet). *Marca* reported Real Madrid's extension will run to the end of 2021/22 and will bring in around €70 million every year, compared to the previous €30 million. That is worth a reported €10.3 million a year more than Manchester United's existing deal with General Motors, which helped lead to GM's global marketing chief being fired 48 hours after the deal was signed in August 2012. Own social media, own TV channels, and own apps have shifted power to the clubs as entertainment/media brands and companies who can capture advertising and marketing dollars more directly.

Video games are adding to the 'reality TV takeover of football'. In his research paper, 'Avastars: The Encoding of Fame within Sport Digital Games', Dr Steven Conway observes that 'the soccer [football] video game wipes the semiotic slate clean and reconstructs a Utopian presentation of the sport aligned with the mathematical precision and neutrality of the machine, with the potential for any political, social, or cultural subversion of the sport (as sometimes practiced by the players and fans themselves) nullified … By transforming the celebrity into a hyper-ludic game piece primed for heroic acts, the developers propagate a form of cult worship synchronic with mass-media production.' The neutrality offered by the gaming platforms takes away the history of football and makes many of the gamers mere celebrity worshippers.

Remember Cristiano Ronaldo's bicycle-kick goal against Juventus in the quarter-finals of the Champions League? A few years ago the digital avatar of Cristiano Ronaldo also scored a crucial goal in a promotional animated video for Samsung Galaxy. The Galaxy 11 had been made up of world-class footballers who had come together under the German legend Franz Beckenbauer as the manager in an attempt to save earth from aliens in a crazy match where the winner will have the control of the planet. In the futuristic animated video of around 20 minutes, Ronaldo scores the winning goal for the humans by an overhead kick in injury time from a cross by Lionel Messi. The goal Ronaldo scored against Juventus on 3 April could well be taken as a 'translation' of that animated goal into real life.

I Want to be Him (Player Incorporated)

The reality TV takeover of football will make players bigger global stars. The global superstars will become even more valuable brands. The star culture of football is supported by the promotion and advertising from shoe companies. The advertising campaigns promote being like (wearing the same shoes) your favourite player. It is also supported by the social media of the players who have an ability to let fans into their lives directly. Cristiano Ronaldo, Messi and Neymar have over 120 million, 88 million and 60 million Facebook followers, respectively. Ronaldo has more followers than Real Madrid (105 million) and Neymar has more than PSG (33 million). Justin Bieber and Taylor Swift have around 70–75 million each. Kim Kardashian has 29 million Facebook followers, more than NBA stars Lebron James (23 million), Kobe Bryant (21 million) and Stephen Curry (8 million). Just to put these numbers into perspective, compare them to global multi-billion dollar corporations with well-known brands. Starbucks and Ferrari have 36 million and 16 million, respectively.

A part of 'I want to be him' is the cross-marketing synergies of athletes and other performers. Gerard Pique has 19 million Facebook followers, while Shakira has 98 million, more than Messi. Victoria Beckham and David Beckham also combine for a powerful social force.

'I want to be him' is also supported by video games. Fans can 'be' Ronaldo or Messi. The games are starting to incorporate more and more elements than just playing football.

Selecting local players or players from the academy or ethnic groups or countries with large fan bases or players from the national team will be utilised more and more by clubs to tap into 'I want to be him' to attract fans because of some sort of identification with players' backgrounds. Local academy players will be more valuable as the players who do the dirty work and fans feel a special connection to. Buying their shirts (even though they are not 'stars') means something special. If they turn into stars, then even better for their clubs.

There will be increased competition for Americas (USA and Mexico) and Asian players that play on their national teams to attract their fans. For example, a Barcelona executive stated: 'One of our dreams is to have a Chinese player in our first football team.'[15] In another example, AS Roma and other clubs are investing in player development in the United States. Roma has partner academies in ten states. Building on its renowned youth academy at home in Italy, Roma brings a unique partnership approach to its development programme in the US. Dedicated Roma staff provide ongoing coaching education as well as tailored physical and tactical performance programming. Partner clubs are invited to participate in training camps

---

15 http://www.thedrum.com/news/2018/01/31/fc-barcelona-investing-globally-become-more-club

and showcase events in the US and Rome, and in competitions worldwide. Pallotta said: 'Player development in the United States continues to be a top priority for us. We are confident this initiative will be great for the country and club and produce many star players of tomorrow...There's a lot of talent here [in the United States] and the club recognises that.'

Smaller New Stadiums with More Unique Experiences

The stadium experience is critical to the TV experience so the seats need to be full and the fans loud. The stadium needs to be fun and safe and the place to be. However, with tastes and attitudes changing and more fans conditioned to watching sports in different ways than just going to a match, the stadiums will not need to be as large for most clubs and as an incentive to go to the match there needs to be unique experience offerings that can be immediately shared on social media. Instead of adding more seats, space will be used to enhance experiences (more restaurants, boxes, and even hotel rooms looking down on the pitch). Fans will expect to have more seating options, to be able to meet players and legends, take photos on the pitch, watch players in the tunnel, see movie stars sitting near them, and have incredible dining options. The match must be like going to a movie or an event with more entertainment and participation and energy. The clubs will encourage fans dressing up, showing their passion, and participating in the event. They will want high quality entertainment during half-time and a reason to come to the game early (dining, entertainment, American football tailgating). The need to be a season ticket holder is decreasing because by utilising technology fans can purchase tickets to the matches they want to see and generally where they want to sit. Fans can sit in the best seats without being season ticket holders. Sports clubs will focus more and more on the in-game experiences. Stadiums will have dedicated sections that are unique and solidify their brands. Utilising technology, the clubs are gathering and analysing fans' preferences when they enter the stadium. When did they last come to a match? What do the fans do first when they arrive? What do they eat? What are they posting on social media? What social media are they using? Which data and statistics are they reviewing? What are they buying? When and where are there lines to wait? Who are their favourite players? Whose jersey do they buy? What music do they listen to? Who else do they follow? Answering these questions, the sports club can then direct special marketing and unique experiences to specific fans and make better business decisions. The focus for most clubs will be on making the most money per seat versus adding more seats. 70% of millennials say funding travel or experiences is the biggest motivation to work after paying for basic necessities. This is a dramatic change from when people worked to buy material goods. People want to share what they are doing or where they are, not as much what they have. Clubs will have to provide that to them.

More International Matches and Match Times During Convenient International Prime TV Time

European football clubs are training in the USA and Asia and playing in summer friendly series. This will continue to expand. The International Champions Cup (ICC) will continue to become a fixture on the football calendar and expand.

The NFL plays regular season American football games outside America, in London and Mexico City. European football leagues and competitions will most likely do the same. More European football matches will start at non-traditional times to be prime time in major global markets.

Sports Theme Parks

As clubs become entertainment brands, over time it's possible that clubs will have theme parks filled with rides and restaurants and multi-functional amphitheatres for concerts and corporate events that would draw tourists-fans and locals. Instead of characters like Mickey Mouse, the characters would be legendary players. Already, the museums of clubs such as Real Madrid and Barcelona are tremendous draws. The parks would reflect the history, legends and values of the clubs. They would serve as another meeting and interaction point for fans as their identities are further intertwined with the clubs.

FC Barcelona is opening up their football academy and the Barça Experience museum in Haikou in China. They also set up a New York office and opened their first US football school in the city, as well as their first residential football academy in Arizona. They recently announced a partnership with Parques Reunidos which will see the club open a series of FC Barcelona-branded leisure and entertainment centres worldwide.

Club Memberships

Even if clubs are not 'member-owned', we believe clubs will move to a subscription membership model. Just like how Real Madrid has 'Madridista' cards or Harley Davidson has Harley Davidson Ownership Group ('HOG'), European football clubs will have memberships with special events and gatherings. For example, HOG membership gives members access to benefits that are designed exclusively for members. HOG members participate in anything from local chapter rides to pin stops, to state and national rallies; they receive complementary admission to the Harley-Davidson Museum; they receive *HOG* magazine, which is published five times a year and is packed with riding stories, product information and member stories; and they receive the HOG Touring Handbook which features road maps and references to dealer information. The cost is €37 for one year, €70 for two years or €98 for three years. There is also Associate HOG membership which is designed for family and friends of Harley-Davidson motorcycle owners which require sponsorship from a full HOG member. There are 1,400 official HOG chapters around the world.

Most likely, the subscription model will also involve some sort of content. In March 2018, Vivienne Walt at Fortune reported one candidate for president of Barcelona believes it makes no sense that a global club like Barcelona doesn't do more to monetise its massive fan base. (Today, Barcelona has 143,855 official member-owners paying 180 euros per year in dues. All Barcelona members over 18 years old vote for the president and the board, as well as on key issues at yearly assemblies.) The candidate estimates each fan spends just €1.6 a year on Barcelona related items today. If the club found a way to charge each fan one dollar per month by subscribing to video-streamed matches, then 400 million fans would generate €4.9 billion in revenue a year (more than the €570 million today). The candidate also believes Barcelona should own its image rights and sell merchandise directly, rather than allowing Nike, adidas, and others to make the profit.[16]

Off the Pitch: League
Financial Gap

'The big clubs have taken over football. The financial gap is big and getting bigger. It seems the only way to consistently win trophies nowadays is to have a global brand and fan base (like Bayern Munich, Barcelona or Real Madrid), a billionaire owner (like Manchester United, Chelsea or Juventus) or an owner controlling other entities to sponsor the club (PSG, Manchester City or clubs of a similar historical status to Leeds) or to play in London, the city with the highest ticket prices on earth. (Three London clubs – Arsenal, Chelsea and Spurs – are now among the 11 with the highest revenues in global football, according to Deloitte's annual 'Money League' report.)'[17]

The European Club Footballing Landscape report for the financial year 2016 by UEFA shows that the financial and other off-the-pitch developments in European club football have been changing significantly and rapidly. The report does show that UEFA's regulatory role in Financial Fair Play has improved European football finances overall. In 2011, European clubs recorded operating losses of €382 million while the most recent data available shows operating profits of €832 million, with 70% of top-flight clubs from Europe's big five leagues reporting bottom-line profits. Financial Fair Play regulations (first introduced in 2011) have contributed to keeping costs down. It also shows that there is a 'polarisation of commercial and sponsorship revenues' between the top tier of clubs and the rest, and this is accelerating. The top 12 'global' clubs generated a dramatic increase in commercial and sponsorship revenues of €1.58 billion in six years – more than double the increase of all other European top-division clubs combined. The other 88 clubs in the top 100 saw far more modest increases, on average of less than 25%. Massive financial gaps are being created by societal and technological changes and globalisation. For example, wages, which correlate to success on the

---

16 http://fortune.com/2018/03/21/inside-fc-barcelona-global-football-empire/

17 https://www.ft.com/content/19455408-0b96-11e8-839d-41ca06376bf2

pitch, are highly concentrated. There are ten clubs with wage bills of €221 million or above. Then there's a €60 million gap to the club in 11th place (AC Milan). Large disparities exist within individual leagues. The top four clubs in England have an average wage bill that is almost twice as high as the next four. In Italy and Germany, it's more than twice as high; in Spain it is three-and-a-half times as high.

The reason this disparity exists is revenue and, excluding Champions League revenues, it is mostly commercial revenue. Nine clubs earn at least €25 million from shirt sponsorship. Another 20 are between €3 million and €25 million. Every other club earns less than €3 million, but often much less. Manchester United, Barcelona and Real Madrid all earn more than €75 million on kit deals, which are many multiples higher than most in their same leagues. The gap is getting bigger and bigger.

Advertisers are likely to concentrate on the biggest and most glamorous clubs with global fan bases. Those clubs with astute commercial departments, like Real Madrid, Manchester United, and Barcelona will snap up the sponsors. As technology improves, far-reaching sponsorships could become even more profitable. For example, perimeter advertising could show different adverts to televisions in different markets. A club may have a US partner whose products would be promoted in the US while, at the same time, European, South American, or African viewers could see messages advertising sponsors in those markets.

Broadcast revenues used to be the big difference maker between the 'global' clubs and others. Today, this is still true on a league-by-league basis. For example, the average English Premier League club receives more than twice what the average Italian club receives. For now, television is driving the divide between leagues. Current Premier League deals, which kicked in at the start of the 2016/17 season, are worth more than €9.8 billion. Domestic British rights for 2016, 2017 and 2018 were sold to Sky and British Telecom for €6.2 billion, a 71% increase on the previous three-year cycle. Leicester City's surprise 2015/16 title triumph helped drive up the demand for overseas rights, because it added to a perception of the Premier League's unpredictability, which is one of its great selling points. However, within the leagues, thanks to centralised collective deals, the earnings gap has, in part, been eroded. This puts more pressure on generating commercial revenues which are dependent on brand identity and value.

English Premier League Develops into the NBA of Football

In the sink-or-swim world of European football, where there's no salary cap and the richest teams can outspend most of their competitors, the English Premier League has gained an edge in becoming the richest league. When we refer to the 'NBA of Football', we are referring to the idea that all basketball players in Europe want to go to the NBA because it's recognised globally as the highest level of basketball competition and has the highest average salaries. 'We run the risk of having the Premier League become the NBA of football in the next five years, with the rest of the European leagues turning into secondary tournaments,' according to Spanish league president Javier Tebas. English Premier League football is growing ever more popular worldwide. Also, there is a fear that with the largest TV contracts owners in the English Premier League have the resources to sign the most talent in any league and to increase its big lead over the other leagues in its broadcasting and marketing revenue opportunities. In total, 14 of the 30 richest football teams in the world (based on 2013/14 revenue) are from the English Premier League. Three London clubs, Arsenal, Chelsea and Tottenham, are in the top 11 of the highest revenues in global football, according to Deloitte's annual 'Money League' report. This may raise the question of whether clubs in Italy, Spain and Germany can be perceived as global leaders and/or make enough money in broadcasting and marketing if the clubs are not regularly playing the clubs with the most talent or interesting cultures, identities and stories.

To adapt, clubs in other leagues will need large investments by entities with significant resources and reach, regardless of their home country. In addition, ideally these entities have ties and synergies to other entities that can sponsor the clubs or access more fans. The concern that the English Premier League's new TV deal 'poses a great threat to all the other European leagues' is leading to more speculation of a European Super League. The idea of creating a European (or even global) Super League is often opposed by football purists who celebrate the local traditions of each national league. Yet the money such a league might command is a compelling argument on its own, at least to team owners and marketers. It also may provide a mechanism of more parity between the big clubs.

In 2016, the Bayern Munich CEO said that he is not ruling out a potential European Super League that consists of 20 teams from England,

France, Germany, Italy and Spain. The income of the European Super League's participants would be much greater than the present income from the UEFA Champions League. In 2009, Florentino Pérez of Real Madrid said he would consider an alternative to the Champions League that 'guarantees that the best always play the best'. He added that he hoped a new system could be designed 'without abandoning the national leagues'. Arsène Wenger has previously said that he expected such a league to be created 'because the income of the Champions League is basically owned by UEFA and they distribute the money to the clubs'. In the future, those matches could be held in the United States or Asia to increase global interest and revenues.

Juventus defender Giorgio Chiellini has predicted that elite level football is heading towards a future of a 'European Super League' that will pit the best teams on the continent together on a weekly basis. He told *El Mundo*, 'In Europe, [football will move] towards the European Super League. It will take 10, 20 or 30 years, but it will arrive. With respect for the smaller teams, Juve fans want to see [Real] Madrid, United, Barça, PSG . . . Imagine a Sunday with a Juve–Madrid, a City–Barça and an Atlético–Liverpool? It will be necessary to harmonise the local leagues, of course, but it will be the biggest show in the world, more than the Super Bowl, because there is no mass phenomenon like football.' Chiellini graduated *cum laude* from the University of Turin's School of Management and Economics with a Masters degree in Business Administration in 2017.

The 'global' non-English clubs will certainly increasingly feel the difference in broadcasting revenues. Eventually, they may capitulate to a Super League to compete. In addition, the top global English Premier League clubs may feel that as overseas rights grow larger and because the foreign market's interest is concentrated on a few clubs, overseas broadcast income should be distributed differently in the EPL, or these clubs will support a Super League. (A change in the EPL would require 14 Premier League clubs to vote in favour of it, and they might not because they believe every club benefits from a stronger league and the Leicester City story.) To reduce the pressure, UEFA announced some restructurings of the Champions League, including the top four leagues in its coefficients – currently Spain, Germany, England and Italy – will be guaranteed four places each in the group stages starting from the 2018/19 season.

In 2017/18, Bayern Munich won its sixth Bundesliga crown in a row. The mark of six straight titles has been reached twice before in Europe's top five leagues. The early 2000s Lyon squad won seven straight Ligue 1 championships, and the current Juventus squad won their seventh straight Serie A championship in 2018. Before this current run by Bayern, the most championships won in a row in the Bundesliga was three. PSG has won the French title five out of the last six years. In the last 14 years, every year except one either Real Madrid or Barcelona have won La Liga. Since the English Premier League was founded in 1992, every year a club from Manchester or London have won the title, except two years. As the financial gap gets larger (discussed earlier), the bigger clubs are dominating more and more.

With casual fans overwhelmed with many football options, almost daily, and watching less and less TV overall, there will be more focus on the Champions League. The Champions League is where there is an opportunity to reach a global audience. Clubs have to prioritise limited resources (healthy, fresh players) for matches that will help drive exposure and revenues. Star players will be rested in the domestic leagues with more frequency. Now with four guaranteed spots for the Champions League in the top leagues, there is less pressure on the big clubs each week. The one exception is the English Premier League, in which there are usually six clubs from London and Manchester fighting for four spots. In addition, over the last 12 seasons ending 2016 just five clubs have claimed 46 of the 49 Champions League berths in the EPL: Arsenal, Man United, Man City, Chelsea and Liverpool. (Everton in 2005, Tottenham in 2010 and Leicester in 2016 are the only exceptions.) Two clubs potentially missing out is another reason there will be pressure to increase the spots from the EPL or for a Super League to be created. Most club executives understand that a global brand is built in the Champions League. For example, Paris Saint-Germain chairman Nasser Al-Khelaifi reiterated the Champions League remained the club's major goal after a stunning 7-1 win over Monaco saw them reclaim the Ligue 1 title from their rivals. After the game he said, 'Of course, everyone knows, our big goal is the Champions League. But today we are very proud and happy with this title.' It was a glorious display which established an unassailable 17-point lead at the summit but the coach who has overseen it from the technical area, Unai Emery, left to join Arsenal at the end of the season. Emery looks to have paid the price for failing to advance the club's European ambitions even after six trophies in three years (all domestic), a fact effectively acknowledged by Al-Khelaifi. In another example, in 2017/18 Barcelona won two domestic trophies and have set an unbeaten record in La Liga. However, coach Ernesto Valverde is under fire after his club's Champions League exit against Roma, especially after failing to rest his players before and establish a rotation policy to keep his players fresh for the Champions League. Of course, Barcelona's Champions League exit was about much more than just fatigue, but a fitter and fresher squad may have held on in Italy to advance to the semi-finals. In the future, we could see 'A' teams and 'B' teams on the first team of big clubs, where the 'B' team plays most of the domestic league matches, while the 'stars' are rested for Champions League and other important matches. This will require greater squad depth, which will require more money. Stars playing less could cause fans to lose interest in the domestic league.

One thing supporting domestic leagues and domestic cup tournaments is that the community wants to win trophies and celebrate. And the odds of winning the Champions League are so small.

In addition, the clubs at the bottom of the tables are further and further behind. As previously mentioned, in no year, in any league, did the bottom four achieve more than 28 points against the top four. Notably, in the EPL, Bundesliga and La Liga, the significant trend is towards the bottom four teams performing far worse against the top four. If games and leagues become too predictable it's possible that fans will lose interest. It's possible that as pressure builds for a European Super League and stars play fewer domestic league matches, a compromise solution will be domestic leagues will get smaller to increase revenues of the top clubs and reduce the number of domestic matches.

More Women's Teams

More European football clubs will have or will start women teams and sign international star players. USA stars Alex Morgan (Olympic gold medallist, FIFA Women's World Cup champion, FIFA World Player of the Year finalist) played for Olympique Lyon on loan from the Orlando Pride and Carli Lloyd (two-time Olympic gold medallist, FIFA Women's World Cup champion, 2015 and 2016 FIFA Player of the Year) played for Manchester City on loan from the Houston Dash. Signing these star women players with large fan bases exposes American girls to European clubs and attracts them as fans. The women's teams wear the same jerseys and play under the same brand. Alex Morgan appeared alongside Lionel Messi on covers of FIFA 16 sold in the United States. Carli Lloyd has or had endorsement deals with Nike, Beats by Dre, and other major companies. One of the biggest growth markets for American sports teams is women. The NFL's line of merchandise geared for women fans has been the fastest and biggest merchandise growth area over the last several years.

Off the Pitch: Management
Owners That Control Other Entities for
Sponsorship Synergies

Spanish league president Javier Tebas has expressed his concern about the economic future of European football with the possibility of state-owned clubs beginning to dominate leagues. Tebas and others have been critical of wealthy clubs like Manchester City and PSG, accusing them of using 'made-up sponsors', backed by states, to invest heavy sums of money. Tebas even said that PSG were 'cheating economically' after they secured the signature of Neymar for a world record. 'The football industry is not the same as it was ten years ago. It's a situation that lacks regulation so football does not get destroyed in many countries… The appearance of state-owned football clubs is really worrying; the numbers are there. The fact that PSG and Manchester City have, in the last four years, made the biggest investment in players, 30% more than the next biggest investors, says everything.'[18]

Multinational Football Companies

City Football Group (CFC), which controls Manchester City, already owns, or co-owns, six clubs in four continents with 240 male professional

---

[18] https://www.si.com/soccer/2018/01/17/la-liga-chief-javier-tebas-really-worried-about-future-european-football

players. It has hundreds more at academies who aspire to play at the highest level. CFC has lots of players training at state-of-the-art academies and training facilities with experienced staff across several continents selling them or sending them to the appropriate clubs it owns to develop. Similarly, the idea is to take local brands and fans, tie them to similar bigger global brands and turn them into fans of the bigger global brands. Best practices in marketing and operations can be shared among clubs. For example, CFC owns a stake in New York City FC (NYCFC) with the New York Yankees. The colours are similar to the colours of Manchester City. CFC is not the only owner of multiple clubs – and some other teams are experimenting with modest forms of integration – but for the most part the others are more like investment portfolios. While being a sports entertainment media company is the first priority of many big clubs now, priority number two is player development. The sky-high transfer fees are making player development important to both make money and save money. Most big clubs used to just 'buy' players in the 'buy versus build' argument, but finding, developing and building players will be increasingly more important. Having lots of ways to help this development at various levels and to control the player for the entire way is an interesting differentiator. For example, CFC purchased a minority stake in Girona, who were in the second division in Spain at the time but are in the first division now. CFC can now send young players to develop in the Spanish league in difficult, competitive and well-attended games to get experience. Players could progress from NYCFC to Girona to Manchester City. Also, as the player develops, the local fans can follow them to other clubs controlled by CFC.[19]

Off the Pitch: Technology
Move from Traditional Broadcasting to Social Media/Technology Companies

NBC retained Premier League rights for six seasons through to 2022/23 for around €800 million, doubling the amount it had been paying per season. However, Twitter agreed to a deal in July 2016 to show Premier League highlights, opening the possibility that other technology or social media companies, such as Google and Apple, could enter the bidding

---

[19] https://www.theguardian.com/news/2017/dec/15/manchester-city-football-group-ferran-soriano

in future years. Wayne Rooney's August 2016 testimonial between Manchester United and Everton was streamed live on Facebook, another possible bidder. Francesco Totti's final farewell to fans was streamed on the Official AS Roma Facebook page and viewed by over 7 million people.

Netflix, Amazon, Facebook, Twitter, YouTube and others want sports to drive traffic. Short highlights and 'behind the scenes access' shows fit perfectly with on-demand social media that covets video.

Many traditional broadcast companies are relatively small players in global terms, but if Google or Amazon bought the rights and started streaming games to billions of people around the world, they may want a guarantee of the biggest clubs, whether that is the EPL or a Super League. The new technology companies know that Rupert Murdoch created valuable broadcasting franchises by securing large sports deals as a key driver of traffic.

Football's reliance on broadcast income could also put it in a perilous position. While many view games on tablets and smartphones, broadcasting is still something of a traditional model. One warning is that those who pay to consume football via satellite or cable TV are an ageing generation that is also adopting new technologies. Technology and tastes change rapidly. Fewer young people watch a match from end to end. They just watch snippets. These new attitudes are slowly being adopted by older generations.

According to a June 2017 report from McKinsey & Company, TV trends – including declining ratings and cord cutting – present a long-term challenge for traditional sports. But the belief that millennials are to blame is misplaced. Sport isn't losing fans, sport is fighting short attention spans and the interest in fabulous people's lives (reality TV, TMZ, etc). With so many sports options across so many screens, fans of all ages – not just millennials – are watching fewer games and quitting them faster. Overall reach for sport on TV hasn't declined; ratings have dropped because fans are watching fewer and shorter sessions. In addition, in a world with so many sports options across so many screens, sports fans of all ages are clicking away from low-stakes or lopsided games. Despite millennials' heavier use of streaming and social media for sports (24% of media time on social media), the gap is closing with Gen X (22%) and Baby Boomers (20%).

In 2017, PWC conducted a survey to consumers of sports TV to understand changing tastes and attitudes. This is what they found: 91% of sports fans subscribe to pay TV for access to live games; 82% of traditional pay-TV subscribers would scale back/cancel their subscription if they no longer needed it to access live sports; and 56% of sports fans want access to more interactive content like stats, interviews and chat while watching live sports.

VAR and TV Commercials

Most likely, more football leagues and European tournaments will slowly incorporate some version of VAR. The general feeling seems to be there is too much money on the line to have human error, and transparency should be increased.

The vast majority of the VAR's tasks are initial checks, with a typical length of 20–30 seconds. Full reviews typically last around a minute but were surprisingly rare. They occurred in just under a third of games, with only 5% of matches needing more than one review. Generally, VAR decisions used up less than 1% of playing time, compared to the 28% lost during free kicks, throw-ins, goal kicks and corner kicks.

From a commercial perspective, one thing is unique during these 30–90 second reviews and stoppages of play: no one will leave their TV set in order to see the replays and decisions. The review is not like half-time where fans know the approximate time the match will restart. These 30–90 second breaks with captive audiences have high commercial value. This stoppage time may be more valuable than a similar slot during half-time. We guess that it is likely the leagues and tournaments will consider selling some sort of TV commercial time or sponsorship during these reviews to make more money.

CONCLUSION

THE WINNER OF THE 2017/18 UEFA CHAMPIONS LEAGUE QUARTER-FINALS – ITALY'S SERIE A

Roma's 2018 Champions League Quarter-final Win Over Barcelona

The week of 2 April 2018 was a bad week for Italian football. Juventus were thrashed 3-0 at home by Real Madrid, and Roma fell 4-1 to Barcelona in the Camp Nou. Italian football fans and the press mourned the death of calcio. *La Gazzetta dello Sport* read: 'Three to zero for Real against Juve, four to one for Barça against Roma. If further proof were needed here it is: right now, for us, Spain is an inaccessible planet.' The newspaper went one step further, commenting on the Roma defeat: 'The Spaniards are too strong . . . Let's not tell stories about a "comeback" at the Olimpico'.

Oh, how Roma proved them wrong.

Roma secured a thrilling 3-0 victory over Barcelona at the Stadio Olimpico on Tuesday, 10 April 2018, overturning the 4-1 deficit from the first leg and advancing to the Champions League semi-finals against all odds. Roma advanced on away goals after centre back Kostas Manolas scored the decider with a header from a corner in the 82nd minute amid a deafening atmosphere. This is the furthest they have gone in a European Cup since Liverpool beat them in the 1984 final.

The victory was richly deserved. Roma employed a high-tempo, energetic performance. They dominated possession for long stretches and stifled the Catalan club with high pressure. In addition, in the early stages in the competition, Roma had won their group, which included Chelsea and Atlético Madrid.

Regardless of who their primary favourite club were, fans across Italy were united in celebrating the Giallorossi. In overturning a three-goal deficit they became one of only three sides to do so in Europe's elite competition. Immediately after the final whistle, there were even surprising scenes of jubilation from some of the world's biggest names in football journalism, not just Italian journalists, sitting within the press box. As with most supporters across Europe, even journalists outside of Italy who hadn't given Serie A football a second look in the years before that Tuesday night just became the most passionate of calcio fans. Car horns blaring, flags waving, fans singing in the streets, wild cheers pouring from every household and tears of joy being shed; the Italian capital came alive after the miracle comeback.

Arguably, it was the Roma president, Jim Pallotta, who had the most notable celebrations that Tuesday evening. After the match, Pallotta found himself in a large courtyard in Rome with hundreds of flag-waving Roma fans who were still celebrating after their win. Rather than just stand among the fans and sing with the faithful supporters, the 60-year-old Pallotta performed a backward somersault in his dress shirt and pants into the fountain in the Piazza del Popolo (literally 'People's Square'). The next day Pallotta was told by authorities he had to pay a €450 fine according to city ordinances for wading into a historic fountain. Not only did Pallotta agree, he apologised to the Mayor of Rome, Virginia Raggi, and donated €230,000 towards the restoration of the famous fountain. (Roma's president jumping into a fountain reminded some fans of another crazy celebration. On the night of 20 May 1992, then-vice president of Barcelona Joan Gaspart, known for sometimes sitting in the stands instead of the executive box, famously jumped into the filthy water of the Thames River in London to celebrate Barcelona finally winning the European Cup, beating Sampdoria at Wembley.)

Did Pallotta regret jumping into the fountain? 'There was no point where I thought I shouldn't have done it . . . I have a history of going one step too far, going all the way back to college, so it didn't faze me at all . . . I thought, 'Why not start a thing called fix a fountain?' If you jump in one you have to buy or fix one . . .'

What did Pallotta feel after the win? 'What a feeling . . . the atmosphere in the stadium and looking around at a lot of the people who work at Roma and seeing how much it meant to them as well as the fans . . . I wasn't happy so much for myself. I was happy with what I was seeing and it didn't really strike me until that point how important it was for the city and how Rome . . . and all of Italy . . . really needed it and wanted it and deserved it.'

What did he do after the final whistle? 'I stayed in the stands at Stadio Olimpico and hugged fans before going down to greet each player individually as they came off the pitch...I didn't go into the locker room after because it's all about them...I didn't see how crazy they were in there until I saw some videos later on...I'm not one of those owners who think they have to be in the dressing room. In many cases they are going to have much more enjoyment without the owner around.'[1]

The financial implications of the win are obvious. Roma earned upwards of €70 million from their European run, a significant amount for a club that posted losses of more than €40 million after missing out of the group stage last season. The social media engagement implications were less obvious. The videos of celebrations went viral and were effective in highlighting what Roma are and how they are unique – less traditional and more fun, inclusive and engaging.

Below is a chart of the total Twitter followers of Liverpool and Roma who both advanced to the semi-finals of the Champions League. Liverpool has six times more followers, but immediately after their respective second matches, Roma had 500,000 Likes and Retweets, 11 times more than Liverpool's 45,000.

---

[1] http://www.bbc.com/sport/football/43744526

Total Twitter Followers (Main Account), Tweets After QF Second Leg Match and Retweets & Likes

Club:	Liverpool	Roma
Total Twitter Followers:	10.1M	1.6M
Tweets After Match:		
Likes	30,000	318,000
Retweets	15,000	182,000
Total Retweets & Likes:	45,000	500,000

Source: https://frntofficesport.com/how-hope-and-emotion-powered-as-romas-social-media-to-win-the-champions-league-quarter-finals/

The drama of the comeback powered Roma to enormous engagement that greatly exceeded that of clubs with a much higher social media following. Roma broke their records across all social media platforms. The stage was so big, and the opposition was one of the two most followed clubs in the world on social media. What fans wanted around the world was content that captured the sheer joy of the moment; the sheer madness of the night. So that's what Roma's digital and social media team gave them. (Roma admits they don't always get it right and don't think they are the best club on social media by a long way, but on that particular night, the content worked.)

Roma captured the attention of casual global fans. And in doing so, raised the profile of Serie A.

Juventus's Gutsy 2018 Champions League Quarter-final Fight with Real Madrid

Roma reminded fans why they should always believe. The question was would Roma's comeback inspire Juventus to adopt a similarly courageous mentality and fight with all the desire it takes to beat a big Spanish giant? Of course, the difference between Roma and Juve is that the Bianconeri lost at home and conceded three away goals. They didn't simply need a 3-0, they needed at least four without reply to advance to the semi-finals.

Juventus almost pulled off an amazing comeback. Real Madrid narrowly escaped the same fate as their bitter rivals Barcelona, in part, thanks to a controversial refereeing decision and Cristiano Ronaldo's fearless penalty kick. Madrid was only able to breathe in the 92nd minute when Lucas Vazquez was brought down by Benatia and the referee awarded a penalty. More than four minutes passed before the penalty was taken and Ronaldo didn't miss. Real Madrid progressed with a 4-3 aggregate triumph in the quarter-final tie. Unfortunately, it was just an awful, agonising, way to end what had been such a spectacular match.

Juventus's hard work, teamwork and determination highlighted what Juventus are. The result was heart-breaking, but Juventus's gutsy fight captured the attention and sympathies of casual global fans. And in doing so, like Roma, Juventus raised the profile of Serie A.

Serie A could have had two clubs in the Champions League 2017/18 semi-finals. The last time that happened was 2002/03.

The last time leagues had at least two clubs in the semi-finals are below.

Last Time When Top Four Leagues Had At Least Two Semi-Finalists in Champions League

League	Year	Clubs
Serie A	2003	Inter, Juventus, Milan
EPL	2009	Arsenal, Chelsea, Manchester United
Bundesliga	2013	Bayern Munich, Borussia Dortmund
La Liga	2017	Atlético Madrid, Real Madrid

Change Needed, But the Authentic Passion from the Fans Is Electric

Lost amongst the controversy of the Juventus penalty is that there are signs that a revival is going on in Serie A. The first signs on the pitch may have been Juventus reaching the finals in 2015 and 2017. But maybe people were sceptical because it was just one club, and it was Agnelli-backed, historical leader Juventus. But Roma's win caused people to give Serie A a second look. Serie A is the only top-five European league with a very exciting fight for the domestic league between Juventus and Napoli. Lazio was on its way to a semi-final in the Europa League before letting it slip away. In addition, three storied clubs, Lazio, Roma and Inter, were fighting it out for the two remaining spots of the four guaranteed Champions League places for Serie A clubs for the following year.

With Lazio's and Roma's runs, there are signs of a football revival in Italy's capital and enthusiasm in the streets. Just five days after Roma's win, on 15 April 2018, fortuitously previous scheduled on the Serie A calendar was the Derby della Capitale – Lazio versus Roma – at the Stadio Olimpico, with a kick-off time of 20:45 CET/2:45 EDT. Average attendances at both Rome's clubs' matches had risen by more than 4,000 from the previous year. With both clubs in a three-way tie for third place in Serie A (with the Lazio/Roma game to be played) and Champions League qualification implications, there was tension and excitement. There have been bigger derbies between them, but not many in recent times. To make the match even more scintillating, the match also pitted the current season's leading Serie A goal scorer Ciro Immobile of Lazio against last season's title holder Edin Džeko of Roma as well as two young and ambitious managers. At the time, Lazio were Serie A's top team scorers, with 75 goals in 31 games, however, they had also conceded 40 times in the league, more than Juventus and Napoli combined.

Maybe unnoticed in Italy, in America, where due to the financial implications it is crucial to grow a fan base, excited fans eager to watch the match were hit with a disappointing reality. Real Madrid were playing Málaga, which was in last place in La Liga, at the same exact time. In securing the broadcasting rights for La Liga and the attraction of Real Madrid and Barcelona to advertisers, BeIN Sports (USA) contractually agreed to always televise the Real Madrid and Barcelona matches. So, one of the most anticipated Derbies della Capitale was not on mainstream subscription TV in America.

The derby not being on TV in America illustrates one of the core challenges to Italy's Serie A. As discussed, there is a circular link between on- and off-the-pitch results. More accessibility around the world leads to a larger the social media conversation. The larger social media conversation leads to more active fan engagement. More active fan engagement leads to more loyalty and passion. More loyalty and passion lead to higher commercial opportunities and revenues. More revenues have a high correlation to winning, a higher correlation than winning to revenues.

The disappointment of the derby match not being on TV in America serves as a reminder that challenges exist and changes, like the TV contract, need to be made to continue the progress of the revival. At the same time, the authentic energy emanating from the fans at the game was electric and serves as a reminder that the spirit of football in Italy is strong, passionate and never-failing.

Looking to the Future

Ronaldo / Juventus

On 10 July, 2018, Real Madrid announced that global superstar Cristiano Ronaldo had been sold to Juventus, per his request, for €100 million, a higher transfer fee amount than the reported €94 million Real Madrid paid to Manchester United for Ronaldo in 2009. While Ronaldo is 33 years old (born 5 February, 1985), it was the seventh-highest transfer fee of all time.

While we use Zidane's leaving Juventus to join Madrid in 2001 as a sign that Serie A was losing world class players, Ronaldo joining Juventus from Madrid in 2018 is another sign of optimism for Serie A. Juventus knew they were signing a superstar whose impact would be as seismic off the pitch as it would be on the pitch, and the social media reaction was an indication of how much of an impact his name will have on the club's brand. Before the 2017 Champions League final Ronaldo had more social media followers than the entire Juventus team combined. Real Madrid had 740 million followers compared to 117 million for Juventus. However, just over a day after the announcement, Juventus gained more than 1.5 million followers on its social media networks and reportedly sold 520,000 Ronaldo jerseys in just 24 hours. To put that figure into context, PSG reportedly sold 10,000 Neymar jerseys within the first 24 hours of his signing and 120,000 within the first month, and Juventus reportedly sold 850,000 jerseys in total in 2016. Ronaldo brings Juventus a much bigger presence and profile in the markets they are in and gives them access to markets they aren't. The 'Ronaldo Effect' will help boost ticket, merchandise and commercial rights sales, as well as provide a point of engagement for new fans all around the world. As discussed, until 2017/2018 Juventus had won Serie A with 80 goals or less for six years in row, while clubs like Real Madrid and Barcelona typically win their leagues with 100 goals or more. Casual global fans want to see the world's best players score lots of exciting goals and those goals make the highlight shows. And it's not just the casual fans. After Ronaldo scored a spectacular bicycle kick in Real Madrid's 3-0 victory in the first leg of the 2017/18 Champions League quarter-final, not only did the goal receive worldwide acclaim, but the home Juventus fans inside the stadium immediately rose to their feet to applaud what they had seen.

Ronaldo will help Juventus transcend Serie A, which they have recently dominated both on and off the pitch and will aim to help realise the club's Champions League aspirations. Ronaldo has scored more goals against Juventus (10) than any other club in the Champions League; therefore, by signing him, Juventus have eliminated one of their biggest nemeses. More importantly, Juventus now have a world class finisher. As discussed previously, Serie A clubs have won the Champions League when they had a striker that was equally effective in Europe as in Serie A. Most strikers, including the current players in the Juventus squad, see a drop-off in scoring when appearing in the Champions League – but Ronaldo doesn't. He also adds a special leadership and drive to an already strong culture at Juventus. In training and on the pitch, Ronaldo has a contagious hyper-competitive edge that drives other players to push themselves. Ronaldo's professionalism in training and preparation sets a positive example for other players to emulate in a way a coach can't.

However, while Ronaldo will help generate attention, revenues and victories, Juventus will now have the high costs and management challenges of a player who will need to accept more and more player rotations to protect his performance that has past his biological peak age. In addition, while good overall for Serie A, Ronaldo's move increases the separation of Juventus, who have won seven Serie A titles in a row, from its Italian rivals.

Lastly, the contract of 40-year-old Gianluigi Buffon, winner of nine Serie A titles and the 2006 World Cup (but unfortunately not a Champions League title), ended at Juventus, and after 17 years with the club, the beloved Juventus captain joined PSG on a free transfer. While Buffon had around 11 million social media followers at the 2017 Champions League final, that would not have even placed in the top 14 at Real Madrid.

AC Milan

AC Milan were taken over by Elliott Management after Li Yonghong missed a 6 July, 2018 deadline to repay a high interest rate loan from the hedge fund. We have discussed why and predict that there will be more foreign ownership in Serie A, which we believe will be good for the league. So far two American billionaires – the Ricketts family, owner of Major League Baseball's Chicago Cubs, and Rocco Commisso, owner of the North American Soccer League's New York Cosmos – have reportedly expressed interest in the club. However, the American fund has stated it has a plan to restore the club's financial stability before any sale. On 20 July, 2018, the Court of Arbitration for Sport (CAS) overturned a UEFA Europa League ban in the 2018/19 season for AC Milan for infringing financial fair play (FFP) rules.

Second Teams Set to Enter Serie C Starting from the 2018/19 Season

In May 2018, the Italian Football Federation announced that Serie A clubs will be allowed to field B teams in the Italian third tier, Serie C, starting in the 2018/19 season. The top sides will have the opportunity to deploy 23-man squads, including 19 players born after 1 January, 1996. This will give a lot of young players the chance to mature in a lower league and ultimately improve the quality of Serie A and the national team. As is the case in Spain and Germany, second teams will be allowed to win promotion to Serie B (but not compete in the national cup), unless the first team is relegated to Serie B, at which time the B team will also be demoted.

FINAL REMARKS

CHANGE NEEDED, BUT THE SPIRIT OF ITALIAN FOOTBALL IS ETERNAL

In January 2018, Rachel Sanderson and Murad Ahmed wrote in the *Financial Times*:

> 'Italian football is in need of a radical overhaul if the game is to attract foreign investment and return to form after its shock failure to qualify for the World Cup finals, according to one of Europe's most powerful football executives. Michele Uva, vice president of European football's governing body UEFA, and director-general of Italian football federation Federazione Italiana Giuoco Calcio (Federcalcio), told the Financial Times that the game's leadership in the country was in "crisis". He said the country's game needed a "rapid change of direction" and new investment to reverse its fortunes. Italian clubs are laggards in the competition for valuable international investment that has helped transform the fortunes of the English Premier League and Spain's La Liga, allowing teams to pay for the best players and attract large international audiences.'[1]

---

[1] https://www.ft.com/content/2163bf7c-02ad-11e8-9650-9c0ad2d7c5b5

We discovered in our research that there isn't just one reason why Italy's Serie A declined. There are several factors to explain the drop-off in Italian football, both on and off the pitch. The important thing to remember is that the two are strongly linked. Academic research shows that club revenues have a higher correlation to winning (e.g. clubs can afford better and more talent) than winning does to revenues (e.g. just because you win doesn't mean you attract as many new loyal and passionate fans as you might think). It's not just the results on the pitch – it is about why the club wins, how the club wins and with whom the club wins. Fan experience, fan identity, fan entertainment and active fan engagement matter today in order to build a global brand to generate the revenues necessary to compete.

A 'radical overhaul' to get Serie A back to the pinnacle requires more than changing a few rules and securing a new TV contract. It goes beyond improving talent and overall fan experience. We identified challenges both on and off the pitch in the league, club management, country, technology and legal/regulatory system. Further improvements will require a more global and long-term vision. However, football in Italy is more than a sport or a business or entertainment; *calcio* is interpreted as an element of identity and pride. This is one reason that made studying Italian football in particular so compelling and engrossing. Italian club owners have to balance the loyalty and passion of local Italian fans with trying to attract global fans.

Club owners and executives can work together to try to adopt necessary league changes, but they do have more control over their own clubs. Aligning strategy, culture and identity requires commitment from their entire management team. It takes courage to rethink organisational design. It takes time and patience to find and support a culture and identity that is based on the community. It takes confidence to depend on the community for directing the mission and values. Doing so authenticates brand meanings and, combined with active engagement, produces the loyalty and passion of both community members and employees to grow the business. This alignment is powerful if it is approached with openness, accountability and transparency, and can deliver superior and sustainable returns and performance. The world has changed. Football is no longer just a sporting event with results on the pitch. The European football industry has changed into a global entertainment business with community brands that produce revenues from many sources.

There are signs that, albeit slowly, selected Italian clubs are adapting to changes and even taking advantage of them, so we are optimistic about the potential opportunities for football in Italy. It is not too late. Success will depend on access to more capital for investment, but, more importantly, commitment to, and the quality of, professional execution.

While change is needed, we are encouraged because we discovered football in Italy is forever in fans' hearts. It is authentic. It is complicated. It is Italy. The spirit of Italian football is eternal.

APPENDIX A

BACKGROUND ON ITALIAN FOOTBALL BEFORE 2000

The first Italian football club (Internazionale Torino) was founded in 1881. The Italian Football Federation (Federazione Italiana Giuoco Calcio – FIGC) was born on 16 March 1898 under the name of FIF (Federazione Italiana Football). The FIGC was recognised by FIFA (Féderation Internationale de Football Association), which was founded in 1904 as the international governing body of football, in 1905. Italy's national team's first match was on 15 May 1910 in Milan. Italy defeated France by a score of 6-2, and the players received some cigarette packets thrown by the 4,000 spectators as a prize. From 1898 to the 1920s, Italian football competition was primarily organised into regional groups. Serie A, the top professional football league in all of Italy, started in the 1929/30 season. The Serie A championship title is often referred to as the *Scudetto* ("small shield") because the winning club are granted the right to wear a small coat of arms with the Italian tricolour in the following season. After declining to participate in the first World Cup (1930, in Uruguay) the Italian national team won two consecutive tournaments in 1934 (Italy) and 1938 (France) with Giuseppe Meazza. In 1949, 10 of the 11 players in the national team's initial line-up were killed in an aeroplane crash that claimed the lives of the entire Torino team, winners of the previous five Serie A titles. In 1949, another important step towards the growth of football in Italy took place. The FIGC granted clubs the ability to register foreign players. This had a significant positive impact in terms of football popularity and attendance in the Italian stadiums.

FIGC was recognised by UEFA (Union of European Football Associations), which was founded in 1954 as the governing body of European football, in 1954. The first European Cup was held in 1954/55 with 16 different clubs representing their respective countries, with AC Milan representing Italy. The advent of floodlighting helped matches to be played in midweek. AC Milan, with Swedes Gunnar Nordahl and Nils Liedholm, Italian-Uruguayan 'Pepe' Schiaffino, Italian-Argentinean Eduardo Ricagni, and Italian Cesare Maldini, lost in the semi-finals to eventual champions Real Madrid (4-5 on aggregate). Stadiums were enlarged to increase revenues, especially with increased demand from the European Cup tournament, and players' salaries increased. For the Real Madrid–Milan semi-finals, the capacity at the San Siro stadium in Milan was 85,000 (which was expanded from 35,000 in 1955), compared to 125,000 at the Santiago Bernabéu stadium in Madrid (which was expanded from 75,000 in 1955). In 1958, Italy did not qualify for the World Cup. In 1968, the *Azzurri*, (plural form of the colour blue, the colour of the Italian jerseys) won the European Championship, their first major competition since the 1938 World Cup. In the 1978 World Cup, a new generation of Italian players, the most famous being Paolo Rossi, came to the international stage. Italy finished fourth but were the only team in the tournament to beat the eventual champions and host team Argentina.

Football was starting to change financially. In 1979, the Italian Federation made shirt sponsorship deals an option for clubs. Juventus was the first big club to have a shirt sponsor with Italian domestic appliance manufacturer, Ariston, in 1979. (In 1979 Liverpool signed a €147,700 two-year deal with Japanese electrical company Hitachi. Written into the contract were clauses that the shirts couldn't be worn in European competitions or any live televised domestic games because the BBC and ITV refused to show any teams who wore shirt sponsors at the time. Real Madrid were La Liga's first to

have a shirt sponsor in 1982. https://footballpink.net/2015/10/22/5475/)
In 1981 AC Milan signed with Pooh Jeans and Roma signed with pasta
maker Barilla. However, it wasn't until midway though the 1990s that most
Italian clubs had shirt sponsors. Broadcast TV was changing around the
world. Until the late 1970s state-owned RAI (Radiotelevisione Italiana)
had a monopoly on football broadcasting rights in Italy. New entrants
were emerging and viewed football as valuable content. The first major
Italian national private television group was created in the early 1980s
through the acquisitions, including the Canale 5 (Channel Five) television
channel, by the Fininvest group, controlled by Silvio Berlusconi. The first
football event shown by the new television group was the inaugural 1981
Coppa Supermondiale Clubs (Cup Super Clubs), an unofficial summer
invitational tournament at the San Siro in Milan organised by Canale 5,
won by Internazionale and with Santos FC of Brazil as runners-up. (In the
UK, the demand for football grew through the 1970s and early 1980s. A
deal was struck for the 1983/84 season and the first live league match since
1960 was televised on ITV between Tottenham Hotspur and Nottingham
Forest on 2 October 1983. The two-year contract for the TV rights in
1983 cost €9 million and the four-year contract in 1988 cost €66 million,
a fourfold increase per year.)

The following provides a background of key milestones in Italian
football from the early 1980s to the turn of the century.

Not-for-Profit Clubs to Companies 1981

Until 1981, professional football clubs in Italy were organised as
recreational associations and not-for-profit organisations. Over the years,
expenses continued to grow, therefore the club members decided to turn
to wealthy regional industrial families to financially support the clubs to
compete. These families realised that the sporting success, both nationally
and internationally, could reward them with important popularity and
consequently with an indirect economic return. The role of the 'mecenate'
(patron), one who promotes and financially supports an artistic activity,
in this case football, was born.

On 23 March 1981, the Italian legislators issued the law 91/81 governing
sports and football for the first time. The law clearly establishes the criteria

for distinguishing professional and amateur sports and regulating the relationships between professional athletes and sports clubs. Moreover, this law also sets out the essential elements in order to establish, manage and liquidate clubs, as well as to establish the specific powers of the sports federations. In addition, law 91/81 establishes important fiscal requisites regarding VAT with reference to contracts stipulated between clubs and athletes. Finally, it establishes the procedures for the application of taxes with regards to transactions involving the transformation of associations into limited companies.

The new law clarified the non-profit-making purpose of football and sports clubs. Article 10 of the law states: 'Only sports clubs founded as limited companies or limited liability companies can enter into contracts with professional athletes. The articles of association must provide that profits are fully reinvested in the club for the exclusive pursuit of sports activity.' As a result, football clubs could freely generate profits, but it was forbidden to distribute the profits among members. Clubs' members could only benefit indirectly from these profits.

In addition, the new law provided more freedoms to athletes. Prior to Law 91, the contractual freedom of the athlete was generally restricted. For example, the athlete could not move to another club without the agreement of the club that first engaged him, even after his contract ended. However, Article 6 of Law 91 provides that once a player's contractual relationship with the club has ended, the athlete's new club may be required to pay the player's former club a 'training and promotion indemnity' to be fixed pursuant to criteria established by the relevant sporting federation. The criteria was normally the average salary paid to the player over the last two seasons, plus bonuses plus any share of the club's sponsorship and promotional revenues paid to the player over that period. This is a 'post-contractual transfer fee'. This type of fee would be challenged in the Bosman court case in 1995.

Italy Wins FIFA World Cup 1982

In 1980, Italian football was full of controversy when a match-fixing, betting scandal (often referred to as Totonero) involving five top teams (Avellino, Bologna, Lazio, Milan and Perugia) was uncovered. Players were arrested in dressing rooms and investigations led to severe punishments, including disqualification. Among those banned was Paolo Rossi (who played for Perugia), then the most expensive player in the world. (Despite the ban, Rossi always claimed to be innocent and stated that he had been the victim of an injustice.)

Initially suspended for three years, Rossi had his suspension reduced to two on appeal. At this point in time, many in Italy were anxious about the direction in which football was heading. Some believed players were being paid far too much and that the traditions of the game were being lost.

Rossi did not play a single game until two months before the FIFA World Cup 1982 in Spain and few experts in Italy expected the coach to include the striker in his World Cup squad. However, the coach placed Rossi in the starting XI for the first game. Rossi had no impact, as Italy drew all their group stage matches and neither of their two goals was scored by Rossi. Italian journalists and fans complained that Rossi was in very poor shape.

Italy only managed to edge past Cameroon for the second spot in the group on goals scored and Rossi and the team were lambasted by their media.[1]

The Italy manager Enzo Bearzot gave his blessing when the entire squad wanted to boycott the press in response. There had been previous, one-off occasions in which players had refused to speak to the media, but such a uniform strike was unheard of. 'Silenzio stampa' had been born and a siege mentality united the players.[2]

The fiercely independent-minded manager staunchly confirmed Rossi for the decisive round robin in the second round, in which his team was to face Argentina, the reigning world champions, and Brazil, the favourites to win the title, with a team consisting of world-class players such as Sócrates, Zico, and Falcão. After Italy defeated Argentina 2-1, also thanks to the defensive work of Claudio Gentile and Gaetano Scirea, who shut down the young Argentinian star Diego Maradona, Rossi scored three memorable goals to defeat Brazil 3-2 to qualify for the semi-finals. In the semi-final match against Poland, Rossi's two goals won the match for Italy once again, granting them a place in the 1982 World Cup final. In the final against West Germany,

1 https://www.theguardian.com/football/2014/may/30/brazil-falcao-1982-world-cup-italy
2 http://www.thegentlemanultra.com/gazzetta/enzo-bearzot-and-the-birth-of-silenzio-stampa

Rossi scored the first of Italy's three goals, from an indirect set piece assist from Gentile, helping Italy to win the match 3-1, giving his team their third World Cup title, after a 44-year wait. Bruno Conti, a one-club legend at Roma, was instrumental in creating Italy's third goal as he set up Alessandro Altobelli with a great cross.

With six goals in total, Rossi won the tournament's Golden Boot award as the top scorer of the tournament, as well as the Golden Ball Award for the best player of the tournament. Rossi's accomplishments gained him the title of European Footballer of the Year and World Player of the Year in 1982, as well as the 1982 Ballon d'Or Award. The enduring image from the 1982 final came from Marco Tardelli, an energetic and hard-tackling yet technically skilful Juventus midfielder. After 69 minutes, a quick ball across the box was controlled with a deft touch before he blasted the ball into the bottom corner for a 2-0 lead. Not only was it a high-quality goal, but Tardelli's emotional reaction and celebration that followed expressed perfectly just how much the goal meant.

There are few international teams that captured the hearts of their fans as completely as that Italy side. The team and its accomplishments are still revered. The team also set a standard for how all 11 players can work together. The goalkeeper and his defenders were like an impregnable, immovable object. They didn't make mistakes and worked closely together with a 'take no prisoners' attitude. Any striker, especially Maradona, who dared to attack was the recipient of hard challenges and tackles from tough Italian full backs. (Gentile and Scirea, rather impressively, were never sent off during a match during their entire careers.) The midfielders provided steel in the centre of the pitch and constantly harassed opponents to regain possession. The midfielders also used skill, guile and touch to quickly connect the defence to attack to create chances, and they also scored goals. The strikers were cool under pressure and clinical finishers.[3]

The 1982 Italy World Cup team set an identity, brand, standard and style of play that Italian clubs would try to emulate and world-class players would want to be a part of. Even today, Italian football, and the global perception of the league, rightly or wrongly, is still influenced by the style of play in 1982.

---

[3] http://bleacherreport.com/articles/2098493-the-italy-side-of-1982-would-win-the-2014-world-cup

Roma Lose to Liverpool in Rome 1984

The 1984 European Cup final was held on 30 May at the Stadio Olimpico in Rome, Italy. Liverpool were appearing in their fourth final, having won the competition in 1977, 1978 and 1981. Roma qualified for the competition by winning the 1982/83 Serie A, becoming Italian champions. They beat Dundee United 3-2 on aggregate in the semi-finals, although it was later revealed that a Roma director had bribed the French referee in the second leg of the semi-final with 100 million lire (€85,000) before the match. Roma were appearing in their first European Cup final. As the final was being held in Roma's hot and hostile backyard, Roma went into the match as the favourites, despite Liverpool's previous success. It was the third final of its kind where a finalist was playing at home with the first two occasions yielding home triumphs for Real Madrid in 1957 and Inter in 1965. In addition, Roma had a 100% home record en route to the final and clinched the Coppa Italia four days earlier in Rome with victory over Hellas Verona. Watched by a crowd of 69,693, Liverpool took the lead in the first half when Phil Neal scored, but Roma equalised before half-time through Roberto Pruzzo. With the scores level at 1-1 through full time and extra time, the match went to a penalty shoot-out. Liverpool won the shoot-out 4-2 to claim their fourth European Cup. (Liverpool's young defender Steve Nicol missed his penalty kick over the crossbar.) The shoot-out is famous for Liverpool goalkeeper Bruce Grobbelaar's use of wobbly or 'spaghetti' legs and other tactics to distract Roma players about to take their penalty kicks. Facing Italian legends Bruno Conti and Francesco Graziani, Liverpool's flamboyant stopper began swaying his legs one way then another on the goal line. He did it only to Roma's two most renowned players, who both missed. In 1986, Roma's president was banned by UEFA for attempting to bribe the referee with €75,000 before the final match.

Platini and Juventus 1983–85
(Five-Year Ban of English Teams from UEFA Competitions)

After early success in the late 1970s, Juventus's domination in Serie A continued on into the early part of the 1980s, winning the Serie A league title six times between 1977 and 1986. This meant Juventus had won 20

Italian league titles and were allowed to add a second golden star to their shirt, thus becoming the only Italian club to achieve this. Around this time the club's players were attracting considerable attention; Paolo Rossi was named European Footballer of the Year following his contribution to Italy's victory in the 1982 FIFA World Cup, where he was also named player of the tournament.

Frenchman Michel Platini of Juventus was also awarded the European Footballer of the Year title for three years in a row – 1983, 1984 and 1985 – which was a record until Lionel Messi won four in a row between 2009 and 2012. (Platini is considered essentially Italian by many native Italians due to his Italian origins. There is a long history of French players playing for Juventus including Zidane, Trezeguet and Deschamps, but Platini was considered the most 'Italian' which made him especially beloved.)

Juventus came close to winning a European Cup in 1983, but suffered a surprising defeat at the hands of Hamburg in the Athens final, finishing as runners-up. In the 1985 European Cup final against Liverpool at the Heysel Stadium in Brussels, Belgium, Juventus were appearing in their third European Cup final, having lost their previous two appearances in 1973 and 1983 but Liverpool were appearing in their fifth final. Liverpool were also the reigning champions, having beaten Italian team Roma 4-2 in a penalty shoot-out after the 1984 final finished 1-1 (Liverpool also won in 1977, 1978 and 1981). Juventus beat Liverpool 1-0, after a 56th minute goal from Michel Platini scored from a penalty, winning their first European Cup. However, the win was marred by a tragedy which changed European football. The Heysel Stadium disaster, in which 39 people (mostly Juventus fans) were killed and 600 were injured when a stadium wall collapsed after a confrontation, resulted in the banning of all English clubs from European competition indefinitely.[4]

The ban eventually lasted for five years, with English clubs returning to European competition in the 1990/91 season. Liverpool returned to European competition a season later in the 1991/92 UEFA Cup. With English clubs being banned from UEFA competition, Serie A and the Italian clubs became a more attractive market for international players and helped Serie A solidify both on- and off-the-field dominance.

[4] http://pesstatsdatabase.com/forum/viewtopic.php?t=12804. Some English fans believe that the tension with Italian fans was partly a carry-over of confrontations between Liverpool and Roma fans in Rome the previous year

Naples is Italy's third largest city with 1 million people, behind Rome (2.8 million) and Milan (1.6 million). Its football club Napoli were a consistent top six side in Serie A for much of the late 1970s. Even into the earliest two seasons of the 1980s, the club were performing respectably with a third-place finish in 1980/81. However, by 1983, they had slipped dramatically and were involved in relegation battles.

Then, something extraordinary happened. Napoli broke the world transfer fee record by acquiring Diego Maradona in a €12 million deal from Barcelona in June 1984. Maradona was considered the greatest footballer on earth at the time. Italians saw his talents first hand on TV in the World Cup in 1982. Italy, and especially the city of Naples, went crazy with his arrival. Even with the excitement, there were questions as to how the money for the transfer fee was raised by the owners, and so quickly. Naples was a poorer and more neglected city in Italy than the major cities in the north, where the benefits of industrial production had concentrated. In addition, in Napoli's 60-year history they had never won Serie A. Even today at football matches, a few fans of the clubs in northern Italy poke fun at the people of Naples, highlighting the regional identification.[5]

The squad was gradually rebuilt, and the rise up Serie A was steady. By 1985/86, they had a third-place finish. In the 1986 World Cup in Mexico, Maradona scored two of the most famous goals in World Cup history against England, and then added two more goals in the semi-finals en route to Argentina winning the trophy. Now unquestionably at the peak of his fame and skill, he returned to Naples with his mind set on bringing the city its first Scudetto. The 1986/87 season was the landmark in Napoli's history; they won the double, the Serie A title and the Coppa Italia. Before Maradona, no team from Italy's south had won Serie A. Napoli added their second Serie A title in 1989/90. In the end, with Maradona, Napoli won two Scudetti, a UEFA Cup and a Coppa Italia. Just as importantly, perhaps, he made Napoli relevant and attracted fans from around the world to the club.

---

5 http://inbedwithmaradona.com/retro/2016/1/6/maradona-arrives-at-napoli

When Italy staged the World Cup in 1990, it seemed that football had come to its spiritual home.[6]

Argentina, the defending champions, boasted not only Maradona, but also Abel Balbo, Claudio Caniggia and Roberto Sensini, who all played in Serie A. The link between Argentina and Italy is very important. A long time ago, Italian used to be a current language in Argentina, and it is estimated that roughly 20–30% of Argentinians have Italian parents or grandparents, so many people in Italy always considered some Argentinians as Italians. Therefore, it was very easy for them to play in Italy, which is still true today. In addition, having parents or grandparents from Italy would allow many Argentinian players to request Italian passports and claim they were Italian. Before 1995, each country had restrictions on foreigners. The Argentinian-born Italians did not count as foreigners in Italian teams' quotas, a big advantage. In 1995, UEFA was warned that its European competitions would be deemed illegal unless the controversial foreigner restrictions were eliminated. In addition, the Bosman ruling allowed players to be free agents.

Despite a shock early loss to Cameroon, Argentina beat the Soviet Union, Brazil and Yugoslavia to set up a semi-final with the hosts Italy. The game was scheduled to be played, and you can't make this up, in Naples.[7]

As the teams walked onto the field, the banner on the Curva read: 'Maradona, Naples loves you, but Italy is our country'. Argentina won the match on penalties and the Neapolitans, though devastated, applauded Maradona as he bowed to the crowd.[8]

Maradona created controversy at the 1990 FIFA World Cup. Recognising the regional identification, Maradona made comments

---

[6] http://www.newsweek.com/2014/09/26/how-italy-became-sick-man-european-football-270924.html

[7] The semi-finalists consisted of Argentina, England, Italy and West Germany, all previous World Cup winners, with a total of eight previous titles between them. The tournament generated a record low goals-per-game average and a then-record 16 red cards were handed out. In the knockout stage, many teams played defensively for 120 minutes, with the intention of trying their luck in the penalty shoot-out, rather than risk going forward. Two exceptions were the eventual champions West Germany and hosts Italy, the only teams to win three of their four knockout matches in normal time. Two changes were made as a result of 1990. Firstly, FIFA introduced the back-pass rule in time for the 1994 tournament to make it harder for teams to time-waste by repeatedly passing the ball back for their goalkeepers to pick up. Secondly, three, rather than two points would be awarded for victories at future tournaments to help further encourage attacking play.

[8] https://sports.vice.com/en_us/article/yp8b9b/our-darling-our-diego-how-naples-fell-in-love-with-maradona

pertaining to North–South inequality in the country, asking Neapolitans to root for Argentina in the semi-finals against Italy in Naples. 'I don't like the fact that now everybody is asking Neapolitans to be Italian and to support their national team. Naples has always been marginalised by the rest of Italy. It is a city that suffers the most unfair racism.' However, after the final, the Italian Football Federation (FIGC) forced Maradona to take a doping test, which he failed, testing positive for cocaine. Napoli and Maradona later claimed the test was a revenge plot for events at the World Cup. Maradona was banned for 15 months and would never play for Napoli again. Though Napoli finished fourth during the 1991/92 season, Napoli gradually went into decline after that season, both financially and on the field.

The game took place at the Stadio Olimpico in Rome, and was won 1-0 by West Germany, their third World Cup title, with a late penalty kick taken by Andreas Brehme being the game's only goal. It was a rematch of the previous final four years earlier. Italy finished third and England fourth, after both lost their semi-finals in penalty shoot-outs.

Of the 11 starters on West Germany's team, six played in Serie A, while the rest played in Germany. West Germany's star players Andreas Brehme, Jürgen Klinsmann and Lothar Matthäus played for Inter; Thomas Berthold and Rudi Völler played for Roma; Thomas Häßler played at Juventus (then Roma in 1991). Another West German starter, Jürgen Kohler, would join Juventus in 1991.

Salvatore Schillaci of Juventus received the Golden Boot and Golden Ball awards for scoring six goals in the World Cup and being the best player. He became the second Italian footballer to win the Golden Boot, after Paolo Rossi won the award in 1982.

1990 Serie A Starts Being Televised in the United Kingdom

After the success of the 1990 World Cup in Italy and the wide recognition that the best players in the World Cup played in the Italian league, Serie A first appeared in the United Kingdom on BSB Sports Channel in 1990/91, then the following year it was on Sky Sports. In 1992, Serie A was shown on Channel 4. Channel 4 paid €2 million for the rights for the 1992/93 season. In the 1990s, Serie A was at its most popular in the United Kingdom when it was shown on Channel 4 from 1992 to 2002. *Football Italia* was a popular television programme in the United Kingdom showing Italian football on Channel 4, at its peak attracting over 3 million viewers. James Richardson presented the show for a large part of its existence. *Gazzetta Football Italia*, a highlights show, became the highest rated Saturday morning programme in Channel 4's history at the time, with around 800,000 viewers a week. The English top flight was no longer on free-to-air terrestrial TV but on BSkyB and England star player Paul Gascoigne had transferred to Lazio in 1992 for €7.3 million. In addition, the quality of English football was seen as lower than Italy's, partly due to English football's 1985–90 ban from UEFA competitions, brought on by hooliganism.

1989, 1990 Back to Back for AC Milan

In February 1986, entrepreneur Silvio Berlusconi (who would become prime minister for the first time in 1994) acquired AC Milan and saved it from bankruptcy after investing vast amounts of money, appointing rising manager Arrigo Sacchi to the helm of the Rossoneri and signing Dutch internationals Ruud Gullit, Marco van Basten and Frank Rijkaard. At the time, Italian league rules allowed three foreigners on each team. The Dutch trio added an attacking impetus to the team, and complemented the club's Italian internationals Paolo Maldini, Franco Baresi, Alessandro Costacurta, Roberto Donadoni and Carlo Ancelotti. The Dutch trio provided the flair (and the goals), the Italian players provided the steel and Sacchi provided the tactical discipline. Together they changed the face of Italian and also European football with an attack-minded, pressing game.[9]

Committed to concepts like 'collective intelligence', Sacchi demanded 'eleven active players in every moment of the game, both in defence and attack'. Remarkably, he used to stage full matches in training without a ball, telling players where the imaginary ball was so they could respond – and position themselves – accordingly. 'The only way you can build a side is by getting players who can play a team game,' Sacchi said. 'You can't achieve anything on your own, and if you do, it doesn't last long. I often quote what Michelangelo said: "The spirit guides the hand."' After this innovative training approach, the press nicknamed Sacchi's side 'Gli Immortali' ('The Immortals') because of the imaginary situations repeated

---

[9] http://www.telegraph.co.uk/sport/2317066/The-greatest-teams-of-all-time.html

every day at practice. At the end of training, players were reportedly exhausted and usually had headaches because of the incredibly high number of simulations of play. Sacchi's sides played in a 4-4-2 system with zonal marking, the distance between the defence and midfield lines never greater than 25 to 30 metres. That high defensive line – and an efficient offside trap – maintained pressure on opponents not used to being hurried. Sacchi started a revolution in Italian football, at a mental and tactical level. They had their style of playing and they were trying to impose it on all opponents. Carlo Ancelotti said: 'Arrigo completely changed Italian football – the philosophy, the training methods, the intensity, the tactics. Italian teams used to focus on defending – we defended by attacking and pressing.'[10]

Under Sacchi, Milan won its first Scudetto in nine years in the 1987/88 season. The following year, beating Real Madrid, the defending champions, in the semi-final of the 1988/89 European Cup was a watershed moment for Milan. The club won its first European Cup in two decades, beating Romanian club Steaua București 4-0 in the final. Milan repeated the feat and were champions again after a 1-0 win over Benfica a year later and were the last team to win back-to-back European Cups before Real Madrid's win in 2017. UEFA ranked the 1989/90 Milan side as one of the greatest teams of all time that changed football.[11]

Milan 1992 to 1995, Three Champions League Finals in a Row

In 1992, Milan returned to the glorious days they had had under Arrigo Sacchi, with Fabio Capello as their new coach. Marco van Basten scored 25 goals as Milan went through the Serie A season unbeaten. The unbeaten run totalled 58 matches, including the next season as well. In that title-winning campaign, Milan only conceded 21 goals. In 1993, Milan would win Serie A again, and make it to the final of the Champions League, losing to Marseille 1-0 in Munich. The season also saw Milan set the world transfer fee record following an intensive bidding battle against Juventus to sign Gianluigi Lentini from Torino. In 1994, Milan would win both Serie A and the Champions League,

---

10 http://www.uefa.com/uefachampionsleague/news/newsid=2213362.html
11 http://fr.uefa.com/uefachampionsleague/news/newsid=2213362.html

beating a Johan Cruyff-coached Barcelona 4-0 in the final in Athens. Milan played in their all-white away strip, which historically they use in finals of the European Cup/UEFA Champions League. That game saw a goal explosion from a Milan side that had been extremely defensive during the entire league season, which in part caused the Italian Football Federation to introduce three points for a win starting in the autumn of 1994. Milan won Serie A with a mere 36 goals scored in 34 games, but conceding only 15, which meant they had the defensive line, with Franco Baresi and Paolo Maldini as key players, to thank for their third consecutive domestic success.[12]

Baresi and Maldini played 1,621 matches together, and in the 196 matches they played as a central defensive partnership they conceded just 23 goals. Paolo was the son of former European Cup-winning Milan captain, Cesare Maldini. In 1995, Milan reached their third consecutive Champions League final, but lost to Ajax 1-0 in Vienna. It was the first final aired by private broadcasters, and the first year that shirts with sponsorship had been worn in the European Cup or Champions League final.

1995 Bosman Ruling

Jean-Marc Bosman was a player for RFC Liège in the Belgian First Division whose contract had expired in 1990. He wanted to change teams and move to Dunkerque, a French club. However, Dunkerque refused to meet his Belgian club's transfer fee demand, so Liège refused to release Bosman. He took his case to the European Court of Justice in Luxembourg and sued for restraint of trade, citing FIFA's rules regarding football. In December 1995, the court ruled in his favour.

Prior to the Bosman ruling, professional clubs in some parts of Europe (but not, for example, in Spain and France) were able to prevent players from joining a club in another country, even if their contracts had expired. The Bosman ruling meant that players could move to a new club at the end of their contract without their old club receiving a fee. Players can now agree a pre-contract with another club for a free transfer if the player's contract with their existing club has six months or less remaining.

---

12 https://www.thesun.co.uk/sport/football/1833874/franco-baresi-and-paolo-maldini-conceded-just-23-goals-at-heart-of-ac-milan-in-196-matches/

The Bosman ruling also prohibited domestic football leagues in EU member states, and also UEFA, from imposing quotas on foreign players to the extent that they discriminated against nationals of EU states. At that time, many leagues placed quotas restricting the number of non-nationals allowed on member teams. Also, UEFA had a rule that prohibited teams in its competitions, namely the Champions League and UEFA Cup/Europa League, from naming more than three 'foreign' players in their squads for any game. After the ruling, quotas could still be imposed, but could only be used to restrict the number of non-EU players on each team.

The Bosman ruling coincided directly with a new era of football becoming a global entertainment business. After the ruling, player salaries and transfer fees rose dramatically. In 1996, Edgar Davids became Europe's first high-profile player to benefit from the ruling when he moved from Ajax to Milan. The big four leagues at the time (England, Italy, Germany and Spain) benefited from the Bosman rule, because just a few clubs outside of these four big leagues made it to a Champions League final after 1995 – Ajax in 1996 and Monaco and Porto in 2004. Great players in the Netherlands or Portugal or another European country will go to the big clubs in the big leagues thanks to the unlimited number of foreigners because of the Bosman rule.

1996 New Laws: Football Clubs Can Now Distribute Profits

Law n. 91/1981 was amended on the basis of the law n. 586/1996 of conversion of the legislative decree n. 485 of 20 September 1996 (referred to as the *'spalma perdite'* decree). The definitive abolition of the transfer indemnity for training or promotion changed many of the plans of Italian clubs that suddenly realised they could no longer count on this relevant source of revenue. The clubs were making money on players who went to other clubs even after their contracts had expired. The Bosman ruling changed this.

The law n. 586/1996 removed the prohibition on the distribution of profits to shareholders (thus eliminating the anomaly that prevented sports clubs from pursuing subjective gainful purposes), and allowing the public listing of football clubs. The only limitation consisted in the 10% of the profits to be allocated to youth academies for training and technical education.

With the new law, clubs considered the capital markets as a cheap source of capital to spend on players or reduce debt or both. Many owners wanted to maintain control but reduce their financial obligations and risks. The owners knew there were lots of loyal and passionate local (and typically unsophisticated) fans willing to invest in their clubs' winning, even if they didn't completely understand the financial risks.

The mid-1990s saw a wave of initial public offerings (IPOs) as soccer teams transformed themselves into fully-fledged businesses. The first IPOs were seen in the smaller market countries, such as Denmark and the Netherlands. The United Kingdom soon took the lead, with more than 20 clubs going public by the turn of the century. In 1998, Lazio joined the trend, becoming the first Italian club to go public on the Italian stock exchange. Two years later, Lazio celebrated their 100th anniversary in style, capturing Serie A for only the second time in their history in 1999/2000. In 1999, Roma went public and also won Serie A two years later in 2000/01 for their third time. In 2001, Juventus went public and would win Serie A in 2001/02 and 2002/03. In a press release at the time, Juventus stated they are 'the football club with the largest number of supporters in Europe, with 17 million. In Italy some 11 million, more than one-third of all Italian football fans, support Juve.'

Juventus in Three Champions League Finals in a Row 1996–98

Marcello Lippi took over as Juventus manager at the start of the 1994/95 season. His first season at the helm of the club was a successful one, as Juventus recorded their first Serie A championship title since the mid-1980s. The players during this period included Ciro Ferrara, Gianluca Vialli and a young Alessandro Del Piero. The following season in 1996, Juventus won the Champions League, beating Ajax on penalties after a 1-1 draw in which Fabrizio Ravanelli scored for Juventus.

The club looked to improve even after winning the European Cup, signing Zinedine Zidane, Filippo Inzaghi and Edgar Davids. At home, Juventus won the 1997 and 1998 Serie A titles. In Europe, Juventus reached the 1997 and 1998 Champions League finals during this period, but lost to Borussia Dortmund and Real Madrid, respectively.[13]

Reaching three Champions League finals in three years, Juventus was dominant in the mid-1990s. The 1998 team may have been better than the 1996 team that won the Champions League. Based on a typically tight Italian defence there was also a succession of great Italian forwards (Ravanelli and Vialli being replaced by Del Piero and Inzaghi) and foreign midfield dynamos such as Paolo Sousa and Edgar Davids. The greatest import was the Frenchman Zidane, providing the genius to this Juventus side in the same way Platini did in the previous decade.[14]

Juventus Lose to Real Madrid in 1998 and Then Lose Zidane to Real Madrid in 2001

Juventus made their third consecutive UEFA Champions League final appearance in 1998 but lost the game 1-0 to Real Madrid. In 1998, Zidane was named FIFA World Player of the Year, and won the Ballon d'Or. Juventus finished second in 2001 in Serie A, but were eliminated in the group stage of the Champions League. In 2001, Zidane was named Serie A Foreign Footballer of the Year for the second time.

In 2001, the world's best player became its most expensive when Zidane swapped Juventus for Real Madrid for a world record fee of about €77.5 million in instalments and signed a four-year contract. Partly using the Zidane money, in 2001 Juventus signed Italian goalkeeper 'Gigi' Buffon from Parma for €51.6 million, French defender Lilian Thuram from Parma for €41.3 million and Czech winger Pavel Nedvěd from Lazio for €38.7 million.

The fee dwarfed the €60.7 million Real Madrid paid Barcelona for Luis Figo the previous year. Zidane was the latest addition to the 'Galácticos era' of global stars signed by Real Madrid every year starting in 2000.

'I have been waiting impatiently for this moment and, after five years at Juventus, I think it was the right time to make a move,' said the World Player of the Year of 1998 and 2000 after being presented

---

[13] Christian 'Bobo' Vieri made 23 appearances and scored eight goals in Serie A in the 1996/97 season, and six goals in ten matches in Europe, making him joint top scorer for Juventus that season along with Alen Bokšić. He ended his season at Juventus by winning the Scudetto and starting in the 3-1 UEFA Champions League final loss to Borussia Dortmund.

[14] http://footballsgreatest.weebly.com/juventus-1996-1998.html

with his number five shirt and introduced to the media by the former Real Madrid legend Alfredo di Stéfano, an honorary president. Zidane's immediate goal was to help Real Madrid win their ninth European Cup and add that ultimate club trophy to his World Cup and European Championship international trophies.

At the time, it was widely believed that the best players played in Italy and wanted to play in Italy. Zidane leaving Italy was the signal that things were changing. Football was becoming entertainment content for digital TV (highlighted by BSkyB's first media rights deal for the English Premier League) and corporate sponsors were looking for global brands with global reach. In hindsight, it also highlighted that the newly elected president of Real Madrid, Florentino Pérez, who was an engineer running a large construction company, recognised the changes happening in football which was why Zidane was coveted by Real Madrid. Besides being considered the best footballer, Zidane was multicultural and represented beautiful football and class. He was a global superstar and would attract global fans and sponsors, besides helping win on the pitch. In his first season at Real Madrid, Zidane scored one of the most famous match-winning goals in history, in Real Madrid's 2-1 win over Bayer Leverkusen in the 2002 UEFA Champions League final.

APPENDIX B

BACKGROUND ON SELECTED FOOTBALL INDUSTRY DISRUPTIONS SINCE 2000 THAT IMPACTED ITALIAN SERIE A

In 2000, Florentino Pérez was elected president of Real Madrid. Real Madrid began to execute a sustainable economic-sport model with a global community brand which was centred on community values, and started with the best players in the world with the values of the community. One of the business model inspirations was Disney. He and his management team polled fans to determine what they wanted which led to a written mission and values statement, and the signing of superstars Figo in 2000, Zidane in 2001, Brazilian Ronaldo in 2002 and David Beckham in 2003. While Beckham was the only one of the four that did not win the Ballon d'Or (runner up in 1999), he had the biggest fan base by far, especially in America and Asia, and was a cross-over global superstar, along with his wife Victoria, who transcended the sport and attracted casual global fans to Real Madrid. In 2003 Real Madrid had five players (Zidane #5, Raúl #7, Roberto Carlos #8, Beckham #10 and Ronaldo #11) in the top 11 in the Ballon d'Or voting. With their global superstars playing beautiful attacking football, Real Madrid became a must-see spectacle. Just like a Disney movie, Real Madrid had stars that people liked and wanted to see putting on a show. Not only did fans around the world want to watch the entertainment, they also bought the licensed commercial products and supported the sponsors. In addition, Real Madrid would spend €240 million on enlarging and modernising the Bernabéu Stadium to improve the fan experience.

In 2002, adidas paid around €75 million to take an 8.33% stake in Bayern Munich. In 2010/11, Audi paid around €90 million for its 8.33% stake. In 2014, German insurer Allianz took an 8.33% stake in Bayern Munich for €110 million as part of a deal to help the club pay down debts on its stadium and to sponsor a youth academy.

In 2003, Chelsea was bought by Russian billionaire Roman Abramovich in a deal worth €202 million. Long-time chairman Ken Bates bought Chelsea in 1982 for just £1, while taking on debts of €2.6 million. Although the club prospered, debts had grown and it was estimated Abramovich would pay an additional €141 million to €169 million to cover the debt. The Russian billionaire pledged to plough even more resources into the club. Funded by Abramovich, Chelsea would sign over €150 million worth of talent in their first summer.[1] In 2003/04 Chelsea's main player purchases were Damien Duff €24.5 million, Hernan Crespo €24.3 million, Claude Makélélé €24 million, Adrian Mutu €22.8 million and Juan Sebastian Veron €21.7 million. Wages were €165.7 million and losses were €126.8 million. Claudio Ranieri was replaced as manager by Jose Mourinho. In 2004/05 Chelsea's main player purchases were Didier Drogba €35.4 million, Ricardo Carvalho €29.5 million, Paulo Ferreira €19.5 million and Arjen Robben €17.7 million. Wages were €160.5 million and losses were €206.3 million.

In 2005, Malcolm Glazer purchased Manchester United in a deal valuing the club at almost €1.17 billion. In 2012, the Glazers took Manchester United public on the New York Stock Exchange. In 2012, Manchester United signed a shirt sponsorship deal with General Motors' Chevrolet worth €435 million over seven years. In 2014, Manchester United spent €169 million in transfer fees.

---

[1] While this may not be that impressive in today's market, it was an enormous sum then and as much as the value of the club itself.

In 2008, Sheikh Mansour bought Manchester City for €263 million in a much-publicised deal and has since accumulated annual losses of €608 million, excluding approximately €227 million on facility upgrades. In 2015 and 2016, Manchester City spent €215 million and €214 million respectively on transfer fees. In 2015, Manchester City sold a 13% stake to a Chinese consortium, CMC Holdings and CITIC Capital.

In 2010, Barcelona announced what was then the most lucrative shirt sponsorship deal in football history, worth €150 million with the Qatar Foundation. Barcelona had previously refused shirt deals and, for the previous five years, had instead paid international children's charity Unicef to carry their logo. In 2017, Barcelona dropped Qatar Airways as their main shirt sponsor and signed a more lucrative deal with Japanese company Rakuten worth around €214.5 million over four years.

In the 2011/12 season, Financial Fair Play was implemented to prevent professional football clubs spending more than they earn in the pursuit of success and in doing so getting into financial problems which might threaten their long-term survival. The terms were agreed to in principle in 2009 by the Financial Control Panel of football's governing body in Europe (Union of European Football Associations – UEFA). Although the intentions of encouraging greater financial caution in football have been well received, FFP has been criticised for limiting the internal market, failing to reduce football club debt and protecting the status quo. In 2015, UEFA announced FFP would be 'eased' in response to a number of lawsuits that are currently ongoing in courts.

In 2011, Oryx Qatar Sports Investments (QSi) purchased Paris Saint-Germain for an estimated €100 million. Previously, PSG was a capital city club floundering in the middle of the Ligue 1 table due to a history of mismanagement and a lack of direction. PSG would spend over €212 million in the first 14 months in transfer fees, making it clear that PSG's ambitions were to compete with the big clubs in Europe.[2] In the summer of 2011, the club signed Javier Pastore for €42 million, and in 2012, Thiago Motta for €10 million, Ezequiel Lavezzi for €30 million, Thiago Silva for €42 million, Zlatan Ibrahimović for €23 million and Marco Verratti for €10 million. In July 2013, Uruguay striker Edinson Cavani joined the club for €70 million. In the summer of 2017 PSG set a world

---

[2] In the first 14 months of new ownership Chelsea spent €283.6 million, Manchester City €234.3 million and PSG €212.6 million.

record transfer fee for Brazilian Neymar of €220 million and followed it with signing 18-year-old French prodigy Kylian Mbappé for around €180 million.

In 2011, Juventus opened its new stadium. Built at a cost of €155 million, it featured modern executive boxes, among other new developments. In 2014, Juventus signed a shirt sponsorship deal with Fiat's Jeep worth around €17 million per season, with additional performance-based bonuses available. In 2016, Juventus spent €193 million in transfer fees.

In 2011, Xi Jinping, President of the People's Republic of China, said that he had three dreams for Chinese football: to qualify, to host and to win a World Cup. As part of his football plans, the president has decreed that China will have 20,000 training centres and 70,000 pitches in place by 2020. Chinese investors hold stakes in AC Milan (2017), Inter Milan (2016), Aston Villa (2016), Manchester City (2015) and Atlético Madrid (2015).

In 2015, Chinese conglomerate Dalian Wanda Group, operating in sectors such as entertainment, hotels and real estate with an extensive footprint in its domestic market and strong growth in Europe and the US, purchased a 20% stake worth €45 million in Atlético Madrid to significantly shore up its balance sheet, as well as accelerate the growth of its brand globally. As part of the agreement, Atlético and Wanda will work together towards opening three football schools in China. Atlético will also be invited to play in China every year and the Spanish outfit will provide special training programmes in Madrid for Chinese youngsters. In 2017, Quantum Pacific Group, an Israeli industrial conglomerate, acquired a 15% stake in Atlético Madrid for €50 million. In 2017, Atlético's newly built Wanda Metropolitano Stadium was opened.

In 2016, Chinese company Suning Holdings Group purchased 68.55% of Inter Milan for €270 million, in the highest-profile takeover so far of a European club by a Chinese firm. In addition to the equity stake, Suning would also take on a large portion of the loss-making club's debt.

In 2016, Barcelona confirmed a long-term contract extension with American kit manufacturers Nike for at least €155 million a season from 2018. The initial deal, which smashes Manchester United's previous record €835 million 10-year deal with adidas, will run until 2023 when

Barca's members will have the chance to vote in favour of a further five-year extension.[3]

In 2017, after two years of negotiations, Silvio Berlusconi agreed to sell AC Milan to a Chinese consortium for €740 million. The new Chinese owners have promised to inject €350 million into the club over three years, with the first €100 million due within the first year. In 2017, Milan spent €192 million in transfer fees, the fifth most in one year in history.

In 2017, Real Madrid extended their sponsorship agreement with Fly Emirates by signing a world-record kit deal, surpassing the previous record held by Manchester United and General Motors (Chevrolet). *Marca* reported Real Madrid's extension will run to the end of 2021/22 and bring in around €70 million every year. That is worth a reported €10.3 million-a-year more than Manchester United's existing deal with General Motors, which helped lead to GM's global marketing chief being fired 48 hours after the deal was signed in August 2012.[4] Manchester United made public it has a €25 million penalty clause from adidas for failure to exhibit their kit brand on the European and global platform provided by Champions League participation, highlighting the importance of the Champions League.[5]

[3] http://www.skysports.com/football/news/11833/10637904/barcelona-confirm-record-kit-deal-with-nike

[4] http://www.marca.com/en/football/real-madrid/2017/09/21/59c3c8be22601d2b118b45aa.html; https://talksport.com/football/real-madrid-surpass-manchester-united-and-sign-biggest-kit-deal-penning-new-fly-emirates

[5] https://www.theguardian.com/football/blog/2017/may/19/champions-league-still-financial-sporting-lure-premier-league-clubs

APPENDIX C

BACKGROUND ON TOP FIVE CLUBS IN DELOITTE FOOTBALL REVENUES RANKINGS 2000/01

Deloitte Football Revenues Rankings
2000/01

Rank	Club	Revenues	European Cups (at the time)
1	Manchester United	€217.2 million	1968, 1999
2	Juventus	173.5	1985, 1996
3	Bayern Munich	173.2	1974, 1975, 1976, 2001
4	AC Milan	164.6	1963, 1969, 1989, 1990, 1994
5	Real Madrid	138.2	1956, 1957, 1958, 1959, 1960, 1966, 1998, 2000

Manchester United: Manchester United were originally founded as a club in 1878. In 1902, majority ownership passed to the four local businessmen who invested £500 (€568 with today's exchange rate) to save the club from bankruptcy. After the Munich air disaster in 1958, when 23 people died out of 44 on a Manchester United team flight back from Munich, Louis Edwards began acquiring shares of the club and in 1964 had acquired control, 54%, of the club for approximately €45,000. Over time, he and his descendants accumulated more shares. Media tycoon Robert Maxwell attempted to buy the club in 1984 from Louis Edwards' son Martin, but did not meet Edwards' asking price. In 1989, chairman Martin Edwards attempted to sell the club to Michael Knighton for €29 million, but the sale fell through and Knighton joined the board of directors instead. Manchester United were floated on the stock market in June 1991 (raising €9.8 million).

In the autumn of 1991, talks were held for the broadcast rights for the Premier League for a five-year period, from the 1992/93 season. ITV were the current rights holders and fought hard to retain the new rights. ITV had increased its offer from €25.2m to €47.6m per year to keep control of the rights. Rupert Murdoch's BSkyB joined forces with the BBC to make a counter-bid. The BBC was given the highlights of most of the matches, with BSkyB paying €425.8m for the Premier League rights, which would give them a monopoly of all live matches, up to 60 per year from the 1992/93 season. Murdoch described football as a 'battering ram' for pay television, providing a strong customer base.

Manchester United received a takeover bid in 1998 from Rupert Murdoch's British Sky Broadcasting Corporation. The Manchester United board accepted a €926.7 million offer, but the takeover was blocked by the Monopolies and Mergers Commission in 1999.

Manchester United did not win any English First Division titles in the 1970s or 1980s. In the 1990s they won in 1993, 1994, 1996, 1997 and 1999, and also won the Champions League in 1999. Keep in mind that the English were banned from European competition from 1985/86 to the 1990/91 season.

Juventus: Juventus were founded in 1897. The Agnelli family, who have controlled Fiat since 1899, have controlled Juventus since 1923. Gianni Agnelli, the grandson of founder Giovanni Agnelli, was Fiat's chairman from 1966 until 1996; he then served as honorary chairman from 1996 until his death in 2003. He was very well respected and connected. Despite offering a relatively competitive range of cars, Fiat was not immune from economic cycles in the car industry. In 1976 it was announced that the Libyan government was to take a 9.6% shareholding in Fiat in return for a necessary capital injection worth an equivalent of €376 million. The 1980s were also a struggle for Fiat. In 1986, 15% of Fiat company stock was still owned by Libya, an investment dating back to the mid-seventies. However, the financial challenges of Fiat didn't seem to impact Juventus. The 1970s and 1980s saw Juventus further solidify their strong position in Italian football. They won the Scudetto in 1972, 1973, 1975, 1977, 1978, 1981, 1982, 1984 and 1986. They won their first ever major European title (the UEFA Cup) in 1977 and the European Cup in 1985. Juventus went public on the Borsa Italiana to raise capital in 2001. The *Wall Street Journal* reported at the time that 'Juventus joins a sector whose shares have been battered. Football clubs' soaring wage costs have been outstripping revenue growth, while lucrative television deals could lose their luster. AS Roma SpA shares are down 46% since their May 2000 public-market debut, despite winning the Italian championship this summer...with profitability dented by the increasingly high cost of attracting star players...Studies by Deloitte & Touche indicate that in England and Italy, salaries eat up two-thirds of clubs' revenues...In such a bleak environment, Italian clubs that don't own the stadiums they play in have further suffered due to weak merchandising and commercial activities.' A fund manager quoted in the article stated, 'Juventus also has the potential to generate cash outside of TV revenue, like Manchester United, but has to prove to investors it can do it.'[1]

Bayern Munich: FC Bayern were founded in 1900. Until 2002, Bayern were 100% owned by club members. Although Bayern won their first national championship in 1932, the club were not selected for the Bundesliga at its inception in 1963. The club had their period of greatest success in the middle of the 1970s when, under the captaincy of Franz Beckenbauer, they won the European Cup three times in a row (1974–76). The 1980s were a period of off-field turmoil for Bayern, with many changes in personnel and major financial problems. The club was in debt and even bankruptcy loomed over them. In 1984 Bayern paid off their debt with the sale of Karl-Heinz Rummenigge to Inter Milan for a record fee of more than €5 million. In 1992, Bayern sold Stefan Effenberg and Brian Laudrup for €8.5 million to Fiorentina to pay players' expenses.

---

[1] https://www.wsj.com/articles/SB1008622946372043000

During the financial turmoil, Bayern were German champions in 1980, 1981, 1985, 1986, 1987, 1989, 1990, 1994 and 1997.

AC Milan: AC Milan were founded as a club in 1899 by an English businessman in Milan. Piero Pirelli, son of Giovanni Pirelli, the founder of the Pirelli rubber and car tyre company, funded AC Milan from 1909 to 1928. From 1954 to 1963, Andrea Rizzoli, son of the founder of the Rizzoli publishing empire in Italy, funded the club. In 1974, Rizzoli bought the Milan newspaper *Corriere della Sera* and made it part of the Rizzoli group.

In 1980, Milan had been sent down to Serie B in disgrace as part of an illegal betting scandal punishment, just a year after winning their tenth Scudetto (and with it the right to wear a gold star on their shirts, one for every ten titles). They came straight up again but, riddled with debt and struggling to attract any decent players, were duly relegated once more. Despite being a member of the Euro 1980 Italy squad that had finished fourth, and the 1982 World Cup-winning team, Franco Baresi elected to stay with Milan, winning the Serie B title for the second time during the 1982/83 season and bringing Milan back to Serie A, endearing him to Milan fans forever.

In 1986, Silvio Berlusconi acquired the club and saved it from bankruptcy. Berlusconi's Fininvest holding company began investing in the burgeoning cable TV market in the late 1970s. Immediately, there were concerns Berlusconi would disrupt the transfer market, causing too much of an imbalance. Berlusconi started a publicity campaign on Fininvest's channels. The ads suggested viewers give themselves a 'little gift this Sunday, with the blue of the sky, the green of the grass and the red and black of the new Milan'. A record number of season ticket holders, over 60,000, took up the offer. Perhaps more than that, though, Berlusconi appreciated football as more than just a sport. At a press conference a few days after buying the club he declared: 'Milan is a team, but it's also a product to sell; something to offer on the market.'

Compared with the still very patriarchal ownership style of Juventus, Milan were a modern, progressive club, applying the business strategies and entrepreneurial spirit of a large-scale conglomerate to the still largely family-run world of Italian football. However, the Rossoneri became another outpost of his commercial empire. The difference versus old industrial

Italian families was that his club fed off and was to feed the core business of his main media-oriented company Fininvest. Television rights became a crucial factor, which was a catalyst for all the glitz and glamour that was to follow. Worth €2.2 million in 1982, they had jumped to €906 million in 1988. Berlusconi's channels were awash with football discussion shows, highlights packages and news programmes (often working as thinly veiled advertorials for new pay TV services). 'Customer' loyalty was introduced because season ticket holders provided the perfect database for marketing opportunities and 'cross-fertilisation' of other Fininvest products (and, later, politics). A psychologist was brought in to teach everyone at the club the company way and to foster a new corporate mentality.

Berlusconi invested vast amounts of money, appointing rising manager Arrigo Sacchi to the helm of the Rossoneri and signing Dutch internationals Ruud Gullit, Marco van Basten and Frank Rijkaard. The Dutch trio added an attacking impetus to the team, and complemented the club's Italian internationals. Before Berlusconi, Milan's last three Scudetti were in 1962, 1968 and 1979. With Berlusconi, in the 1980s and 1990s Milan won in 1988, 1992, 1993, 1994, 1996 and 1999. Milan won the European Cup in 1989, 1990 and 1994.

In the early 1990s, with Italian politics still reeling from a series of corruption scandals, Berlusconi formed the Forza Italia party, filling a vacuum, just as he had in 1986 when he took over Milan. Berlusconi helped to reinvent the game. He set a template for saturated television coverage, ushering in Serie A's golden age in the process. In addition, he helped with the formation of the Champions League (from the European Cup). Introduced in 1992/93, the Champions League replaced the European Cup, which had run since 1955/56, adding a group stage to the competition and allowing multiple entrants from certain countries. The pre-1992 competition was initially a straight knockout tournament open only to the champion club of each country. This meant more opportunities for more big clubs to qualify and more big match-ups on TV which resulted in expanding revenues to the participating clubs.

Real Madrid: Real Madrid were founded in 1902 as a not-for-profit membership club, and today has 92,000 owners/members. In 1947, Real Madrid's president Santiago Bernabéu wanted to get the best players for

Real Madrid. To pay for them, he did something innovative at the time. He took a huge financial risk and built one of the biggest football stadiums to increase ticket revenues, predicting that the best playing stars would not only win there but would also draw large crowds to the stadium to see them do it. To finance the stadium, which would one day be named after him, he sold bonds to the club members and fans. At the time, many thought it was 'too much stadium for so little a club'. Bernabéu's gamble paid off, and with the larger ticket receipts, Real Madrid were able to afford better players. Real Madrid won La Liga in 1953/54 over defending champions Barcelona. It took Bernabéu ten years to win his first La Liga championship as president (the club's third Spanish title). One factor in that success was that in 1953 Bernabéu had done something on a scale that was unheard of at the time. He had embarked upon an ambitious strategy of signing the best world-class players from abroad, the most famous being Argentinian forward Alfredo Di Stéfano. In the mid-1950s, Bernabéu helped create the European Champion Clubs' Cup, simply referred to as the European Cup (later renamed as the UEFA Champions League), to showcase the team and build the Real Madrid brand beyond Spain.

After Bernabéu proved the sustainable economic-sport model works, other clubs quickly copied elements of it. Barcelona, for example, began construction of a new stadium called Camp Nou in 1954, which was much larger than Real Madrid's stadium (Barcelona's 106,146 capacity versus Real Madrid's 75,145 in 1957). So, although Real Madrid won the first five European Cups (from 1955/56 through 1959/60), the other teams eventually caught up. Real Madrid would only win one more European Cup in the 1960s with an all-Spanish team that had three of the starting 11 players as graduates of the Real Madrid youth academy. After that, the team would not win another European Cup until the late 1990s.

When Bernabéu passed away in 1978, he had been the club's president for 35 years, during which time Real Madrid had won six European Cups and 16 Spanish league titles. In the later years of his presidency, Real Madrid failed to continue to innovate or tweak the model and found itself struggling financially. During this time, Ajax, Bayern Munich, Benfica, Inter Milan and Liverpool were starting to have consistent success in the European Cup, sometimes taking elements from the 1955–60 Real Madrid model. For example, Inter Milan won the 1965 European Cup, for the second year in a row, with the Italian team having two starters from Spain and one from Brazil.

By the early 1980s, Real Madrid had lost its grasp on the Spanish league title and no longer had the resources to sign even the best Spanish players, impacting on strategy. The club's new strategy was to develop and promote players from within (from the academy). A new cohort of five home-grown stars dominated Spanish football in the 1980s with two UEFA Cups and five Spanish championships in a row. They had the nickname 'La Quinta del Buitre' ('Vulture's Cohort'), which was derived from the nickname given to the most charismatic and prominent player of the group, Emilio Butragueño ('El Buitre', 'The Vulture'). The other four members were Sanchís, Rafael Martín Vázquez, Míchel and Miguel Pardeza. All five players were graduates of Real Madrid's youth academy, referred to as La Fábrica.

In 1995, Lorenzo Sanz, who had been a board member from 1985 to 1995 during the presidency of Ramón Mendoza, became president of the club. Mendoza resigned after admitting the club had undisclosed large debts. Sanz tried to turn around the club by bringing in star players to play with home-grown star striker Raúl. The club borrowed more money to sign new players but was not successful in creating an economic model or financial strategy to pay off the debt. Generally, it was assumed that if the club won, it would make money. The assumption was wrong. The club won on the field, but it did not lead to off-the-field financial success. Financially, the club sank deeper into trouble.

Between 1997 and 2000, Real Madrid's net debt doubled, reaching €162 million on recurring revenues of only €118 million. The club teetered on the brink of bankruptcy, despite impressive on-the-field success in the Champions League. Real Madrid won their seventh European title in May 1998, breaking a 32-year drought, and won its eighth in May 2000. Even delivering two Champions League titles, the incumbent lost the presidential election to Florentino Pérez, demonstrating that fans don't only care about winning.

APPENDIX D

BACKGROUND ON SERIE A FINANCIALS AND REVENUE COMPOSITION

Serie A Balance Sheets 2016/17
€ in millions

Team	Revenue	Costs	Plus-Minus	Net Result 2016/17	Net Result 2015/16	Net Debt	Net Wealth
Atalanta	60.6	78.9	22.3	0.3	-1.9	39.6	8
Bologna	59.1	86.9	13.2	-16	-32.6	39.1	18.4
Cagliari	61.3	65.3	6.5	0.7	Serie B	8.5	22.6
Chievo	50	67	19.3	0.3	0.3	64	4.5
Crotone	18.4	21.3	5	1.1	Serie B	3.2	1.9
Empoli	38.3	43.6	6.3	-0.2	1.6	13.3	2
Fiorentina	108	136.4	28	-1.6	-14.2	6.5	55.8
Genoa	59.3	89	29.7	-4.1	-10.6	76.9	0.07
Inter	273.7	301.9	44.3	-24.6	-59.6	472.3	-83.4
Juventus	422.4	495.2	139.8	42.6	4.1	524	93.8
Lazio	100.2	114.2	28.8	11.4	-12.6	109.7	20.3
Milan	223.9	292.4	10.3	-74.9	-89.3	183.5	-50.4
Napoli	203.7	207.4	104.4	66.6	-3.2	73	122.6
Palermo	56.3	64.7	19	4	-0.4	-6.1	15.7

Pescara	35.9	47.6	6	-7.3	Serie B	13.3	-0.6
Roma	183.3	292.9	94.8	-41.7	-14.6	353.4	-88.9
Sampdoria	66.4	94.5	34.6	3.2	-1.4	20.8	23.7
Sassuolo	78.4	90	20.6	3.8	-0.3	36.6	13
Torino	66.4	73.3	9.6	1.4	9.5	12.5	23.3
Udinese	70.8	96.8	36	-1	-27	55.7	18.5

Source: La Gazzetta dello Sport

Serie A Revenue Composition 2016/17
€ in millions

	Revenue	*%*
TV Rights	1,262	56%
Commercial	496	22%
Stadium	230	10%
Other	279	12%
Total	2,267	100%

Source: La Gazzetta dello Sport

Serie A Team Revenue Composition 2016/17
€ in millions

TV Rights		*Commercial*		*Stadium*	
Juventus	232.8	Inter	112.2	Juventus	63.4
Napoli	145.4	Juventus	104	Roma	29.2
Roma	111.6	Milan	77.7	Inter	28
Milan	96.8	Napoli	32.3	Milan	25.5
Inter	94.3	Sassuolo	31.7	Napoli	19.7
Lazio	73.4	Roma	24.3	Fiorentina	8.4
Fiorentina	71.2	Fiorentina	17.2	Lazio	7.6
Torino	44.6	Lazio	14.5	Udinese	6.4
Udinese	39.6	Cagliari	13.1	Torino	5.2
Sassuolo	38.8	Atalanta	11.3	Atalanta	5.1
Atalanta	36.4	Bologna	10.6	Bologna	4.8
Bologna	35.9	Torino	7.8	Sampdoria	4.7
Cagliari	35.5	Sampdoria	7.6	Genoa	4.3
Genoa	35.5	Udinese	6.4	Cagliari	3.5

410

Chievo	35.2	Palermo	5.5	Pescara	3.2
Sampdoria	35	Chievo	5.3	Palermo	3
Palermo	32.1	Pescara	5.2	Sassuolo	2.9
Empoli	29.1	Genoa	4.7	Chievo	2
Pescara	25.4	Empoli	2.3	Empoli	1.9
Crotone	13.6	Crotone	2.2	Crotone	1.4

Source: La Gaz

Serie A Total League Revenues v. Total League Salaries and Growth
2012/13–2016/17
€ in millions

Season	Total Revenues	% Growth	Total Salaries	% Growth
2012/13	2,696		1,158	
2013/14	2,727	1.1%	1,225	5.8%
2014/15	2,625	-3.7%	1,250	2.0%
2015/16	2,858	8.9%	1,350	8.0%
2016/17	2,267	-20.7%	1,401	3.8%

Source: La Gazzetta dello Sport

Serie A Total League Debts 2012/13–2016/17
€ in millions

Season	Debts net of Receivables	Bank Debt (and factoring institutions)	% Growth
2012/13	1,572	977	
2013/14	1,715	1,056	9.1%
2014/15	1,724	1,118	0.5%
2015/16	1,871	1,175	8.5%
2016/17	2,100	1,289	12.2%

Source: La Gazzetta dello Sport

APPENDIX E

BACKGROUND ON SELECT EUROPEAN LEAGUE KEY STATISTICS (FROM PWC REPORT CALCIO 2017)

Five Top European Leagues:
Economic Profile–Average Per Club Data
€ in millions

Country	Number of Clubs	Revenues (€)	Costs (€)	Net Result	Avg Annual Rev Growth (2010-15)	Avg Annual Growth GDP/Capita (2010-15)
England	20	220.2	215.8	4.4	10.4%	3.0%
Germany	18	134.5	130.4	4.1	8.1%	3.2%
Spain	20	102.5	99.3	3.2	4.6%	1.6%
Italy	20	95.2	109.8	-14.6	3.9%	0.4%
France	20	70.9	74.1	-3.2	5.7%	2.2%

Source: Analysis by FIGC–Study and Research Division with data provided by UEFA

Sponsorships in Top Four Leagues
by country of origin and industry

	England	Germany	Spain	Italy
Number of sponsorship deals	311	354	223	560
% of national sponsors	37.6%	76.8%	59.2%	85.0%
% of foreign sponsors	62.4%	23.2%	40.8%	15.0%
Clothing & fashion	6%	4%	3%	9%
Food	2%	5%	4%	10%
Automotive	7%	10%	7%	7%
Banking, insurance & financial services	15%	10%	14%	4%
Betting	11%	5%	6%	3%
Beverages	11%	10%	23%	7%
Public institutions/no profit	0%	0%	3%	0%
Healthcare	4%	3%	9%	7%
Media	4%	5%	3%	8%
Services & consultancy/other	7%	8%	1%	12%
Technology & electronics	5%	10%	3%	8%
Tourism & accommodations	3%	3%	7%	3%
Other	26%	30%	16%	21%
Total	100%	100%	100%	100%

Source: Analysis by FIGC–Study and Research Division. Data updated at 31 December, 2016

Incidence of average ticket price over average daily wage 2015

Country	Incidence	Total Gate Receipts (€ in millions)	Total Attendance	Avg Ticket Price (€)	Avg Daily Wage 2015 (€)
Turkey	69.9%	79.3	2,444,617	32.5	46.4
Spain	53.7%	420.0	10,197,376	41.2	76.6
England	53.7%	718.0	13,747,982	52.2	97.2
Germany	39.8%	473.4	13,318,871	35.5	89.4
Italy	36.2%	204.0	8,202,731	24.9	68.7
Greece	33.4%	18.7	874,070	21.4	64.0

Source: Analysis by FIGC–Study and Research Division with data provided by UEFA, Lega Serie A and OECD

Total Attendance in Serie A:
Number of Spectators and YoY Growth

Year	Attendance	YoY Growth (%)
2010/11	8,945,763	
2011/12	8,362,025	-6.5%
2012/13	8,584,596	2.7%
2013/14	8,744,116	1.9%
2014/15	8,202,731	-6.2%
2015/16	8,466,512	3.2%

Source: FIGC Stadia Database, Lega Serie A, Lega Serie B, Lega Pro and public data

Top Division Clubs' Attendance Figures 2015/16

	Germany	England	Spain	Italy	France	Total
Number of clubs	18	20	20	20	20	98
Number of league matches	307	380	380	380	380	1827
Avg attendance for league matches	43,327	36,461	28,568	22,280	20,896	29,786
Total attendance for league matches	13,301,300	13,855,180	10,855,840	8,466,512	7,940,480	54,419,312
Average capacity	47,029	38,155	38,864	39,608	31,208	38,651
Occupancy rate (%)	92%	96%	74%	56%	67%	77%
Total potential attendance	14,437,835	14,498,900	14,768,396	15,051,211	11,859,097	70,615,439
Total unsold seats	1,136,535	643,720	3,912,556	6,584,699	3,918,617	16,196,127

Source: Analysis by FIGC–Study and Research Division with data provided by UEFA, Lega Serie A, transfermarkt.i.
europeanfootballstatistics.co.uk and soccerway.com

ACKNOWLEDGEMENTS

WE WOULD like to thank the many kind people involved with European and Italian football who allowed us to interview them, answered our many questions, made introductions, and provided us with information. You were incredibly kind, forthcoming, thoughtful, professional, responsive, and patient. We would love to recognise your contributions and time on an individual basis, but we want to respect your privacy and not cause any potential issues. We hope that you feel our genuine, heart felt gratitude and know the book benefited tremendously from your involvement.

The book is a result of the love and support of our families and friends. The book was a very serious undertaking and required us to spend a lot of our time away from our loved ones. Thank you for your understanding and patience. With three authors we can't specifically tell each and every one of you how much we love you, but we hope that we do that each and every day.

We would like to give a special thank you to Frank Castiglione, marketing executive, and Marcantonio Antamoro, financial executive, who read a number of drafts of the book and gave us feedback as well as encouragement.

We would like to express our deepest gratitude to David Stern, NBA commissioner emeritus; Gary Bettman, commissioner of the NHL; Her

Excellency Ms. Isabelle Picco Monaco's Ambassador and Permanent Representative to the United Nations; Gabriele Marcotti, most recently *Hail, Claudio!*; Stefan Szymanski, most recently *Money and Football*; Terry Daley of ESPN; Dermot Corrigan of ESPN; Paddy Agnew, *Forza Italia*; James Horncastle of ESPN; Rory Smith of *The New York Times*; Philippe Moggio, General Secretary of CONCACAF; Kiyan Sobhani and Gabe Lezra of ManagingMadrid.com; Michael Berland of Edelman Berland; Inigo Lopez de la Osa Escribano; Francesca Franco; Borja Arteaga of PJT Partners; Alberto Cribiore of Citigroup; the community of Columbia University Business School; and the community of the master's degree programme in Sports Management.

We want to thank our friends at beIN Sports. Their family make watching European football so much fun. Their shows (*The Locker Room*, *The Xtra*, *The Express*, *Coach's Corner*, *Football Crazy Podcast*), commentary, and insights helped inform us. The quotes in the book from Ray Hudson didn't really happen; they are just what we imagined he would have said. How could we make up a quote for living legend Christian 'Bobo' Vieri? A special thank you to Gabrielle Amado, Gary Bailey, Matteo Bonetti (The Calcio Guy), Andrés Cordero, Jamie Easton, Kevin Egan, Terri Leigh, George Metellus, Kay Murray, Tancredi Palmeri, Thomas Rongen, Carlos Ruiz, Phil Schoen, and Jeremy St. Louis.

We want to thank Charlie Stillitano, the Executive Chairman of Relevent Sports, the company that hosts the International Champions Cup, and a host of *The Football Show* on SiriusXM. His commentary and insights (and humour) helped inform us.

We would like to express our deepest gratitude to Alfonso Mastrantonio, Program Assistant for RAI2 football and comedy show *Quelli Che Il Calcio*. He was instrumental in providing detailed and thoughtful feedback with extremely helpful information and analysis. He also challenged, and provided examples to better illustrate, some of our analysis and conclusions.

We would like to thank Alessandro Mosca, legal consultant at Ruiz-Huerta & Crespo and a Columbia University, Master of Science in Sports Management and ISDE, Master in Global Sports Law graduate. He was instrumental in helping analyse current and historical legal issues of Italian football.

We would like to thank Alberto Favaretto, a corporate lawyer from Milan, who provided feedback with nuances and subtleties. The same exact thank you for Stefano Faccendini; Alexandre Cassanovas, who also helped edit and translate *The Real Madrid Way* (even though he is a Barcelona supporter!); Míchel Acosta of http://messi-vs-cristiano.com; and Joaquin Berral.

Many thanks to the professionals who helped with ideas, encouragement, debate and introductions for the book: Cynthia Curry of Colliers International; Dewey Shay of the New York Islanders; William Reid of Reid Capital; Ashley Berhard of Haven Hill; Shawn Doss of Elevate Sports Ventures; Richard Hinman of *The Gentleman Ultra*, Chris Hanson and Matthew Green of Deloitte, Lorenzo Bettoni of *Calciomercato*, Battista Severgnini of Copenhagen Business School, Craig Depken III of UNCC, Miguel Blanco Callejo of Universidad Rey Juan Carlos, Cristian Nyari of Bayern Munich, Mark Godfrey of *The Football Pink*, Matt Caldwell and Shawn Thornton of the Florida Panthers, Paul Ingram, Damon Phillips, Bruce Kogut and Michael Mauskapf of Columbia Business School; Scott Rosner of Columbia University's master's degree programme in Sports Management; Marisa Saenz of Universidad Europea de Madrid; Carlos Gomez Arroyo of Rabobank; Ben Cherington of the Toronto Blue Jays; Vince Gennaro of New York University; Jesse Fioranelli of San Jose Earthquakes; Bren of https://www.chiesaditotti.com; and Manolo Zubiria of CONCACAF.

We would like to thank the following for providing suggestions and support: Thomas Dunipace, Bren, Wayne Girard, Luca Martano, Tad Burns, Marco Ciarla, Marcus Ranney, Francesco Ricati, Alessandro Ciarla, Eric Simons, Ross Catanzariti, Eric Buckmeyer, David Pauletti, Giovanni D'Alessandro, Bastien Carta, Benjamin Izuel, Yann Lonca, Kevin Appaule, Nadim El-Choufani, Juan Garcia Camara, Alberto Rigotto, Fabio A.L. De Araujo, Francesco Ricatti, Davide Lauritano, Muhammad Azeem, Darren Holland, Massimo Benassi, Jakub Fila, Ahmed Hashim, Raul Caruso, Dr Michele Colucci, Durante Rapacciuolo, Salvatore Civale, Allessandro Coni, Anrico Lubrano, Sean Hamil, Stephen Morrow, Catherine Idle, Giambattista Rossi, Mark Nervegna, Jaime Rodrigo, Baraka Nasari, Michele Pasquali, Matthew Clark, Tim Kraus, José Alavez, Zito Madu, Bryan Nelson, David Amoyal, John Henderson,

Liam Fitzpatrick, Tal Moriah, Steve Mitchell, Karla Morales, Vincenzo Cioffi, José Alavez, Richard Hall, Samson Delgado, Darren Holland, and Nima Tavallaey Roodsari.

The authors want to give special thanks for the inspiration from Sam Tinaglia Jr, who is a Palermo fan like his father Sam. Tinaglia Jr was first diagnosed with B-cell Acute Lymphoblastic Leukaemia right before his fifth birthday in 2003. He then got it again in 2005, 2011, 2013 and 2015. He has been in remission since receiving CAR T-cell therapy in 2016. His father Sam, second generation Italian (Sicilian)-American, and mother Suzie have also been an incredible inspiration.

Lastly, we want to thank those that took special care of us while we were researching and writing. Our good friends at Harry Cipriani Restaurant on 5th Avenue (Sergio Vacca, the maître d's, the bartenders, and staff). We always look forward to speaking with you about football at both breakfast and dinner. The bartenders at PDT in NYC and Jerry Thomas in Rome, the two best speakeasies in the world, for being so welcoming. Salvatore and Marilena Barberi of Walks Inside Rome, who are the most fantastic tour guides and hosts in Rome. The generous owners of Antica Pesa Restaurant of Rome and Williamsburg, Brooklyn. Finally, we want to thank Tim Monaghan, the bartender at 1020 for his friendship.

ABOUT THE AUTHORS

Steven G. Mandis is an adjunct associate professor in finance and economics at Columbia University Business School and an instructor in the master's degree program in Sports Management, having previously worked at Goldman Sachs and Citigroup and as a senior advisor to McKinsey. He is the author of award-winning books, *What Happened to Goldman Sachs: An Insider's Story of Organizational Drift and its Unintended Consequences* and *The Real Madrid Way: How Values Created the Most Successful Sports Team on the Planet.* Mandis holds an AB from The University of Chicago and an MA, MPhil, and PhD from Columbia University. Mandis was a two-sport varsity athlete in college and currently competes in triathlons, including having completed the IRONMAN World Championships in Kailua-Kona, Hawaii and Escape from Alcatraz in San Francisco, California. He was awarded the prestigious Ellis Island Medal of Honor, given to children of immigrants who exemplify a life dedicated to community service.

Thomas Lombardi works in asset management at Crédit Agricole Pyrénées Gascogne. Lombardi holds a BS from the University of Pau (France), a MS from the University of Lugano (Switzerland) and an MBA from Columbia University Business School.

Sarah Parsons Wolter works at Morgan Stanley. Wolter holds a BA from Dartmouth College and MBA from Columbia University Business School. Wolter was the youngest player on the USA women's hockey team that won a bronze medal at the 2006 Winter Olympics in Turin, Italy. Wolter played hockey in college and was awarded the Kenneth Archibald Prize, which is Dartmouth's highest athletic honour. Wolter played soccer (football), lacrosse and hockey at Noble and Greenough School in Massachusetts, where she is the school's record holder for most goals in a career in soccer and hockey. While she was there, her soccer team also won a New England Class A Championship and her hockey team won three. She also qualified for, and completed, the Boston Marathon.